Sixth Linguistic Annotation Workshop 2012

(LAW VI)

Held in conjunction with the 50th Annual Meeting of the Association for Computational Linguistics 2012 (ACL 2012)

Jeju Island, Korea
12 – 13 July 2012

ISBN: 978-1-62276-597-3

Printed from e-media with permission by:

Curran Associates, Inc.
57 Morehouse Lane
Red Hook, NY 12571

CURRAN ASSOCIATES INC. proceedings.com

Some format issues inherent in the e-media version may also appear in this print version.

Printed by Curran Associates, Inc. (2012)

Association for Computational Linguistics
209 N. Eighth Street
Stroudsburg, Pennsylvania 18360

Phone: 1-570-476-8006
Fax: 1-570-476-0860

acl@aclweb.org

Additional copies of this publication are available from:

Curran Associates, Inc.
57 Morehouse Lane
Red Hook, NY 12571 USA
Phone: 845-758-0400
Fax: 845-758-2634
Email: curran@proceedings.com
Web: www.proceedings.com

Introduction

The Linguistic Annotation Workshop (The LAW) is organized annually by the Association for Computational Linguistics Special Interest Group for Annotation (ACL SIGANN). It provides a forum to facilitate the exchange and propagation of research results concerned with the annotation, manipulation, and exploitation of corpora; work towards the harmonization and interoperability from the perspective of the increasingly large number of tools and frameworks for annotated language resources; and work towards a consensus on all issues crucial to the advancement of the field of corpus annotation. These proceedings include papers presented at LAW VI, held in Jeju, Korea, on 12-13 July 2012.

This year's call for papers was answered by over 40 submissions. After careful review, the Program Committee accepted 14 long papers, together with nine additional papers to be presented as posters. This year's submissions addressed many topics of interest for resource annotation, with a particularly strong representation of papers describing annotation schemes devised to handle phenomena at a wide range of linguistic levels, from particles in Korean to social actions in discourse. Another topic that received considerable attention concerned strategies to evaluate and improve the reliability of annotations, especially those that are manually produced as well as annotations obtained via crowdsourcing. Annotated written and spoken resources in a variety of languages, including Korean, Urdu, Hindi, and Indonesian, were also represented.

The LAW VI call for papers included a new and special component: a call for submissions to answer *The LAW Challenge*, sponsored by the U.S. National Science Foundation (IIS 0948101 Content of Linguistic Annotation: Standards and Practices (CLASP)) and the ACL Special Interest Group on Annotation (ACL SIGANN). The challenge was established this year to promote the use and collaborative development of open, shared resources, and to identify and promote best practices for annotation interoperability. The evaluation criteria included the following:

- innovative use of linguistic information from different annotation layers;
- demonstrable interoperability with at least one other annotation scheme or format developed by others;
- quality of the annotated resource in terms of scheme design, documentation, tool support, etc.;
- open availability of developed resources for community use;
- usability and reusability of the annotation scheme or annotated resource;
- outstanding contribution to the development of annotation best practices.

The winner of the first LAW Challenge was *Who Did What to Whom? A Contrastive Study of Syntacto-Semantic Dependencies*, which examines interoperability among a broad range of common annotation schemes for syntacto-semantic dependencies within the LinGO Redwoods Treebank project. The strengths of the project were seen to be its design and focus on interoperability, as well as its potential to promote work on interoperability that will help the community to develop larger, richer representations to train various linguistic tools. The winning paper received a monetary award to cover the authors' travel expenses and workshop registration. The selection process for the winner of the first LAW Challenge was extremely difficult, and therefore, the committee decided to acknowledge a strong runner-up, entitled *Prague Markup Language Framework*, which was recognized for the extensive influence of the described scheme on the community and the extent to which the scheme and tools have been applied to other languages.

We would like to thank SIGANN for its continuing organization of the LAW workshops, as well as the support of the ACL 2012 workshop committee chairs, Massimo Poesio and Satoshi Sekine. Most of all, we would like to thank all the authors for submitting their papers to the workshop and our program committee members and reviewers for their dedication and informative reviews.

Nancy Ide and Fei Xia, Program Committee Co-chairs

Program Committee Chairs:

Nancy Ide (Vassar College)
Fei Xia (University of Washington)

Program Committee:

Collin Baker (ICSI/UC Berkeley)
Emily Bender (University of Washington)
Nicoletta Calzolari (ILC/CNR)
Steve Cassidy (Macquarie University)
Christopher Cieri (LDC/University of Pennsylvania)
Stefanie Dipper (Ruhr-Universitaet Bochum)
Tomaz Erjavec (Josef Stefan Institute)
Alex Chengyu Fang (City University of Hong Kong)
Christiane Fellbaum (Princeton University)
Dan Flickinger (Stanford University)
Udo Hahn (Friedrich Schiller Universität Jena)
Chu-Ren Huang (Hong Kong Polytechnic)
Aravind Joshi (University of Pennsylvania)
Adam Meyers (New York University)
Antonio Pareja Lora (UCM / ATLAS-UNED)
Martha Palmer (University of Colorado)
Massimo Poesio (University of Trento)
Christopher Potts (Stanford University)
Sameer Pradhan (BBN Technologies)
James Pustejovsky (Brandeis University)
Owen Rambow (Columbia University)
Manfred Stede (Universitat Potsdam)
Mihai Surdeanu (Yahoo! Research, Barcelona)
Katrin Tomanek (Universitaet Dordrecht)
Theresa Wilson (University of Edinburgh)
Andreas Witt (IDS Mannheim)
Nianwen Xue (Brandeis University)

Table of Contents

This page intentionally left blank.

Workshop Program

Thursday, July 12, 2012

8:45–9:00 Opening Remarks

Invited talk

9:00–9:35 *The Role of Linguistic Models and Language Annotation in Feature Selection for Machine Learning*
James Pustejovsky

Special Session: The LAW Challenge

9:35–9:40 Presentation of LAW Challenge Award

9:40–10:05 Challenge Winner: *Who Did What to Whom? A Contrastive Study of Syntacto-Semantic Dependencies*
Angelina Ivanova, Stephan Oepen, Lilja Øvrelid and Dan Flickinger

10:05–10:30 Special Recognition: *Prague Markup Language Framework*
Jirka Hana and Jan Štěpánek

10:30–11:00 Morning coffee break

Paper Session 1

11:00–11:25 *Exploiting naive vs expert discourse annotations: an experiment using lexical cohesion to predict Elaboration / Entity-Elaboration confusions*
Clémentine Adam and Marianne Vergez-Couret

11:25–11:50 *Pair Annotation: Adaption of Pair Programming to Corpus Annotation*
Isin Demirsahin, Ihsan Yalcinkaya and Deniz Zeyrek

11:50–12:15 *Structured Named Entities in two distinct press corpora: Contemporary Broadcast News and Old Newspapers*
Sophie Rosset, Cyril Grouin, Karën Fort, Olivier Galibert, Juliette Kahn and Pierre Zweigenbaum

12:15–12:40 *Intra-Chunk Dependency Annotation : Expanding Hindi Inter-Chunk Annotated Treebank*
Prudhvi Kosaraju, Bharat Ram Ambati, Samar Husain, Dipti Misra Sharma and Rajeev Sangal

12:40–14:15 Lunch

Thursday, July 12, 2012 (continued)

Paper Session 2

14:15–14:40 *A Model for Linguistic Resource Description*
Nancy Ide and Keith Suderman

14:40–15:05 *A GrAF-compliant Indonesian Speech Recognition Web Service on the Language Grid for Transcription Crowdsourcing*
Bayu Distiawan and Ruli Manurung

15:05–15:30 *Towards Adaptation of Linguistic Annotations to Scholarly Annotation Formalisms on the Semantic Web*
Karin Verspoor and Kevin Livingston

15:30–16:00 Afternoon coffee break

Paper Session 3

16:00–16:25 *Intonosyntactic Data Structures: The Rhapsodie Treebank of Spoken French*
Kim Gerdes, Sylvain Kahane, Anne Lacheret, Paola Pietandrea and Arthur Truong

16:25–16:50 *Annotation Schemes to Encode Domain Knowledge in Medical Narratives*
Wilson McCoy, Cecilia Ovesdotter Alm, Cara Calvelli, Rui Li, Jeff B. Pelz, Pengcheng Shi and Anne Haake

16:50–17:15 *Usability Recommendations for Annotation Tools*
Manuel Burghardt

17:15–17:30 SIGANN business meeting

Friday, July 13, 2012

Poster Session (9:00-10:05am)

Search Result Diversification Methods to Assist Lexicographers
Lars Borin, Markus Forsberg, Karin Friberg Heppin, Richard Johansson and Annika Kjellandsson

Simultaneous error detection at two levels of syntactic annotation
Adam Przepiórkowski and Michał Lenart

Exploring Temporal Vagueness with Mechanical Turk
Yuping Zhou and Nianwen Xue

Developing Learner Corpus Annotation for Korean Particle Errors
Sun-Hee Lee, Markus Dickinson and Ross Israel

Annotating Archaeological Texts: An Example of Domain-Specific Annotation in the Humanities
Francesca Bonin, Fabio Cavulli, Aronne Noriller, Massimo Poesio and Egon W. Stemle

Annotating Preferences in Chats for Strategic Games
Anais Cadilhac, Nicholas Asher and Farah Benamara

Morpheme Segmentation in the METU-Sabancı Turkish Treebank
Ruket Cakici

AlvisAE: a collaborative Web text annotation editor for knowledge acquisition
Frédéric Papazian, Robert Bossy and Claire Nédellec

CSAF - a community-sourcing annotation framework
Jin-Dong Kim and Yue Wang

Friday, July 13, 2012 (continued)

Paper Session 4

10:05–10:30 *Dependency Treebank of Urdu and its Evaluation*
Riyaz Ahmad Bhat and Dr. Dipti Misra Sharma

10:30-11:30: Morning coffee break

Paper Session 5

11:00–11:25 *Annotating Coordination in the Penn Treebank*
Wolfgang Maier, Sandra Kübler, Erhard Hinrichs and Julia Kriwanek

11:25–11:50 *Annotating Particle Realization and Ellipsis in Korean*
Sun-Hee Lee and Jae-Young Song

11:50–12:15 *Annotation of Adversarial and Collegial Social Actions in Discourse*
David Bracewell, Marc Tomlinson, Mary Brunson, Jesse Plymale, Jiajun Bracewell and Daniel Boerger

12:15–12:30 Closing

The Role of Linguistic Models and Language Annotation in Feature Selection for Machine Learning

James Pustejovsky
Department of Computer Science
Brandeis University
Waltham, MA 02454, USA
jamesp@cs.brandeis.edu

Abstract

As NLP confronts the challenge of Big Data for natural language text, the role played by linguistically annotated data in training machine learning algorithms is reaching a critical question. Namely, what role can annotated corpora play for supervised learning algorithms when the datasets become significantly outsized, compared to the gold standards used for training? The use of semi-supervised learning techniques to help solve this problem is a good next step, one that requires not less adherence to annotated data, but an even stricter adherence to linguistic models and the features that are derived from these models for subsequent annotation.

Who Did What to Whom?

A Contrastive Study of Syntacto-Semantic Dependencies

Angelina Ivanova♣, Stephan Oepen♣, Lilja Øvrelid♣, and Dan Flickinger♡

♣ University of Oslo, Department of Informatics

♡ Stanford University, Center for the Study of Language and Information

{angelii|oe|liljao}@ifi.uio.no, danf@stanford.edu

Abstract

We investigate aspects of interoperability between a broad range of common annotation schemes for syntacto-semantic dependencies. With the practical goal of making the LinGO Redwoods Treebank accessible to broader usage, we contrast seven distinct annotation schemes of functor–argument structure, both in terms of syntactic and semantic relations. Drawing examples from a multi-annotated gold standard, we show how abstractly similar information can take quite different forms across frameworks. We further seek to shed light on the representational 'distance' between pure bilexical dependencies, on the one hand, and full-blown logical-form propositional semantics, on the other hand. Furthermore, we propose a fully automated conversion procedure from (logical-form) meaning representation to bilexical semantic dependencies.[†]

1 Introduction—Motivation

Dependency representations have in recent years received considerable attention from the NLP community, and have proven useful in diverse tasks such as Machine Translation (Ding & Palmer, 2005), Semantic Search (Poon & Domingos, 2009), and Sentiment Analysis (Wilson et al., 2009). Dependency representations are often claimed to be more 'semantic' in spirit, in the sense that they directly express predicate–argument relations, i.e. *Who did What to Whom?* Several of the shared tasks of the Conference on Natural Language Learning (CoNLL) in the past years have focused on data-driven dependency parsing—producing both syntactic (Nivre et al., 2007) and semantic dependencies (Hajič et al., 2009)—and have made available gold standard data sets (dependency banks) for a range of different languages. These data sets have enabled rigorous evaluation of parsers and have spurred considerable progress in the field of data-driven dependency parsing (McDonald & Nivre, 2011).

Despite widespread use, dependency grammar does not represent a unified grammatical framework and there are large representational differences across communities, frameworks, and languages. Moreover, many of the gold-standard dependency banks were created by automated conversion from pre-existing constituency treebanks—notably the venerable Penn Treebank for English (PTB; Marcus et al., 1993)—and there exist several conversion toolkits which convert from constituent structures to dependency structures. This conversion is not always trivial, and the outputs can differ notably in choices concerning head status, relation inventories, and formal graph properties of the resulting depedency structure. Incompatibilty of representations and differences in the 'granularity' of linguistic information hinder the evaluation of parsers across communities (Sagae et al., 2008).

In this paper, we pursue theoretical as well as practical goals. First, we hope to shed more light on commonalities and differences between a broad range of dependency formats—some syntactic, others semantic in spirit. Here, divergent representations are in part owed to relatively superficial design decisions, as well as in part to more contentful differences in underlying linguistic assumptions; thus, for some classes of syntagmatic relations there may be one-to-one correspondences across families of dependency formats, while for other classes (or other subsets of formats), interconversion may not be possible in general. Building on freely available gold-standard annotations in seven different formats, we contrast these representations both qualitatively and quantitatively. A better understanding

[†]We are indebted to Emily Bender, Rebecca Dridan, and four anonymous reviewers for their feedback on this work.

of such cross-representational relations and related trade-offs will be beneficial to creators and users of syntacto-semantic annotations alike.

Our notion of *syntacto-semantic* information encompasses dependencies ranging from 'classic' syntactically defined grammatical functions (like *subject*, *complement*, or *adjunct*) to more abstract (proto-)roles in propositional semantics (like *agent* or *location*). Indeed, we observe that 'syntactic' vs. 'semantic' representations are anything but clearly separated universes, and that dependency schemes often seek to bring into equilibrium syntactic as well as semantic considerations. At the same time, our focus (and that of much recent and current work in annotation and parsing) is on *bilexical* dependencies, i.e. representations that limit themselves to directed and labeled relations between observable, lexical units of the linguistic signal.

Second, our work is grounded in the practical goal of making pre-existing, large and framework-specific treebanks accessible to a broader range of potential users. Specifically, the Deep Linguistic Processing with HPSG Initiative (DELPH-IN[1]) has produced both manually and automatically annotated resources making available comparatively fine-grained syntactic and semantic analyses in the framework of Head-Driven Phrase Structure Grammar (HPSG; Pollard & Sag, 1994). For English, the so-called LinGO Redwoods Treebank (Oepen et al., 2004) contains gold-standard annotations for some 45,000 utterances in five broad genres and domains; comparable resources exist for Japanese (Bond et al., 2004) and are currently under construction for Portuguese and Spanish (Branco et al., 2010; Marimon, 2010). We develop an automated, parameterizable conversion procedure for these resources that maps HPSG analyses into either syntactic or semantic bilexical dependencies. Similar conversion procedures have recently been formulated for functional structures within the LFG framework (Øvrelid et al., 2009; Cetinoglu et al., 2010). In the design of this unidirectional (i.e. lossy) mapping, we apply and corroborate the cross-framework observations made in the more linguistic part of this study.

The paper has the following structure: Section 2 introduces the corpus and annotations we take as our point of departure; Section 3 contrasts analyses of select linguistic phenomena by example; and Section 4 develops an automated conversion from HPSG analyses to bilexical dependencies.

2 The Multi-Annotated PEST Corpus

At the 2008 Conference on Computational Linguistics (COLING), a workshop on *Cross-Framework and Cross-Domain Parser Evaluation* organized a shared task on comparing different target representations for grammatical analysis (Bos et al., 2008). For a selection of ten sentences from the PTB, the organizers encouraged contrastive studies over a set of parallel, gold-standard annotations in eight different formats. This collection, dubbed PEST (*Parser Evaluation Shared Task*), remains a uniquely valuable resource, despite its small size, for its careful selection of grammatical phenomena, broad coverage across frameworks, and general availability.[2] In the following we briefly review our selection of dependency representations from the PEST data set that provide the vantage point for the current work—using the dimensions identified earlier: head status, relation types, and graph properties.

In the dependency parsing community, it is commonly assumed that dependency structures are directed trees: labeled, directed graphs, where the word tokens in a sentence constitute the nodes, and (i) every token in the sentence is a node in the graph (combined with a designated root node, conventionally numbered as 0), (ii) the graph is (weakly) connected, (iii) every node in the graph has at most one head, and (iv) the graph is acyclic (Nivre et al., 2007). Although these formal constraints facilitate efficient syntactic parsing, they are not necessarily warranted from a pure linguistic point of view. In fact, many of the more theoretical accounts of dependency grammar do not adhere to these requirements (Hudson, 1984). The choice of heads in a dependency representation is another area where individual schools differ substantially. Generally speaking, we may distinguish between formats that take

[1] See `http://www.delph-in.net` for background.

[2] See `http://lingo.stanford.edu/events/08/pe/` for details. Note that, in addition to the gold-standard 'core' of ten PTB sentences, the full PEST collection includes another three dozen sentences from other corpora with some cross-framework annotations, though not in all of the formats and in some cases not manually validated.

	Description	H	T	C
CD	CoNLL Syntactic Dependencies	F	+	+
CP	CoNLL PropBank Semantics	S	–	–
SB	Stanford Basic Dependencies	S	+	+
SD	Stanford Collapsed Dependencies	S	–	–
EP	Enju Predicate – Argument Structures	S	–	+
DT	DELPH-IN Syntactic Derivation Tree	F	+	+
DM	DELPH-IN Minimal Recursion Semantics	S	–	–

Table 1: Summary of dependency formats, where the columns labeled *H* indicate the head status (functional vs. substantive), *T* whether or not structures are acyclic trees, and *C* whether or not all tokens are weakly connected.

a largely functional view of head status—e.g. functional elements like auxiliaries, subjunctions, and infinitival markers are heads—and more substantive or content-centered approaches where the lexical verbs or arguments of the copula are heads. The inventory of dependency relations constitutes another dimension of variation between frameworks. Typically, these relations are largely based on syntactic functions; however, there is also a tradition for using relations more akin to semantic roles, e.g. in the so-called tectogrammatical layer of the Prague Dependency Treebank (Sgall et al., 1986).

Specifically, we look at the 'core' part of the PEST data set that contains ten sentences from the Wall Street Journal portion of the PTB in the following formats: CoNLL 2008 (a) Syntactic Dependencies and (b) PropBank Semantics, Stanford (c) basic and (d) collapsed dependencies, and (e) Enju predicate–argument structures. For comparison to the DELPH-IN HPSG resources, we augment these annotations with gold-standard (f) syntactic and (g) semantic analyses from the LinGO English Resource Grammar (ERG; Flickinger, 2000).[3]

CoNLL Syntactic Dependencies (CD) As discussed earlier, several of the CoNLL shared tasks in the past decade addressed the identification of syntactic or semantic bilexical relations. For English, syntactic dependencies in the PEST collection were obtained by converting PTB trees with the PennConverter software (Johansson & Nugues, 2007), which relies on head finding rules (Magerman, 1994; Collins, 1999) and the functional annotation already present in the PTB annotation. In this format, the dependency representations adhere to the formal graph constraints mentioned above and syntactic heads are largely functional. The dependency relations are mostly syntactic, but also express a few more semantic distinctions like different types of adverbial modification—temporal, locative, etc.

CoNLL PropBank Semantics (CP) For the 2008 CoNLL shared task on joint learning of syntactic and semantic dependencies (Surdeanu et al., 2008), the PropBank and NomBank annotations 'on top' of the PTB syntax (Palmer et al., 2005; Meyers et al., 2004) were converted to bilexical dependency form. This conversion was based on the dependency syntax already obtained for the same data set (CD, above) and heuristics which identify the semantic head of an argument with its syntactic head.The conversion further devotes special attention to arguments with several syntactic heads, discontinuous arguments, and empty categories (Surdeanu et al., 2008). The representation does not adhere to the formal constraints posed above; it lacks a designated root node, the graph is not connected, and the graph is not acyclic. The choices with respect to head status are largely substantive. The dependency relations employed for this representation are PropBank semantic roles, such as `A0` (proto-agent), `A1` (proto-patient), and various modifier roles.

Stanford Basic Dependencies (SB) The Stanford Dependency scheme, a popular alternative to CoNLL-style syntactic dependencies (CD), was originally provided as an additional output format for the Stanford parser (Klein & Manning, 2003). It is a result of a conversion from PTB-style phrase structure trees (be they gold standard or automatically produced)—combining 'classic' head finding rules with rules that target specific linguistic constructions, such as passives or attributive adjectives (Marneffe et al., 2006). The so-called *basic* format provides a dependency graph which conforms to the criteria listed above, and the heads are largely content rather than function words. The grammatical relations are organized in a hierarchy, rooted in the generic relation 'dependent' and containing 56 different relations (Marneffe & Manning, 2008), largely based on syntactic functions.

[3]Among others, annotations in the Prague Dependency format would be interesting to compare to, but currently these are unfortunately not among the formats represented in the PEST corpus.

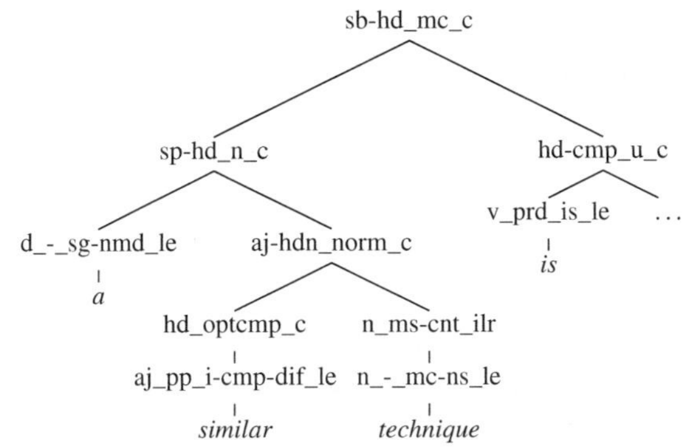

Figure 1: Syntactic derivation tree from the ERG.

{ e_{12}
$\_{1}$:_a_q(BV x_6)
e_9:_similar_a_to(ARG1 x_6)
x_6:_technique_n_1
e_{12}:_almost_a_1(ARG1 e_3)
e_3:_impossible_a_for(ARG1 e_{18})
e_{18}:_apply_v_to(ARG2 x_6, ARG3 x_{19})
$\_{2}$:udef_q(BV x_{19})
e_{25}:_other_a_1(ARG1 x_{19})
x_{19}:_crop_n_1
e_{26}:_such+as_p(ARG1 x_{19}, ARG2 x_{27})
$\_{3}$:udef_q(BV x_{27})
$\_{4}$:udef_q(BV x_{33})
x_{33}:_cotton_n_1
$\_{5}$:udef_q(BV i_{38})
x_{27}:implicit_conj(L-INDEX x_{33}, R-INDEX i_{38})
$\_{6}$:udef_q(BV x_{43})
x_{43}:_soybeans/nns_u_unknown
i_{38}:_and_c(L-INDEX x_{43}, R-INDEX x_{47})
$\_{7}$:udef_q(BV x_{47})
x_{47}:_rice_n_1
}

Figure 2: ERG Elementary Dependency Structure.

Stanford Collapsed Dependencies (SD) Stanford Dependencies also come in a so-called *collapsed* version[4], where certain function words, such as prepositions, introduce dependency relations (rather than acting as nodes in the graph). Moreover, certain dependents—such as subjects of control verbs—have more than one head. The collapsed representation thus does not meet the formal graph criteria mentioned above: it is not connected, since not all tokens in the sentence are connected to the graph, a node may have more than one head, and there may also be cycles in the graph.

Enju Predicate–Argument Structures (EP) The Enju system is a robust, statistical parser obtained by learning from a conversion of the PTB into HPSG (Miyao, 2006). Enju outputs so-called predicate–argument structures (often dubbed PAS, but in our context henceforth EP), which primarily aim to capture semantic relations and hence prefer substantive heads over functional ones and encode most types of syntactic modifiers as predicates (i.e. heads) rather than arguments. The gold-standard Enju predicate–argument structures in the PEST collection were obtained semi-automatically from the HPSG conversion of the PTB;[5] they do not obey our formal graph constraints, much for the same reasons as we see in CP or SD.

DELPH-IN Syntactic Derivation Tree (DT) Similar to Enju, the LinGO English Resource Grammar (ERG; Flickinger, 2000) is couched in the HPSG framework; in contrast to Enju, however, the ERG has been engineered fully analytically (fully independent of the PTB), growing grammatical coverage continuously since the early 1990s. Figure 1 shows the ERG derivation tree for part of our running example (see below), which provides a compact 'recipe' for construction of the full HPSG analysis. Internal nodes in the tree are labeled with identifiers of HPSG constructions (subject–head, specifier–head, and head–complement, in the top of the tree), leaf nodes with types of lexical entries. In Section 4 below, we convert DELPH-IN derivations into syntactic bilexical dependencies.

DELPH-IN Minimal Recursion Semantics (DM) As part of the full HPSG sign, the ERG also makes available a logical-form representation of propositional semantics in the format of Minimal Recursion Semantics (MRS; Copestake et al., 2005). While MRS proper utilizes a variant of predicate calculus that affords underspecification of scopal relations, for our goal of projecting semantic forms onto bilexical dependencies, we start from the reduction of MRS into the Elementary Dependency Structures (EDS) of Oepen & Lønning (2006), as shown in Fig-

[4]The collapsed scheme actually is the default option when running the Stanford converter, whereas the basic format must be requested by a specific command-line flag ('-basic').

[5]For unknown reasons, the original PEST release lacks Enju annotations for one of the ten 'core' sentences. We were able to obtain a stand-in analysis with the help of Prof. Yusuke Miyao (one of the original PEST coordinators), however, which we will include in our re-release of the extended resource.

ure 2. EDS is a lossy (i.e. non-reversible) conversion from MRS into a variable-free dependency graph; graph nodes (one per line in Figure 2) correspond to elementary predications from the original logical form and are connected by arcs labeled with MRS argument indices: ARG1, ARG2, etc. (where BV is reserved for what is the bound variable of a quantifier in the full MRS).[6] Note that, while EDS already brings us relatively close to the other formats, there are graph nodes that do not correspond to individual words from our running example, for example the underspecified quantifiers for the bare noun phrases (udef_q) and the binary conjunction implicit_conj that ties together *cotton* with *soybeans and rice*. Furthermore, some words are semantically empty (the predicative copula, infinitival *to*, and argument-marking preposition), and the EDS does not form a tree (*technique*, for example, is the ARG1 of *similar*, ARG2 of *apply*, and bound variable of *a*). In Section 4 below, we develop a mapping from DELPH-IN Elementary Dependency Structures to 'pure' bilexical semantic dependencies.

3 Contrasting Analyses by Example

Availability of the ten PEST sentences in different dependency representations allows us to observe and visualize cross-format differences both qualitatively and quantitatively.[7] To illustrate some pertinent contrasts, Figure 3 visualizes syntacto-semantic dependencies in seven formats for the PEST example:

(1) *A similar technique is almost impossible to apply to other crops, such as cotton, soybeans and rice.*

For the CoNLL, Stanford, and DELPH-IN formats, which each come in two variants, we present the more syntactic dependencies above (in red) and the more semantic dependencies below (blue) the actual string. This running example illustrates a range of linguistic phenomena such as coordination, verbal chains, argument and modifier prepositional phrases, complex noun phrases, and the so-called *tough* construction.

Figure 3 reveals a range of disagreements across formats. The analysis of coordination represents a well-known area of differences between various dependency schemes, and this is also the case for our example. Strikingly, none of the formats agree on the analysis of the coordination *cotton, soybeans and rice*. CoNLL Syntactic Dependencies (CD) exhibit the so-called Mel'čuk-style analysis of coordination (Mel'čuk, 1988), where the first conjunct is regarded as the head of coordinated structures, and the consequent conjuncts and coordinating construction are sequentially linked to each other. DELPH-IN MRS (DM) is similar, but the coordinating conjunction is treated as functional and therefore does not contribute a dependency node. CoNLL Propositional Semantic (CP) has no analysis for the coordinated structure, since it only analyzes main arguments in the sentence. In both Stanford schemes, the first conjunct is the head of the coordination construction, and the other conjuncts depend on it—but the basic (SB) and collapsed (SD) representations differ because a coordination relation is propagated to all conjuncts in SD. In the DELPH-IN Derivation (DT), finally, the coordinating conjunction is the head for all conjuncts.

Above, we proposed a distinction between more functional vs. more substantive dependency formats, and although this distinction does not clearly separate the different analyses in Figure 3, it points to some interesting differences. Where the majority of the schemes identify the root of the sentence as the finite verb *is*, the Stanford schemes—being largely substantive in their choices concerning syntactic heads—annotate the predicative adjective *impossible* as the root. Further, the infinitive *to apply* receives different interpretations in the formats. The infinitival marker depends on the main verb in CP, SB, and SD—whereas CD, EP, and DT regard it as the head. In CD, SB, and DT, prepositions are dependents, as illustrated by *(such) as*; in EP and DM, prepositional modifiers are heads; and SD 'collapses' prepositions to yield direct relations between the nominal head of the preposition (*crops*) and its internal argument.

The treatment of noun phrases cuts across this distinction between functional and substantive ap-

[6] In the textual rendering of our EDS in Figure 2, nodes are prefixed with unique identifiers, which serve to denote node reentracy and the targets of outgoing dependency arcs.

[7] In this section, we use bilexical dependency variants of the DELPH-IN analyses, anticipating the conversion procedure sketched in Section 4 below.

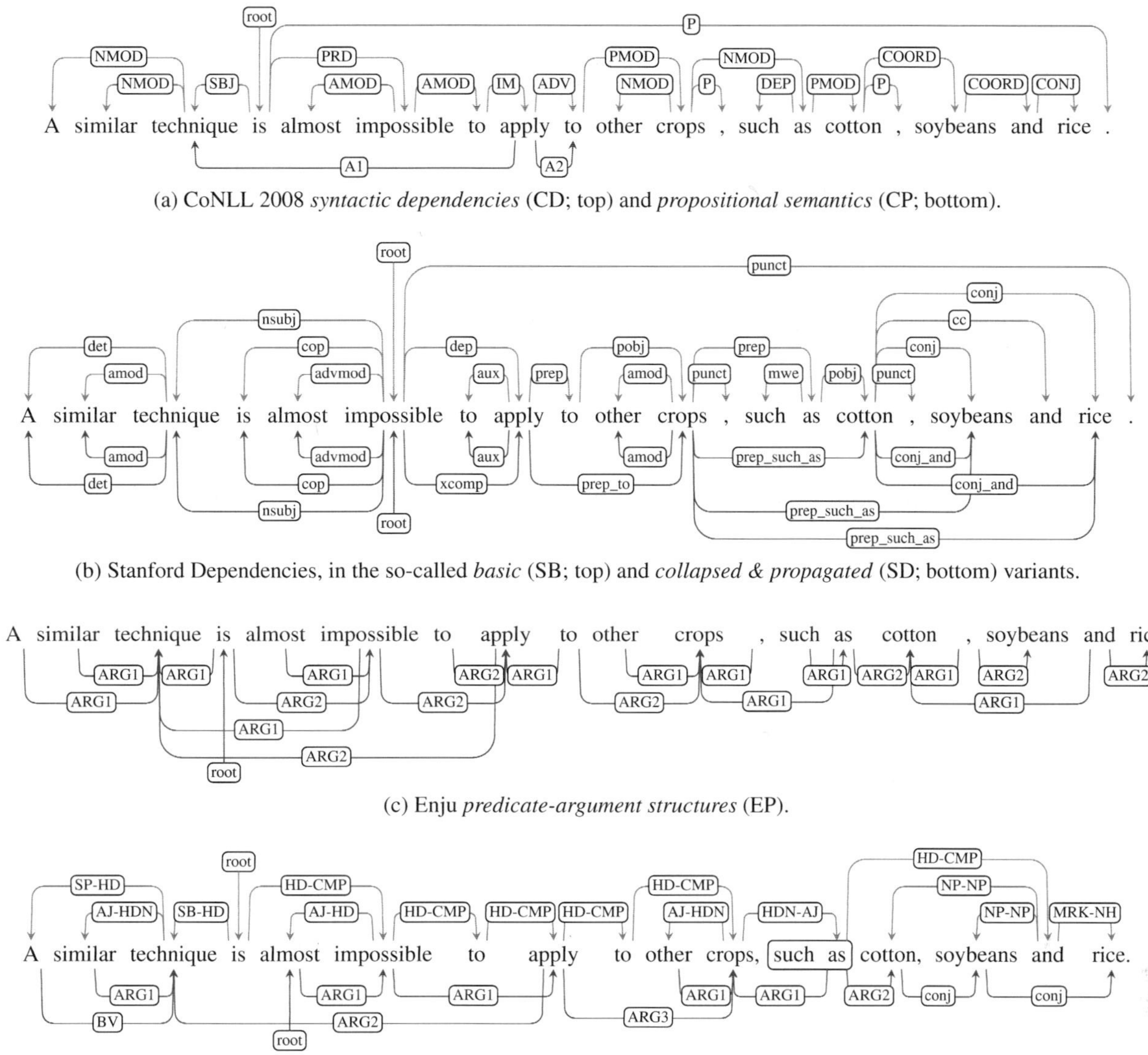

(a) CoNLL 2008 *syntactic dependencies* (CD; top) and *propositional semantics* (CP; bottom).

(b) Stanford Dependencies, in the so-called *basic* (SB; top) and *collapsed & propagated* (SD; bottom) variants.

(c) Enju *predicate-argument structures* (EP).

(d) DELPH-IN *syntactic derivation tree* (DT; top) and *Minimal Recursion Semantics* (DM; bottom).

Figure 3: Dependency representations in (a) CoNLL, (b) Stanford, (c) Enju, and (d) DELPH-IN formats.

proaches. In *a similar technique*, one can treat the determiner and attributive adjective as dependents of the noun, which is what we find in the CD, SB, SD, and DT schemes. Alternatively, one may consider the noun to be a dependent of both the determiner and the adjective, as is the case in the schemes deriving from predicate logic (EP and DM).

Our running example also invokes the so-called *tough* construction, where a restricted class of adjectives (*impossible* in our case) select for infinitival VPs containing an object gap and, thus, create a long-distance dependency (Rosenbaum, 1967; Nanni, 1980, inter alios). In the dependency analyses in Figure 3, we observe three possible heads for the noun *technique*, viz. *is* (CD, EP, DT), *impossible* (SB and SD), and *apply* (CP, EP, and DM). The long-distance dependency (between *technique* and *apply*) is marked only in the more semantic schemes: CP, EP, and DM.

Our comparison shows a range of pertinent qualitative differences. To further quantify the degree of overlap between different analyses in the PEST data, we abstract from tokenization subtleties by aligning representations across formats in terms of native PTB tokenization. For example, in the ERG punctuation is attached to the words (e.g. *crops,*), multiword expressions (*such as*) act as one entity, and unlike in the PTB hyphenated words (like *arms-*

	CD	CP	SB	SD	EP	DT	DM
CD	*19*	1	12	5	6	12	2
CP	1	*2*	1	0	1	1	1
SB	12	1	*19*	10	4	7	3
SD	5	0	10	*14*	2	4	3
EP	6	1	4	2	*20*	6	8
DT	12	1	7	4	6	*15*	0
DM	2	1	3	3	8	0	*11*

Table 2: Pairwise unlabelled dependency overlap.

	CD	CP	SB	SD	EP	DT	DM
CD		.171	.427	.248	.187	.488	.115
CP	.171		.171	.177	.122	.158	.173
SB	.427	.171		.541	.123	.319	.147
SD	.248	.177	.541		.14	.264	.144
EP	.187	.122	.123	.14		.192	.462
DT	.488	.158	.319	.264	.192		.13
DM	.115	.173	.147	.144	.462	.13	

Table 3: Pairwise Jaccard similarity on PEST 'core'.

control, not present in our example) are split into component parts (a similar, but not identical splitting is also used in CD). Conversely, in the PTB-derived formats punctuation marks are separate tokens, but EP consistently drops sentence-final punctuation.

Table 2 shows how many *unlabelled* dependency arcs each pair of formats have in common for our running example. The most similar pairs here are CD and DT, CD and SB, and SB and SD. The values in the diagonal of the table expose the total number of dependencies in a given representation.

For each pair of formats we computed its Jaccard similarity index $\frac{|A \cap B|}{|A \cup B|}$, by macro-averaging over all ten sentences, i.e. computing total counts for the union and intersection for each pair of formats $\langle A, B \rangle$. The results are presented in Table 3, where we observe that Jaccard indices are comparatively low across the board and do not exceed 55 % for any pair. This measure (unsurprisingly) shows that SB and SD are the most similar formats among all seven. The DELPH-IN dependency representations demonstrate comparatively strong interoperability with other schemes, since CD corresponds well with DT syntactically, while EP correlates with DM among the more semantic formats.

4 Automated Conversion from HPSG

In the following paragraphs, we outline an automated, parameterizable, and lossy conversion from the native DELPH-IN analyses to bilexical dependencies, both syntactic and semantic ones.

Background: LinGO Redwoods The LinGO Redwoods Treebank (Oepen et al., 2004) is a collection of English corpora annotated with gold-standard HPSG analyses from the ERG. The annotations result from manual disambiguation among candidate analyses by the grammar, such that the treebank is entirely composed of structures derived from the ERG as an explicit, underlying model.[8] Synchronized to major releases of the ERG, Redwoods has been continuously updated to take advantage of improved coverage and precision of the grammar. The current, so-called Seventh Growth provides manually validated analyses for some 45,000 sentences from five domains, which also represent different genres of text. Automatically parsed and disambiguated versions of the English Wikipedia and comprehensive samples of user-generated web content are available in the exact same formats (so-called *treecaches*; Flickinger et al., 2010; Read et al., 2012).

Syntax: Derivations to Dependencies The transformation of DELPH-IN derivation trees to syntactic dependencies is, in principle, straightforward—as the HPSG constructions labeling internal nodes of the tree (see Figure 1) directly determine syntactic head daughters. Thus, for the conversion it is sufficient to (a) eliminate unary nodes and (b) extract bilexical dependencies in a single tree traversal. Here, HPSG constructions (like sb-hd_mc_c in Figure 1, i.e. a subject–head combination in a main clause) introduce dependency relations holding between the (lexical head of) the head daughter and (that of) each non-head daughter. Note that we further generalize the 150 or so fine-grained ERG constructions to 50 major construction types, e.g. sb-hd_mc_c to just sb-hd in Figure 3d.

Semantics: Logical Form to Dependencies The complete ERG Elementary Dependency Structure for our running example is shown in Figure 2 (al-

[8] The downside of this grammar-driven approach to treebank creation is that the collection can contain gaps for inputs that the grammar is unable to analyze and ones where annotators reject all available candidates as inadequate. At present, between ten and twenty percent of all utterances in Redwoods lack a gold-standard analysis for one of these reasons.

```
[transparent]
implicit_conj L-INDEX
/_c$/ L-INDEX
[relational]
/_c$/ conj L-INDEX R-INDEX
implicit_conj conj L-INDEX R-INDEX
```

Figure 4: Excerpt from the ERG configuration file.

though we are not showing some additional information on each node, relating EDS components to input tokens). The conversion procedure for 'regular' *lexical* relations, i.e. ones that correspond to actual tokens, is simple. For example, _other_a_1(ARG1 x_{19}) in Figure 2 contributes an ARG1 dependency between *other* and *crops* in Figure 3d, because x_{19} is the identifier of the EDS node labelled _crop_n_1.

Besides this basic mechanism, our converter supports three 'special' classes of relations, which we call (a) *transparent*, (b) *relational*, and (c) *redundant*. The latter class is of a more technical nature and avoids duplicates in cases where the EDS gave rise to multiple dependencies that only differ in their label (and where labels are considered equivalent), as can at times be the case in coordinate structures.[9]

Our class of so-called *transparent* relations includes the semantic relation associated with, for example, nominalization, where in the underlying logic a referential instance variable is explicitly derived from an event. In terms of bilexical dependencies, however, we want to conceptually equate the two EDS nodes involved. In our running example, in fact, coordination provides an example of transparency: in the EDS, there are two binary conjunction relations (implicit_conj and _and_c), which conceptually correspond to group formation; node i_{38} (corresponding to *and*) is the second argument of the implicit conjunction. For our semantic bilexical dependencies, however, we opt for the analysis of Mel'čuk (see Section 3 above), which we achieve by making interchangeable conjunction nodes with their left arguments, i.e. nodes i_{38} and x_{43}, as well as x_{27} and x_{33}, in Figure 2.

Finally, somewhat similar to the 'collapsing' available in Stanford Dependencies, our class of so-called *relational* predicates allows the creation of dependency labels transcending EDS role indices, which we apply for, among others, possession, subordination, apposition, and conjunction. The two conj dependencies in Figure 3d, for example, hold between left and right arguments of the two conjunctions, as per the excerpt from the ERG-specific conversion specification shown in Figure 4.[10]

5 Conclusions—Outlook

With the goal of making the Redwoods Treebank resources accessible to the broader NLP community, we have presented both a qualitative and quantitative comparison of a range of syntacto-semantic dependency formats, in order to make explicit the information contained in the treebank representations, as well as contrasting these to already existing formats. Our comparative analysis shows a large variation across formats and—although this is not surprising per se—highlights the importance of contrastive studies. In this article we have furthermore presented an automatic conversion procedure, which converts the HPSG representations in the treebanks to a set of syntactic and semantic dependencies.

In terms of next steps, we will release the transformed Redwoods Treebank and conversion software in the hope that the new resources will enable various follow-up activities. Both the CoNLL and Stanford formats have been used to train data-driven dependency parsers, and it is a natural next step to train and evaluate parsers on the converted DELPH-IN formats. In order to do so, further adjustments may have to be made to the DM format to convert it into a dependency tree. In light of the broader variety of domains available in Redwoods, the converted data will enable experimentation in domain and genre adaptation for parsers. As a further step in gauging the utility of the various dependency formats, it would also be interesting to contrast these in a downstream application making use of dependency representations.

[9] The full underlying logical forms make a distinction between scopal vs. non-scopal arguments, which is washed out in the EDS. The existence of seemingly redundant links in coordinate structures is owed to this formal reduction.

[10] Our conversion software is fully parameterizable in terms of the different classes of relations, to allow for easy experimentation and adaptation to other DELPH-IN grammars. We plan to contribute the converter, extended PEST collection, and a version of Redwoods transformed to bilexical dependencies into the open-source DELPH-IN repository; see `http://www.delph-in.net/lds/` for details and access.

References

Bond, F., Fujita, S., Hashimoto, C., Kasahara, K., Nariyama, S., Nichols, E., Ohtani, A., Tanaka, T., & Amano, S. (2004). The Hinoki treebank. A treebank for text understanding. In *Proceedings of the 1st International Joint Conference on Natural Language Processing* (pp. 158 – 167). Hainan Island, China.

Bos, J., Briscoe, E., Cahill, A., Carroll, J., Clark, S., Copestake, A., Flickinger, D., Genabith, J. van, Hockenmaier, J., Joshi, A., Kaplan, R., King, T. H., Kuebler, S., Lin, D., Loenning, J. T., Manning, C., Miyao, Y., Nivre, J., Oepen, S., Sagae, K., Xue, N., & Zhang, Y. (Eds.). (2008). *Proceedings of the COLING 2008 Workshop on Cross-Framework and Cross-Domain Parser Evaluation.* Manchester, UK: Coling 2008 Organizing Committee.

Branco, A., Costa, F., Silva, J., Silveira, S., Castro, S., Avelãs, M., Pinto, C., & Graça, J. (2010). Developing a deep linguistic databank supporting a collection of treebanks. The CINTIL DeepGramBank. In *Proceedings of the 7th International Conference on Language Resources and Evaluation.* Valletta, Malta.

Cetinoglu, O., Foster, J., Nivre, J., Hogan, D., Cahill, A., & Genabith, J. van. (2010). Lfg without c-structures. In *Proceedings of the 9th international workshop on treebanks and linguistic theories.* Tartu, Estonia.

Collins, M. J. (1999). *Head-driven statistical models for natural language parsing.* Unpublished doctoral dissertation, University of Pennsylvania, Philadelphia.

Copestake, A., Flickinger, D., Pollard, C., & Sag, I. A. (2005). Minimal Recursion Semantics. An introduction. *Journal of Research on Language and Computation, 3*(4), 281 – 332.

Ding, Y., & Palmer, M. (2005). Machine translation using probabilistic synchronous dependency insertion grammars. In *Proceedings of the 43rd Meeting of the Association for Computational Linguistics* (pp. 541 – 548). Ann Arbor, MI, USA.

Flickinger, D. (2000). On building a more efficient grammar by exploiting types. *Natural Language Engineering, 6 (1)*, 15 – 28.

Flickinger, D., Oepen, S., & Ytrestøl, G. (2010). WikiWoods. Syntacto-semantic annotation for English Wikipedia. In *Proceedings of the 7th International Conference on Language Resources and Evaluation.* Valletta, Malta.

Hajič, J., Ciaramita, M., Johansson, R., Kawahara, D., Martí, M. A., Màrquez, L., Meyers, A., Nivre, J., Padó, S., Štěpanek, J., Straňák, P., Surdeanu, M., Xue, N., & Zhang, Y. (2009). The CoNLL-2009 Shared Task: Syntactic and semantic dependencies in multiple languages. In *Proceedings of the 13th Conference on Natural Language Learning.*

Hudson, R. A. (1984). *Word grammar.* Blackwell.

Johansson, R., & Nugues, P. (2007). Extended constituent-to-dependency conversion for English. In J. Nivre, H.-J. Kaalep, & M. Koit (Eds.), *Proceedings of NODALIDA 2007* (pp. 105 – 112).

Klein, D., & Manning, C. D. (2003). Accurate unlexicalized parsing. In *Proceedings of the 41st Meeting of the Association for Computational Linguistics* (pp. 423 – 430).

Magerman, D. M. (1994). *Natural language parsing as statistical pattern recognition.* Unpublished doctoral dissertation, Stanford University.

Marcus, M. P., Santorini, B., & Marcinkiewicz, M. A. (1993). Building a large annotated corpus of English. The Penn Treebank. *Computational Linguistics, 19*, 313 – 330.

Marimon, M. (2010). The Spanish Resource Grammar. In *Proceedings of the 7th International Conference on Language Resources and Evaluation.* Valletta, Malta.

Marneffe, M.-C. de, MacCartney, B., & Manning, C. D. (2006). Generating typed dependency parses from phrase structure parses. In *Proceedings of the 5th International Conference on Language Resources and Evaluation.* Genova, Italy.

Marneffe, M.-C. de, & Manning, C. D. (2008). The Stanford typed dependencies representation.

In *Proceedings of the COLING08 Workshop on Cross-Framework Parser Evaluation* (pp. 1 – 8).

McDonald, R., & Nivre, J. (2011). Analyzing and integrating dependency parsers. *Computational Linguistics*, *37*(1), 197 – 230.

Mel'čuk, I. (1988). *Dependency syntax: Theory and practice.* Albany: SUNY Press.

Meyers, A., Reeves, R., Macleod, C., Szekely, R., Zielinska, V., Young, B., , & Grishman, R. (2004). The NomBank project: An interim report. In *Proceedings of HLT-EACL Workshop: Frontiers in Corpus Annotation.*

Miyao, Y. (2006). *From linguistic theory to syntactic analysis. Corpus-oriented grammar development and feature forest model.* Unpublished doctoral dissertation, University of Tokyo, Tokyo, Japan.

Nanni, D. (1980). On the surface syntax of constructions with *easy*-type adjectives. *Language*, *56*(3), 568–591.

Nivre, J., Hall, J., Kübler, S., McDonald, R., Nilsson, J., Riedel, S., & Yuret, D. (2007). CoNLL 2007 Shared Task on Dependency Parsing. In *Proceedings of the CoNLL Shared Task session of EMNLP-CoNLL 2007* (pp. 915 – 932).

Nivre, J., Hall, J., Nilsson, J., Chanev, A., Eryiğit, G., Kübler, S., Marinov, S., & Marsi, E. (2007). Maltparser: A language-independent system for data-driven dependency parsing. *Natural Language Engineering*, *13*(2), 95 – 135.

Oepen, S., Flickinger, D., Toutanova, K., & Manning, C. D. (2004). LinGO Redwoods. A rich and dynamic treebank for HPSG. *Journal of Research on Language and Computation*, *2*(4), 575 – 596.

Oepen, S., & Lønning, J. T. (2006). Discriminant-based MRS banking. In *Proceedings of the 5th International Conference on Language Resources and Evaluation* (pp. 1250 – 1255). Genoa, Italy.

Øvrelid, L., Kuhn, J., & Spreyer, K. (2009). Improving data-driven dependency parsing using large-scale lfg grammars. In *Proceedings of the 47th Meeting of the Association for Computational Linguistics.*

Palmer, M., Gildea, D., & Kingsbury, P. (2005). The Proposition Bank: An annotated corpus of semantic roles. *Computational Linguistics*, *31*(1), 71 – 105.

Pollard, C., & Sag, I. A. (1994). *Head-Driven Phrase Structure Grammar.* Chicago, IL and Stanford, CA: The University of Chicago Press and CSLI Publications.

Poon, H., & Domingos, P. (2009). Unsupervised semantic parsing. In *Proceedings of the 2009 Conference on Empirical Methods in Natural Language Processing.* Singapore.

Read, J., Flickinger, D., Dridan, R., Oepen, S., & Øvrelid, L. (2012). The WeSearch Corpus, Treebank, and Treecache. A comprehensive sample of user-generated content. In *Proceedings of the 8th International Conference on Language Resources and Evaluation.* Istanbul, Turkey.

Rosenbaum, P. S. (1967). *The grammar of English predicate complement constructions* (Vol. 46). MIT Press.

Sagae, K., Miyao, Y., Matsuzaki, T., & Tsujii, J. (2008). Challenges in mapping of syntactic representations for framework-independent parser evaluation. In *Proceedings of the Workshop on Automated Syntactic Annotations for Interoperable Language Resources at ICGL'08.* Hong Kong.

Sgall, P., Hajičová, E., & Panevová, J. (1986). *The meaning of the sentence in its pragmatic aspects.* Dordrecht: Reidel.

Surdeanu, M., Johansson, R., Meyers, A., Màrquez, L., & Nivre, J. (2008). The CoNLL-2008 Shared Task on joint parsing of syntactic and semantic dependencies. In *Proceedings of the 12th Conference on Natural Language Learning* (p. 159-177).

Wilson, T., Wiebe, J., & Hoffman, P. (2009). Recognizing contextual polarity: An exploration of features for phrase-level sentiment analysis. *Computational Linguistics*, *35*(3), 399 – 433.

Prague Markup Language Framework

Jirka Hana and **Jan Štěpánek**
Charles University in Prague, Faculty of Mathematics and Physics
lastname@ufal.mff.cuni.cz

Abstract

In this paper we describe the Prague Markup Language (PML), a generic and open XML-based format intended to define format of linguistic resources, mainly annotated corpora. We also provide an overview of existing tools supporting PML, including annotation editors, a corpus query system, software libraries, etc.

1 Introduction

Constructing a linguistic resource is a complicated process. Among other things it requires a good choice of tools, varying from elementary data conversion scripts over annotation tools and tools for consistency checking, to tools used for semi-automatic treebank building (POS taggers, syntactic parsers). If no existing tool fits the needs, a new one has to be developed (or some existing tool adapted or extended, which, however, seldom happens in practice). The variety of tools that exist and emerged from various NLP projects shows that there is no simple solution that would fit all. It is sometimes a small missing feature or an incompatible data format that disqualifies certain otherwise well-established tools in the eyes of those who decide which tools to use for their annotation project.

This paper presents an annotation framework that was from its very beginning designed to be extensible and independent of any particular annotation schema. While reflecting the feedback from several annotation projects, it evolved into a set of generic tools that is open to all kinds of annotations.

The first section describes the Prague Markup Language and the way it is used to define format of linguistic resources; follows a section on annotation tools, a query engine and programming libraries. Finally, we discuss related work and future plans.

2 Data Format

The base data format selected for the described annotation framework, both for data exchange and as a memory-model reference, is Prague Markup Language (PML, Pajas and Štěpánek, 2006). While designing PML, we have followed the following set of desiderata:

- Stand-off annotation principles: Each layer of the linguistic annotation should be cleanly separated from the other annotation layers as well as from the original data. This allows for making changes only to a particular layer without affecting the other parts of the annotation and data.

- Cross-referencing and linking: Both links to external document and data resources and links within a document should be represented coherently. Diverse flexible types of external links are required by the stand-off approach. Supposed that most data resources (data, tagsets, and dictionaries) use the same principles, they can be more tightly interconnected.

- Linearity and structure: The data format ought to be able to capture both linear and structure types of annotation.

- Structured attributes: The representation should allow for associating the annotated units with complex and descriptive data structures, similar to feature-structures.

- Alternatives: The vague nature of language often leads to more than one linguistic interpretation and hence to alternative annotations. This phenomenon occurs on many levels, from atomic values to compound parts of the annotation, and should be treated in a unified manner.

- Human-readability: The data format should be human-readable. This is very useful not only in the first phases of the annotation process, when the tools are not yet mature enough to reflect all evolving aspects of the annotation, but also later, especially for emergency situations when for example an unexpected data corruption occur that breaks the tools and can only be repaired manually. It also helps the programmers while creating and debugging new tools.

- Extensibility: The format should be extensible to allow new data types, link types, and similar properties to be added. The same should apply to all specific annotation formats derived from the general one, so that one could incrementally extend the vocabulary with markup for additional information.

- XML based: XML format is widely used for exchange and storing of information; it offers a wide variety of tools and libraries for many programming languages.

Thus PML is an abstract XML-based format intended to be generally applicable to all types of annotation purposes, and especially suitable for multi-layered treebank annotations following the stand-off principles. A notable feature that distinguishes PML from other encoding schemes existing at the time of its creation (see Section 4) is its generic and open nature. Rather than being targeted to one particular annotation schema or being a set of specifically targeted encoding conventions, PML is an open system, where a new type of annotation can be introduced easily by creating a simple XML file called PML schema, which describes the annotation by means of declaring the relevant data types (see Figure 1 for an example).

The types used by PML include the following:

Attribute-value structures (AVS's), i.e. structures consisting of attribute-value pairs. For each pair, the name of the attribute and the type of the value is specified. The type can be any PML type, including an AVS. A typical usage example of an AVS structure is, for example a structure gathering the annotation of several independent morphological categories (lemma, case, gender, number). A special type of AVS is a *container*, a structure with just one non-attribute member.

Lists allowing several values of the same type to be aggregated, either in an ordered or unordered manner. For example, a sentence can be represented as an ordered list of tokens, whereas a set of pointers to an ontology lexicon could be captured as an unordered list.

Alternatives used for aggregating alternative annotations, ambiguity, etc. For example, `noun` and `verb` can be alternative values of the part-of-speech attribute in the morphological analysis of the word *flies*: only one of them is the correct value, but we do not know (yet) which one.

Sequences representing sequences of values of different types. Unlike list members, the members of a sequence do not need to be of the same type and they may be further annotated using XML attributes. There is also a basic support for XML-like mixed content (a sequence can contain both text and other elements). A simple regular expression might be used to specify the order and optionality of the members. To give a typical usage example, consider the phrase structure tree: each node has a sequence of child nodes of two data types, terminals and non-terminals. The content of each node would typically be an AVS capturing the phrase type for non-terminals and morphological information for terminals.

Links providing a uniform method for cross-referencing within a PML instance, referencing among various PML instances (e.g. between layers of annotation), and linking to other external resources (lexicons, audio data, etc.).

Enumerated types which are atomic data types whose values are literal strings from a fixed fi-

```
<?xml version="1.0"?>
<pml_schema version="1.1" xmlns="http://ufal.mff.cuni.cz/pdt/pml/schema/">
  <description>Example of constituency tree annotation</description>
  <root name="annotation">
    <sequence role="#TREES" content_pattern="meta, nt+">
      <element name="meta" type="meta.type"/>
      <element name="nt" type="nonterminal.type"/>
    </sequence>
  </root>
  <type name="meta.type">
    <structure>
      <member name="annotator"><cdata format="any"/></member>
      <member name="datetime"><cdata format="any"/></member>
    </structure>
  </type>
  <type name="nonterminal.type">
    <container role="#NODE">
      <attribute name="label" type="label.type"/>
      <sequence role="#CHILDNODES">
        <element name="nt" type="nonterminal.type"/>
        <element name="form" type="terminal.type"/>
      </sequence>
    </container>
  </type>
  <type name="terminal.type">
    <container role="#NODE">
      <cdata format="any"/>
    </container>
  </type>
  <type name="label.type">
    <choice>
      <value>S</value>
      <value>VP</value>
      <value>NP</value>
        <!-- etc. -->
    </choice>
  </type>
</pml_schema>
```

Figure 1: A PML schema defining a simple format for representation of phrase structure trees

```
<?xml version="1.0"?>
<annotation xmlns="http://ufal.mff.cuni.cz/pdt/pml/">
  <head>
    <schema href="example_schema.xml"/>
  </head>
  <meta>
    <annotator>John Smith</annotator>
    <datetime>Sun May 1 18:56:55 2005</datetime>
  </meta>
  <nt label="S">
    <nt label="NP">
      <form>John</form>
    </nt>
    <nt label="VP">
      <form>loves</form>
      <nt label="NP">
        <form>Mary</form>
      </nt>
    </nt>
  </nt>
</annotation>
```

Figure 2: A sample phrase structure encoded in the format defined in Figure 1

nite set. A typical example is a boolean type with only two possible values, 0 and 1.

CData type representing all character-based data without internal structure or whose internal structure is not expressed by means of XML. For improved validation and optimal in-memory representation, the cdata type declaration can be accompanied by a simple format specification (identifier, reference, and the standard W3C XML Schema simple types for numbers, date, time, language, ...).

A PML schema can also assign roles to particular annotation constructions. The roles are labels from a pre-defined set indicating the purpose of the declarations. For instance, the roles indicate which data structures represent the nodes of the trees, how the node data structures are nested to form a tree, which field in a data structure carries its unique ID (if any), or which field carries a link to the annotated data or other layers of annotation, and so on.

A new PML schema can be derived from an existing one by just mentioning the reference to the old one and listing the differences in special PML elements.

A PML schema can define all kinds of annotations varying from linear annotations of morphology, through constituency or dependency trees, to complex graph-oriented annotation systems (coreference, valency, discourse relations). The schema provides information for validating the annotation data as well as for creating a relevant data model for their in-memory or database representation.

To give a complex example, the annotation of the Prague Dependency Treebank 2.0 (PDT 2.0, Hajič et al., 2006) was published in the PML format. It consists of four annotation layers, each defined by its own PML schema:

- a lowest word-form layer consisting of tokenized text segmented just into documents and paragraphs;
- a morphological layer segmenting the token stream of the previous layer into sentences and attaching the appropriate morphological form, lemma, and tag to each token;
- an analytical layer building a morpho-syntactic dependency tree from the words of each sentence (morphologically analysed on the previous layer);
- a tectogrammatical layer consisting of deep-syntactic dependency trees interlinked in a $m{:}n$ manner with the analytical layer and a valency lexicon and carrying further relational annotation, such as coreference and quotation sets.

Many other corpora were encoded in the format, including the Prague English Dependency Treebank,[1] the Prague Arabic Dependency Treebank,[2] the Prague Dependency Treebank of Spoken Language,[3] the Prague Czech-English Dependency Treebank,[4] Czesl (an error tagged corpus of Czech as a second language, (Hana et al., 2010)), the Latvian Treebank,[5] a part of the National Corpus of Polish,[6] the Index Thomisticus Treebank,[7] etc.

Moreover, several treebanks were converted into the PML format, mostly to be searchable in the query tool (see Section 3.3); e.g. the Penn Treebank 3, the TIGER Treebank 1.0, the Penn – CU Chinese Treebank 6.0, the Penn Arabic Treebank 2 – version 2.0, the Hyderabad Treebank (ICON 2009 version), the Sinica Treebank 3.0 (both constituency and CoNLL dependency trees), the CoNLL 2009 ST data, etc. The conversion programs are usually distributed as "extensions" (plug-ins) of TrEd (see Section 3.2), but they can be run without the editor as well.

3 Tools

A data format is worthless without tools to process it. PML comes with both low level tools (validation, libraries to load and save data) and higher level tools like annotation editors or querying and conversion tools. Since the last published description of the framework (Pajas and Štěpánek, 2008), the

[1] `http://ufal.mff.cuni.cz/pedt2.0/`

[2] `http://ufal.mff.cuni.cz/padt/PADT_1.0/docs/index.html`

[3] `http://ufal.mff.cuni.cz/pdtsl/`

[4] `http://ufal.mff.cuni.cz/pcedt2.0/`

[5] `http://dspace.utlib.ee/dspace/bitstream/handle/10062/17359/Pretkalnina_Nespore_etal_74.pdf`

[6] `http://nkjp.pl/`

[7] `http://itreebank.marginalia.it/`

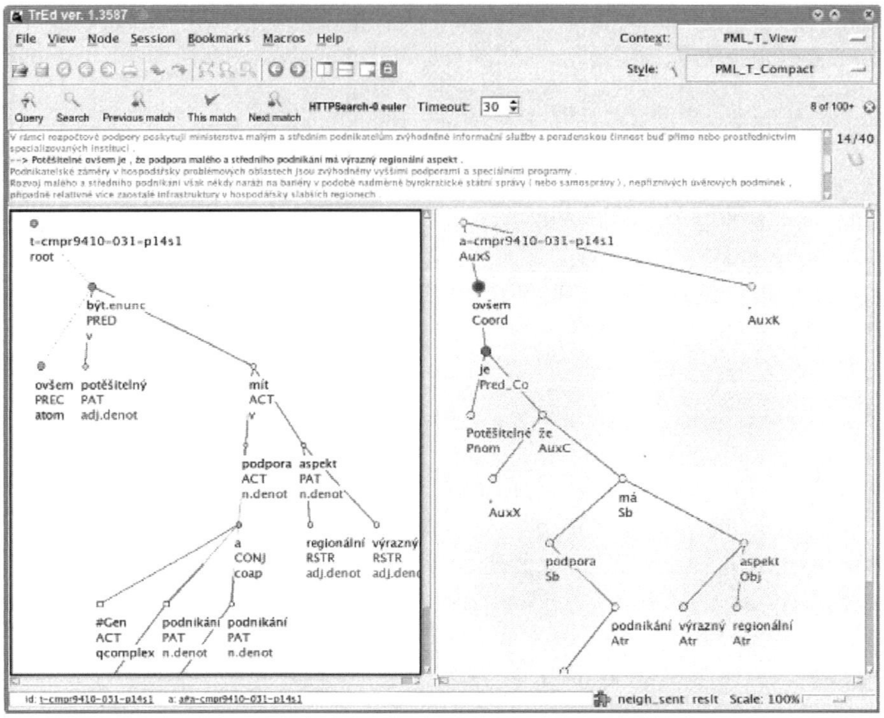

Figure 3: Sample sentence in the TrEd tree annotation tool

tools were further improved and several new ones emerged.

3.1 Low Level Tools

PML documents can be easily validated against their schemas. The validation is implemented by translating the PML schema into a Relax NG schema (plus some Schematron rules) and then validating the documents using existing validation tools for Relax NG. For schemas themselves, there exists another Relax NG schema that can validate them.

Most PML-related tools are written in Perl. The `Treex::PML` package (available at CPAN[8]) provides object-oriented API to PML schemas and documents. The library first loads the schema and then generates API tailored to the instances of the schema.

Applications written in Java can build on a library providing objects supporting basic PML types and utilities for reading and writing them to streams, etc. Moreover, additional libraries provide support for several PML instances (e.g. the PDT corpus and the Czesl corpus (Hana et al., 2010)). While adding support for additional instances is rather straightforward, it must be done manually, as we have not yet implemented an automatic API generator as we did for Perl.

3.2 Tree Editor TrEd

TrEd, a graphical tree editor, is probably the most frequently used tool from the PML framework. It is a highly extensible and configurable multi-platform program (running on MS Windows, Max OS and Linux). TrEd can work with any PML data[9] whose PML schema correctly defines (via roles) at least one sequence of trees. Besides the PML format, TrEd can work with many other data formats, either by means of the modular input/output interface of the PML library or using its own input/output backends.

The basic editing capabilities of TrEd allow the user to easily modify the tree structure with drag-and-drop operations and to easily edit the associated data. Although this is sufficient for most annotation

[8] `http://www.cpan.org/`

[9] TrEd can open data in other formats, too, because it is able to convert the data to PML and back on the fly, the conversion can be implemented as an XSLT transformation, Perl code or executable program.

tasks, the annotation process can be greatly accelerated by a set of custom extension functions, called *macros*, written in Perl. Macros are usually created to simplify the most common tasks done by the annotators. For example, by pressing "(", the annotator toggles the attribute `is_parenthesis` of the whole subtree of the current node.

While macros provide means to extend, accelerate and control the annotation capabilities of TrEd, the concept of *style-sheets* gives users full control over the visual presentation of the annotated data.

So far, TrEd has been used as an annotation tool for PDT 2.0 and several similarly structured treebanking projects like Slovene (Džeroski et al., 2006), Croatian (Tadić, 2007), or Greek Dependency Treebanks (Prokopidis et al., 2005), but also for Penn-style Alpino Treebank (van der Beek et al., 2002), the semantic annotation in the Dutch language Corpus Initiative project (Trapman and Monachesi, 2006), the annotation of French sentences with PropBank information (van der Plas et al., 2010), as well as for annotation of morphology using so-called MorphoTrees (Smrž and Pajas, 2004) in the Prague Arabic Dependency Treebank (where it was also used for annotation of the dependency trees in the PDT 2.0 style).

TrEd is also one of the client applications to the querying system, see Section 3.3.

The editor can also be used without the GUI just to run macros over given files. This mode supports several types of parallelization (e.g. Sun Grid Engine) to speed up processing of larger treebanks. This inspired the Treex project (Popel and Žabokrtský, 2010), a modular NLP software system implemented in Perl under Linux. It is primarily aimed at machine translation, making use of the ideas and technology created during the Prague Dependency Treebank project. It also significantly facilitates and accelerates development of software solutions of many other NLP tasks, especially due to re-usability of the numerous integrated processing modules (called blocks), which are equipped with uniform object-oriented interfaces.

3.3 Tree Query

Data in the PML format can be queried in a query tool called PML-Tree Query (PML-TQ, Pajas and Štěpánek, 2009). The system consists of three main components:

- an expressive *query language* supporting cross-layer queries, arbitrary boolean combinations of statements, able to query complex data structures. It also includes a sub-language for generating listings and non-trivial statistical reports, which goes far beyond statistical features of e.g. TigerSearch.
- client interfaces: a graphical user interface with a graphical query builder, a customizable visualization of the results, web-client interface, and a command-line interface.
- two interchangeable engines that evaluate queries: a very efficient engine that requires the treebank to be converted into a relational database, and a somewhat slower engine which operates directly on treebank files and is useful especially for data in the process of annotation.

The PML-TQ language offers the following distinctive features:

- selecting all occurrences of one or more nodes from the treebanks with given properties and in given relations with respect to the tree topology, cross-referencing, surface ordering, etc.
- support for bounded or unbounded iteration (i.e. transitive closure) of relations[10]
- support for multi-layered or aligned treebanks with structured attribute values
- quantified or negated subqueries (as in "find all clauses with exactly three objects but no subject")
- referencing among nodes (find parent and child that have the same case and gender but different number)
- natural textual and graphical representation of the query (the structure of the query usually corresponds to the structure of the matched subtree)

[10] For example, `descendant{1,3}` (iterating parent relation) or `coref_gram.rf{1,}` (iterating coreference pointer in PDT), `sibling{-1,1}` (immediately preceding or following sibling), `order-precedes{-1,1}` (immediately preceding or following node in the ordering of the sentence)

- sublanguage for post-processing and generating reports (extracting values from the matched nodes and applying one or more layers of filtering, grouping, aggregating, and sorting)
- support for regular expressions, basic arithmetic and string operations in the query and post-processing

For example, to get a frequency table of functions in the Penn Treebank, one can use the following query:

```
nonterminal $n := []
>> for $n.functions
       give $1, count()
       sort by $2 desc
```

Which means: select all non-terminals. Take their functions and count the number of occurrences of each of them, sort them by this number. The output starts like the following:

```
        738953
SBJ     116577
TMP     27189
LOC     19919
PRD     19793
CLR     18345
  ...
```

To extract a grammar behind the tree annotation of the Penn Treebank is a bit more complex task:

```
nonterminal $p := [ * $ch := [ ] ]
>> give $p, $p.cat,
   first_defined($ch.cat,$ch.pos),
   lbrothers($ch)
>> give $2 & " -> "
   & concat($3," " over $1 sort by $4)
>> for $1 give count(),$1
   sort by $1 desc
```

Which means: search for all non-terminals with a child of any type. Return the identifier of the parent, its category, the category or part-of-speech of the child, and the number of the child's left brothers. From this list, return the second column (the parent's category), add an arrow, and concatenate the third column (child's category or part-of-speech) of all the children with the same parent (first column) sorted according to the original word order. In this list, output number of occurrences of each line plus the line itself, sorted by the number of occurrences.

Running it on the Penn Treebank produces the following output:

```
189856    PP -> IN NP
128140     S -> NP VP
 87402    NP -> NP PP
72106     NP -> DT NN
65508      S -> NP VP .
45995     NP -> -NONE-
36078     NP -> DT JJ NN
31916     VP -> TO VP
28796     NP -> NNP NNP
23272   SBAR -> IN S
...
```

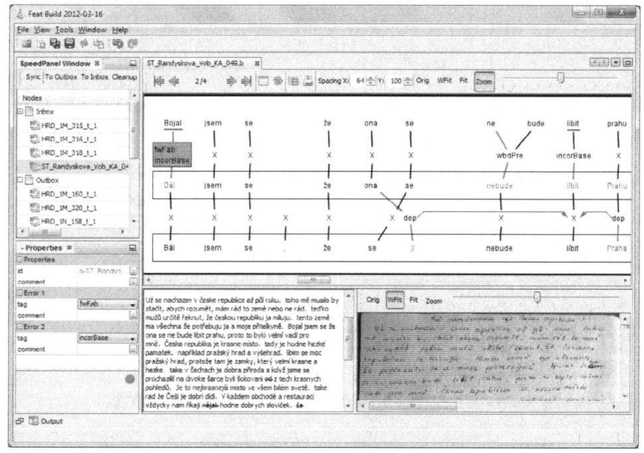

Figure 4: Sample sentence in the *feat* annotation tool

More elaborate examples can be found in (Pajas and Štěpánek, 2009; Štěpánek and Pajas, 2010).

3.4 Other Tools

In addition to the versatile TrEd tree editor, there are several tools intended for annotation of non-tree structures or for specific purposes:

MEd is an annotation tool in which linearly-structured annotations of text or audio data can be created and edited. The tool supports multiple stacked layers of annotations that can be interconnected by links. MEd can also be used for other purposes, such as word-to-word alignment of parallel corpora.

Law (Lexical Annotation Workbench) is an editor for morphological annotation. It supports simple morphological annotation (assigning a lemma and tag to a word), integration and comparison of different annotations of the same text, searching for particular word, tag etc. It natively supports PML but can import from and export to several additional formats.

[11] http://ufal.mff.cuni.cz/~hana/feat.html

Feat[11] is an environment for layered error annotation of learners corpora (see Figure 4). It has been used in the Czesl project (e.g. Hana et al., 2010; Hana et al., 2012) to correct and annotate texts produced by non-native speakers of Czech. The corpus and its annotation is encoded in several interconnected layers: scan of the original document, its transcription, tokenized text encoding author's corrections and two layers of error correction and annotation. Tokens on the latter three layers are connected by hyper-edges.

Capek[12] (e.g. Hana and Hladká, 2012) is an annotation editor tailored to school children to involve them in text annotation. Using this editor, they practice morphology and dependency-based syntax in the same way as they normally do at (Czech) schools, without any special training.

The last three of the above tools are written Java on top of the Netbeans platform, they are open and can be extended via plugins. Moreover, the Capek editor also has an iOS version for iPad.

4 Related Work

TEI The Text Encoding Initiative (TEI) provides guidelines[13] for representing a variety of literary and linguistic texts. The XML-based format is very rich and among other provides means for encoding linguistic annotation as well as some generic markup for graphs, networks, trees, feature-structures, and links. On the other hand, it lacks explicit support for stand-off annotation style and makes use of entities, an almost obsoleted feature of XML, that originates in SGML. There are no tools supporting the full specification.

ISO LAF, MAF, SynAF, GrAF The Linguistic Annotation Format (LAF; Ide and Romary, 2004; Suderman and Ide, 2006) was developed roughly at the same time as PML. It encodes linguistics structures as directed graphs; both nodes and edges might be annotated with feature structures. LAF is very similar to PML, they both support stand-off annotations, feature structures, alternatives, etc. The following points are probably the main differences between the frameworks:

- LAF is an abstract format, independent of its serialization to XML, which is specified by the Graph Annotation Format (GrAF; Ide and Suderman, 2007). PML is an XML based format, but in principle it could be encoded in other structured languages such as JSON.
- While PML allows encoding general graphs in the same way as GrAF, for certain specific graphs it is recommended to use encoding by XML structures: simple paths by a sequence of XML elements and trees by embedding. This greatly simplifies parsing and validation and prevent lots of errors. (In theory, these errors should be prevented by the use of appropriate applications, but in practice the data are often modified by hand or low level tools.) In addition, many problems can be solved significantly faster for trees or sequences than for general graphs.
- PML is supported with a rich set of tools (TrEd and other tools described in this paper). We were not able to find a similar set of tools for LAF.

Plain text There are many advantages of a structured format over a plain-text vertical format (e.g. popular CoNLL Shared Task format). The main drawbacks of the simpler plain-text format is that it does not support standard encoding of meta information, and that complex structures (e.g. lists of lists) and relations in multi-layered annotation are encoded in an ad-hoc fashion which is prone to errors. For details, see (Straňák and Štěpánek, 2010).

EXMARaLDA We have also used PML to encode the Czesl learner corpus. As the corpus uses layered annotation, the only established alternative was the tabular format used by EXMARaLDA (Schmidt, 2009). However, the format has several disadvantages (see, e.g. Hana et al., 2010; Hana et al., 2012). Most importantly, the correspondences between the original word form and its corrected equivalents or annotations at other levels may be lost, especially

[12] `http://ufal.mff.cuni.cz/styx/`

[13] `http://www.tei-c.org/Guidelines/P5/`

for errors in discontinuous phrases. The feat editor supports import from and export to several formats, including EXMARaLDA.

5 Future Work

In the current specification, PML instances use a dedicated namespace. A better solution would be to let the user specify his or her own namespace in a PML schema. Support for handling additional namespaces would also be desirable (one might use it e.g. to add documentation or comments to schemas and data), however, this feature need much more work: if some PML elements are moved or deleted by an application, should it also move or delete the foreign namespace content?

List members and alternative members are always represented by `<LM>`, resp. `<AM>` XML elements. Several users requested a possibility to define a different name in a PML schema. This change would make the data more readable for human eyes, but it might complicate the internal data representation.

We would also like to extend support of PML in Java and add support for additional languages.

Finally, we plan to perform a detailed comparison with the LAF-based formats and create conversion tools between PML and LAF.

Acknowledgements

This work has been using language resources developed and/or stored and/or distributed by the LINDAT-Clarin project of the Ministry of Education of the Czech Republic (project LM2010013). This paper and the development of the framework were also supported by the Grant Agency of the Czech Republic (grants 406/10/P193 and 406/10/P328).

References

Sašo Džeroski, Tomaž Erjavec, Nina Ledinek, Petr Pajas, Zdeněk Žabokrtský, and Andreja Žele. 2006. Towards a Slovene Dependency Treebank. In *Proceedings of the 5th International Conference on Language Resources and Evaluation (LREC 2006)*, pages 1388–1391.

Jan Hajič, Jarmila Panevová, Eva Hajičová, Petr Sgall, Petr Pajas, Jan Štěpánek, Jiří Havelka, Marie Mikulová, Zdeněk Žabokrtský, and Magda Ševčíková-Razímová. 2006. *Prague Dependency Treebank 2.0.* Linguistic Data Consortium, Philadelphia. CD-ROM, CAT: LDC2001T10.

Jirka Hana and Barbora Hladká. 2012. Getting more data – Schoolkids as annotators. In *Proceedings of the Eighth Conference on Language Resources and Evaluation (LREC 2012)*, Istanbul. accepted.

Jirka Hana, Alexandr Rosen, Svatava Škodová, and Barbora Štindlová. 2010. Error-tagged Learner Corpus of Czech. In *Proceedings of The Fourth Linguistic Annotation Workshop (LAW IV)*, Uppsala.

Jirka Hana, Alexandr Rosen, Barbora Štindlová, and Petr Jäger. 2012. Building a learner corpus. In *Proceedings of the Eighth Conference on Language Resources and Evaluation (LREC 2012)*, Istanbul. accepted.

Nancy Ide and Laurent Romary. 2004. International standard for a linguistic annotation framework. *Nat. Lang. Eng.*, 10(3-4):211–225, September.

Nancy Ide and Keith Suderman. 2007. Graf: a graph-based format for linguistic annotations. In *Proceedings of the Linguistic Annotation Workshop*, LAW '07, pages 1–8.

Petr Pajas and Jan Štěpánek. 2006. XML-based representation of multi-layered annotation in the PDT 2.0. In Richard Erhard Hinrichs, Nancy Ide, Martha Palmer, and James Pustejovsky, editors, *Proceedings of the LREC Workshop on Merging and Layering Linguistic Information (LREC 2006)*, pages 40–47.

Petr Pajas and Jan Štěpánek. 2008. Recent advances in a feature-rich framework for treebank annotation. In Donia Scott and Hans Uszkoreit, editors, *The 22nd International Conference on Computational Linguistics – Proceedings of the Conference*, volume 2, pages 673–680, Manchester.

Petr Pajas and Jan Štěpánek. 2009. System for querying syntactically annotated corpora. In Gary Lee and Sabine Schulte im Walde, editors, *Proceedings of the ACL-IJCNLP 2009 Software Demonstrations*, pages 33–36, Singapore. Association for Computational Linguistics.

Martin Popel and Zdeněk Žabokrtský. 2010. TectoMT: Modular NLP framework. In *Proceedings of IceTAL, 7th International Conference on Natural Language Processing*, pages 293–304, Reykjavik.

Prokopis Prokopidis, Elina Desypri, Maria Koutsombogera, Haris Papageorgiou, and Stelios Piperidis. 2005. Theoretical and practical issues in the construction of a Greek dependency treebank. In *In Proc. of the 4th Workshop on Treebanks and Linguistic Theories (TLT)*, pages 149–160.

Thomas Schmidt. 2009. Creating and working with spoken language corpora in EXMARaLDA. In *LULCL II: Lesser Used Languages & Computer Linguistics II*, pages 151–164.

Otakar Smrž and Petr Pajas. 2004. MorphoTrees of Arabic and their annotation in the TrEd environment. In Mahtab Nikkhou, editor, *Proceedings of the NEMLAR International Conference on Arabic Language Resources and Tools*, pages 38–41, Cairo. ELDA.

Jan Štěpánek and Petr Pajas. 2010. Querying diverse treebanks in a uniform way. In *Proceedings of the 7th International Conference on Language Resources and Evaluation (LREC 2010)*, pages 1828–1835. European Language Resources Association.

Pavel Straňák and Jan Štěpánek. 2010. Representing layered and structured data in the CoNLL-ST format. In Alex Fang, Nancy Ide, and Jonathan Webster, editors, *Proceedings of the Second International Conference on Global Interoperability for Language Resources*, pages 143–152, Hong Kong.

Keith Suderman and Nancy Ide. 2006. Layering and merging linguistic annotations. In *Proceedings of the 5th Workshop on NLP and XML: Multi-Dimensional Markup in Natural Language Processing*, NLPXML '06, pages 89–92.

Marko Tadić. 2007. Building the Croatian Dependency Treebank: the initial stages. In *Contemporary Linguistics*, volume 63, pages 85–92.

Jantine Trapman and Paola Monachesi. 2006. Manual for the annotation of semantic roles in D-Coi. Technical report, University of Utrecht.

Leonoor van der Beek, Gosse Bouma, Robert Malouf, and Gertjan van Noord. 2002. The Alpino Dependency Treebank. In *Computational Linguistics in the Netherlands CLIN 2001*, Amsterdam.

Lonneke van der Plas, Tanja Samardzic, and Paola Merlo. 2010. Cross-lingual validity of PropBank in the manual annotation of French. In *Proceedings of The Fourth Linguistic Annotation Workshop (LAW IV)*, Uppsala.

Exploiting naive *vs* expert discourse annotations: an experiment using lexical cohesion to predict Elaboration / Entity-Elaboration confusions

Clémentine Adam
CLLE & University of Toulouse
adam@univ-tlse2.fr

Marianne Vergez-Couret
LPL, Aix-Marseille University
and Hong-Kong Polytechnic University
marianne.vergez@gmail.com

Abstract

This paper brings a contribution to the field of discourse annotation of corpora. Using ANNODIS, a french corpus annotated with discourse relations by naive and expert annotators, we focus on two of them, Elaboration and Entity-Elaboration. These two very frequent relations are (a) often confused by naive annotators (b) difficult to detect automatically as their signalling is poorly studied. We propose to use lexical cohesion to differentiate between them, and show that Elaboration is more cohesive than Entity-Elaboration. We then integrate lexical cohesion cues in a classification experiment, obtaining highly satisfying results.

1 Introduction

This paper brings a contribution to the field of corpus annotation at the discourse level. Discourse structure is based on coherence links existing between discourse units. These links can be captured using the notion of discourse relations (Mann and Thompson, 1987; Asher and Lascarides, 2003). Handling and detecting elements of discourse structure is very challenging for Natural Language Processing. Applications such as natural language generation (Bateman and Zock, 2005), automatic summarization (Marcu, 2000), among others, could take advantage of discourse level information detection. In the current state of research, providing reliably annotated corpora at the discourse level is really groundbreaking and opens new possibilities of investigation in discourse studies.

The ANNODIS project (Péry-Woodley et al., 2009; Afantenos et al., 2012) will provide the scientific community with access to such a corpus for French (see section 2). It is the first ressource in French annotated with discourse relations. Similar corpora have already been developped for English, including the Penn Discourse TreeBank (Prasad et al., 2007), the RST Tree Bank (Carlson et al., 2001) or the Discor corpus (Reese et al., 2007). But ANNODIS has distinct characteristics. For our concern, the main difference is the two-level annotation: first a pre-annotation done by naive annotators (called "naive annotation") and then a revised annotation done by expert annotators (called "expert annotation"). This allows investigation on the whole process of annotation.

In this paper, we focus on Elaboration and Entity-Elaboration, the two most frequent and frequently confused relations (see section 3). We propose a new approach based on lexical cohesion cues to differentiate between these relations, and show its reliability using expert annotation (see section 4). We integrate this approach in a machine learning experiment and highlight the improvement it brings (see section 5). We show how the obtained classifier can be used to automatically improve naive annotation or to reduce the experts' workload.

2 The ANNODIS corpus

The ANNODIS corpus[1], enriched with annotations at the discourse level, considers two different approaches of discourse organization, a top-down ap-

[1] http://w3.erss.univ-tlse2.fr/annodis

proach[2] and a bottom-up approach. Here, we focus only on the bottom-up approach which aims at constructing the structure of discourse, starting from elementary discourse units (EDUs) and recursively building more complex discourse units (CDUs) via discourse relations (EDUs contain at least one eventuality, most of the time only one). At the end, a hierarchical structure is defined for the whole text. This part of the corpus is composed of newspaper articles (from *Est Républicain*) and extracts from Wikipedia articles.

The specifications in the annotation manual were adapted from the SDRT model, a semantic approach of discourse structure (Asher and Lascarides, 2003), but were also inspired by other discourse models such as the RST framework (Mann and Thompson, 1987), the Linguistic Discourse Model (Polanyi, 1988), the graphbank model (Wolf and Gibson, 2005) etc. The discourse relations linking discourse units described in the manual are a set of relations[3] largely inspired from discourse relations common to most discourse theories mentioned above.

The ANNODIS corpus was annotated using a three-step process: it contains preliminary, naive and expert annotations of discourse relations. During the first preliminary phase, 50 documents were annotated by 2 postgraduate students in language sciences. The key purpose of this initial phase was to assist the drafting of the annotation manual which was used afterwards for the second main phase of annotation. 86 different texts were then doubly annotated with the help of the aforementioned manual by 3 postgraduate students in language sciences. The naive annotation was performed in order to discover cognitive principles of discourse organization (Afantenos et al., 2012). The double annotation allowed evaluating the inter-annotators agreement. The Kappa score (Cohen, 1960) on common attached discourse units for the full set of relations is 0.4, which indicates a moderate to weak agreement and reveals the difficulty of the discourse annotation task. The expert annotation was performed as a third phase. 42 texts randomly selected from naive annotation were then reviewed and corrected by expert annotators. 44 texts from naive annotations remain to be reviewed and corrected.

This paper will focus on one of the frequent mistakes concerning two close relations: Elaboration and Entity-Elaboration (hereafter E-Elaboration) in the naive annotation and their correction in the expert annotation.

3 On Elaboration and Entity-Elaboration

The distinction between an elaboration of a state or an event (Elaboration) and an elaboration of an entity (E-Elaboration) is common in discourse theories. But the status of E-Elaboration as a discourse relation is not obvious and divides the scientific community. In the RST framework (Mann and Thompson, 1987), distinction points exist between Elaboration and E-Elaboration but both are regrouped in a single discourse relation. Knott (1996) considers discourse markers as the basis to motivate a set of coherence relations. Therefore Knott et al. (2001) reject E-Elaboration as a discourse relation for two reasons. The first is absence of obvious discourse markers. The second is that the E-Elaboration relation does not relate two propositions, as discourse relations usually do. Conversely, Fabricius-Hansen and Behrens (2001) introduce separate relations (called E[ventuality] Elaboration and I[ndividual] Elaboration). Prévot et al. (2009) note the need to introduce this relation in order to avoid confusions in annotation, arguing that keeping all the embedded segments in one discourse segment smudges the discourse contribution of the including segment. In ANNODIS, the choice was made to consider two different relations for annotation.

3.1 Elaboration and Entity-Elaboration in ANNODIS

For each relation, the annotation manual gives an informal description, several illustrations and additional information on the possible confusions between the described relation and other discourse relations. Here are the descriptions of Elaboration and

[2]The top-down approach focuses on the selective annotation of multi-level discourse structure such as enumerative structures (Ho-Dac et al., 2009).

[3]Alternation, Attribution, Background, Comment, Continuation, Contrast, Elaboration, Entity-Elaboration, Explanation, Flashback, Frame, Goal, Narration, Parallel, Result, Temporal Location. Fusion is also used when expert annotation disagreed with segmentation. Fusion(1,2) means that segments 1 and 2 are considered one segment.

E-Elaboration in the annotation manual of ANNODIS:

The Elaboration relation relates two propositions only if the second proposition describes a sub-state or sub-event of the state or event described in the first proposition. Elaboration also includes exemplification, reformulation and paraphrase cases.

The E-Elaboration relation relates two segments for which the second one specifies a property of one of the involved entities in the first segment. This property can be important (e.g. identificatory) or marginal.

Example (1) illustrates both relations. Each segment corresponding to one EDU is numbered. Segments sharing a same rhetorical role in the discourse must be joined into complex segments.

(1) [La Lausitz, [une région pauvre de l'est de l'Allemagne,]$_1$ [réputée pour ses mines de charbon à ciel ouvert,]$_2$ a été le théâtre d'une première mondiale, mardi 9 septembre.]$_3$ [Le groupe suédois Vattenfall a inauguré, dans la petite ville de Spremberg, une centrale électrique à charbon expérimentale]$_4$ [qui met en œuvre toute la chaîne des techniques de captage et de stockage du carbone]$_5$
[Lausitz, [a poor region in east Germany,]$_1$ [famous for its open air coal mines,]$_2$ was the scene of a world first, on Tuesday September 9th.]$_3$ [The swedish group Vattenfall inaugurated, in the small town of Spremberg, an experimental coal power plant]$_4$ [involving the complete carbon capture and storage chain.]$_5$

The expert annotation for this mini-discourse is given below :

E-Elaboration (3,[1-2])
Elaboration (3,4)
E-Elaboration (4,5)

Complex segment [1-2] is embedded in segment 3 and is given properties of the entity "La Lausitz". It is therefore attached to this segment by Entity-Elaboration. Segment 4 describes the event "to inaugurate a power plant" which is a reformulation of "to be the scene of a world first" and is attached to segment 3 with Elaboration. Finally, segment 5 gives a property of the entity "a power plant" in segment 4 and is attached to it via E-Elaboration.

The annotation manual also discusses possible confusions between Elaboration and E-Elaboration (and conversely). The discussion mostly highlights how the distinction between state and event could help to avoid confusion. It also reminds the reader of the major distinction between the two relations, e.g. Elaboration gives details on a state or an event while E-Elaboration gives details on an entity.

Despite these precautions, the naive annotators are often prone to error when confronted with these two relations.

3.2 Quantitative analysis in ANNODIS

Elaboration and E-Elaboration are the more frequent relations in the ANNODIS corpus, both in the naive annotation with 50% of the annotated relations and in the expert annotation with 35% of the annotated relations. The low inter-agreement for these relations in the naive annotation indicates that the relations are not well-understood. This hypothesis is reinforced by overestimation of annotated Elaboration and E-Elaboration: in 60% of the cases, an agreement between two naive annotators does not ensure that the annotation is correct (Vergez-Couret, 2010).

Note that when experts review and correct naive annotation, most of the corrections involve wrong annotations of Elaboration and E-Elaboration. Table 1 presents the expert annotation for each Elaborations and E-Elaborations annotated by the naives.

		Naive		
		Elab	E-Elab	Total
Expert	Elab	302	70	372
	E-Elab	158	216	374
	Total	460	286	746
Expert	Fusion	81	57	
	Continuation	70	32	
	Background	32	18	
	Other	150	59	

Table 1: Expert annotations for E-Elaborations and Elaborations in naive annotation

This table shows that confusions between Elaboration and E-Elaboration are the most important compared to confusions with other discourse relations. Elaboration is mistaken for E-Elaboration (hereafter Elaboration $\rightarrow$ E-Elaboration) and more importantly E-Elaboration is mistaken for Elaboration (here after noted E-Elaboration → Elaboration). This paper only focuses on these two relations for methodological reasons: this choice allows first to give careful considerations to the linguistic features involved in the two relations (see section 3.3) and also to highlight and evaluate the improvements brought by using new kinds of linguistic cues (see section 4).

3.3 Linguistic features of Elaboration and Entity-Elaboration

Annotating Elaboration and E-Elaboration, manually or automatically, is very challenging since no prototypical marker exists for the two relations (Knott, 1996, among others). Some possible markers given in the ANNODIS manual (*à savoir, c'est-à-dire, notamment*, etc.) are not discriminatory for one of the two relations, and they are relatively rare.

One could think of other possible linguistic features of Elaboration and E-Elaboration. Prévot et al. (2009) underline possible linguistic realisations of E-Elaboration such as relative clauses and appositions (nominal and adjectival appositions, brackets...). Adam and Vergez-Couret (2010) point out that French gerund clauses may express serveral discourse relations including Elaboration but not E-Elaboration. Even if these syntactic features are not discriminatory with respect to all discourse relations (for instance gerund clauses and appositions may express Explanation or Background), we will see in section 4 if these syntactic features allow to distinguish Elaboration and E-Elaboration.

But more importantly, we would like to focus on one of the major distinctions between the two relations, e.g. Elaboration provides details on a state or an event while E-Elaboration provides detail on an entity, and how to highlight this distinction. The hypothesis we are testing is that this distinction results in differences concerning the lexical cohesion between the two segments. Cohesion includes all the links holding a text together as a whole, including reference, ellipsis and lexical cohesion. Lexical cohesion encompasses relations such as synonymy, hyperonymy, lexical similarity, etc. Our hypothesis is that Elaboration involves more lexical cohesion links since it relates two propositions and its interpretation involves information given by lexical semantics and world knowledge (Asher and Lascarides, 2003). Adam and Vergez-Couret (2010) show that the use of lexical cohesion cues reliably detect gerund clauses which are Elaborations. In contrast, E-Elaboration only relates a proposition to an entity. In example (2), where Elaboration relates [17-19] to the target segment 16, it is indeed possible to highlight lexical cohesion links playing a role in Elaboration.

(2) [Un soir, il faisait un temps horrible,]$_{16}$ [les éclairs se croisaient,]$_{17}$ [le tonnerre grondait,]$_{18}$ [la pluie tombait à torrent.]$_{19}$
[One night, the weather was horrible,]$_{16}$ [flashes of lightning were crossing,]$_{17}$ [thunder growled,]$_{18}$ [rain fell heavily.]$_{19}$

In this case, cohesion lexical links between "temps" (weather) in 16 and "éclair" (flash of lightning), "tonnerre" (thunder) and "pluie" (rain) in [17-19] play a role in the interpretation of Elaboration.

On the other hand, E-Elaboration does not provide details about the whole proposition in the target segment, but provides details on an entity of this segment. Lexical cohesion links are not expected in this case.

(3) [Pourquoi a-t-on abattu Paul Mariani, [cinquante-cinq ans]$_4$, [attaché au cabinet de M. François Doubin,]$_5$?]$_6$
[Why was Paul Mariani, [fifty-five]$_4$, [personal assistant to M. François Doubin,]$_5$ gunned down?]$_6$

In example (3), the age and the profession of Paul Mariani is not lexically linked to the fact that he was gunned down.

In the next section, we discuss how to highlight lexical cohesion links in order to differenciate Elaboration and E-Elaboration.

4 Differentiating between Elaboration and Entity-Elaboration using lexical cohesion

4.1 Preamble

The interplay of lexical cohesion and discourse structure is an often studied but still not fully understood issue (Barzilay, 2008; Berzlánovich et al., 2008). Lexical cohesion cues are typically used in diverse automated approaches of discourse, but as these cues are used among others, their impact is not precisely evaluated. We aim at demonstrating that lexical cohesion cues can be successfully applied to differentiation between Elaboration and E-Elaboration.

Adam and Morlane-Hondère (2009) propose to use a distributional semantic model (Baroni and Lenci, 2010) in order to detect lexical cohesion. Adam and Vergez-Couret (2010) use the lexical links identified by this method in a practical experiment of Elaboration detection. They show that the use of distributional neighbors in combination with an ambiguous marker of Elaboration (the gerund clause) very reliably detects some cases of Elaboration. This result confirms that Elaboration implies lexical cohesion, and that a distributional semantic model is a good lexical resource for identifying lexical cohesion links in texts.

As an extension to those studies, we want to use lexical cohesion cues to help differentiating between Elaboration and E-Elaboration. We first present how distributional neighbors can be used to estimate lexical cohesion between two text segments (section 4.2). Then, we compare the lexical cohesion of Elaboration and E-Elaboration and show that Elaboration is significatively more cohesive than E-Elaboration (section 4.3).

4.2 Methods: How to evaluate the strength of lexical cohesion between two segments

In order to evaluate the strength of lexical cohesion between two text segments S_a and S_b, we proceed in two steps. First, the two segments are annotated with part-of-speech and lemma information using the TreeTagger (Schmid, 1994). Then, all the lexical proximity links between the two segments are annotated. To detect these links, we use a lexical proximity measure based on the distributional analysis of the french Wikipedia (Bourigault, 2002). Internal links in a segment are not considered.

The number of lexical links N_ℓ can be directly interpreted as a cohesion cue. But this cue is skewed since this number is correlated to the segment's size (longer segments have more items to be linked). To reduce this skew, we built a score where the number of lexical links is normalized. Calling N_a the number of neighbours (linked or not) in the first segment (S_a) and N_b the number of neighbours in the second segment (S_b), our normalized score Sc is defined as:

$$Sc = \frac{N_\ell}{\sqrt{N_a \cdot N_b}}$$

4.3 Application to Elaboration and E-Elaboration relations in ANNODIS

From the ANNODIS corpus, we extracted all the Elaboration and E-Elaboration relations according to the expert annotation. Then, we projected the neighbourhood links as described in section 4.2. The results are given in the Table 2.

	Elab.	E-elab.
Number of cases	625	527
Average segment length	54.61	27.84
Average # of proj. links N_ℓ	**5.99**	1.39
Average cohesion score Sc	**0.61**	0.32

Table 2: Comparison between Elaboration and E-Elaboration lexical cohesion

Table 2 shows that Elaborations contain much more lexical links than E-Elaborations (4 to 5 times more). This can partially be explained by the length of Elaboration segments : Elaborations are typically 2 times longer than E-Elaborations. From an application point of view, the skew on N_ℓ is not a problem. Using N_ℓ as a cue is then equivalent to combining two cues: the higher lexical cohesion of Elaboration relation and the fact than Elaborations are longer than E-Elaborations. From a theoretical point of view, we expect to observe that Elaboration is more lexically cohesive than E-Elaboration even for the normalized score Sc. Data in Table 2 confirms this expectation. This first result is interesting in itself, as it provides an experimental validation based on a corpus for the theoretical descriptions of Elaboration and E-Elaboration (Asher and Lascarides, 2003; Prévot et al., 2009).

Based on this result, we propose to use lexical cohesion cues to improve ANNODIS annotations, by predicting the errors of the annotators. In the next section (5) we present an experiment set up in order to reach this goal.

5 Predicting the confusions between Elaboration and E-Elaboration: implementation

In section 3, we highlighted that Elaboration and E-Elaboration are the relations that are most frequently mistaken in the naive annotation of ANNODIS corpus. However, as shown in section 4, Elaboration and E-Elaboration can be distinguished using their lexical cohesion, which can be evaluated by using distributional neighbours. In this section, we present a machine learning experiment aiming at automatically classifying Elaboration and E-Elaboration using lexical cohesion cues, among other features.

5.1 Experiment methodology

From the ANNODIS corpus, we extracted all Elaboration and E-Elaboration relations according to the naive annotation. We restricted this subset to relations having an Elaboration or E-Elaboration annotation in the expert annotation. Indeed, we only defined cues for these two relations; considering other relations would require specifying markers for them. Then, for each $< S_a, S_b >$ couple, we computed the attributes listed in Table 3.

Att.	Description	Values
N_ℓ	see section 4.2	$N_\ell \in \mathbb{N}$
Sc	see section 4.2	$Sc \in \mathbb{R}^+$
rel	S_b is a relative clause	boolean
app	S_b is a nom. / adj. apposition	boolean
ger	S_b is a gerund clause	boolean
bra	S_b is in brackets	boolean
emb	S_b is an embedded segment	boolean
w_{Sa}	# of words in S_b	$w_{S1} \in \mathbb{N}$
w_{Sb}	# of words in S_b	$w_{S2} \in \mathbb{N}$
w_{tot}	$w_{Sa} + w_{Sb}$	$w_{tot} \in \mathbb{N}$
s_{Sa}	# of segments in S_a	$s_{S1} \in \mathbb{N}$
s_{Sb}	# of segments in S_b	$s_{S2} \in \mathbb{N}$
s_{tot}	$s_{Sa} + s_{Sb}$	$s_{tot} \in \mathbb{N}$

Table 3: Attributes computed

Thus, we considered:

- lexical cohesion cues described in section 4.2 (N_ℓ and Sc);
- linguistic features presented in section 3.3 (rel, app, ger and bra): these features were detected using patterns based on the part-of-speech annotation of the segments;
- structural features regarding the two segments: is S_b embedded in S_a? (emb) How many words are there in the two segments? (w_{Sa}, w_{Sb} and w_{tot}) Are they simple segments or complex segments? (s_{Sa}, s_{Sb} and s_{tot}).

We then processed the data produced using the machine learning software Weka (Hall et al., 2009). More specifically, we used Weka's implementation of the Random Forest classifier (Breiman, 2001). In the following sections, we present our results (section 5.2) and discuss the way they could be exploited in an annotation campaign (section 5.3).

5.2 Classification results

Table 4 shows again the results for naive annotation when compared to the annotation provided by experts. The accuracy is satisfying at 69.4%, but closer examination reveals that a large set of E-Elaboration are mistakenly classified as Elaboration by the naive annotators. Using the classifier introduced in section 5.1, we performed a classification experiment on this data set, considering the naive annotation as an additional unreliable cue. Results from this experiment, using 10-fold cross-validation, are presented in Table 5. The accuracy increases to 75.7% and both E-Elaboration→Elaboration and Elaboration→E-Elaboration confusions are significantly reduced. This 6.3% improvement on the naive annotation is highly satisfying.

↑Expert annot. \ ← Naive annot.	elab	e-elab
elab	302	70
e-elab	158	216

Accuracy : 69.4%

Table 4: Confusion matrix for naive annotation

↑Expert annot. \ ← Naive-aided auto. annot.	elab	e-elab
elab	306	66
e-elab	115	259

Accuracy : 75.7%

Table 5: Confusion matrix for naive-aided automatic annotation

In order to evaluate the impact of the different attributes used in the classifier (see Table 3), we repeated the classification experiment, using a single attributes category at a time. The results are summarized in Table 6. Structural attributes bring only a

Attributes used	Accuracy
Naive annotation	69.4%
Naive + lexical cohesion cues	72.3% (+2.9%)
Naive + linguistic cues	71.7% (+2.3%)
Naive + structural cues	69.7% (+0.3%)
All	75.7% (+6.3%)

Table 6: Impact of the different attributes categories

0.3% gain. As expected, lexical cohesion cues bring a noticeable improvement (+2.9%). Moreover, this improvement is stronger than the one brought by all linguistic features combined (+2.3%). This confirms the importance of lexical cohesion to differentiate between Elaboration and E-Elaboration. The synergy between the attributes categories is highlighted by the gain brought by the combination of all attributes, significantly higher than the sum of individual gains.

5.3 Exploiting our classifier's results in an annotation campaign

In the context of an iterative annotation campaign such as ANNODIS, an automatic classifier could hold different roles: (a) providing a first annotation, *i.e.* replacing the naive annotation (b) improving the naive annotation, *i.e.* replacing the expert annotation (c) helping the expert annotation, with an intermediate process between naive and expert annotation.

Role (a) is irrelevant to the present study. Indeed, the automatic annotations experiments were performed only on cases identified by naive annotators as Elaboration or E-Elaboration. In its current form, the automatic annotation system developed can only be used as a processing step following the required naive annotation (in the ANNODIS context, naive annotation is the only one available for 44 texts, see section 2). As demonstrated by the results of section 5.2, our system can directly be used to improve the naive annotation (b): a significant amount of confusions between the frequent relations Elaboration and E-Elaboration can be corrected (from 69.4% to 75.7% accuracy).

Finally, we show below how our classifier can be exploited to help expert annotation (c). This last proposal is relevant to workload reduction for the experts annotators, which are still required here (contrary to proposal (b)) . We have seen (Table 4) that naive annotators are not very reliable for E-Elaboration identification, so that in practice this classification should always be reviewed. However, presenting all naive E-Elaboration results to the expert introduces a significant overhead. Automatic classification can be used to isolate the most critical cases, allowing to reduce this overhead by presenting only those cases to the expert.

Table 8 illustrates the expected performance for such a system. From 286 relations classified as E-Elaboration by the naive annotators, 159 are automatically validated as E-Elaboration and not presented to the experts. Aiming for an error rate below 10%, we used the cost matrix presented in Table 7. Thus, only 8.2% of the accepted annotations are erroneous. The experts are then presented with the 127 cases that the automated classifier identified as possible Elaborations. For the data on which Table 8 is based, this represents a $159/286 = 55.6\%$ workload reduction for expert annotators.

0	10
1	0

Table 7: Cost matrix

	elab	e-elab	← automatic annot. (naive annot=e-elab)
elab	57	13	
e-elab	70	146	
↑Expert	127	159	
	↙ second look by expert	↘ accepted annot. (error : 8.2%)	

Table 8: Confusion matrix for naive e-elab second-look setup

Going further, our system could also be used to suggest improvements to the annotation manual, by highlighting the causes for frequent mistakes and by allowing an analysis of the reliability of the different cues taken in consideration (or not) by the annotators

6 Conclusion

In this paper, we used ANNODIS, a french corpus annotated with discourse relations, which provides the results of two annotation steps, to study two particular discourse relations: Elaboration and E-Elaboration. These two very frequent relations are (a) often erroneously interchanged by annotators (b) difficult to detect automatically as their signalling is poorly studied. We considered these relations from a lexical cohesion viewpoint.

We introduced a method to evaluate the lexical cohesion between two segments, using distributional neighbors. This approach allowed us to confirm that Elaboration is more cohesive than E-Elaboration. We therefore integrated lexical cohesion cues in a machine learning system, employed in a classification experiment with promising results.

These results bring improvements that could be used to facilitate future annotation campaigns. Going further, this study is especially interesting because (a) it fully exploits two levels of annotation, which is very rare; (b) it enhances the linguistic description of the considered relations, based on attested data; (c) it validates our approach based on lexical cohesion detection.

References

C. Adam and F. Morlane-Hondère. 2009. Détection de la cohésion lexicale par voisinage distributionnel : application à la segmentation thématique. In *RECITAL'09*, Senlis, France, juin 2009.

C. Adam and M. Vergez-Couret. 2010. Signalling elaboration: Combining gerund clauses with lexical cues. In *Multidisciplinay Approaches to Discourse (MAD 2010)*, Moissac, France, 17-20 March.

S. Afantenos, N. Asher, F. Benamara, M. Bras, C. Fabre, M. Ho-dac, A. Le Draoulec, P. Muller, M.-P. Péry-Woodley, L. Prévot, J. Rebeyrolle, L. Tanguy, M. Vergez-Couret, and L. Vieu. 2012. An empirical resource for discovering cognitive principles of discourse organisation: the annodis corpus. In *Eighth Language Resources and Evaluation Conference (LREC 2012)*, Istanbul (Turkey), 21-22 May.

N. Asher and A. Lascarides. 2003. *Logics of conversation*. Cambridge:CUP.

M. Baroni and A. Lenci. 2010. Distributional memory: A general framework for corpus-based semantics. *Computational Linguistics*, 36(4):673–721.

M. Barzilay, R. & Lapata. 2008. Modeling local coherence: An entity-based approach. *Computational Linguistics*, 34(1):1–34.

J. Bateman and M. Zock, 2005. *The Oxford Handbook of Computational Linguistics*, chapter Natural Language Generation, pages 284–304. Oxford Universtity Press, New York.

I. Berzlánovich, M. Egg, and G. Redeker. 2008. Coherence structure and lexical cohesion in expository and persuasive texts. In *Proceedings of the Workshop Constraints in Discourse III*, pages 19–26, Potsdam, Germany.

D. Bourigault. 2002. UPERY : un outil d'analyse distributionnelle étendue pour la construction d'ontologies à partir de corpus. In *Actes de la 9ème confrence sur le Traitement Automatique de la Langue Naturelle*, pages 75–84, Nancy.

L. Breiman. 2001. Random forests. *Machine Learning*, 45(1):5–32.

L. Carlson, D. Marcu, and M. E. Okurowski. 2001. Building a discourse-tagged corpus in the framework of rhetorical structure theory. In *Proceedings of the 2nd SigDial Workshop on Discourse and Dialogue*. version papier + version lectronique.

J. Cohen. 1960. A coefficient of agreement for nominal scales. *Educational and Psychological Measurement*, 20 (1):37–46.

C. Fabricius-Hansen and B. Behrens. 2001. Elaboration and related discourse relations viewed from an interlingual perspective. In *Proceedings from Third Workshop on Text Structure*, Austin, Texas.

M. Hall, E. Frank, G. Holmes, B. Pfahringer, P. Reutemann, and I. H. Witten. 2009. The weka data mining software: An update. *SIGKDD Explorations*, 11(1).

L.-M. Ho-Dac, C. Fabre, M.-P. Péry-Woodley, and J. Rebeyrolle. 2009. A top-down approach to discourse-level annotation. In *Corpus linguistic Conference*, Liverpool, UK, 20-23 juillet.

A. Knott, J. Oberlander, M. O'Donnell, and C. Mellish. 2001. Beyond elaboration : the interaction of relations and focus in coherent text. In T. Sanders, J. Schilperoord, and W. Spooren, editors, *Text representation : linguistic and psycholinguistic aspects*, pages 181–196. Amsterdam : Benjamins.

A. Knott. 1996. *A data-driven methodology for motivate a set of coherence relations*. Ph.D. thesis, University of Edinburgh.

W. C. Mann and S. A. Thompson. 1987. Rhetorical structure theory : a theory of text organisation. Technical report, Technical report ISI/RS-87-190, Information Sciences Intitute.

D. Marcu. 2000. The rhetorical parsing of unrestricted texts : a surface-based approach. *Computational Linguistics*, 26(3):395–448.

M.-P. Péry-Woodley, N. Asher, P. Enjalbert, F. Benamara, M. Bras, C. Fabre, S. Ferrari, L.-M. Ho-Dac, A. Le Draoulec, Y. Mathet, P. Muller, L. Prévot, J. Rebeyrolle, M. Vergez-Couret, L. Vieu, and A. Widlöcher. 2009. Annodis : une approche outillée de l'annotation de structures discursives. In *Actes de la conférence TALN*, Senlis, France.

L. Polanyi. 1988. A formal model of the structure of discourse. *Journal of Pragmatics*, 12:601–638.

R. Prasad, E. Miltsakaki, N. Dinesh, A. Lee, A. Joshi, L. Robaldo, and B-L. Webber. 2007. The penn discourse treebank 2.0. annotation manual. Technical report, IRCS, Institute for Research in Cognitive Science, University of Pennsylvania.

L. Prévot, L. Vieu, and N. Asher. 2009. Une formalisation plus précise pour une annotation moins confuse: la relation d'elaboration d'entité. *Journal of French Language Studies*, 19(2):207–228.

B. Reese, P. Denis, N. Asher, J. Baldridge, and J. Hunter. 2007. Reference manual for the analysis and annotation of rhetorical structure. Technical report, University of Texas at Austin.

H. Schmid. 1994. Probabilistic part-of-speech tagging using decision trees. In *Proceedings of the Conference on New Methods in Language Processing*, Manchester, UK.

M. Vergez-Couret. 2010. *Etude en corpus des réalisations linguistiques de la relation d'Elaboration*. Ph.D. thesis, Université de Toulouse.

F. Wolf and E. Gibson. 2005. Representing discourse coherence: A corpus-based study. *Computational Linguistics*, 31(2):249–287, June.

Pair Annotation: Adaption of Pair Programming to Corpus Annotation

Işın Demirşahin
Cognitive Science Program
Middle East Technical University
Ankara, Turkey
disin@metu.edu.tr

İhsan Yalçınkaya
Cognitive Science Program
Middle East Technical University
Ankara, Turkey
yalcinkaya.ihsan@gmail.com

Deniz Zeyrek
Cognitive Science Program
Middle East Technical University
Ankara, Turkey
dezeyrek@metu.edu.tr

Abstract

This paper will introduce a procedure that we call pair annotation after pair programming. We describe initial annotation procedure of the TDB, followed by the inception of the pair annotation idea and how it came to be used in the Turkish Discourse Bank. We discuss the observed benefits and issues encountered during the process, and conclude by discussing the major benefit of pair annotation, namely higher inter-annotator agreement values.

1 Introduction

The Turkish Discourse Bank (TDB) is a 500,000-word subcorpus of METU Turkish Corpus (Say et al., 2002), which is annotated for discourse connectives in the style of Penn Discourse Tree Bank (PDTB) (Prasad et al., 2008). As in the PDTB; discourse connectives are annotated along with the two text spans they link. The text spans can be single or multiple verb phrases, clauses, or sentences that can be interpreted as abstract objects (Asher, 1993). The text span that syntactically hosts the connective is labeled the second argument (Arg2), while the other text span is labeled the first argument (Arg1). The TDB annotations were carried out using the Discourse Annotation Tool for Turkish (DATT) (Aktaş, et al., 2010). In the first release of TDB, a total of 8482 relations are annotatannotated for 147 connectives.[1]

In this paper, we first describe the initial annotation procedure. Then, we introduce how the pair annotation (PA) procedure emerged. We continue with agreement statistics on some connectives annotated via the PA procedure, and finally we discuss the advantages and disadvantages of PA.

2 Initial Annotation Procedure in the TDB

2.1 Independent Annotations

The initial step in the TDB project was to determine which instances of the connectives would be annotated as discourse connectives. First, the connective tokens were revealed. Using each token as a search unit, three annotators went through the whole corpus and annotated all discourse connective instances of the token, together with the texts spans they link. Each annotator worked individually and independently, and did not have access to the annotations of other annotators.

Some search units corresponded to several discourse connectives. For example, the search for the unit *halde* 'although, despite' results in four discourse connectives. It appears as a complex subordinator that expects a nominalizing suffix -DIK and a case marker on its second argument as in (1). In the examples, Arg1 is shown in italics, and Arg2 is set in bold. The connective is underlined and the modifier is in square brackets when present.

(1) **Doğu Beyazıt'da geceledigimiz** <u>halde</u> *bir dünya şaheseri olan İshak Paşa medresesini göremeden Ankara'ya döndük.*

[1] The current TDB release can be requested online from the project website at http://medid.ii.metu.edu.tr

Although **we spent the night in Doğu Beyazıt**, *we returned to Ankara without seeing the İshak Paşa Medresseh, which is a masterpiece.*

It also appears with anaphoric elements: *o halde* 'then, in that case' as in (2), and *şu halde* 'in the current situation, in this specific case' as in (3).

(2) *Beyin delgi ameliyatı, hangi gerekçeyle yapılırsa yapılsın, insanoğlunun gerçekleştirdiği ilk cerrahi müdahaledir.* O halde, **nöroşirürjiyi Neolitik Çağ'a, hatta Mezolitik Çağ'a kadar götürebiliriz**.
Trepanation operations, regardless of the justifications for which they have been carried out, are the first surgical operation ever attempted by mankind. Then, **we can trace neurosurgery back to Neolithic Era, even to Mesolithic Era**.

(3) *Bu seçim, eskisinin devamı niteliğinde olsaydı, 60 günlük bir süreye ihtiyaç duyulmaması ve en kısa zamanda seçime gidil-mesi gerekirdi.* Şu halde **60 günlük süre yeni bir seçimin yapılması için gerekli prosedürün uygulanması ve hazırlıkların tamamlanmasını sağlamak için öngörül-müş bir süredir.**
If the nature of this election was the continuation of the old one, a period of 60 days wouldn't have been necessary and and the elections would have to be held immediately. In the current situation, **the 60-day period is the anticipated period for the application of the necessary procedure and the completion of the preperations.**

Finally, it appears with the adjective *aksi* 'opposite' to form *aksi halde* 'otherwise' as in (4).

(4) Feyzi Bey *böyle bir durumda mebusluktan istifa edeceğini*, aksi halde [de] **Falih Rıfkı Bey'in istifa etmesi gerektiğini** belirtmiş.
Mr. Fevzi stated that *in such a situation he would resign from parliament membership*, otherwise **Mr. Falih Rıfkı would have to resign.**

All such occurrences were annotated when searching with the unit *halde*, but are counted as different discourse connectives. There is no label for instances of search units that are not discourse connectives, so all other occurrences were left unannotated. For example, the adverbial clause forming *bir halde* 'in such a manner' in (5), which takes the clause *ne yapacağımı bilmez-* 'doesn't know what I will do' and builds and the adverbial clause *ne yapacağımı bilmez bir halde* 'not knowing what to do', was not annotated at all.

(5) O gün akşama kadar ne yapacağımı bilmez bir halde dolaştım evin içinde.
I walked around the house till evening that day, not knowing what to do.

2.2 Agreement Procedure

Upon the completion of independent annotations, disagreements were determined and brought to agreement meetings. The agreement meetings were open to the whole research group, which included four researchers in addition to the three annotators. All researchers, annotator and non-annotator, were native speakers of Turkish. In any given agreement meeting at least one non-annotator researcher and at least two annotators were present.

The preferred method for agreement was discussion among the annotators and researchers. The final annotation was not necessarily selected from the independent annotations. Sometimes a partial or complete combination of different annotations was agreed upon, and in few cases, a novel annotation emerged as the agreed annotation.

In cases where the discussion proved to be inconclusive, a non-annotator adjudicator decided how the agreed annotation should be. The adjudicator was constant throughout the project, and had the deepest and most thorough understanding of the annotation guidelines among the research group. When deciding on the agreed annotation, the adjudicator took the preceding consideration into account, as well as the native speaker intuitions of the annotators and the researchers. The adjudicator sometimes consulted the majority vote of the annotations or the research group, but only as long as the majority vote was completely in accord with the annotation guidelines.

The agreement meetings sometimes resulted in additions and/or changes to the annotation guidelines. In such cases, all annotations were checked to preserve consistency across annotations, and the final version was produced, which may be referred to as the gold standard.[2]

2.3 Common Divergences among Independent Annotations

There are five common types of divergence in the annotations.

(a) The first case is a physical error in selecting a connective or argument span. The annotation guidelines state that all the punctuation marks and spaces around argument spans and discourse connectives should be left out, with one exception: when one of a pair of quotation marks or dashes is in the argument span, the matching one is included in the span, too. Sometimes space characters or punctuation marks that should be left out are included in the selection or a quotation mark or dash is excluded although its pair is in the annotated span; or one or more letters of a word is not selected. These errors arise because the DATT allows continuous selection of text and do not snap to word boundaries automatically. The tool is designed in this way so as to allow the annotation of simple subordinators which are single suffixes such as *–dan* in (6).

(6) **Başka kimse olmadığın**dan *iki kadının da yüzü açıktı.*
'Since **there was no one else**, *the faces of both women were unveiled.*'

In some cases, type (a) divergences occur in a larger scale. The annotation guidelines exclude some text spans such as salutations, commentaries and parenthetical form arguments when they are not vital to the understanding of the discourse connection between the two arguments. Sometimes annotators may overlook this rule and include intrusions of several words that should not be in the argument. Since these cases are explicitly ruled out by the annotation guidelines, these divergences are taken to be errors, rather than genuine cases of disagreement.

(b) The second type of divergence arises when the annotators more or less agree on what the arguments are, but there is a syntactic or semantic ambiguity in the text that prevents them from agreeing on the argument span. For example one annotator may include a temporal adverb in an argument whereas the other annotates the same adverb as "shared", i.e. applying to both arguments. Similarly, some adverbs like *salt* 'only, just' may be understood by one annotator to take an argument as its scope and thus should be included in that argument (7a), whereas the same adverb is considered by another annotator to take the connective as its scope, and as a result it might be annotated as a modifier (7b).

(7a) **Salt gülmek** için *gelmişlerdi.*
They came to **just laugh**.

(7b) [Salt] **gülmek** için *gelmişlerdi.*
They came [only] to **laugh**.

(c) A third type of divergence occurs when the annotators annotate relations differently, because they get different meanings from that part of the text. In these cases, the span annotated by one of the annotators might include, overlap with, or completely differ from the spans of the other annotators, as in (8a) and (8b). (8a) shows that the annotator interpreted the temporal sequence as between the speech and the moving of the funeral, whereas (8b) shows that another annotator believed that the relation was between the ceremony and the moving of the funeral.

(8a) Usumi için ilk tören, Türkiye Gazeteciler Cemiyeti (TGC) önünde düzenlendi. *TGC Başkanı Orhan Erinç, konuşmasında Usumi'nin yokluğunu hissedeceklerini vurguladı.* **Usumi'nin cenazesi** [daha] sonra **Sultanahmet Camii'ne götürüldü**.
The first ceremony for Usumi was arranged in front of the Association of the Journalists of Turkey (TGC). *Orhan Erinç, the chairman the TGC, emphasized that Usumi would be missed.* Then, **the Usumi's funeral was moved to the Sultan Ahmed Mosque**.

[2] This so called gold standard is suitable for linguistic explorations and descriptive studies as it tries to be as exhaustive as possible, i.e., all located instances of discourse connectives were annotated, including even the hardest of the cases. The inclusion of the hard cases in the data may increase the noise, requiring caution when using the data for benchmarking (Reidsma and Carletta, 2008). A benchmarking version of TDB that excludes the hard cases and includes the noise levels following Klebanov and Beigman (2008) is in preparation.

(8b) *Usumi için ilk tören, Türkiye Gazeteciler Cemiyeti (TGC) önünde düzenlendi.* TGC Başkanı Orhan Erinç, konuşmasında Usumi'nin yokluğunu hissedeceklerini vurguladı. **Usumi'nin cenazesi** [daha] <u>sonra</u> **Sultanahmet Camii'ne götürüldü**.
The first ceremony for Usumi was arranged in front of the Association of the Journalists of Turkey (TGC). Orhan Erinç, the chairman the TGC, emphasized that Usumi would be missed. <u>Then</u>, **the Usumi's funeral was moved to the Sultan Ahmed Mosque**.

Divergences of type (b) and (c) are cases of genuine disagreement, pointing to hard cases; whereas type (a) is a simple case of human error and may arise even in the easiest cases.

(d) Another type of divergence is the case when one or more annotators did not annotate an instance of the search unit, whereas the others have annotated it. This might be because one annotator believed this specific instance of the search unit to be a non-discourse connective, or it might simply be overlooked. The former cases are genuine disagreements, whereas the latter cases are errors in annotation.

(e) The last type of divergence emerges due to cases underdetermined in annotation guidelines. An example of this type of divergence resulted from the case of shared copula during the annotation of *ve* 'and'.

(9) Kızın saçları *siyah* <u>ve</u> **kıvırcıktı**.
The girl's hair was *black* <u>and</u> **curly**.

Because in present tense the copula is often dropped and *Kızın saçları siyah* 'The girl's hair is black' is interpreted as an abstract object, (9) was interpreted by some annotators and researchers as coordination of two abstract objects; whereas others interpreted it as simple adjective coordination, where *ve* 'and' links the two adjectives *siyah* 'black' and *kıvırcık* 'curly'.

During the annotation phase, the guidelines were not clear concerning instances like (9) and were only finalized after further consideration and more exposure to data. Obviously, such underdetermination by annotation guidelines can and does result in major disagreements. However, since this type of disagreement should be settled in the guidelines and cannot be improved by the annotators, type (e) divergences will not be considered further in this paper.

The divergences resulting form human errors were the easiest to resolve during the agreement meetings. Of the genuine disagreements, types (b) and (c) were the harder to resolve because they resulted from ambiguities, and in some cases various annotations seemed plausible.

It was during this discussion of hard cases when the annotators came up with the need to incorporate some sort of discussion into the annotation procedure. When the inter-annotator reliability among three annotators stabilized, it was proposed to use a pair of annotators to carry out the task together while the third annotator continued her task independently in an attempt to accelerate the annotations. This team approach quickly led to the procedure we call pair annotation after the pair programming procedure in software engineering.

3 Pair Programming

Pair programming (PP), also referred to as collaborative programming, is the process where two programmers work together at the same piece of algorithm or code (Williams, et al, 2000; Williams and Kessler, 2000). PP can be taken as a method for software development by itself (Williams and Kessler, 2003), or it can be integrated into other development schemes as in the case of extreme programming (XP) (Beck, 2000).

In pair programming, one of the programmers, the driver, is responsible for physically producing the code or the algorithm. The driver is the one that uses the keyboard to actually write the code. The other programmer, the navigator, continuously monitors the driver and actively takes part in the creation of the code by watching for errors, thinking of alternative strategies or better ways to implement the algorithm and looking up resources that might be needed during coding.

The division of labor and the fact that the driver is the one actually producing the code, however, do not imply that the driver takes a leading role, or has greater part in ownership or responsibility. The ownership of the piece of code developed in PP, and the responsibility for the errors it may contain, belong to both programmers equally. Therefore, the navigator needs to be actively involved at all times, for they will be held equally responsible if anything goes wrong. The role of the driver is switched periodically, so in the overall process, both programmers have equal roles as well as equal credit and equal responsibility.

3.1 Advantages of Pair Programming

Programmers observe that when they work in pairs, they produce higher quality software in less time than it would take to produce the software by means of individual programming. They also report that they have higher motivation while programming, because they feel responsibility towards their partner. They put less time in irrelevant or personal tasks and concentrate more on the job at hand because they feel otherwise they would be wasting their partner's time. In addition, working together with a partner and creating a jointly owned product brings the programmers close, leading to a case called pair jelling (Williams, et al., 2000) in which "the sum is greater than its parts" (DeMarco and Lister, 1977, as cited in Williams, et al, 2000), which in turn facilitates the pair performance to exceed the performance of the individual programmers, or even their individual performances combined.

One of the major costs in the budget of a project, and an often overlooked one, is the time spent for communication between the teams or programmers who take part in the development of software. The cost of the project is usually calculated on the basis of programmer hours and these hours usually indicate only the actual coding hours, but Brooks (1975) states that the time spent for communication should also be included in the overall cost of the project. Williams and Kessler (2000) report that PP decreases this communication time thanks to the already established communication channels and protocols within the programming pair.

3.2 Disadvantages of Pair Programming

The fact that PP takes a shorter period of time to produce a piece of software does not mean that it takes up less resource. The most prominent disadvantage of PP for those who encounter the idea the first time is that it is a waste of time to put two programmers to a job that could have been carried out by only one. Even if the software is produced quicker than when it was produced by an individual programmer, the overall programmer hours is expected to be so high that the procedure is not likely to be cost efficient. Research shows that this is not necessarily the case. Although it might take more time to complete a task compared to individual programmers when the programmers are newly introduced to the PP, as they become more experienced, the overall programming hours spent on the task come close to time spent when the programming is done individually.

In one case, when the programmers are first introduced to PP, the pairs completed a task faster and more accurately then individual programmers, but the overall programming hours was 60% higher that individual programmers. However, as the programmers adapted to the procedure, the increase was reduced to 15% (Williams, et al., 2000). Considering the fact that a less accurate code will need much debugging, this 15% increase in programming time seems to be acceptable.

4 Pair Annotation

To keep the annotations as unbiased as possible while accelerating the annotation process, the TDB group decided to keep one of the individual annotators independent. Two other annotators teamed up and annotated as a pair, which would be treated as a single annotator in the agreement process.

At the time of the introduction of the pair annotation (PA) procedure to the project, two of the annotators had some degree of familiarity with the idea of pair programming; but it did not immediately occur to them to relate software programming and corpus annotation processes. As pair annotation advanced, the most basic principles of PP emerged on their own accord. It was more practical to let one of the annotators handle the input for the whole session, so the roles of the driver and navigator arose. The corrective and the supportive role of the navigator also emerged because of the self-imposed responsibility of the person who was not actually handling the keyboard-mouse. She neither wanted to leave the entire job to the other person, nor to be left out of the annotation process. For similar reasons, switching of the driver/navigator roles followed. As the PA routine became more and more established, the similarities between the PA and PP routines became more prominent.

The agreement process for PA is similar to independent annotations; but the pair is treated as a single entity, especially where majority vote is concerned. The annotators in the pair are free to voice their opinions; however, care is taken to prevent the pair from biasing the gold standard.

4.1 Observed Benefits of Pair Annotation

During the PA experience, the annotators observed that the frequency of errors, especially that of type (a) decreased; because even if the driver made as many mistakes as an individual annotator, the navigator almost always warned her. The mistake was immediately corrected, and therefore they would not appear as disagreements in later phases.

When done in pairs, annotation of the hard cases of type (b) and (c) was faster, too. Sometimes the pair had to carry out lengthy discussions until they agreed on an annotation. Although this seems like it might prolong the annotation time, it did not.

In the cases when a relation is hard to annotate due to ambiguities, all individual annotators would spend a long time on the same relation to understand the larger context to resolve the ambiguity. Sometimes they would have to recall, or search for, a piece of background knowledge that is necessary to process the text. In fact, it usually takes an individual longer than a pair to complete such difficult annotations because the pair can search twice as fast, as well as sharing their knowledge about the context, sometimes eliminating the need to spend any time at all. As a result, a pair annotates a set of relations faster than an individual does.

As mentioned in the PP literature, yet another benefit is higher motivation during annotation. Annotating the same connective in the corpus can sometimes become a tedious job, but having a partner to discuss cases, or even just share complaints or jokes lightens up the process considerably. A repetitive and tedious job becomes interactive and even enjoyable. Moreover, similar to PP, pair annotations are done more efficiently because the partners spend less time on unrelated or personal activities during the designated PA times due to the fact that they do not want to waste each other's time.

In addition to decreasing the time spent during annotation, PA decreases the overall time spent on the agreement procedures just as PP decreases the time spent on communication between programmers. In those cases when the pair have already discussed a particular annotation, they summarize the results of this discussion in a notes field provided in the annotation tool. These discussion summaries present their justification for their annotation to the research group during the agreement meeting. Although the notes field contributes to agreement of individual annotations in a similar manner, the notes of a pair include the already compared and evaluated views of two annotators and a proposed resolution, which results in agreement in a shorter time.

4.2 Issues in Pair Annotation

Questions arise against PA similar to those that arise against PP. Is it not a waste of time to ask three annotators to work if all we are going to have are two sets of annotations? If we can put three annotators to the job, is it not preferable to have three sets of annotations instead of two? From one point of view, the more sets of independent annotations, the better. However, it is common practice for corpus annotation projects to decrease the number of annotators once disagreement stabilizes, as in the example of the PDTB (Miltsakaki, et al, 2004) and it is this practice that we adopted in the TDB.

Another concern that arises for both PP and PA is what if one partner -the usual candidate is the navigator- does not participate in the process actively? Or what if one partner constantly dominates the process and ignores the opinions of the other? The TDB has not encountered this specific problem mainly because the annotators have been involved in the process from the beginning of the project, and have taken active roles in building the annotation principles. In other projects where certain annotators have to contribute for a limited amount of time only, this may become an important caveat. To circumvent the potential problem, the pairs might be asked for feedback periodically to make sure that the PA procedure is working as intended.

Finally, there are annotation specific questions concerning PA. There is always the threat that a pair's annotation could be biased, because the pair interacts constantly. As a result of their discussions or the persuasive powers of one of the partners, the resulting annotations may diverge from the initial native speaker intuitions of the annotators; or while trying to combine two different annotations, the result may end up being counterintuitive. In the TDB, we did not come across this problem thanks to the productive utilization of the notes field.

As explained above, the annotators use the notes field to summarize their discussions of the hard cases. By doing so, they include the first intuitions of both annotators and the reasoning process of their resulting annotation. In some cases they use the field to declare that a joint annotation could not be reached. These comments have been very useful during the agreement meetings for the pair annotation and also contributed to the improvement of annotation schema and annotation guidelines.

Pair annotation is not the solution to all problems in annotation, nor does it offer the perfect annotation procedure. That is why what we propose here is not replacing the entire annotation progress with PA, but having an independent individual annotator in addition to the pair. The procedure we are describing is closer to having two independent annotators, where one of the annotators is like a composite being consisting of two individuals thinking independently, but producing a single set of annotations collaboratively. Similar to the joint ownership of PP, neither partner claims the annotation as her own, but the annotation is treated as it belongs to a single annotator, i.e. the pair. It is treated as a single set of annotations both during the agreement meetings and in calculating the agreement statistics.

4.3 Effect of Pair Annotation on the Agreement Statistics

For four high frequency connectives, *ama* 'but', *sonra* 'after', *ve* 'and' and *ya da* 'or', the first 1/3 of the files were annotated independently by all three annotators (IA). The rest of the files were annotated via the PA procedure. Periodical agreement meetings were held during and after both phases. For six other connectives, *aslında* 'actually', *halde* 'despite', *nedeniyle* 'because of', *nedenle* 'for this reason', *ötürü* 'due to' and *yüzden* 'so, because of this', only PA annotations were carried out.

Table 1 provides the averaged pair-wise averaged inter-annotator agreement, i.e. annotator against annotator agreement, Kappa (K) coefficient values of the IA phase for the first group, where three independent annotators created the annotations independently.

Table 2 shows the K values of the second phase for the same group, where the PA procedure followed the agreement meetings of the independent annotations.

Connective	Arg1	Arg2
ama	0.832	0.901
sonra	0.820	0.902
ve	0.692	0.791
ya da	0.843	0.974

Table 1 – Pair-wise averaged inter-annotator agreement (K) for 3 individual annotators in IA – individual annotator against individual annotator

Connective	Arg1	Arg2
ama	0.956	0.969
sonra	0.889	0.953
ve	0.945	0.964
ya da	0.939	0.973

Table 2 – Inter-annotator agreement (K) for pair vs. individual in PA – individual annotator against pair annotator

In tables 1 and 2, all the cells but one, indicate good agreement ($0.80<K<1.00$). Only the first argument of *ve* 'and' in independent annotation phase shows not good but some agreement ($0.60 < K < 0.80$). Zeyrek et al. (2010) discusses other connectives in TDB with K values below 0.80.

The results show that the K values for both arguments have increased after the transition from the IA to PA. A repeated measures test shows that the increase is significant ($p< 0.01$).

Tables 3 and 4 show the agreement statistics for the second group of connectives, where only PA was conducted. Each set of annotations are compared to the agreed annotations that were produced after the final agreement meeting for that particular connective. In Table 3, the K values show the agreement between the individual's annotations and the agreed annotations, and in Table 4, they indicate the agreement between the pair's annotations and the agreed annotations.

Connective	Arg1	Arg2
aslında	0.766	0.889
halde	0.834	0.898
nedeniyle	0.905	0.984
nedenle	0.952	0.987
ötürü	1.000	0.907
yüzden	0.916	0.983

Table 3 - Individual annotator vs. agreed agreement (K) in PA

Connective	Arg1	Arg2
aslında	0.937	0.984
halde	0.973	1.000
nedeniyle	0.937	0.984
nedenle	1.000	1.000
ötürü	1.000	0.953
yüzden	0.992	1.000

Table 4 – Pair annotator vs. agreed agreement (K) in PA

In Tables 3 and 4, except for the mediocre agreement of Arg1 of *aslında* 'actually', all K values indicate good agreement. A repeated measures test shows that the agreement of the pair and the agreed annotations are significantly higher than the agreement of the individual annotator and the agreed annotations ($p<0.001$).

Since non-discourse connectives were omitted during the annotation phase instead of being marked as non-discourse connectives, there was no easy way to distinguish errors from deliberate omissions in type (d) divergences. In an attempt to find out the missing annotations, we compared the number of relations that were annotated both on the agreed annotations and on the annotators' annotations. At first glance it seems that the individual annotator missed significantly more relations that should be annotated than the pair ($p<0.5$). However, since many of the cases omitted by the individual annotator were of type (e) divergences similar to (9), this comparison does not yield interpretable results.

5 Discussion and Conclusion

For the first group of connectives discussed in this paper, where a 3-annotator independent annotation procedure preceded the PA procedure, there was a significant increase in the K values for inter-annotator agreement, which probably due to the agreement meetings that took place between the two annotation phases. In the agreement meetings, peculiar uses of specific connectives and syntactic structures unique to the connectives were explored. Following the discussions, some annotation guidelines were added, modified or fine-tuned, new principles were added or modified to reflect the annotators' intuitions both about general properties of Turkish discourse structure and the particular discourse connective in question.

As a result, annotators were prepared for the PA phase, leading to less disagreement between the individual annotator and the pair.

For the second group of connectives, where all annotations were carried out with one individual and a pair, the higher K values for the pair vs. agreed annotations than for the individual vs. agreed annotations reflect the benefits of pair programming.

During PA, simple mistakes are corrected during annotation. Ambiguities are discovered more easily because the annotators discover different readings and point them to each other, and discuss productively in an attempt to agree on the more prominent reading. Annotation principles are applied more carefully because the pair is usually more alert than the individual. PA allows for better understanding and analysis of the context, because the sum of the contextual and world knowledge of the partners is greater than that of the individual annotators. As a result, the annotation is more accurate and although not statistically proven yet, it is observed to be faster.

5.1 Conclusion

The benefits of the PA can be summarized as higher annotation clarity due to less annotation errors and faster disagreement resolution due to previous extended discussions. The drawbacks are one less set of annotations for each pair of annotators and the shadow of doubt cast over the unbiased nature of annotations due to the dense interaction of the pair. While pair jelling was beneficial for PP, it might prove problematic for PA, as independent linguistic intuition is valuable in linguistic annotation. We believe that we have minimized this bias by treating the pair as a single annotator for the agreement statistics, and by letting the individual intuitions and ideas leak into the agreement meeting by means of the notes field in the annotation tool. However, this solution was project specific and the problem should be investigated in more detail when applying PA to other projects.

Acknowledgements

We gratefully acknowledge the support of the Turkish Scientific and Technological Research Council of Turkey (TUBITAK) and METU Scientific Research Fund (no. BAP-07-04-2011-005).

References

Nicholas Asher. 1993. *Reference to Abstract Objects in Discourse.* Kluwer Academic Publishers.

Berfin Aktaş, Cem Bozşahin, Deniz Zeyrek. 2010. Discourse Relation Configurations in Turkish and an Annotation Environment. *LAW IV - The Fourth Linguistic Annotation Workshop.* Uppsala, Sweden, July 2010.

Kent Back. 2000. *Extreme Programming Explained: Embrass Change.* Addison Wesley Longman, Reading, Mass.

Frederick, P. J. Brooks. 1975. *The Mythical Man-Month.* Addison-Wesley, Reading, Mass.

Tom DeMarco and Timothy Lister. 1977. *Peopleware.* Dorset House, New York.

Eleni Miltsakaki, Rashmi Prasad, Aravind Joshi, Bonnie Webber. 2004. Annotating Discourse Connectives and Their Arguments. *HLT/NAACL Workshop on Frontiers in Corpus Annotation.* Boston, MA. May 2004.

Beata Beigman Klebanov and Eyal Beigman. 2008. From Annotator Agreement to Noise Models. *Computational Linguistics*, 34(3):495–503.

Rashmi Prasad, Nikhil Dinesh, Alan Lee, Eleni Miltsakaki, Livio Robaldo, Aravind Joshi, Bonnie Webber. 2008. The Penn Discourse Treebank 2.0. *LREC'08 - The sixth international conference on Language Resources and Evaluation.* Marrakech, Morocco, May 2008.

Dennis Reidsma and Jean Carletta. 2008. Reliability measurement without limit. *Computational Linguistics*, 34(3):319–326.

Bilge Say and Deniz Zeyrek and Kemal Oflazer and Umut Ozge. 2002. Development of a Corpus and a Treebank for Present-day Written Turkish. *ICTL 2002 - 11th International Conference on Turkish Linguistics.* Famagusta, TRNC, August 2002.

Laurie Williams, Robert R. Kessler, Ward Cunningham, Ron Jeffries. 2000. Strengthening the Case for Pair Programming. *IEEE Software*, July/August 2000:19–25.

Laurie Williams and Robert R. Kessler. 2000. All I Really Need to Know about Pair Programming I Learned In Kindergarten, *Communications of the ACM*, 43(5):108–114.

Laurie Williams and Robert R. Kessler. 2003. *Pair Programming Illuminated.* Addison Wesley, Reading, Massachusetts.

Deniz Zeyrek, Işın Demirşahin, Ayışığı Sevdik-Çallı, Hale Ögel Balaban, İhsan Yalçınkaya and Ümit Deniz Turan. 2010. The Annotation Scheme of the Turkish Discourse Bank and an Evaluation of Inconsistent Annotations. *LAW IV - The Fourth Linguistic Annotation Workshop* Uppsala, Sweden, July 2010.

Structured Named Entities in two distinct press corpora: Contemporary Broadcast News and Old Newspapers

Sophie Rosset$^{\alpha}$**, Cyril Grouin**$^{\alpha}$**, Karën Fort**$^{\beta,\gamma}$
Olivier Galibert$^{\delta}$**, Juliette Kahn**$^{\delta}$**, Pierre Zweigenbaum**$^{\alpha}$
$^{\alpha}$LIMSI–CNRS, France $^{\beta}$INIST–CNRS, France $^{\gamma}$LIPN, France $^{\delta}$LNE, France
{sophie.rosset,cyril.grouin,pierre.zweigenbaum}@limsi.fr
karen.fort@inist.fr, {olivier.galibert,juliette.kahn}@lne.fr

Abstract

This paper compares the reference annotation of structured named entities in two corpora with different origins and properties. It addresses two questions linked to such a comparison. On the one hand, what specific issues were raised by reusing the same annotation scheme on a corpus that differs from the first in terms of media and that predates it by more than a century? On the other hand, what contrasts were observed in the resulting annotations across the two corpora?

1 Introduction

Named Entity Recognition (NER), and its evaluation methods, constitute an active field of research. NER can be performed on many kinds of documents. On textual data, a few NER applications focus on newspapers, spoken data, as well as digitized data. On specific kinds of data such as historical data, various investigations have been performed to detect named entities (Miller et al., 2000; Crane and Jones, 2006; Byrne, 2007; Grover et al., 2008). From the point of view of both annotation and evaluation campaigns, ACE (Doddington et al., 2004) included NER on OCRed data.

For the French language, an evaluation involving classical named entities was performed a few years ago on old newspapers data (Galibert et al., 2010). More recently, we proposed a definition of structured named entities for broadcast news data (Grouin et al., 2011). We follow this definition in the present work.

After a presentation of related work (Section 2), including the definition of structured named entities, this paper presents the construction of a new annotated corpus of old newspapers (Section 3). The main goal of the paper is to report the comparison of structured named entity annotation in two contrasting press corpora: the pre-existing broadcast news corpus and this new corpus of old newspapers. This comparison is performed at two levels: the annotation process itself (Section 4.1) and the annotation results (Section 4.2).

2 Related Work

2.1 Named Entity Definition

Initially, Named Entity recognition (NER) was described as recognizing proper names (Coates-Stephens, 1992). Since MUC-6 (Grishman and Sundheim, 1996), named entities include three major classes: *person, location* and *organization*. Some numerical types are also often described and used in the literature: *date, time* and *amount* (money and percentages in most cases).

Proposals were made to sub-divide existing categories into finer-grained classes: e.g., *politician* as part of the *person* class (Fleischman and Hovy, 2002), or *city* in the *location* class (Fleischman, 2001). New classes were added during the CONLL conference. More recently, larger extensions were proposed: *product* by (Bick, 2004) while (Sekine, 2004) defined an extensive hierarchy of named entities containing about 200 types. Numerous investigations concern named entities in historical data (Miller et al., 2000; Crane and Jones, 2006;

Byrne, 2007; Grover et al., 2008). In most cases, the definition of named entity follows the classical definition. Nevertheless, in some cases, new categories were added. For example, the Virginia Banks project (Crane and Jones, 2006) added categories such as *ships*, *regiments*, and *railroads* to adapt the definition to the American Civil War period.

2.2 Structured Named Entity Definitions

We proposed a new structure of named entities that relies on two main principles: our extended named entities are both hierarchical and compositional. This structure requires novel methods to evaluate system outputs. Compared to existing named entity definitions, our approach is more general than the extensions proposed for specific domains, and is simpler than the extensive hierarchy defined by Sekine (2004). This structure allows us to cover a large number of named entities with a basic categorization which provides a foundation that facilitates further annotation work. The guidelines are available online (Rosset et al., 2011).

2.2.1 Hierarchy

We defined an extended named entity as being composed of two kinds of elements: *types* and *components*. In our definition, *types* refer to a general segmentation of the world into major categories. Furthermore, we consider that the content of an entity must be structured as well. From this perspective, we defined a second level of annotation for each category, which we call *components*.

Types and sub-types refer to the general category of a named entity. We defined this type of element as being the first level of annotation because they give general information about the annotated expression. Our taxonomy is thus composed of 7 types (*person, location, organization, amount, time, production* and *function*) and 32 sub-types (individual person *pers.ind* vs. group of persons *pers.coll*; law, decree, and agreement *prod.rule* vs. political, philosophical and religious belief *prod.doctr*, etc.).

Components can be considered as internal clues for the annotation of elements: either to determine the type of an extended named entity (a first name is a clue for the individual person *pers.ind* sub-type), or to set the named entity boundaries (a given token is a clue for the named entity, and is within its scope—e.g., a number in a date—, while the next token is not a clue and is outside its scope—e.g., a word that is not a month, nor a part of a date).

Components are second-level elements, and can never be used outside the scope of a type or sub-type element. We specified two kinds of components: transverse components that can be included in all types of entities (*name, kind, qualifier, demonym, val, unit, object* and *range-mark*), and specific components, only used for a reduced set of components (for example, *name.last, name.first, name.middle* and *title* for the *pers.ind* sub-type).

2.2.2 Structure

Three kinds of structures can be found in our annotation schema. First, a sub-type contains a component: the *pers.ind* sub-type (individual person) contains components such as *title* and *name.last*, while the *func.ind* sub-type (individual function) contains other components such as *kind* (the kind of function) and *qualifier* (a qualifier adjective) (see Figure 1).

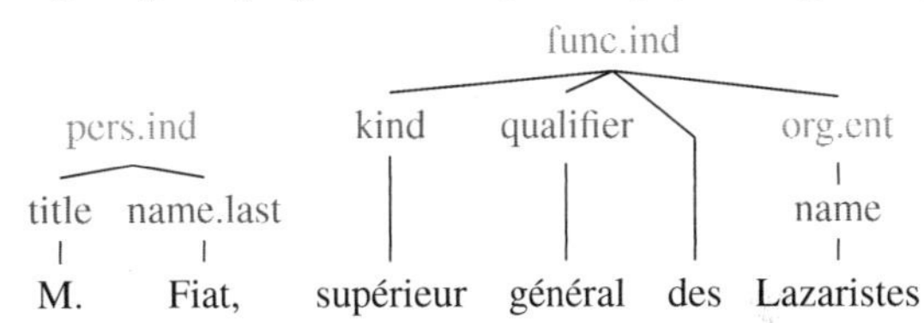

Figure 1: Multi-level annotation of entity sub-types (red tags) and components (blue tags): *Mr Fiat, general Superior of the Lazarists*

Secondly, a sub-type includes another sub-type, used as a component. In Figure 2, the *func.ind* sub-type (individual function), which spans the whole function expression, includes the *loc.adm.town* sub-type (administrative location for a town), which spans the single word of the French town *Versailles*.

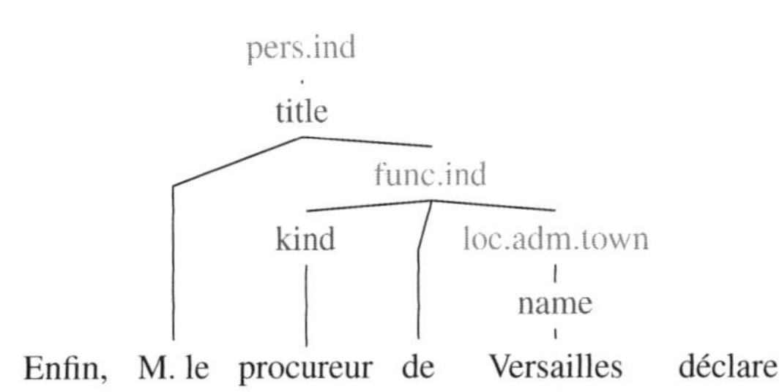

Figure 2: Multi-level annotation of entity sub-types: *Finally, Mr the prosecutor of Versailles declares*

Finally, in cases of metonymy and antonomasia, a sub-type is used to refer to another sub-type (Figure 3). The sub-type to which the entity intrinsically belongs is annotated (the *loc.oro* sub-type, an oronym location). Then, this sub-type is over-annotated with the sub-type to which the expression belongs in the considered context (the *org.adm* sub-type, an administrative organization).

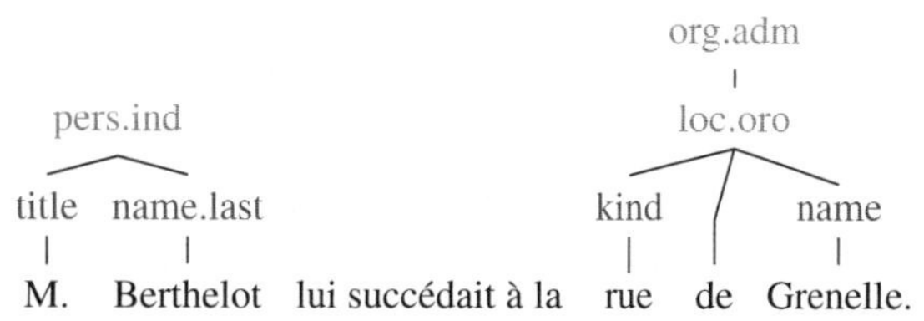

Figure 3: Annotation with sub-types and components including metonymy: *Mr Berthelot was succeeding him at rue de Grenelle* (= Ministry of Education)

2.3 Experiments on Broadcast News Data

In (Grouin et al., 2011), we reported a human annotation campaign using the above-mentioned structured entities on spoken data and the resulting corpus. The training part of the corpus is only composed of broadcast news data while the test corpus is composed of both broadcast news and broadcast conversations data. In order to build a mini-reference corpus for this annotation campaign (a "gold" corpus), we randomly extracted a sub-corpus from the training one. This sub-corpus was annotated by 6 different annotators following a 4-step procedure. Table 1 gives statistics about training, test and gold corpora. These corpora ("BN" in the remainder of the paper) has been used in an evaluation campaign (Galibert et al., 2011).

Inf. \ Data	Training	Test	Gold
# shows	188	18	-
# lines	43,289	5,637	398
# tokens	1,291,225	108,010	11,532
# entity types	113,885	5,523	1,161
# distinct types	41	32	29
# components	146,405	8,902	1,778
# distinct comp.	29	22	22

Table 1: Statistics on the annotated BN corpora

3 Structured Named Entities in Old Newspapers

We performed the same annotations on a corpus composed of OCRed press archives, henceforth the Old Press (OP) corpus. Human annotation was subcontracted to the same team of annotators as for the BN corpus, thus facilitating the consistency of annotations across corpora.

3.1 Corpus

The Old Press corpus consists of 76 newspaper issues published in December 1890 and provided by the French National Library (Bibliothèque Nationale de France). We used three different French titles: *Le Temps*, 54 documents for a total 209 pages, *La Croix*, 21 documents for a total 84 pages, and *Le Figaro*, 1 document with 2 pages.

A newspaper is composed of various parts (*titles, articles, ads,* etc.), some of which are not useful for named entity annotation. A corpus study allowed us to determine parts in which we considered annotation would be useless: *titles, mastheads, ads, tables of numbers, theater programs, stock exchange results, weather reports, etc.* We designed a procedure to filter out these parts in each document, which is fully described in (Galibert et al., 2012). The result consists in a corpus of about 23,586 text blocks extracted from 295 different pages.

3.2 Adaptation of Annotation Guidelines

Given the characteristics of the corpus (OCRed press archives), although the OCR quality rate is good (Character Error Rate at 5.09% and Word Error Rate at 36.59%[1]), we introduced a new XML attribute and a new component into the annotation schema in order to take into account these features and to fulfill annotators' requirements.

Attribute *correction*. Annotators were asked to correct incorrectly recognized entities. To save time and effort, correction was to be performed only on named entities, not on the whole text (see Figure 4 where the entity "*d'Algor*" of type *loc.adm.town* has been corrected into "*d'Alger*" (from Algiers)).

[1]The CER and the WER were computed in terms of Levenshtein distance (Levenshtein, 1965).

00232766/PAG_1_TB000125.png
On nous télégraphie <loc.adm.town correction="d'Alger"> d'Algor </loc.adm.town> Le <prod.object> Comorin, </prod.object> venant du <loc.adm.reg> Tonkin, </loc.adm.reg> est arrivé en rade <loc.adm.town correction="d'Agha"> d'Ag'ha </loc.adm.town> à <time.hour.abs correction="trois heures de l'après-midi;"> <val> trois </val> <unit> heures </unit> do <time-modifier> l'après-midi; </time-modifier> </time.hour.abs> il n'a pu être admis à la libre pratique qu'à <time.hour.abs> <val> cinq </val> <unit> heures </unit> du <time-modifier> soir, </time-modifier> </time.hour.abs> par suite d'un décès survenu devant <prod.object> Bougie. </prod.object> A <time.hour.abs> <val> six </val> <unit> heures, </unit> </time.hour.abs> il mouillait dans le port. Il débarquera ses troupes <time.date.rel> aujourd'hui </time.date.rel> dans la matinée et appareillera ensuite nour <loc.adm.town> Toulon. </loc.adm.town>

Figure 4: Example annotated text block

Component *noisy-entities*. When a character recognition error involves an entity boundary, a segmentation error occurs, either between an entity and other tokens, or between several entities and possibly other tokens. To allow the annotators to annotate the entity in that character span, we defined a new component *noisy-entities* which indicates that an entity is present in the noisy span of characters. A complete description of these adaptations can be found in (Galibert et al., 2012).

3.3 Inter-Annotator Agreement

To evaluate the manual annotations of the annotation team ("Global annotated corpus" in Figure 5), we built a mini reference corpus by selecting 255 blocks from the training corpus. We followed the same procedure as the one used for the BN corpus, as illustrated in Figure 5:

1. The corpus is annotated independently by 2 teams of 2 annotators ("Scientist" boxes).
2. Each team produces an adjudicated annotated corpus from the two teams' annotations ("Institute 1" and "Institute 2" boxes).
3. One team produces an adjudicated annotated corpus from the two previously obtained versions of the corpus ("Institutes" box).
4. Then, one team produces an adjudicated annotated corpus ("Mini-reference" box) from the previous corpus and the corresponding corpus extracted ("Annotated sub-corpus" box) from the global annotated corpus.

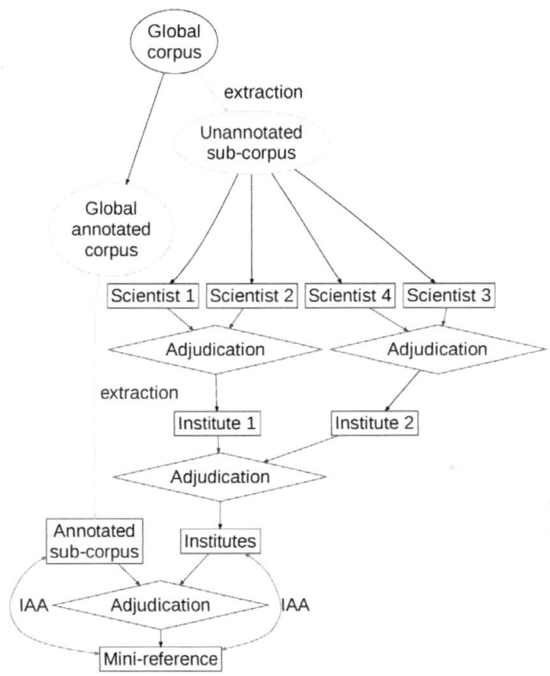

Figure 5: Mini reference corpus constitution procedure. Parts of the figure in green refer to the extraction stage, parts in blue to the adjudication stage and parts in red to the inter-annotator agreement stage

The complete annotated corpus was divided for evaluation purposes into training and test corpora, as described in (Galibert et al., 2012). Table 2 gives statistics about these corpora and the gold corpus.

During the whole annotation process, inter-annotator agreements and disagreements were computed. Here, we present the results in term of inter-annotator agreement between the annotated sub-corpus and the mini reference corpus.

Information \ Data	Training	Test	Gold
# pages	231	64	-
# lines	192,543	61,088	1618
# tokens	1,297,742	363,455	12,263
# distinct tokens	152,655	64,749	5,215
# entity types	114,599	33,083	1,373
# entity types w/ corr.	4,258	1,364	65
# distinct entity types	40	39	29
# components	136,113	40,432	2,053
# components w/ corr.	71	22	51
# distinct components	26	25	23

Table 2: Old Press corpora annotated with extended named entities. *Gold* stands for mini reference corpus; *corr.* for correction attribute

To compute an inter-annotator agreement, we need a 'random baseline' which is dependent on the number of *markables*. We showed that considering as markables all entities annotated at least in one of the two corpora should lead to the lowest possible bound for κ estimation (in our experiment, $\kappa = 0.647$) (Grouin et al., 2011). In contrast, the F-measure can indicate the highest possible bound ($F = 0.799$).

4 Comparisons

We have annotated two different corpora using the same definition of extended and structured named entities. This gives us an opportunity to analyze differences in (*i*) the annotation campaigns for these two corpora, highlighting specific difficulties linked to corpus properties (Section 4.1), and (*ii*) the obtained annotated corpora (Section 4.2).

4.1 Annotation Campaign

4.1.1 From the Source Material Point of View

As mentioned in Section 3.2, the Old Press annotation included an additional task for the annotators: correcting the incorrectly recognized characters in the annotated named entities. Performing this task properly implies to read not only the OCRed text, but also the corresponding source image, as some errors do not appear as such in the text. This is the case, for example, in "*M. Buis*" (Mr Buis) instead of "*M. Buls*" (Mr Buls) or, more importantly, "*touché*" (touched) instead of "*Fouché*" (last name of a person). In addition to this, segmentation issues had to be dealt with. For example, "*M. Montmerqué,ingénieur des ponts etchauasées*" (Mr Montmerqué, highway engineer) has two tokens and a punctuation glued together (*Montmerqué,ingénieur*).

4.1.2 From the Language Point of View

Specific languages. A set of difficulties was due to the specific language types encountered in the corpus, in particular the religious language from the newspaper *La Croix* (17 issues, 68 pages). Some expressions, like "*mandement de Carême*" (Lent pastoral prayer) were found difficult to annotate and required some checking in external sources. The language used in classified ads from *Le Temps* was also quite difficult to annotate due to their format (see Figure 6) and the abbreviations they contain, which are not always easy to understand. For instance, in the same figure, *Cont.* might stand for contiguous.

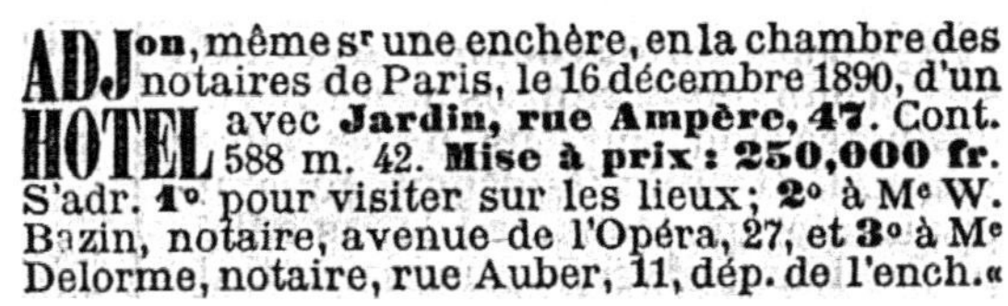
ADJon, même sr une enchère, en la chambre des notaires de Paris, le 16 décembre 1890, d'un HOTEL avec Jardin, rue Ampère, 47. Cont. 588 m. 42. Mise à prix : 250,000 fr. S'adr. 1° pour visiter sur les lieux; 2° à Me W. Bazin, notaire, avenue de l'Opéra, 27, et 3° à Me Delorme, notaire, rue Auber, 11, dép. de l'ench.«

Figure 6: Example of classified ads from *Le Temps*

Cultural context. Another set of difficulties was due to the general cultural context of the time, which is long forgotten now and which the annotators had to rediscover, at least partly. Thus, they had to consult various external sources, like Wikipedia, to check geographical divisions (was "*Tonkin*" a country or a mere region in 1890?), events (in "*le krach Macé*" (Macé crash), does "*Macé*" correspond to a family name?), and even names (is "*Lorys*" a first or a last name?).

More generally, the language of the time (end of the 19th century), though apparently close to present French, presents some specificities that required a re-interpretation of the annotation guide. For example, persons were almost systematically designated by their title (e.g., "Mr X", where "Mr" is a *title* component and "X" a *name.last* component).

Annotation difficulties. During the Broadcast News campaign, we noticed that the distinction made in the annotation guide between a function (which does not include a person) and a title (which is included in a person named entity) was in fact not stable and difficult to use. In the Old Press corpus, with the high frequency of usage of a title with a name of a person, this distinction generated even more questions, mistakes and inconsistencies in the annotations. These differences, though minor and more or less expected, made the annotation more complex, as it depended on realities that are much less frequent nowadays.

Finally, difficulties regarding boundary delimitation were more frequent, most probably due to the written form of the OP corpus (as opposed to the spoken form of the BN corpus). Figure 7 shows a long entity which should probably include *France*.

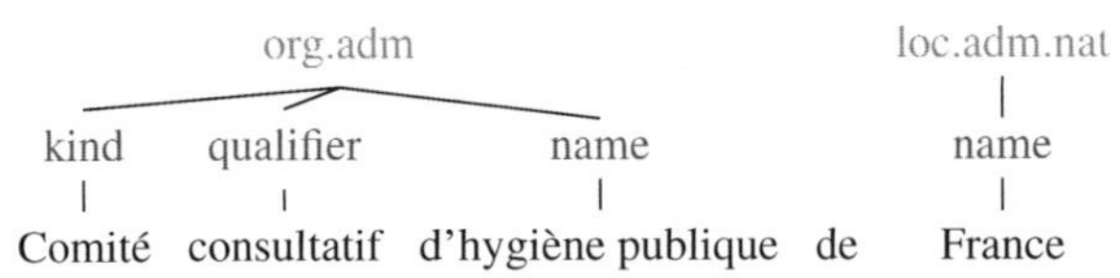

Figure 7: Boundary delimitation difficulties: *consultative committee for public hygiene of France*

4.2 Study of Annotated Corpora

The Broadcast News (BN) corpus and the Old Press (OP) corpus have different temporal and genre properties. Intuitively, we expect these differences to be reflected in the types of named entities they contain.

Having these two corpora consistently annotated with the same types of named entities makes it easier to test this hypothesis. Furthermore, the structure of these entities opens avenues for more detailed contrastive analysis than plain, one-level entities. We sketch some of them in this section.

We used two methods to test the above hypothesis. First, we used a statistical test to compare the distributions of entity types and components across the two corpora. Second, we checked whether documents of these two corpora could be discriminated based on their entity types and components.

4.2.1 Statistical Analysis

We study in this section whether there is a significant difference between the two corpora in terms of entity types and components. Let us stress that we examine only the labels of these entities (e.g., org.adm or name), not their contents (e.g., *Comité consultatif...*).

We first examined the density of entities in documents of the two corpora. For each document, the entity-token ratio is computed as follows: the total number of occurrences of entity types and entity components (*tags*), divided by the number of tokens in the document (*tokens*): $\frac{\text{tags}}{\text{tokens}}$. A Welch Two Sample t-test (computed with the R t.test function) was performed to check whether the mean entity-token ratio was significantly different across the Old Press and Broadcast News documents. It shows that the two means (0.233 and 0.251) have a slightly significant difference (95% confidence interval, $p < 0.01$).

We then applied the same test to each entity type and each entity component. To remove the difference in entity-token ratios, the variable we examine for each entity type or component is the proportion of occurrences of this type or component (tag_i) among all occurrences of entity types and components (*tags*) in a document: $\frac{\text{tag}_i}{\text{tags}}$. Entity types and entity components are all the more over-represented in one of the two corpora as the significance level (p) is high.

Figures 8 and 9 respectively rank entity types and components in decreasing order of p. Bar height reflects the significance of the means difference $|\log(p)|$. An ascending bar means that the entity is more present in the Broadcast News corpus, a descending bar in the Old Press corpus. In total, 36 entity types and components out of 73 have a $p < 0.001$, and 6 more have a $p < 0.01$. Therefore, more than half of them have a significant difference across the two corpora.

Entity type analysis. We can see on Figure 8 that BN has a greater proportion of countries and continents (loc.adm.nat, loc.adm.sup: maybe due to more international news in contemporary press), relative dates and times (time.date.rel, time.hour.rel: possibly linked to the media, audio and television, with more immediate references), companies and administrations (org.ent, org.adm), media names (prod.media). OP has a greater proportion of absolute dates (time.date.abs), individual persons and functions (pers.ind, func.ind), physical addresses, including streets, roads, facilities (loc.add.phys, loc.oro, loc.fac: reference is more often given to where something can be found), hydronyms (loc.phys.hydro), and works of art (prod.art: articles about plays in theaters).

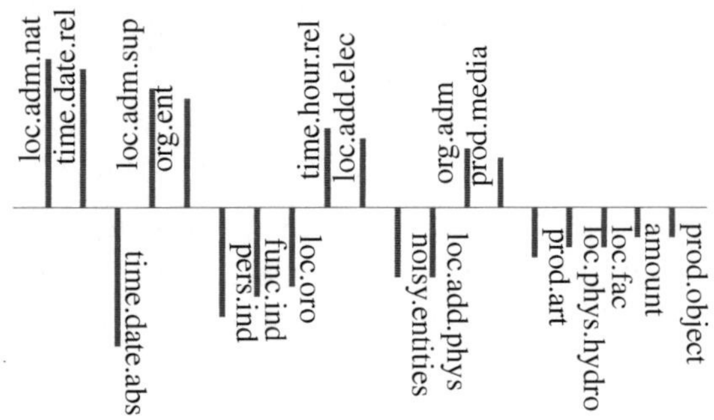

Figure 8: 19 entity types with $p < 0.001$, ranked by decreasing order of significance

Some entity types are only present in one of the corpora. This is indeed the case of the noisy-entities element introduced for OP, but also of electronic addresses and software (loc.add.elec, proc.soft) which did not exist in the nineteenth century.

Entity component analysis. Figure 9 shows that BN has a greater proportion of first names, middle names, and demonyms (name.first, name.middle, demonym), whereas OP has a greater proportion of titles and last names (title, name.last): this reflects differences in time periods (more titles in the nineteenth century, use of first name in addition to last name in contemporary news) and topics (use of demonyms for sports teams in contemporary news). Days, months and years are in greater proportion in OP since they are the components of absolute dates, also in greater proportion in OP (see above).

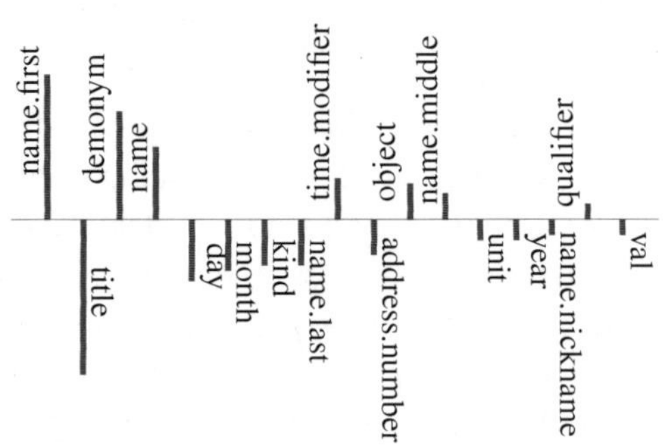

Figure 9: 17 components with $p < 0.001$, ranked by decreasing order of significance

More precise assessments can be performed based on the rich structure of the entities, with their nested types and components. Among person entities (pers.ind and pers.coll), BN has a much larger proportion (52% vs. 6%) of persons composed of a first and a last name (pers_first_last: entities of the form <pers.*> <name.first/> <name.last/> </pers.*>) and of persons with a first name (pers_with_first: entities where <pers.*> includes a <name.first/>: 69% vs. 19%), whereas OP has a much larger proportion (44% vs. 8%) of persons with a title (pers_with_title: entities where <pers.*> includes a <title/>) and of persons composed of a title and a last name (pers_title_last, 34% vs. 2%: *M. Berthelot*). In contrast, there is no significant difference in the proportion of persons with a last name. This refines the individual observations on name components and types, and shows that although OP has a greater proportion of last names, it has in the same way a greater proportion of persons, so that their ratio is constant across both corpora. On the contrary, the greater proportion of titles in OP is confirmed by its greater proportion of persons who include a title.

In another area, OP has a quite large proportion (29% vs. 6%) of administrations (org.adm) that are composed of exactly one <kind> component (orgadm_kind): the most frequent ones are *la Chambre*, *le gouvernement*, *la République*, *l'Etat*, etc., instead of a kind and some precision (e.g., *la <org.adm> <kind> Chambre </kind> des <func.coll> <kind> députés </kind> </func.coll> </org.adm>* [the Chamber of Representatives]). This reflects a particular administrative (here, governmental) system and a conventional reduction of the full name of some of its instances.

4.2.2 Automatic Classification and Feature Selection

If the distributions of entity types and components are sufficiently different across the Broadcast News and Old Press corpora, it should be possible to use them as features in a classifier which detects whether a document of these corpora belongs to BN or OP. To test this hypothesis, we used as features for a document the same variables as in the statistical analysis: the $\frac{\text{tag}_i}{\text{tags}}$ ratio for each entity type and component.

We tested several classifiers (using the Weka toolbox (Hall et al., 2009)), with stratified ten-fold cross-validation over the whole training corpus (188 BN documents and 231 OP documents). Table 3 shows the results for One Rule (OneR), decision trees (J48), Naïve Bayes, and SVM (SMO). False Negative (FN) and False Positive (FP) computation assumes that the target class is Old Press (hence FN is the number of OP documents classified as BN).

	FP	FN	FP+FN	Accuracy
One Rule	22	12	34	0.919
Decision Tree	2	5	7	0.983
Naïve Bayes	2	1	3	0.993
SVM	0	0	0	1.000

Table 3: Classification based on tag ratio

Even a baseline classifier (One Rule) obtained a high accuracy (0.919). It chose the title feature and produced the rule *"if title $<$ 0.0255 then BN, else OP"*. This is consistent with the above observation that it has the second most significant difference in means across the two corpora.

The Decision Tree classifier obtained a much better accuracy, with a tree based on features title, then on name.first and loc.adm.sup (also among the most significant differences), and on func.ind, demonym (very significant differences too). The Naïve Bayes classifier did better (0.993), and the SVM obtained a perfect classification: taken together, the 73 tag ratios are indeed discriminant enough to determine the corpus to which a document belongs.

Performing feature selection is yet another way to test which entity types and components are the most discriminant. Using the default feature selection method in Weka (CfsSubsetEval with Best-First search) selected 21 features, 19 of which had a $p < 0.001$. With only the three features title, demonym, and name.first (the three tag ratios with the most statistically significant differences), the SVM still correctly classified all documents but one. This confirms that some of the entity types and components are highly discriminant. Interestingly enough, the three most discriminant ones are components: this underlines the contribution of this aspect of our structured named entities.

5 Conclusion and Perspectives

We have presented the human annotation of a second reference corpus (Old Press) with Structured Named Entities, using the same annotation scheme as in the previous corpus (Broadcast News). These two corpora have similar overall sizes in tokens and numbers of entity types and components, but are different in terms of time periods and media. This entailed a need to adapt slightly the annotation guidelines.

Having two corpora annotated according to the same annotation scheme makes it possible to perform contrastive studies. We reported a series of observations on the human annotation of these two corpora. We illustrated the impact of OCRed text and of a time-induced cultural distance on the human annotation process. Based on the annotation results, we evidenced significant differences between the entity types and components of the two corpora, as well as discriminant entity types and components.

The structured named entities made it possible to study finer-grained distinctions, such as different naming structures for people (title + last name in Old Press vs. first + last name in Broadcast News), or single-component (in Old Press) vs. multiple-component administrative organizations.

Indeed, the studies reported in this paper are but a small sample of what can be achieved thanks to these structured entities. At the time of writing, we are in the final stages of the paperwork necessary to release the two corpora for free usage by the scientific community. We hope that many colleagues will thus obtain these corpora and use them both to train named entity recognizers and to perform more precise contrastive studies.

Acknowledgments

This work has been partially financed by OSEO under the Quaero program and by the French ANR ETAPE project.

We thank all the annotators *(Jérémy, Matthieu, Orane, and Raoum)* from the Elda company; they worked seriously and with professionalism.

References

Eckhard Bick. 2004. A named entity recognizer for Danish. In *Proc. of LREC*. ELRA.

Kate Byrne. 2007. Nested named entity recognition in historical archive text. In *Proceedings of the first IEEE International Conference on Semantic Computing (ICSC 2007)*, Irvine, California.

Sam Coates-Stephens. 1992. The analysis and acquisition of proper names for the understanding of free text. *Computers and the Humanities*, 26:441–456.

Gregory Crane and Alison Jones. 2006. The challenge of Virginia Banks: an evaluation of named entity analysis in a 19th-century newspaper collection. In *Proceedings of the 6th ACM/IEEE-CS joint conference on Digital libraries*, JCDL'06, pages 31–40, New York, NY, USA. ACM.

George Doddington, Alexis Mitchell, Mark Przybocki, Lance Ramshaw, Stephanie Strassel, and Ralph Weischedel. 2004. The automatic content extraction (ACE) program—tasks, data, and evaluation. In *Proc. of LREC*, pages 837–840. ELRA.

Michael Fleischman and Eduard Hovy. 2002. Fine grained classification of named entities. In *Proc. of COLING*, volume 1, pages 1–7. ACL.

Michael Fleischman. 2001. Automated subcategorization of named entities. In *Proc. of the ACL 2001 Student Research Workshop*, pages 25–30.

Olivier Galibert, Ludovic Quintard, Sophie Rosset, Pierre Zweigenbaum, Claire Nédellec, Sophie Aubin, Laurent Gillard, Jean-Pierre Raysz, Delphine Pois, Xavier Tannier, Louise Deléger, and Dominique Laurent. 2010. Named and specific entity detection in varied data: The Quaero named entity baseline evaluation. In *Proc. of LREC*, Valletta, Malta. ELRA.

Olivier Galibert, Sophie Rosset, Cyril Grouin, Pierre Zweigenbaum, and Ludovic Quintard. 2011. Structured and extended named entity evaluation in automatic speech transcriptions. In *Proc. of IJCNLP*, Chiang Mai, Thailand.

Olivier Galibert, Sophie Rosset, Cyril Grouin, Pierre Zweigenbaum, and Ludovic Quintard. 2012. Extended named entities annotation in ocred documents: From corpus constitution to evaluation campaign. In *Proc. of LREC*, Istanbul, Turkey. ELRA.

Ralph Grishman and Beth Sundheim. 1996. Message Understanding Conference - 6: A brief history. In *Proc. of COLING*, pages 466–471.

Cyril Grouin, Sophie Rosset, Pierre Zweigenbaum, Karën Fort, Olivier Galibert, and Ludovic Quintard. 2011. Proposal for an extension of traditional named entities: From guidelines to evaluation, an overview. In *Proc. of the Fifth Linguistic Annotation Workshop (LAW-V)*, Portland, OR. Association for Computational Linguistics.

Claire Grover, Sharon Givon, Richard Tobin, and Julian Ball. 2008. Named entity recognition for digitised historical texts. In *Proceedings of the Sixth International Language Resources and Evaluation (LREC'08)*, Marrakech, Morocco. ELRA. http://www.lrec-conf.org/proceedings/lrec2008/.

Mark Hall, Eibe Franck, Geoffrey Holmes, Bernhard Pfahringer, Peter Reutemann, and Ian H. Witten. 2009. The weka data mining software: An update. *SIGKDD Explorations*, 11(1).

Vladimir Levenshtein. 1965. Binary codes capable of correction deletions, insertions and reversals. *Doklady Akademii Nauk SSSR*, 163(4):845–848.

David Miller, Sean Boisen, Richard Schwartz, Rebecca Stone, and Ralph Weischedel. 2000. Named entity extraction from noisy input: speech and OCR. In *Proceedings of the sixth conference on Applied natural language processing*, ANLC'00, pages 316–324, Stroudsburg, PA, USA. Association for Computational Linguistics.

Sophie Rosset, Cyril Grouin, and Pierre Zweigenbaum, 2011. *Entités Nommées Structurées : guide d'annotation Quaero*. LIMSI–CNRS, Orsay, France. `http://www.quaero.org/media/files/bibliographie/quaero-guide-annotation-2011.pdf`.

Satoshi Sekine. 2004. Definition, dictionaries and tagger of extended named entity hierarchy. In *Proc. of LREC*. ELRA.

Intra-Chunk Dependency Annotation: Expanding Hindi Inter-Chunk Annotated Treebank

Prudhvi Kosaraju
Intl. Institute of Info. Technology
Hyderabad, India
prudhvi.kosaraju@research.iiit.ac.in

Bharat Ram Ambati
Intl. Institute of Info. Technology
Hyderabad, India
ambati@research.iiit.ac.in

Samar Husain
Univ. of Potsdam
Potsdam, Germany
husain@uni-potsdam.de

Dipti Misra Sharma
Intl. Institute of Info. Technology
Hyderabad,India
dipti@iiit.ac.in

Rajeev Sangal
Intl. Institute of Info. Technology
Hyderabad, India
sangal@mail.iiit.ac.in

Abstract

We present two approaches (rule-based and statistical) for automatically annotating intra-chunk dependencies in Hindi. The intra-chunk dependencies are added to the dependency trees for Hindi which are already annotated with inter-chunk dependencies. Thus, the intra-chunk annotator finally provides a fully parsed dependency tree for a Hindi sentence. In this paper, we first describe the guidelines for marking intra-chunk dependency relations. Although the guidelines are for Hindi, they can easily be extended to other Indian languages. These guidelines are used for framing the rules in the rule-based approach. For the statistical approach, we use MaltParser, a data driven parser. A part of the ICON 2010 tools contest data for Hindi is used for training and testing the MaltParser. The same set is used for testing the rule-based approach.

1 Introduction

Treebanks are corpora in which each sentence pairs with a parse tree. These are linguistic resources in which the morphological, syntactic and lexical information for each sentence has been explicitly marked. Some notable efforts in this direction are the Penn Tree Bank (Marcus et al., 1993) for English and the Prague Dependency Bank (Hajicova, 1998) for Czech. Lack of such treebanks has been a major bottleneck in various efforts in advance research and development of NLP tools and applications for Indian languages.

Treebanks can be created manually or semi-automatically. Manual creation of treebank is a costly task both in terms of money and time. The annotators follow a set of prescribed guidelines for the annotation task. Semi-automatic creation of treebank involves first running of tools/parsers and then manual correction of errors. An accurate annotating parser/tool saves cost and time for both the annotation as well as the validation task.

A multi-layered Hindi treebank is in the process of being created (Bhatt et al., 2009). Dependency treebank forms the first layer in this annotation. To save annotation effort, manual annotation of the dependency relations for Hindi dependency treebank is carried at the inter-chunk level. The intra-chunk relations are marked automatically. The focus of this paper is the task of automatically marking intra-chunk relations. We present both a rule-based and a statistical approach for this expansion process. We call this process 'expansion' since the intra-chunk dependencies are made explicit by removing the chunk encapsulation; one could visualize this as expanding the chunk into sub-trees. The rest of the paper is organized as follows. Sections 2 & 3 give an overview of Hindi treebank and the steps involved in its development. Section 4 describes the guidelines for annotating intra-chunk dependencies. Section 5 shows our approach to building an automatic intra-chunk annotator. Section 6 talks about issues with a couple of dependency relations and how these are handled by the automatic annotator. We conclude in section 7 and present future work in Section 8.

2 Hindi Dependency Treebank

A multi-layered and multi-representational Treebank for Hindi (Bhatt et al., 2009; Xia et al., 2009) is currently being developed. The treebank will have dependency relations, verb-arguments (PropBank, Palmer et al., 2005) and phrase structure (PS) representations. The dependency treebank contains information encoded at the morpho-syntactic (morphological, part-of-speech and chunk information) and syntactico-semantic (dependency) levels The manual annotation of the dependency treebank entails the annotation of part of speech (POS) tag, morphological information for each word, identification of chunk boundary (and chunk tag) and marking inter-chunk dependency relation between word pairs.

The intra-chunk dependencies are left unannotated. The decision to leave intra-chunk relations unmarked is based on the understanding that their identification is quite deterministic and can be automatically annotated with high degree of accuracy. The notion of chunk is, in essence, used as a device for modularity in the process of annotation. The relations among the words in a chunk are not marked in the initial phase of annotation and hence allow us to ignore local details while building the sentence level dependency tree. An example of inter-chunk dependency annotation is given in Figure 1 below. Note how the two chunks (the noun chunk, NP and the verb chunk, VGF) are related to each other using the attribute 'drel' (dependency relation), also note that the relations between the chunk-internal words (e.g. नीली and किताब in the NP chunk) are left unspecified. The annotation is represented in SSF[1]

Sentence1: नीली किताब गिर गई
niilii kitaab gir gaii
'blue' 'book' 'fall' 'go-perf'
The blue book fell down

```
1      ((      NP     <name='NP' drel='k1:VGF'>
1.1    niilii  JJ     <name='niilii'>
1.2    kitaab  NN     <name='kitaab'>
       ))
2      ((      VGF    <name='VGF'>
2.1    gir     VM     <name='gir'>
2.2    gaii    VAUX   <name='gaii'>
       ))
```

Figure 1: SSF representation

Figure 2 shows the schematic dependency tree for sentence 1.

Figure 2: Inter-chunk dependency tree of sentence1

The inter-chunk dependency annotation is done following the dependency guidelines in Bharati et al., (2009) that uses a dependency framework inspired by Panini's grammar of Sanskrit (see, Begum et al., 2008 for more details). Subsequent to inter-chunk dependency annotation, intra-chunk annotation is done automatically following the guidelines described in this paper.

The final treebank for Hindi would have other layers annotation such as Propbank and Phrase structure. The conversion to phrase structure depends on the expanded version of the treebank (i.e. trees with inter-chunk, as well as, intra-chunk relations marked).Hence, it is important to have high quality complete dependency structure for each sentence, and since inter-chunk annotation is manual, this implies that the process of automatic expansion (i.e. the task of making intra-chunk relations explicit) should be very accurate.

[1] SSF: Shakti Standard Format http:// web2py.iiit.ac.in/ publications/default/download/techreport.pdf.c08a8d0a-50ed-4837-8ff0-93d099efbccb.pdf

```
1   niilii  JJ    <fs drel='nmod__adj:kitaab' chunkType='child:NP' name='niilii '>
2   kitaab  NN    <fs drel='k1:gir' name='kitaab' chunkId='NP' chunkType='head:NP'>
3   gir     VM    <fs name='gir' chunkId='VGF' chunkType='head:VGF'>
4   gaii    VAUX  <fs drel='lwg__aux:gir' name='gaii' chunkType='child:VGF'>
```

Figure 3: SSF representation of complete dependency tree

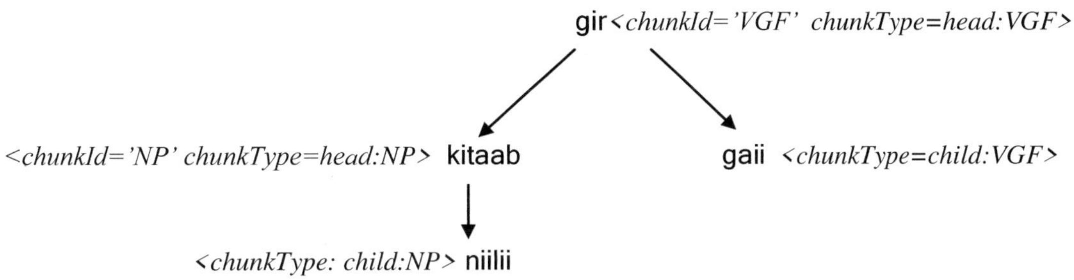

Figure 4: Complete dependency tree of sentence 1

3 Intra-Chunk Annotation

Showing intra-chunk relations and thereby a fully parsed dependency tree implies chunk removal from the inter-chunk dependency annotation. Once the intra-chunk dependencies are made explicit, every sentential token becomes part of the dependency tree. However, it can be useful to retain the chunk information which has been manually validated for inter-chunk dependency annotation. Indeed, previous parsing experiments for Hindi during the ICON2010 tools contest (Husain et al., 2010) have shown that this information consistently improves performance. Thus, during the process of expansion, we introduce two attribute-value pairs for this purpose. This way we maintain chunk information after making the intra-chunk relations explicit. This makes it possible for the users of the treebank to select the chunk head and ignore the intra-chunk information if so desired. Alternatively, it is also possible to access the complete dependency tree.

In Figure 1, the dependency relations are marked between chunk heads, i.e. 'kitaab' is seen related to 'gir' with a 'k1' relation. 'niilii' and 'gaii', on the other hand, are not shown related to any other word. Also note that the chunk boundaries are shown using brackets. Once we show all the tokens as part of the dependency tree, this information goes in the feature structure of individual nodes. This can be seen in figure 3.

The attribute, 'chunkId' and 'chunkType' substitute the bracketing, as well as show the chunk members in the role of head and child. The head node has 'chunkId' that gives it a unique chunk name; note that this is same as the value of 'name' for the original chunk. When multiple chunks with same name occur in a sentence, we append a number along with the name. For example, if there are multiple NP's then the chunk ids will be NP, NP2 and NP3 etc. In addition, all the chunk members have 'chunkType' that gives their membership type. In the example (figure 3), the adjective 'nIlI' modifies the head noun 'kiwAba' with 'nmod__adj' relation. The chunk membership is also shown for both these tokens, nIlI is the 'child of the chunk with chunkId=NP' shown by chunkType. kiwAba on the other hand is the 'head of the chunk with chunkId=NP', it has both chunkType and chunkId.

4 Intra-Chunk Dependency Guidelines

Intra-chunk labels are used when the dependencies within a chunk are made explicit. There are a total of 12 major intra-chunk tags. The tags are of three types: (a) normal dependencies, eg. *nmod__adj, jjmod__intf,* etc., (b) local word group dependencies(lwg), eg. *lwg__psp, lwg__vaux, etc.,* and (c) linking lwg dependencies, eg. *lwg_cont.* Local word dependencies themselves can be broadly classified into two types, one that handles post-positions and auxiliary verbs and the other that handles negations, particles, etc. Following guidelines are used to annotate the intra-chunk dependencies.

1. ***nmod__adj:*** Various types of adjectival modifications are shown using this label. An adjective modifying a head noun is one such instance. The label also incorporates various other modifications such as a demonstrative or a quantifier modifying a noun.

Chunk: नीली किताब

NP ((*niilii*_JJ *kitaab*_NN))
'blue ' 'book'

niilii
↓ *nmod__adj*
kitaab

In the above example NP is the chunk with words 'niilii' (blue) and 'kitaab' (book) with POS tags JJ and NN respectively.

2. ***lwg__psp:*** This relation is used to attach post-positions/auxiliaries associated with the noun or a verb. 'lwg' in the label name stands for local word grouping and associates all the postpositions with the head noun. These relations are distinct from normal dependency relations as they are more morphological in nature.

Chunk: अभिषेक ने

NP((*abhishek*_NNP *ne*_PSP))
'abhishek' 'ERG'

abhishek
↓ *lwg__psp*
ne

3. ***lwg__neg:*** This relation is used for negative particles. Negative particles are normally grouped with a noun/verb. Like postpositions or auxiliaries these are also classified as 'lwg'.

Chunk: नहीं आयेगा

VGF((nahim_NEG aayegaa_VM))
'Never' 'Come'

nahim
↓ *lwg__neg*
aayega

4. ***lwg__vaux:*** This relation is used when an auxiliary verb modifies the main verb.

Chunk: हो गया

VGF((ho_VM gayaa_VAUX))
'be' 'go-perf'

ho
↓ *lwg__vaux*
gayaa

5. ***jjmod_intf :*** This relation is used when an adjectival intensifier modifies an adjective.

Chunk: बहुत तेज़ जानवर

NP((bahut_INTF tez_JJ jaanvar_NN))
'very' 'fast' 'animal'

bahut
↓ *nmod__adj*
tez
↓ *jjmod__intf*
jaanvar

6. ***pof__redup:*** This relation is used when there is reduplication inside a chunk. The POS tag will in almost all the cases help us identify such instances. We see this in the example below.

Chunk: धीरे धीरे

RBP((dhiire_RB dhiire_RDP))
'slowly' 'slowly'

dhiire
↓ *pof__redup*
dhiire

7. ***pof__cn:*** This relation is used for relating the components within a compound noun. Like 'pof__redup' identifying such cases will be straight-forward. The POS will provide us with the relevant information

Chunk: रामबच्चन यादव

NP((raamabachhan_NNPC yaadav_NNP))
'rambachhan' 'yadav'

raamabachhan
↓ *pof__cn*
yaadav

8. ***pof__cv :*** This relation is used for compound verbs. Like the previous 'pof' labels, POS information will be sufficient to identify this relation.

Chunk: उठ बैठा

VGF((uTha_VMC baiThaa_VM))
'rise' 'sit-perf'

uTha
↓ *pof__cv*
baiThaa

9. ***rsym:*** Punctuation marks and symbols like '-' should be attached to the head of the chunk with relation rsym.
10. ***lwg__rp:*** This relation is used when a particle modifies some chunk head.

Chunk: जाना भी था

VGF((jaanaa_VM bhi_RP tha_VAUX))
'go-inf' 'also' 'perf'

jaanaa
lwg__rp ↙ ↘ *lwg__vaux*
bhi tha

11. ***lwg__uh:*** This relation is used when interjection modifies other words.

Chunk : हे भगवान

NP((hei_INJ bhagvaan_NN))

'Oh!' 'God'

bhagvaan
↓ *lwg__uh*
hei

12. ***lwg__cont:*** We use this label to show that a group of lexical items inside a chunk together perform certain function. In such cases, we do not commit on the dependencies between these elements. We see this with complex post-positions associated with a noun/verb or with the auxiliaries of a verb. 'cont' stands for continue.

Chunk: जा सकता है

VGF((*jaa*_VM *sakataa*_VAUX *hai*_VAUX))
'go' 'can' 'be-pres'

jaa
↓ *lwg__vaux*
sakataa
↓ *lwg__cont*
hai

5 Intra-Chunk Dependency Annotator

In this section we discuss our approach to building an intra-chunk dependency annotator/parser for Hindi. We describe three experiments; the first two are rule-based and statistical based, while the third is hybrid in a sense that it adds on a heuristic based post-processing component on top of the statistical technique. We evaluate about approaches in section 5.3 after describing rule-based and statistical approaches in sections 5.1 and 5.2 respectively.

5.1 Rule-Based Dependency Annotator

The rule-based approach identifies the modifier-modified (parent–child) relationship inside a chunk with the help of the rules provided in a rule template. The inter-chunk dependency annotated data is run through a head computation module (a rule-based tool), which marks the head of each chunk. After getting the heads for each chunk, we get the intra-chunk relations using a rule-base that has been manually created. The design of the rule template allows capturing all the information in a SSF representation. The rule template is a 5-columned table with each row representing a rule. Table1 shows a sample rule written using the rule template. The five columns are

1. Chunk Name: Specifies the name of the chunk for which this expansion rule can be applied.

2. Parent Constraints: Lexical item which satisfies these constraints will be identified as the parent. Constraints are designed capturing POS, chunk, word and morphological features. In Table1 the constraint on the parent is specified using its POS category (NN: common noun).

3. Child Constraints: Lexical item satisfying these constraints becomes the child. Constraints are designed similar to the parent constraints. In Table 1 the constraint on the child is specified using its POS category (JJ:adjective).

Chunk Name	Parent Constraints	Child Constraints	Contextual Constraints	Dep. Relation
NP	*POS* == NN	*POS* == JJ	*posn*(parent) > *posn*(child);	nmod__adj

Tablc 1: Sample rule

4. Contextual Constraints: Lexical items satisfying constraints 1, 2 &3 become parent and child in a chunk. One can access the previous and next words of parent and child by applying arithmetic on *posn* attribute. Information about the lexical item can be accessed by applying attributes like POS (for part of speech tag), CAT (category), and LEMMA (for root form of lexical item).

Here an example of a contextual constraint taken from Table1:

***posn*(parent) > *posn*(child)**

Parent and child constraint look at the properties of word but there are cases where the constraint needs to be formed beyond word level information. These constraints involve capturing of word order information. In such cases we use the operator '>'. It can be used only when '*posn*' attribute is used. Here the constraint means that this rule is applicable only when child occurs before parent inside the chunk.

One can also specify constraints in form of:

POS__posn(parent) - 1 == NN

Here the Part of Speech of word preceding parent is accessed and compared with NN. ***posn(parent) – 1*** retrieves the position of preceding word of parent and ***POS__*** on this position gives us the Part of Speech tag of that lexical item.

5. Dependency Relation: If all the constraints are satisfied, then the dependency relation from this column is marked on the parent-child arc.

5.2 Sub-tree Parsing using MaltParser

We use MaltParser (Nivre et al., 2007) as an alternative method to identify the intra-chunk relations. It is well known in the literature that transition-based dependency parsing techniques (e.g. Nivre, 2003) work best for marking short distance dependencies in a sentence. As must be clear by now, intra-chunk relations are in fact short distance dependencies; and we basically use MaltParser to predict the internal structure of a chunk. So instead of using it to parse a sentence, we parse individual chunks. Each chunk is treated as a sub-tree. The training data contains sub-trees with intra-chunk relations marked between chunk-internal nodes, the head of the chunk becomes the root node of the sub-tree. The MaltParser is trained on these sub-trees and a model is created. We run the test data on this model for marking intra-chunk dependencies among the sub-trees and then post-process them to obtain complete dependency tree for the data.

5.3 Results

In this section we evaluate the three approaches that were explored to build the automatic intra-chunk annotator. A total of 320 sentences extracted from the ICON2010 tools contest data for Hindi (Husain et al., 2010) have been manually annotated for intra-chunk relations. Table 2 shows the statistics for this gold data that has been used for evaluation (and training).

Data	Number of Sentences
Training	192
Development	64
Testing	64

Table 2: Gold data

Rule-Based Approach: As discussed in section 5.1, the rule-based approach marks dependency relation mainly by using POS patterns in a chunk. Table 3 shows the result when evaluated for the test data.

LAS	97.89
UAS	98.50
LS	98.38

Table 3: Parsing accuracies[2] obtained using rule-based tool

Statistical/MaltParser-based approach: Table 2 shows the division of data into training, development and test. The experimentation procedure is similar to the one used in Kosaraju et al., (2010). We prepared a list of features with the aim of getting a better parse. A simple forward selector is used to prune the list and prepare the best feature template. The selector's task is to include the feature into feature template if this

[2] Parsing Accuracies- LAS: labeled attachment score, UAS: Unlabeled attachment score, LS: label score.

template improves the LAS score over the previous template. These feature optimization experiments were conducted over 5-fold cross-validation of the combined training and development data. The best feature template was used to get the final accuracies for the test data. Table 4 shows results on the basic template, template capturing POS patterns and best template that included POS, lemma and other information present in the SSF data.

	LAS	UAS	LS
Base line	95.70	97.07	96.80
POS template	96.80	97.62	97.80
Best template	**97.35**	**98.26**	**97.90**

Table 4: Parsing accuracies using MaltParser

The POS-based template scores can be compared with the results obtained from the rule-based scores (Table 3) since the rules are formed using POS patterns.

We see that both rule-based and statistical approach give very high accuracies on the test data. These results validate our initial intuition that identification of intra-chunk relations is quite deterministic. These results also support our annotation design choice of leaving the annotation of intra-chunk relations out of the initial manual phase. Table 5 shows percentage error contribution of some major tags to total Error of their respective systems. Table 6 shows precision (P) and recall (R) of some major tags.

Depn. Relation	Rule-based appraoch	Statistical appraoch
pof__cn	28.33	26.7
nmod__adj	13.3	13.3
lwg__rp	6.6	0
rsym	16.7	20.0

Table 5: Percentage Contribution of error by each tag to the total error of the system

Hybrid approach: Table 5 & 6 shows error analysis of both approaches. For some tags like *nmod__adj* we see the rule-based appraoch shows better results. Therefore we decided to include rules as a post-processing step in the statistical approach.

Depn. Relation	Rule-based		Statistical	
	P	R	P	R
pof__cn	95.63	**94.50**	91.07	92.73
nmod__adj	96.33	**98.33**	95.28	98.06
lwg__rp	97.62	95.35	100	**100**
rsym	96.71	**97.63**	92.41	96.05

Table 6: Error analysis of both methods

We made the statistical approach hybrid by post-processing the output of the MaltParser. This involves correction of some dependency relations based on heuristics framed from the rules of the rule-based tool. Heuristics are formed for those dependency relations that have higher recall in the rule-based approach compared to the statistical approach. The modification resulted in improvement in parsing accuracies. This can be seen in Table 7.

Approach	LAS	UAS	LS
Rule-based	97.89	98.50	98.38
Statistical	97.35	98.26	97.90
Hybrid	**98.17**	**98.81**	**98.63**

Table 7: Parsing accuracies

6 Special Cases

The neat division between the task of inter-chunk parsing and intra-chunk parsing is based on the following assumption: 'Chunks are self contained units. Intra-chunk dependencies are chunk internal and do not span outside a chunk.' However, there are two special cases where this constraint does not hold, i.e. in these two cases a chunk internal element that is not the head of the chunk has a relation with a lexical item outside its chunk and therefore, these two relations have to be handled separately. These are related to punctuation and co-ordination.

1. rsym__eos: The EOS (end-of-sentence) marker occurs in the last chunk of the sentence. It attaches to the head of the sentence (which may lie in the same chunk or another chunk) with this relation.

2. lwg__psp: As noted in section 4, a PSP (postposition) attaches to the head of its chunk with a lwg__psp relation. However, if the right most child of a CCP (conjunction chunk) is a nominal (NP or VGNN), one needs to attach the PSP of this nominal child to the head of the CCP during expansion. If there are multiple PSP then the first PSP gets lwg__psp and the following gets lwg__cont relation. Take the following example

NP(*raama*_NNP) CCP(*aur*_CC) NP(*siitaa*_NNP
'ram' 'and' 'sita'
*ne*_PSP)
'ERG'

In this case the PSP connects to the CC with the relation lwg__psp. The subtree after expansion is shown in figure 6.

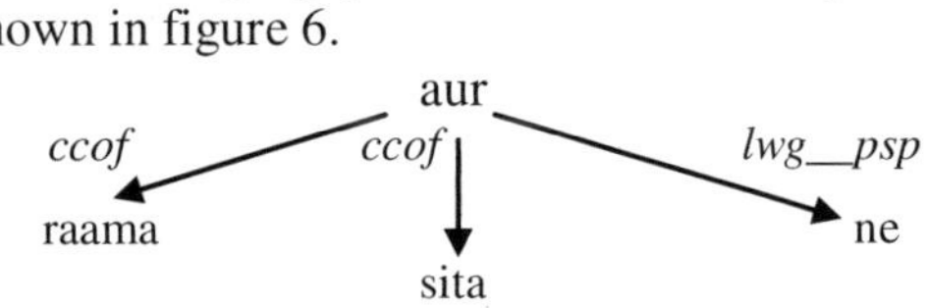

Figure 6: Expanded sub-tree with PSP connected with CC.

7 Conclusion

In this paper we described annotation guidelines for marking intra-chunk dependency relations. We then went on to show that these relations can be automatically identified with high accuracy. This was illustrated using (1) a rule-based approach that mainly used intra-chunk POS patterns, and (2) a statistical approach using MaltParser. We also showed that these two systems can be combined together to achieve even higher accuracy.

From the report of error analysis, it is been shown that there are certain relations that are not being marked successfully. This is good news because then one can make very targeted manual corrections after the automatic tool is run.

Acknowledgments

We would like to thank Karthik Gali for his initial efforts in building the annotator. The work reported in this paper is supported by the NSF grant (Award Number: CNS 0751202; CFDA Number: 47.070).

References

A. Bharati, D. M. Sharma S. Husain, L. Bai, R. Begam and R. Sangal. 2009. AnnCorra: TreeBanks for Indian Languages, Guidelines for Annotating Hindi TreeBank (version–2.0). http://ltrc.iiit.ac.in/MachineTrans/research/tb/DSguidelines/DS-guidelines-ver2-28-05-09.pdf

E. Hajicova. 1998. Prague Dependency Treebank: From Analytic to Tectogrammatical Annotation. *In Proc. TSD'98.*

F. Xia, O. Rambow, R. Bhatt, M. Palmer, and D. M. Sharma. 2009. Towards a Multi-Representational Treebank. *In Proceedings of the 7th International Workshop on Treebanks and Linguistic Theories (TLT 2009), Groningen, Netherlands.*

J. Nivre, An Efficient Algorithm for Projective Dependency Parsing. *In Proceedings of the 8th International Workshop on Parsing Technologies (IWPT 03), Nancy, France, 23-25 April 2003, pp. 149-160.*

J. Nivre, J. Hall, J. Nilsson, A. Chanev, G. Eryigit, S. Kübler, S. Marinov and E Marsi. 2007. MaltParser: A language-independent system for data-driven dependency parsing. *Natural Language Engineering, 13(2), 95-135.*

M. Marcus, B. Santorini, and M.A. Marcinkiewicz. 1993. Building a large annotated corpus of English : The Penn Treebank. *Computational Linguistics 1993.*

P. Kosaraju, S. R. Kesidi, V. B. R. Ainavolu and P. Kukkadapu. 2010. Experiments on Indian Language Dependency Parsing. *In Proceedings of the ICON10 NLP Tools Contest: Indian Language Dependency Parsing.*

R. Begum, S. Husain, A. Dhwaj, D. M. Sharma, L. Bai, and R. Sangal. 2008. Dependency annotation scheme for Indian languages. *In Proceedings of IJCNLP-2008.*

R. Bhatt, B. Narasimhan, M. Palmer, O. Rambow, D. M. Sharma and F. Xia. 2009. MultiRepresentational and Multi-Layered Treebank for Hindi/Urdu. *In Proc. of the Third Linguistic Annotation Workshop at 47th ACL and 4th IJCNLP.*

A Model for Linguistic Resource Description

Nancy Ide
Department of Computer Science
Vassar College
Poughkeepsie, New York, USA
ide@cs.vassar.edu

Keith Suderman
Department of Computer Science
Vassar College
Poughkeepsie, New York, USA
suderman@anc.org

Abstract

This paper describes a comprehensive standard for resource description developed within ISO TC37 SC4). The standard is instantiated in a system of XML headers that accompany data and annotation documents represented using the the Linguistic Annotation Framework's Graph Annotation Format (GrAF) (Ide and Suderman, 2007; Ide and Suderman, Submitted). It provides mechanisms for describing the organization of the resource, documenting the conventions used in the resource, associating data and annotation documents, and defining and selecting defined portions of the resource and its annotations. It has been designed to accommodate the use of XML technologies for processing, including XPath, XSLT, and, by virtue of the system's linkage strategy, RDF/OWL, and to accommodate linkage to web-based ontologies and data category registries such as the OLiA ontologies (Chiarcos, 2012) and ISOCat (Marc Kemps-Snijders and Wright, 2008).

1 Introduction

While substantial effort has gone into defining standardized representation formats for linguistically annotated language resources, very little attention has been paid to standardizing the metadata and documentation practices associated with these resources (see, for example, (Ide and Pustejovsky, 2010)). Multiple techniques have been proposed to represent resource provenance, and a W3C Working Group[1] has recently been convened to devise means to enable provenance information to be exchanged, in particular for data originating from and/or distributed over the web. Beyond this, there exist some standard practices for resource publication through established data distribution centers such as the Linguistic Data Consortium (LDC)[2] and ELRA[3], but they are not completely consistent among different centers, and they are not comprehensive. Whether a resource is distributed from a data center or via the web, detailed information about methodology, annotation schemes, etc. is often sparse. However, users need this kind of information to not only use but also assess the quality of a resource, replicate processes and results, and deal with idiosyncrasies or documented errors.

Another area that has received virtually no attention involves standardized strategies for formally describing the structure and organization of a resource. Information about directory structure and relations among files is typically provided in accompanying README files that provide no means to ensure that the requisite components are in place or perform systematic processing without developing customized scripts. Formalized description of resource organization would enable automatic validation as well as enhanced processing capabilities.

This paper describes a comprehensive standard for resource description developed within ISO TC37 SC4[4]. The standard is instantiated in a system of XML headers that accompany data and annotation documents represented using the the Linguis-

[1] http://www.w3.org/2011/01/prov-wg-charter.html

[2] http://www.ldc.upenn.edu

[3] http://www.elra.info

[4] http://www.tc37sc4.org

tic Annotation Framework's Graph Annotation Format (GrAF) (Ide and Suderman, 2007; Ide and Suderman, Submitted). It provides mechanisms for describing the organization of the resource, documenting the conventions used in the resource, associating data and annotation documents, and defining and selecting defined portions of the resource and its annotations. It has been designed to accommodate the use of XML technologies for processing, including XPath, XSLT, and, by virtue of the system's linkage strategy, RDF/OWL, and to accommodate linkage to web-based ontologies and data category registries such as the OLiA ontologies (Chiarcos, 2012) and ISOCat (Marc Kemps-Snijders and Wright, 2008). We first describe the general architecture of resources rendered in GrAF, followed by a description of the headers that instantiate the resource description standard.

2 GrAF Overview

GrAF has been developed with ISO TC37 SC4 to provide a general framework for representing linguistically annotated resources. Its design has been informed by previous and current approaches and tools, including but not limited to UIMA CAS(Ferrucci and Lally, 2004), GATE (Cunningham et al., 2002), ANVIL (Kipp, Forthcoming), ELAN (Auer et al., 2010), and the NLP Interchange Format (NIF)[5] under development within the Linked Open Data (LOD) effort[6]. The approach has been to develop a *lingua franca* or "pivot" format into and out of which other models may be translated in order to enable exchange among systems.[7] In order to serve this purpose, the GrAF data model was designed to capture the *relevant structural generalization* underlying best practices for linguistic annotation, which is the directed (acyclic) graph.

The overall architecture of a linguistically-annotated resource rendered in GrAF consists of the following:

- One or more *primary data documents*, in any medium;
- One or more documents defining a set of regions over each primary data document, each of which may serve as a *base segmentation* for annotations;
- Any number of *annotation documents* containing feature structures associated with nodes and/or edges in a directed graph; all nodes reference either a base segmentation document (in which case the node is a 0-degree node with no outgoing edges) or are connected to other nodes in the same or other annotation documents via outgoing edges;
- *Header documents* associated with each primary data document and annotation document, and a resource header that provides information about the resource as whole.

We describe the GrAF headers below, followed by a brief overview of how header elements are used in primary data, segmentation, and annotation documents. Note that the full description of GrAF, including GrAF schemas and a description of all components, elements, and attributes, appears in the LAF ISO Candidate Draft; similar GrAF documentation together with schemas in a variety of formats are available at `http://www.anc.org/graf`.

3 The GrAF Headers

In GrAF, all primary data, segmentation, and annotation documents, as well as the resource as a whole, require a header to provide a formal description of the various properties of the resource component. All of the headers have been designed with the aim of facilitating the automatic processing and validation of the resource content and structure.

3.1 Resource header

The GrAF resource header provides metadata for the resource by establishing resource-wide definitions and relations among files, datatypes, and annotations that support automatic validation of the resource file structure and contents. The resource header is based on the XML Corpus Encoding Standard (XCES

[5]http://blog.aksw.org/2011/nlp-interchange-format-nif-1-0-spec-demo-and-reference-implementation/

[6]http://linkeddata.org/

[7]This approach that has been widely adopted in the standardization field as the most pragmatic way to provide interoperability among tools, systems, and descriptive information such as metadata and linguistic annotations.

)header[8], omitting the information that is relevant only to single documents. A `resourceDesc` (resource description) element is added that describes the resource's characteristics and provides pointers to supporting documentation. The relevant elements in the resource description are as follows:

fileStruct: Provides the file structure of the resource, including the directory structure and the contents of each directory (additional directories and individual files). A set of fileType declarations describe the data files in the resource. Each is associated via attributes with a medium (content type), a set of annotation types, an optional name suffix, an indication of whether or not the file type is required to be present for each primary data document in the resource, and a list of one or more file types required by this filetype for processing.

annotationSpaces: Provides a set of one or more annotation spaces, which are used in a way similar to XML namespaces. AnnotationSpaces are needed especially when multiple annotations of the same data are merged, to provide context and resolve name conflicts.

annotationDecls: A set of one or more annotation declarations, which provide information about each annotation type included in the resource, including the annotation space it belongs to, a prose description, URI for the responsible party (creator), the method of creation (automatic, manual, etc.), URI for external documentation, and an optional URI for a schema or schemas providing a formal specification of the annotation scheme.

media: Provides a set of one or more medium types that files may contain, the type, encoding (e.g., utf-8), and the file extension used on files containing data of this type.

anchorTypes: a set of one or more types of anchors used to ground annotations in primary data (e.g., character-anchor, time-stamp, line-segment, etc.), the medium with which these anchor types are used, and a URI for a formal specification of the anchor type.[9] Via this mechanism, different anchor types have different semantics, but all GrAF anchors are represented in the same way so that a processor can transform the representation without consulting the definition or having to know the semantics of the representation, which is provided externally by the formal specification.

groups: Definition of one or more groups of annotations that are to be regarded as a logical unit for any purpose. The most common use of groups is to associate annotations that represent a "layer" or "tier"[10], such as a morpho-syntactic or syntactic layer. However, grouping can be applied to virtually any set of annotations. GrAF provides five types of grouping mechanisms:

1. *annotation*: annotations with specific values for their labels (as given on the @LABEL attribute of an `a` element in an annotation document) and/or annotation space. Wildcards may be used to select sets of annotations with common labels or annotation spaces, e.g., `*:tok` selects all annotations with label *tok*, in any annotation space (designated with "*:"), `xces:*` selects all annotations in the xces annotation space.

2. *type*: annotations of a specific type or types, by referencing the id of an annotation declaration defined in the resource header;

3. *file*: annotations appearing in a specific file type or types, by referring to the id of a file type defined in the resource header;

4. *enumeration*: an enumerated list of annotation ids appearing in a specified annotation document;

5. *expression*: an xPath-like expression that can navigate through annotations–for example, the expression @SPEAKER='ALICE' would choose all annotations with a feature named *speaker* that has the value *Alice*;

[8]http://www.cs.vassar.edu/CES/CES1-3.html

[9]Note that all anchor types are associated with one or more media, but a medium is not necessarily associated with an anchor type–in particular, media types associated with documents other than primary data documents (notably, annotation documents) are not associated with an anchor type.

[10]Groupings into layers/tiers are frequently defined in speech systems such as ELAN and ANVIL.

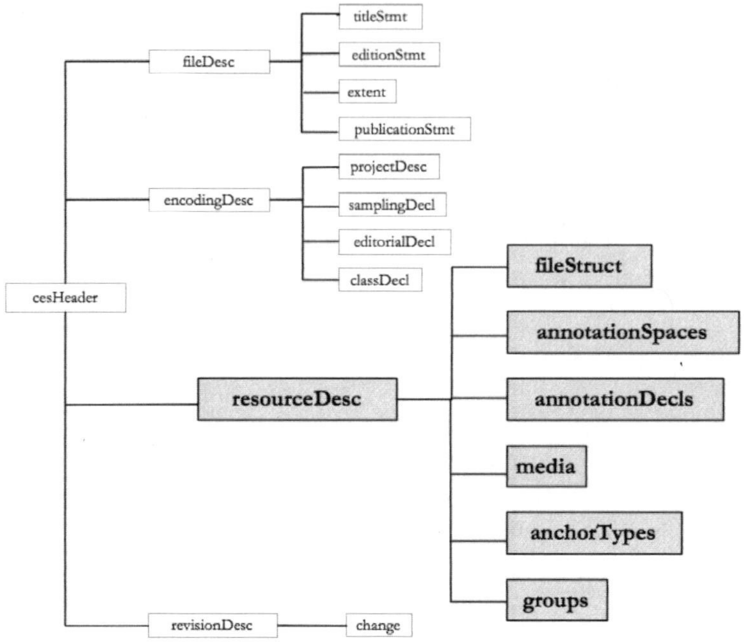

Figure 1: Main elements of the resourceDesc element in the GrAF resource header.

6. *group*: another group or set of groups. This can be used, for example, to group several enumeration groups in order to group enumerated annotation ids in multiple annotation documents.

All files, annotation spaces, annotations, media, anchors, and groups have an @xml:id attribute, which is used to relate object definitions where applicable. Figure 3 provides an example of a groups definition illustrating the different grouping mechanisms as well as the use of ids for cross-reference among objects defined in the header. It assumes declarations of the form shown in Figure 2 elsewhere in the resource header. The dependencies for several of these elements are shown graphically in Figure 4, which also shows the use of the @SUFFIX attribute for file types and the @EXTENSION attribute for media in a sample file name.

3.2 Primary data document header

The primary document header is stored in a separate XML document with root element `documentHeader`. The document header contains TEI-like elements for describing the primary data document, including its title, author, size, source of the original, language and encoding used in the document, etc., as well as a `textClass` element that provides genre/domain information by referring to classes defined in the resource header. Additional elements provide the locations of the primary data document and all associated annotation documents, using either a path relative to the root (declared on a `directory` element in the resource header) or a URI or persistent identifier (PID).

3.3 Annotation document header

Annotation documents contain both a header and the graph of feature structures comprising the annotation. The annotation document header is brief; it provides four pieces of information:

1. a list of the annotation labels used in the document and their frequencies;

2. a list of documents required to process the annotations, which will include a segmentation document and/or any annotation documents directly referenced in the document;

3. a list of annotationSpaces referenced in the document, one of which may be designated as a default for annotations in the document;

```
<fileType xml:id="f.entities" suffix="ne" a.ids="a.ne"
       medium="xml" requires="f.ptbtok"/>
...
<annotationSpace xml:id="xces" pid="http://www.xces.org/schema/2003"/>
...
<annotationDecl xml:id="a.ne" as="xces">
   <a.desc>named entities</a.desc>
   <a.resp lnk:href="http://www.anc.org">ANC project</a.resp>
   <a.method type="automatic-validated"/>
   <a.doc lnk:href="https://www.anc.org/wiki/wiki/NamedEntities"/>
</annotationDecl>
...
 <medium xml:id="text" type="text/plain" encoding="utf-8" extension="txt"/>
 <medium xml:id="xml" type="text/xml" encoding="utf-8" extension="xml"/>
...
 <anchorType medium="text" default="true"
        lnk:href="http://www.xces.org/ns/GrAF/1.0/#character-anchor"/>
```

Figure 2: Definitions in the GrAF resource header

```
<groups>
   <group xml:id="g.token">
      <!-- all annotations in any annotation space with label "tok" -->
      <g.member value="*:tok" type="annotation"/>
   </group>
   <group xml:id="g.example">
            <!-- all annotations of type logical -->
            <g.member value="a.logical" type="type"/>
            <!-- all files of containing entity annotations -->
            <g.member value="f.entities" type="file"/>
            <!-- all annotations with a feature "speaker" with value "Alice" -->
            <g.member value="@speaker='alice'" type="expression"/>
            <!-- annotations with ids "id_1" to "id_n" in file "myfile.xml"-->
            <g.member xml:base="myfile.xml" value="id1 id2 ... idN"
                      type="enumeration"/>
            <!-- the annotations included in group g.token, as defined earlier -->
            <g.member value="g.token" type="group"/>
   </group>
</groups>
```

Figure 3: Group definitions in the GrAF resource header

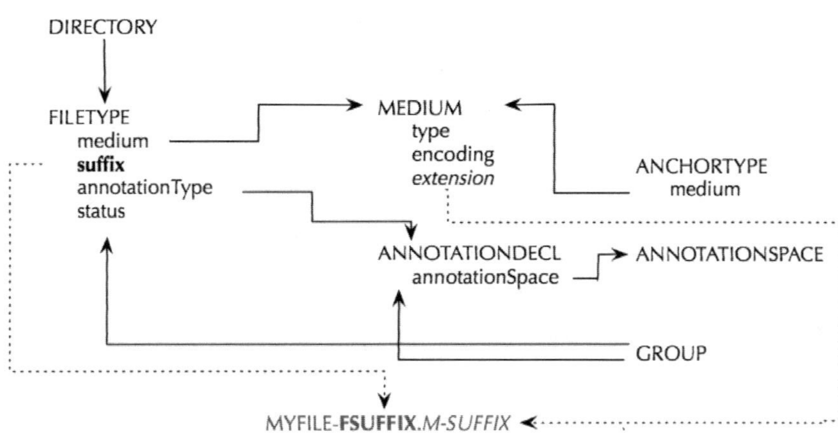

Figure 4: Dependencies among objects in the resource header

4. (optional) The root node(s) in the graph, when the graph contains one or more graphs that comprise a well-formed tree.

Information about references to other documents is intended for use by processing software, to both validate the resource (ensure all required documents are present) and facilitate the loading of required documents for proper processing. Information about annotation spaces provides a reference to required information in the resource header. When there is more than one tree in a graph, specification of their root nodes is required for proper processing. An example annotation document header is shown in Figure 5.

Following the header, annotation documents contain a graph or graphs and their associated annotations. LAF recommends that each annotation type or layer be placed in a separate annotation document, although in the absence of a standard definition of layers it is likely that there will be considerable variation in how this is implemented in practice. A newly-proposed ISO work item will address this and other organization principles in the near future.

4 Using Resource Header Elements

4.1 Primary data documents

Primary data in a LAF-compliant resource is frozen as read-only to preserve the integrity of references to locations within the document or documents. This, a primary data document will contain only the data that is being annotated. Corrections and modifications to the primary data are treated as annotations and stored in a separate annotation document.

In the general case, primary data does not contain markup of any kind. If markup appears in primary data (e.g., HTML or XML tags), it is treated as a part of the data stream by referring annotations; no distinction is made between markup and other characters in the data when referring to locations in the document. Although LAF does not recommend anchoring annotations in primary data by referencing markup, when necessary, XML elements in a document that is valid XML may be referenced by defining a medium type as XML and defining the associated anchor type as an XPath expression. References to locations within these XML elements (i.e., XML element content) can be made using standard offsets, which will be computed by including the markup as part of the data stream; in this case, two media types would be associated with the primary document's file type, as shown in Figure 6.

4.2 Segmentation: regions and anchors

Segmentation information is specified by defining *regions* over primary data. Regions are defined in terms of *anchors* that directly reference locations in primary data. All anchors are typed; anchor types used in the resource are each defined with an `anchorType` element in the resource header (see Section 3.1). The type of the anchor determines its semantics and therefore how it should be processed by an application. Figure 8 shows a set of region definitions and the associated anchor type and medium definitions from the resource header.[11]

Anchors are first-class objects the LAF data model (see Figure 7) along with regions, nodes, edges, and links. The anchor is the only object in the model that may be represented in two alternative ways in the GrAF serialization: as a the value of an @ANCHORS attribute on the `region` element, or with an `anchor` element. When anchors are represented with the `anchor` element, the `region` element will include a @REFS attribute (and must not include an @ANCHORS attribute) providing the ids of the associated anchors. For example, an alternative representation for region "r2" in Figure 8 is given in Figure 9.

In general, the design of GrAF follows the principle of orthogonality, wherein there is a single means to represent a given phenomenon. The primary reason for allowing alternative representations for anchors is that the proliferation of `anchor` elements in a segmentation document is space-consuming and potentially error-prone. As shown in Figure 8, the attribute representation can accommodate most references into text, video, and audio; the only situation in which use of an `anchor` element may be necessary is one where a given location in a document needs to be interpreted in two or more ways, as, for example, a part of two regions that should not be considered to have a common border point. In this case, multiple `anchor` elements can be de-

[11] Note that the @TYPE attribute on the `region` element specifies the anchor type and not the region type.

```
<graph xmlns="http://www.xces.org/ns/GrAF/1.0/">
 <header>
   <labelsDecl>
     <labelUsage label="Target" occurs="171"/>
     <labelUsage label="FE" occurs="372"/>
     <labelUsage label="sentence" occurs="32"/>
     <labelUsage label="NamedEntity" occurs="32"/>
   </labelsDecl>
   <dependencies>
     <dependsOn file_type.id="fntok"/>
   </dependencies>
   <annotationSpaces>
     <annotationSpace as.id="FrameNet" default="true"/>
   </annotationSpaces>
 </header>
...
```

Figure 5: Annotation document header

```
<fileType xml:id = "f.primary" medium="text xml"/>
<medium xml:id = "text" type="text/plain" encoding = "utf-8" extension = "txt"/>
<medium xml:id = "xml" type = "xml" encoding = "utf-8" extension = "xml"/>
<anchorType medium = "xml" default = "true"
            lnk:href = "http://www.w3.org/TR/xpath20/"/>
<anchorType medium = "text"
            lnk:href = "http://www.xces.org/ns/GrAF/1.0/#character-anchor"/>
```

Figure 6: Referencing XML elements in primary data

```
<anchor xml:id="a1" value="10,59"/>
<anchor xml:id="a2" value="10,173"/>
<anchor xml:id="a3" value="149,173"/>
<anchor xml:id="a4" value="149,59"/>

<region xml:id="r2" refs="a1 a2 a3 a4"
   anchor_type="image-point"/>
```

Figure 9: Region and anchor definitions

fined that reference the same location, and each anchor may then be uniquely referenced. Because of its brevity and in the interests of orthogonality, the attribute representation is recommended in LAF.

4.2.1 Segmentation documents

An annotation document is called a *segmentation document* if it contains only segmentation information–i.e., only `region` and `anchor` elements. Although regions and anchors may also be defined in an annotation document containing the graph of annotations over the data, LAF strongly recommends that when a segmentation is referenced from more than one annotation document, it appears in an independent document in order to avoid a potentially complex jungle of references among annotation documents.

A *base segmentation* for primary data is one that defines minimally granular regions to be used by different annotations, usually annotations of the same type. For example, it is not uncommon that different annotations of the same text–especially annotations created by different projects–are based on different tokenizations. A base segmentation can define a set of regions that include the smallest character span isolated by any of the alternative tokenizations–e.g., for a string such as "three-fold", regions spanning "three", "-", and "fold" may be included; a tokenization that regards "three-fold" as a single token can reference all three regions in the @TARGETS attribute on a `link` element associated with the node with which the token annotation is attached, as shown in Figure 10.

Multiple segmentation documents may be associated with a given primary data document. This is useful when annotations reference very different

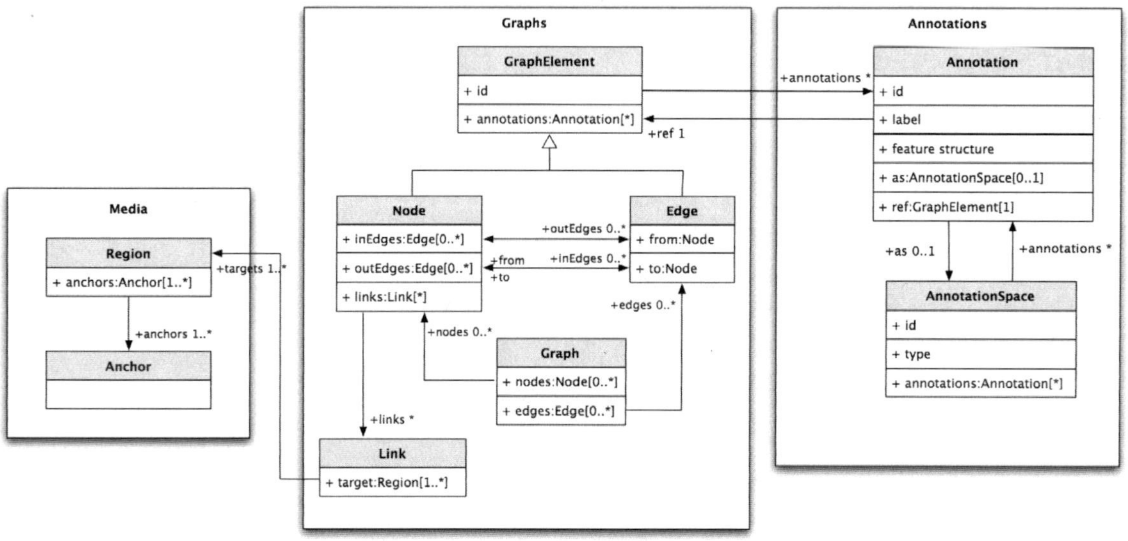

Figure 7: LAF model

```
<!-- Definitions in the resource header -->
<medium xml:id="text" type="text/plain" encoding="utf-8" extension="txt"/>
<medium xml:id="audio" type="audio" encoding="MP4" extension="mpg"/>
<medium xml:id="video" type="video" encoding="Cinepak" extension="mov"/>
<medium xml:id="video" type="image" encoding="jpeg" extension="jpg"/>
...
<anchorType xml:id="text-anchor" medium="text" default="true"
        lnk:href="http://www.xces.org/ns/GrAF/1.0/#character-anchor"/>
<anchorType xml:id="time-slot" medium="audio"
        lnk:href="http://www.xces.org/ns/GrAF/1.0/#audio-anchor"/>
<anchorType xml:id="video-anchor" medium="video"
        lnk:href="http://www.xces.org/ns/GrAF/1.0/#video-anchor"/>
<anchorType xml:id="image-point" medium="image"
        lnk:href="http://www.xces.org/ns/GrAF/1.0/#image-point"/>

<!-- Regions in the segmentation document -->
<region xml:id="r1" anchor_type="time-slot" anchors="980 983"/>
<region xml:id="r2" anchor_type="image-point" anchors="10,59 10,173 149,173 149,59"/>
<region xml:id="r3" anchor_type="video-anchor" anchors="fr1(10,59) fr2(59,85) fr3(85,102)"/>
<region xml:id="r4" anchor_type="text-anchor" anchors="34 42"/>
```

Figure 8: Region and anchor definitions

```
<region xml:id="seg-r770" anchors="211 216"/>
<region xml:id="seg-r771" anchors="216 217"/>
<region xml:id="seg-r772" anchors="217 221"/>

<node xml:id="n1019">
  <link targets="seg-r770 seg-r771 seg-r772"/>
</node>
<a label="tok" ref="n1019" as="xces">
  <fs>
      <f name="msd" value="JJ"/>
  </fs>
</a>
```

Figure 10: Referencing multiple regions

regions of the data; for example, in addition to the base segmentation document containing the minimal character spans that is partially shown in Figure 10, there may also be a segmentation based on sentences, which may in turn be referenced by annotations for which this unit of reference is more appropriate.[12] Alternative segmentations for different granularities, such as phonetic units, may also be useful for some purposes.

4.3 Annotation documents

In addition to the header, annotation documents contain a graph consisting of nodes and edges, either of which may be associated with an annotation. Annotations associated with a node or edge are represented with `a` elements that have a @REF attribute that provides the id of the associated node. The @LABEL attribute on an `a` element gives the main category of the annotation; this may be the string used to identify the annotation as described by the annotation documentation referenced in the annotation type declaration in the resource header, a category identifier from a data category registry such as ISOCat, an identifier from a feature structure library, or any PID reference to an external annotation specification. Each annotation is also associated with an *annotation space*, as defined in the resource header, which is referenced in the annotation document header. Figure 11 shows an example of an annotation for FrameNet that includes the annotation

```
<node xml:id="fn-n2"/>
<a label="FE" ref="fn-n2"  as="FrameNet">
 <fs>
  <f name="name" value="Recipient"/>
  <f name="GF" value="Obj"/>
  <f name="PT" value="NP"/>
 </fs>
</a>
```

Figure 11: Node with associated annotation

space in the AS attribute of the `a` element.[13]

5 Conclusion

We provide here a general overview of a system for formal description of a linguistically annotated resource, designed to allow automatic validation and processing of the resource. It provides means to define the file structure of a resource and specify interfile requirements and dependencies so that the integrity of the resource can be automatically checked. The scheme also provides links to metadata as well as annotation semantics, which may exist externally to the resource itself in a database or ontology, and provides mechanisms for defining grouping of selected annotations or files based on a wide range of criteria.

Although some of these mechanisms for resource documentation have been implemented in other schemes or systems, to our knowledge this is the first attempt at a comprehensive documentation system for linguistically annotated resources. It addresses a number of requirements for resource documentation and description that have been identified but never implemented formally, such as documentation of annotation scheme provenance, means of production, and resource organization and dependencies. Many of these requirements were first outlined in the Sustainable Interoperability for Language Technology (SILT) project[14], funded by the U.S. National Science Foundation, which drew input from the community at large.

Similar to the graph representation for annotations, the GrAF documentation system is designed to be easily integrated with or mappable to other

[12] Sentences may also be represented as annotations defined over tokens, but for some purposes it is less desirable to consider a sentence as an ordered set of tokens than as a single span of characters.

[13] Note that if the annotation document header in Figure 5 were used, no AS attribute would be needed to specify the FrameNet annotation space, since it is designated as the default.

[14] http://www.anc.org/SILT/

schemes, especially those relying on Semantic Web technologies such as RDF/OWL. However, it should be noted that GrAF is equally suitable for resources that are not primarily web-based (i.e., do not link to information elsewhere on the web) and therefore do not require the often heavy mechanisms required for Semantic Web-based representations.

Due to space constraints, many details of the GrAF scheme are omitted or mentioned only briefly. The MASC corpus (Ide et al., 2008; Ide et al., 2010), freely downloadable from `http://www.anc.org/MASC`, provides an extensive example of a GrAF-encoded resource, including multiple annotation types as well as the resource header and other headers. Other examples of GrAF annotation, including annotation for multi-media, are provided in (Ide and Suderman, Submitted).

Acknowledgments

This work was supported by National Science Foundation grant INT-0753069.

References

Eric Auer, Albert Russel, Han Sloetjes, Peter Wittenburg, Oliver Schreer, S. Masnieri, Daniel Schneider, and Sebastian Tschpel. 2010. Elan as flexible annotation framework for sound and image processing detectors. In *Proceedings of the Seventh International Conference on Language Resources and Evaluation (LREC'10)*, Valletta, Malta. European Language Resources Association (ELRA).

Christian Chiarcos. 2012. Ontologies of linguistic annotation: Survey and perspectives. In *Proceedings of the Eighth International Conference on Language Resources and Evaluation (LREC)*.

Hamish Cunningham, Diana Maynard, Kalina Bontcheva, and Valentin Tablan. 2002. GATE: A framework and graphical development environment for robust nlp tools and applications. In *Proceedings of ACL'02*.

David Ferrucci and Adam Lally. 2004. UIMA: An architectural approach to unstructured information processing in the corporate research environment. *Natural Language Engineering*, 10(3-4):327–348.

Nancy Ide and James Pustejovsky. 2010. What does interoperability mean, anyway? Toward an operational definition of interoperability. In *ICGL 2010: Proceedings of the Second International Conference on Global Interoperability for Language Resources*, Hong Kong, China.

Nancy Ide and Keith Suderman. 2007. GrAF: A graph-based format for linguistic annotations. In *Proceedings of the First Linguistic Annotation Workshop*, pages 1–8, Prague.

Nancy Ide and Keith Suderman. Submitted. The Linguistic Annotation Framework: A Standard for Annotation Interchange and Merging. *Language Resources and Evaluation*.

Nancy Ide, Collin Baker, Christiane Fellbaum, Charles Fillmore, and Rebecca Passonneau. 2008. MASC: The Manually Annotated Sub-Corpus of American English. In *Proceedings of the Sixth International Conference on Language Resources and Evaluation (LREC)*, Marrakech, Morocco.

Nancy Ide, Collin Baker, Christiane Fellbaum, and Rebecca Passonneau. 2010. The Manually Annotated Sub-Corpus : A community resource for and by the people. In *Proceedings of the The 48th Annual Meeting of the Association for Computational Linguistics*, Uppsala, Sweden.

Michael Kipp. Forthcoming. Anvil: A universal video research tool. In G. Kristofferson J. Durand, U. Gut, editor, *Handbook of Corpus Phonology*. Oxford University Press.

Peter Wittenburg Marc Kemps-Snijders, Menzo Windhouwer and Sue Ellen Wright. 2008. Isocat: Corralling data categories in the wild. In et al. Nicoletta Calzolari, editor, *Proceedings of the Sixth International Conference on Language Resources and Evaluation (LREC'08)*, Marrakech, Morocco. European Language Resources Association (ELRA).

A GrAF-compliant Indonesian Speech Recognition Web Service on the Language Grid for Transcription Crowdsourcing

Bayu Distiawan Trisedya
Faculty of Computer Science
Universitas Indonesia
b.distiawan@cs.ui.ac.id

Ruli Manurung
Faculty of Computer Science
Universitas Indonesia
maruli@cs.ui.ac.id

Abstract

This paper describes the development of an Indonesian speech recognition web service which complies with two standards: it operates on the Language Grid, ensuring process interoperability, and its output uses the LAF/GrAF format, ensuring data interoperability. It is part of a larger system, currently in development, that aims to collect speech transcriptions via crowdsourcing methods. Its utility is twofold: it exposes a functional speech recognizer to the web, and allows the incremental construction of a large speech corpus.

1 Background

In recent years, the initial groundwork for developing Indonesian speech recognition systems, i.e. development of phonetic models and dictionaries, as well as language and acoustic models, has been carried out (Baskoro and Adriani, 2008; Zahra et al., 2009; Huntley and Adriani, 2009). However, to build high-quality speech recognition systems, large collections of training data are needed. To achieve this, we can employ a strategy that has emerged in recent times, which capitalizes on the ubiquity of the Internet, known as crowdsourcing, i.e. relying on a large group of individuals to perform specific tasks. One successful example of this is the PodCastle project (Goto and Ogata, 2010).

This paper presents our initial efforts in developing a speech recognition system that utilizes the Language Grid platform (Ishida, 2005) to provide Indonesian speech recognition services accessible through the web and mobile devices in an efficient and practical manner, and support crowdsourcing of speech annotations through an interactive web application. Section 2 will provide an overview of the system, Sections 3 and 4 will discuss related standards, i.e. the Language Grid and the Linguistic Annotation Framework respectively, and Section 5 will present the developed speech recognition service. In Section 6 we briefly discuss the speech transcription crowdsourcing application.

2 System Overview

Building high-quality speech recognition systems requires a large collection of annotated training data in the form of spoken audio data along with validated speech transcriptions. Such resources are very costly to build, which typically involves skilled human resources such as linguistic experts. Our solution is to offer a speech recognition web service whose utility is twofold: it provides a valuable service to users, whilst allowing the construction of a large speech corpus. This service will be supplemented with an interactive web application for transcribing and correcting any arising speech recognition errors.

Furthermore, transcribed speech corpora are useful for many applications, but typically existing collections are restricted in their utility due to formatting issues of metadata. Adopting standards that ensure interoperability will maximize the

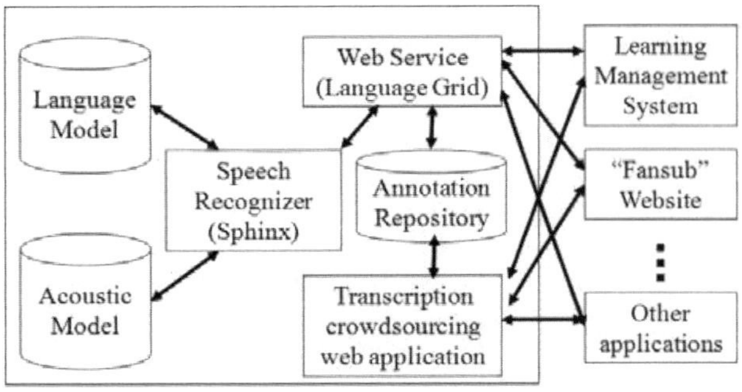

Figure 1. Overview of the system

usefulness of various resources. This can be achieved by integrating standards such as the Linguistic Annotation Framework (Ide and Romary, 2006), which focuses on data and annotation interoperability, with the Language Grid, which focuses on process interoperability. Some work in this area has already been done, e.g. by Hayashi et al. (2010) and Distiawan and Manurung (2010).

The Language Grid specification currently already includes support for speech recognition services. The defined web method requires four parameters: language identifier, speech data in Base 64 encoding, audio type, and voice type. However, the specification of the return results are not precisely defined. By providing return results of speech recognition using interoperable standards, e.g. based on GrAF (Ide and Suderman, 2007), which also provides crucial timestamp information for synchronization between audio and transcription, many further applications can be supported.

Figure 1 presents an overview of the system, which is enclosed in a rectangle. At its core is a speech recognition system, based on the CMU Sphinx open source system [1], which accesses previously developed resources such as a language model and an acoustic model. A standards-compliant "wrapper" web service exposes the functionality of this speech recognizer to the web, and aside from returning the results to the calling application, also stores the primary data along with its annotations in a RESTful annotation repository inspired by the DADA annotation server (Cassidy, 2008). These annotations are then served to a transcription crowdsourcing web application similar to the PodCastle project[2].

We envision various use cases for this system. One instance that we hope to implement is as a support to a Learning Management System, where lecture recordings are automatically transcribed and form valuable learning resources for students, who can also correct the transcriptions and make further annotations, similar to the SyNote project (Li et al., 2009). Another possible application is to support various "fansub" projects, which are Internet-based communities who provide user-created subtitles for TV shows and films in various languages.

3 The Language Grid

The Language Grid was developed in early 2005 involving many researchers from the National Institute of Information and Communication Technology (NICT), universities and research institutes around Kyoto (Ishida, 2005). The aim of the development of the Language Grid is to overcome the language barriers that often inhibit communication between people who have different languages. Many knowledge sources available on the Internet are written in different languages. This happens because there is no standard language used on the Internet: even English only accounts for 35% of the total Internet content. At the beginning of the development of the Language Grid was built machine translation which includes five languages: Chinese, Malaysian, Japanese, Korean, and English.

Researchers in various countries have developed language tools for the purposes of their own language, but unfortunately these resources are often not accessible to the public. In addition, these separate resources are only usable as atomic services that can only be used for a particular language. Therefore, the Language Grid seeks to combine resources that already exist for various languages so that they can be used by parties who need to combine them to become an integrated service. A simple example of integrated service is as follows. Imagine there are two language services for machine translation, Japanese - English (and vice versa) and Chinese - English (and vice versa). If both atomic services are deployed onto the Language Grid, it will be

[1] http://cmusphinx.sourceforge.net

[2] http://www.podcastle.jp

possible to construct a new service, i.e. Japanese - Chinese machine translation and vice versa by using English as an intermediary language.

There are two types of services on the Language Grid; the first is called the horizontal Language Grid, which combines existing language services using web services technology. The second is called the vertical Language Grid, which combines the language services on the horizontal language grid to support inter-cultural activities. An example of the vertical language grid is making a parallel text in the medical field to assist foreign patients at local hospitals (Ishida, 2005).

To support maximum interoperability on the Internet, the Language Grid relies on web services technology, in which there is WSDL, UDDI, and SOAP. The Language Grid has also been equipped with support services such as OWL ontologies, so the Language Grid has supported the Semantic Web and has been providing services for search and automatic configuration of the composite services.

Currently, the Language Grid already has a lot of services, including: Bilingual Dictionaries, Morphological Analyzer Services, Machine Translation, etc. The process of deploying and combining the language services that have been developed on the Language Grid is by the wrapping mechanism of the language resource so that it becomes a web service that can be accessed via a SOAP protocol. Rules and standards to perform the wrapping is already regulated and established by the Language Grid project through standard wrapping libraries. Until now the wrapping standard allows developers to do wrapping into a Java-based web service only using JAX-RPC library.

To combine language resources that are already available, the first step is to conduct the wrapping of language resources. A wrapper is a program that makes language resources accessible through a web service, by adjusting the input and output specifications of the NICT Language Service Interface. Thus, language resources can be registered as a language service on the Language Grid.

After the wrapper of the language resource has been completed, the wrapper is then deployed to a Language Grid Service Node, or a so-called server service provider, and will receive requests from a Language Grid Core Node or the so-called client

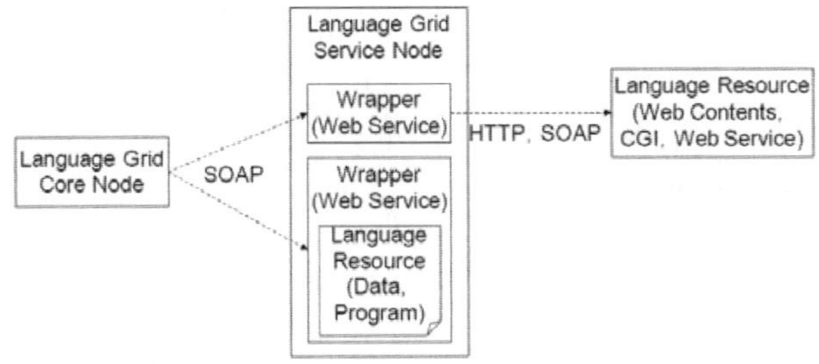

Figure 2. Configuration diagram of wrapper

service requester. Figure 2 shows an illustration of the data flow using the Language Grid wrapper. From Figure 2 we can see that when there is a request from a Language Grid Core Node, the Language Grid Service Node can access the language resources that have been wrapped or access another available language resource on another server using conventional HTTP and SOAP protocols, then return output according to a predetermined format.

4 Linguistic Annotation Framework

The Linguistic Annotation Framework (LAF) is a standard that provides the architecture for the creation, provision of annotation, and manipulation of linguistic resources so that encoders and annotators have the discretion to determine the format of annotation and facilitate the reuse of existing annotation. LAF was developed by ISO TC37 SC WG1-1. The two main objectives of LAF are the provision of tools to utilize and reuse linguistic data from a variety of applications at all levels of linguistic description, and the facilitation of the maintenance of a cycle of documents through various stages of the process and allowing the addition of information on existing data (Ide and Romary, 2003).

To achieve this, various principles are observed, i.e.:

1. The separation between data and annotations. Language data can only be read and not allowed to change its contents (read-only) and contains no annotations. All the annotations are contained in a separate document which is connected to the primary data (related documents). This approach is often called stand-off markup.
2. The separation between user annotation formats and a globally understood exchange,

or 'dump', format. Users can use any format for annotations (XML, LISP, etc.). The only requirement is that the format should be mappable to the structure of data in the dump format.
3. The separation between the structure and contents of the dump format.

The Graph Annotation Format (GrAF) is one of the formats that implement the conceptual standard annotation of the Language Annotation Framework (LAF). GrAF utilizes graph theory to model the linguistic annotation that can provide the flexibility to create, represent, and incorporate some annotations into a single and integrated annotation. By utilizing a pivot LAF (dump) format, the user annotation can be transformed into a graph format. With the ability of transformation, GrAF can combine two or more annotations into a single unitary representation of annotation. To prove the concept, there have been some experiments conducted using several different annotation formats on the Wall Street Journal corpus (Ide and Suderman, 2007).

GrAF itself is an XML file that follows the general structure for the annotation that has been specified by the LAF. A GrAF document represents the structure of an annotation by two XML elements: <node> and <edge>. Either element, whether <node> or <edge>, can be labeled in accordance with the annotation information.

Annotations are saved in a separate graph from primary data. When the annotation is stored in GrAF format, then the process of merging

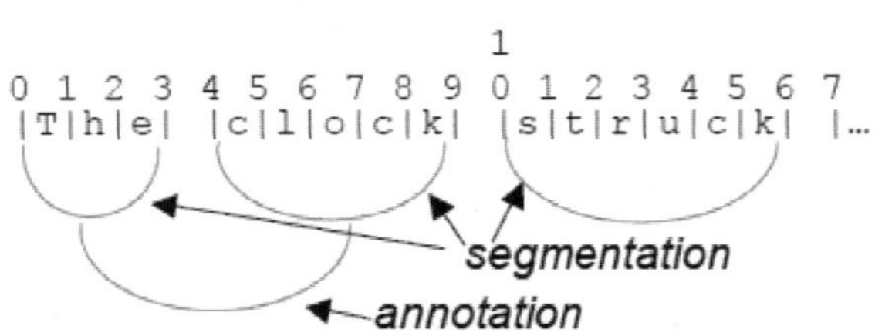


```
<!-- edges over primary data -->
<edge id="e1" from="0" to="3"/>
<edge id="e2" from="4" to="9"/>
<edge id="e2" from="10" to="16"/>
```

Figure 3. Segmentation and Construction of GrAF (Ide and Romary, 2006).

annotations of the same primary data or annotation of the annotation reference to the primary data can be combined with existing graph merging algorithms that have been developed.
Besides the ease to the process of merging graphs, there are many other benefits obtained by the use of graph theory in the GrAF format, since a lot of software is readily available for graph manipulation, for example to show the relevance between node and edge visualization, graph traversal, as well as adding information in the graph.

One important part of GrAF is segmentation. Segmentation needs to be done because the primary data is separated from the annotation. Segmentation is performed on primary data to divide the primary data into smaller elements to be annotated. Segmentation in the primary document will eventually form a set of nodes and edges that form the basis of GrAF. Multiple segmentation documents can be defined over the primary data, and multiple annotation documents may refer to the same segmentation document (Ide and Romary, 2006). Figure 3 provides an illustration of segmentation and annotation.

There is no limitation or standard to perform segmentation. Segmentation in text documents are generally made to divide the document into a word or phrase. The word or phrase itself can still be segmented into smaller elements in the form of characters that form a word or phrase.

In its implementation, the text document segmentation is done by forming edges linking some contiguous tokens (characters) in a document. This is done by determining the position of tokens in a document. Then, the edge will be considered as a node (in this case it can be a word or phrase). The GrAF format requires the specification of the primary data location (i.e. URL) in order to interpret the segmentation information.

5 Integration of Language Grid Web Service and GrAF-based Annotation for Speech Recognition

To facilitate the integration between the services that are available on the Language Grid to provide a LAF-based standard annotation, we use the GrAF-aware Language Grid framework (Distiawan and Manurung, 2010). As shown in Figure 4, this

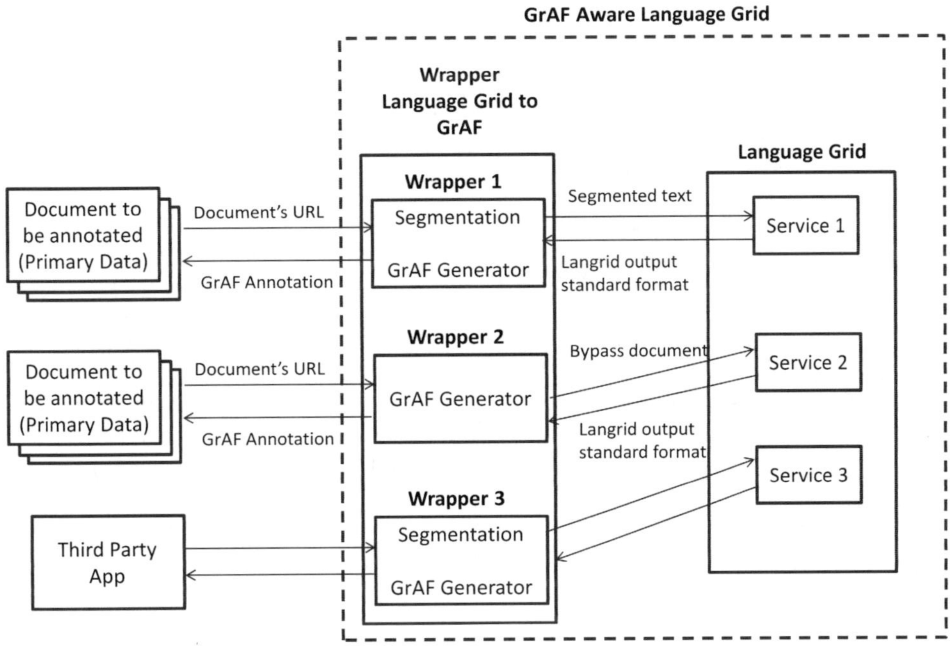

Figure 4. GrAF-aware Language Grid Framework

framework introduces an additional wrapping layer that carries out two processes, namely the segmentation of the primary data (if no segmentation exists previously) and the generation of the GrAF XML document. Segmentation is performed on the primary data, and forms the basis which further linguistic annotations refer to.

This wrapping layer is also responsible for recording the segmentation for matching the generation of GrAF XML documents to the native segmentation of the wrapped Language Grid service. After the segmentation is completed, the additional layer will send each element of segmentation results to obtain the annotation from the existing services on the Language Grid. The Language Grid output generated will then be used to fill the GrAF XML document.

This additional layer is developed as a web service so it is expected to be easily integrated into the Language Grid. One additional layer will correspond with one service on the Language Grid; this is to facilitate modularity and the reusability of additional layers in other applications.

The development of additional layers to combine services on the Language Grid with a standard GrAF annotation is done by using Java SOAP web services technology, but this does not rule out the possibility of an additional layer development using RESTFul web services technology. This additional layer service receives the URL of a document as input and will generate a GrAF XML document.

The first step is to carry out primary data segmentation, because this segmentation will link the information between the primary data with the secondary data, i.e. the Language Grid-produced annotations. For text documents, segmentation is performed by splitting the document into single words, where one word will be inserted into a single token that is marked with an edge tag. Each token has information about the beginning and end index positions relative to a particular document.

Since we are developing a service relating to audio primary data, we assume that the segmentation will be defined in terms of the timestamps when utterances occur in the primary media file, whether audio or video. Thus, an utterance token is marked with an edge tag, and contains information about the beginning and end timestamps.

The second step is communication with the web services on the Language Grid, which produces the linguistic annotation, e.g. in this case, speech recognition. For our purposes, this layer is developed against a previously developed speech recognition service on the Language Grid, which in turn uses the Sphinx open-source speech recognizer.

```
<container xmlns:graf="http://www.tc37sc4.org/graf/v1.0.6b">
  <header>
    <primaryData
      loc="http://fws.cs.ui.ac.id/fedora/objects/Speech:1/datastreams/FILE/content"
      type="audio/wav"/>
  </header>
  <graph>
    <edgeSet id="Speech Segmentation">
      <instant id="e1" from="0.35" to="0.7"/>
      <instant id="e2" from="0.7" to="1.15"/>
      <instant id="e3" from="1.15" to="1.57"/>
      ...
    </edgeSet>
    <edge id="t1" ref="e1">
      <fs type="token">
        <f name="word" sVal="lima"/>
      </fs>
    </edge>
    <edge id="t2" ref="e2">
      <fs type="token">
        <f name="word" sVal="empat"/>
      </fs>
    </edge>
    ...
  </graph>
</container>
```

Figure 5. Sample GrAF segmentation and annotation from the speech recognizer

The third stage consists of the mapping of the Language Grid service output to the initial segmentation produced during the first stage. This approach allows flexibility of utilizing all currently available services on the Language Grid.

Since the initial segmentation of an audio file into utterances is carried out by the speech recognition web service, it is more efficient to conflate the three steps into one: given the source audio file, the web service will pass it on to the Sphinx speech recognition module, which can be configured to output the timestamps of when utterances also occur. Thus, the output will consist of both the segmentation and the annotation.

Figure 5 provides an example of GrAF segmentation and annotation results given an input audio file that consists of an Indonesian utterance (specifically, someone utterring a telephone number).

We adopt GrAF because of its flexibility in the provision of multiple segmentation results. Our system can output the *n*-best recognition results from Sphinx, which will be used to provide alternative recommendations from the speech recognition system to the users. It is possible that these alternative transcriptions have different segmentations. For example, Sphinx can provide two possible outputs for a document, e.g.: the best recognition result contains the word `"sedikitnya"` in the range `4.02-4.3` seconds, whereas an alternative result contains the words `"sedih"` in the range `4.02-4.2` seconds and the word `"kita"` in the range `4.2-4.3` seconds. By using GrAF annotation we can deliver both segmentation results as well as providing an appropriate annotation for each segment as follows:

```
<graph>
    <edgeSet id="Speech Segmentation">
      <instant id="e1" from="4.02" to="4.3"/>
      <instant id="e2" from="4.02" to="4.2"/>
      <instant id="e3" from="4.2" to="4.3"/>
      ...
    </edgeSet>
    <edge id="t1" ref="e1">
      <fs type="token">
        <f name="word" sVal="sedikitnya"/>
      </fs>
    </edge>
    <edge id="t2" ref="e2">
      <fs type="token">
        <f name="word" sVal="sedih"/>
      </fs>
    </edge>
    <edge id="t2" ref="e2">
      <fs type="token">
        <f name="word" sVal="kita"/>
      </fs>
    </edge>
    ...
</graph>
```

This example is still a rough idea of how we represent the primary recognition result and its alternatives in cases of different segmentations found among the results. We are still experimenting with more suitable representations.

This web service has been implemented, and can currently be accessed from the following URL: `http://langrid.cs.ui.ac.id/GRAFSpeechRecognizer/ws/recognize?file=<URL_to_media>`.

To support the crowdsourcing system to be developed, we use our previously developed corpus repository (Manurung et al., 2010), which will be used to store all audio or video data along with its automatic or crowdsourced GrAF annotation.

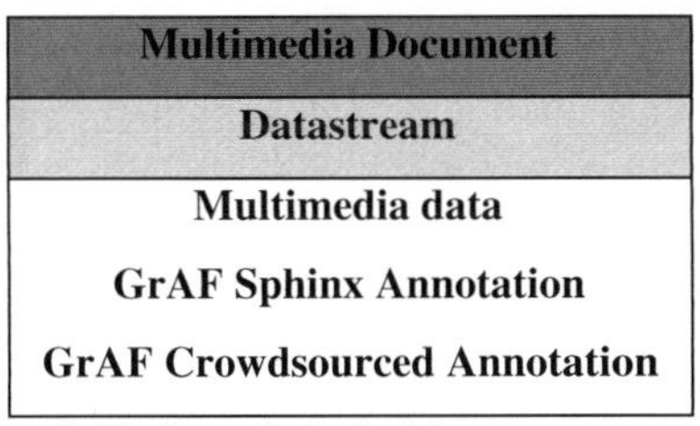

Figure 6. Fedora digital object representation

In this corpus repository, data and its annotations will be represented as a datastream in a Fedora Commons digital object that can be accessed using a persistent and unique URL. An illustration of this is shown in Figure 6. For example, the audio data can be accessed at: `http://fws.cs.ui.ac.id/fedora/objects/Speech:1/datastreams/FILE/content` and the automatic GrAF annotation can be accessed at: `http://fws.cs.ui.ac.id/fedora/objects/Speech:1/datastreams/UserAnnotation-1/content`.

6 Crowdsourcing audio transcriptions

As mentioned in Section 2, one way in which we hope to leverage this standards-compliant speech recognition web service is as a supporting tool for an interactive web application that enables users to correct the automatically produced speech transcription, which will likely still contain errors. Users will be able to play back the primary data, whether in audio or video form, and the transcription will be displayed synchronized to the media playback. They can then view and edit this information in a non-linear fashion. This application is currently under development, utilizing open standards such as HTML5 and Javascript to ensure maximum interoperability.

Several design issues arise, as follows:

1. User interface design. We are currently experimenting with various designs, e.g. displaying the transcriptions as a scrolling "ticker tape", as a full length text field, or in static segments similar to how movie subtitles are displayed.

2. Crowdsourcing incentive scheme. A crucial aspect of successful crowdsourcing initiatives is the appropriate incentive scheme, i.e. providing motivation for users, which may be financial, sociological, or psychological in nature (Shaw et al., 2011). Our aim is to place the transcription task within a context that provides natural motivation for the user, e.g. in a learning management system (LMS), wherein students would benefit from studying and working with lecture transcriptions.

3. Utilizing user corrections. Once user corrections have been collected, we aim to feed them back into the speech recognition system by retraining the acoustic and language models. During this process, we aim to measure inter-annotator reliability to remove outliers.

7 Further Work and Summary

The development of GrAF-compliant Indonesian Speech Recognition Web Service is just the first step to built a robust Bahasa Indonesia speech recognition system. This service will be used to create an interactive website that can be used by the user to see the transcript of a video and also the user can give feedback to the incorrect transcription. Using segmentation from GrAF annotation, the transcription will be displayed adjusted to the video timeline.

We realize that our speech recognition system is still not perfect, therefore, in addition to providing the best recognition results, the GrAF-compliant Indonesian Speech Recognition Web Service will also provide some alternatives recognition result. The alternative recognition result will also displayed alongside the transciption result. By providing the alternative result, we hope the user willing to give feedback about the incorrect transciption. We will use the feedback from user to get a larger and valuable corpus to retrain the speech recognition system.

References

Sadar Baskoro and Mirna Adriani. 2008. "Developing an Indonesian Speech Recognition System". Second MALINDO Workshop. Selangor, Malaysia.

Steve Cassidy. 2008. "A RESTful Interface to Annotations on the Web", in Proceedings of the 2nd Linguistic Annotation Workshop (LAW II), LREC2008, Marrakech.

Masataka Goto and Jun Ogata. 2010. "PodCastle: A Spoken Document Retrieval Service Improved by User Contributions", in Proceedings of the 24th Pacific Asia Conference on Language, Information and Computation (PACLIC 24), pp.3-11.

Yoshihiko Hayashi, Thierry Declerck and Chiharu Narawa. 2010. "LAF/GrAF-grounded Representation of Dependency Structures". LREC 2010, Malta.

Nancy Ide and Laurent Romary. 2003. "Outline of the International Standard Linguistic Annotation Framework," in Proceedings of the ACL'03 Workshop on Linguistic Annotation: Getting the Model Right, Sapporo, pp. 1-5.

Nancy Ide and Laurent Romary. 2006. "Representing Linguistic Corpora and Their Annotations," in Proceedings of LREC 2006, Genoa, Italy.

Nancy Ide and Keith Suderman. 2007. "GrAF: A Graph-based Format for Linguistic Annotations," in Proceedings of the Linguistic Annotation Workshop, held in conjunction with ACL 2007, Prague, June 28-29, pp. 1-8.

Toru Ishida. 2005. "Language Grid: An Infrastructure for Intercultural Collaboration," in Proceedings of the 2005 Symposium on Applications and the Internet (SAINT'06), vol., no., pp. c1- c1.

Myrna Laksman-Huntley and Mirna Adriani. 2009. "Developing Indonesian Pronunciation Dictionary". The Third International MALINDO Workshop, Co-located Event ACL-IJCNLP 2009. Singapore.

Yunjia Li et al. 2009. "Synote: Enhancing Multimedia E-learning with Synchronised Annotation", in Proceedings of the first ACM international workshop on Multimedia technologies for distance learning. Beijing.

Ruli Manurung, Bayu Distiawan, and Desmond Darma Putra. 2010. "Developing an Online Indonesian Corpora Repository". in Proceedings of the 24th Pacific Asia Conference on Language, Information, and Computation (PACLIC 2010), pp.243-249, Sendai, Japan.

Aaron Shaw, John Horton, and Daniel Chen. 2011. "Designing incentives for inexpert human raters". in Proceedings of the ACM 2011 Conference on Computer Supported Cooperative Work (CSCW '11), pp.275-284, Hangzhou, China.

Bayu Distiawan Trisedya and Ruli Manurung. 2010. "Extending the Language Grid for GrAF-based Linguistic Annotations", in Proceedings of the International Conference on Advanced Computer Science and Information Systems (ICACSIS 2010). Bali.

Amalia Zahra, Sadar Baskoro and Mirna Adriani. 2009. "The Performance of Speech Recognition System for Bahasa Indonesia Using Various Speech Corpus". Second Workshop on Technologies and Corpora for Asia-Pacific Speech Translation (TCAST 2009). Singapore.

Towards Adaptation of Linguistic Annotations to Scholarly Annotation Formalisms on the Semantic Web

Karin Verspoor[*†]
[*]National ICT Australia
Victoria Research Lab
Melbourne VIC 3010 Australia
karin.verspoor@nicta.com.au

Kevin Livingston[†]
[†]University of Colorado Denver
12801 E 17th Ave, MS 8303
Aurora, CO 80045 USA
kevin.livingston@ucdenver.edu

Abstract

This paper explores how and why the Linguistic Annotation Framework might be adapted for compatibility with recent more general proposals for the representation of annotations in the Semantic Web, referred to here as the Open Annotation models. We argue that the adapted model, in addition to being interoperable with other annotations and annotation tools, also resolves some representational limitations and semantic ambiguity of the original data model.

1 Introduction

Formal annotation of language data is an activity that dates back at least to the classic work of Kucera and Francis on the Brown Corpus (Kucera 1967). Many annotation representations have been developed; some proposals are specific to a given corpus, e.g., the Penn Treebank (Marcus et al. 1993)) or type of annotation, e.g., CONLL dependency parse representation[1]), while others aim towards standardization and interoperability, most recently the Linguistic Annotation Framework [2] (LAF) (ISO 2008). All such proposals, however, are closely tied to the requirements of linguistic annotation.

Annotation, however, is not an activity limited to language data but rather is a general scholarly activity used both by the humanist and the scientist. It is a method by which scholars organize existing knowledge and facilitate the creation and sharing of new knowledge. Museum artifacts are annotated with meta-data relating to artist or date of creation, or semantic descriptors for portions of the artifacts (e.g. an eye of a statue) (Hunter & Yu 2011). Medieval manuscripts or ancient maps are annotated with details resulting from careful study (Sanderson et al. in press). Beyond scholarship, annotation is becoming increasingly pervasive in the context of social media, such as Flickr tags on images or FaceBook comments on news articles. Recognition of the widespread importance of annotation has resulted in recent efforts to develop standard data models for annotation (Ciccarese et al. 2011; Hunter et al. 2011), specifically targeting Web formalisms in order to take advantage of increasing efforts to expose information on the Web, such as through Linked Data initiatives[3].

In this paper, we will explore the adoption of the more general scholarly annotation proposals for linguistic annotation, and specifically look at LAF in relation to those proposals. We will show that with a few adaptations, LAF could move into use within the Semantic Web context, and, importantly, achieve compatibility with data models under development in the broader scholarly annotation community.

This generalization of the model is particularly pertinent to collaborative annotation scenarios; exposing linguistic annotations in the *de facto* language of the Semantic Web, the W3C's Resource Description Framework (RDF), provides several advantages that we will outline below.

[1] http://conll.cemantix.org/2012/data.html
[2] http://www.cs.vassar.edu/~ide/papers/LAF.pdf
[3] http://linkeddata.org/

2 Characteristics of the Semantic Web

There are two converging cultures within the Semantic Web community (Ankolekar et al. 2008) – one of providing structured data, and one of promoting community sharing of data. Sharing is supported by four principles of linked data (Bizer et al. 2009):

1. Use URIs (Uniform Resource Identifiers) as names for things.
2. Use HTTP URIs so that people can look up those names.
3. When someone looks up a URI, provide useful information, using standards.
4. Include links to other URIs, so that they can discover more things.

These principles are built on top of the basic technology of the Web, HTTP and URIs, and represent best practices for making structured data available on the Web. They are the foundation for any Semantic Web model.

RDF provides a generic graph-based data model for structuring and relating information, through simple assertions. The RDF model encodes data in the form of subject, predicate, object triples. The predicate specifies how the subject and object are related. The linked data principles mean that the subject and predicates of an RDF triple are typically dereferenceable URIs representing concepts or entities.

3 The relevance of the Semantic Web for linguistic annotation

There are several clear reasons to explore a linguistic annotation formalism that is compatible with general Semantic Web annotation efforts. Some are not unique to the Web, but there do exist some special opportunities in the Web context.

3.1 Interoperability

Interoperability refers to enabling different entities (agents, services) to exchange information. Interoperability is impeded by both the syntax and format of data representations, and also by the ability to accurately represent the semantics of one data source in another.

Data can be exchanged in an *ad hoc* manner, for instance by having an individual system understand the syntax and semantics of the information produced by a given source and translating or mapping that information to an internal representation. However, this leads to significant duplication of effort, with each system having to manage data import and conversion from a given source independently.

Data compatibility problems also exist when attempting to use multiple data sources simultaneously. If two independent sources refer to "annotation 1" do they mean the same annotation or different annotations? And if these annotations are different are the tools processing them equally aware of the distinction?

The Semantic Web overcomes syntax and format issues through the use of RDF. While agreeing on semantics will continue to be challenging, the use of unique and resolvable URIs goes a long way toward formalizing meaning, or at least agreeing on references. Additionally as the use of more formal subsets of RDF, such as OWL, grows, more precise definitions of concepts will also become available.

3.2 Information Sharing and Reuse

Interoperability in turn enables reuse of information. The results of any annotation effort are generally intended to be shared. Agreement on a standard representation of annotations, with a consistent semantics, facilitates integration.

With interoperability, tools can directly build on annotations made by others. For the natural language processing community, this has several potentially significant advantages. Individual research groups need not build an end-to-end processing pipeline, but can reuse existing annotations over a common resource. For domains where there are commonly used shared document sets, such as standard annotated corpora used for training or testing, or document repositories that are the primary target of a body of text-related work – e.g. the Medline repository of biomedical journal abstracts – annotations can be made available for incorporation into downstream processing, without the need for re-computation and to ensure consistency. Tokens, parts of speech, even syntactic structures and basic named entities, can all be computed once and made available as a starting point for subsequent processing.

Where there is considerable investment in linked data, such as the biomedical domain, it also opens the possibility of taking advantage of external resources in language processing algorithms: if a document has been semantically annotated by a domain expert, or semantically connected to external information, those annotations can be used to enable more sophisticated analysis of that document. For instance, (Livingston et al. 2010) demonstrated that incorporating existing background knowledge about proteins when extracting biological activation events from biological texts allows some inherent ambiguities in recognizing those events to be resolved.

3.3 Web-scale collaboration and analysis

Targeting the semantic web provides new opportunities in terms of collecting, analyzing and summarizing data both within and across annotation sets on the web. The methods on the Semantic Web for creating and providing data are fundamentally "open-world" and allow for data to be added at any time.

The Web is the natural place for collaborative annotation activities, which is by necessity a distributed activity. Whether a collaborative annotation project is undertaken by a focused community of interest or by crowd sourcing, using semantic models that can represent and document contradiction or multiple competing views allows data to be collected and aggregated from multiple sources.

Collaboration is also about coordinating and cooperating with the consumers of annotation. The Semantic Web has defined ways in which data can be shared and distributed to others. This includes the preference for resolvable URIs, such that automated tools can seek out data and definitions as needed. Additionally data is being provided through access points, such as SPARQL end points. Vocabularies exist for documenting what is in a dataset, such as VoID (Alexander & Hausenblas 2009), and there is work underway to standardize data sharing within domains, for example health care and life science.[4]

The availability of Linked Open Data also enables unforeseen novel use of the data. This is evident in the large number of popular "mash-ups" connecting existing tools and data in new ways to provide additional value. Tools even exist for end-users to create mash-ups, such as Yahoo! Pipes[5].

3.4 Availability of tools

Adoption of Semantic Web standards for annotation makes available mature and sophisticated technologies for annotation storage (e.g. triple-stores) and to query, retrieve, and reason over the annotations (e.g. SPARQL).

Perhaps of particular interest to the computational linguistics community are tools under development to visualize and manipulate annotation information in the dynamic context of the web. For instance, the DOMEO tool (Ciccarese et al. in press) provides support for display of annotation over the text of biomedical journal publications in situ, by adopting strategies for managing dynamic HTML. The Utopia Documents tool (Attwood et al. 2010) is oriented towards annotation of PDF documents and provides visualization of annotations that dynamically link to web content. The Utopia tool has been recently updated to consume Annotation Ontology content[6].

Finally, enabling compatibility of linguistic annotation tools with Semantic Web standards opens up the possibility of making those tools useful to a much broader community of annotators.

4 RDF data models for annotation

Beyond fundamental Semantic Web compatibility, we believe that linguistic annotation formalisms can benefit from compatibility with the Web-based scholarly annotation models. We are aware of two such models, namely, the Annotation Ontology (Ciccarese et al. 2011) and the Open Annotation Collaboration (OAC) (Hunter et al. 2011) models. Each of these models incorporates elements from the earlier Annotea model (Kahan et al. 2002). These two groups have now joined together to bring their existing proposals together, through the Open Annotation W3C community group[7]. As a result, we will focus on their commonalities, and use the OAC model and terminology for the purposes of our discussion. We refer to the models collectively as the Open Annotation models.

4.1 High-level model for scholarly annotation

The basic high-level data model of the two primary Open Annotation models defines an *Annotation* as

[4] http://www.w3.org/blog/hcls/
[5] http://pipes.yahoo.com/pipes/
[6] http://www.scivee.tv/node/26720
[7] http://www.w3.org/community/openannotation/

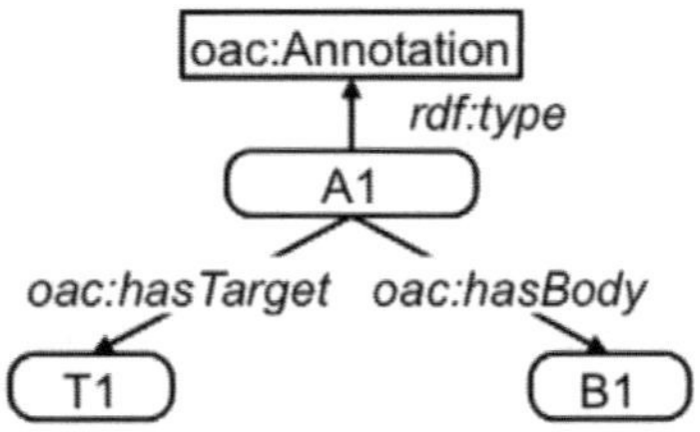

Figure 1: Base model for OAC[8].

an association created between two elements, a *Body* or content resource and (one or more) *Target* resources. The annotation provides some information about the target through the connection to the body. For instance, an annotation may relate the token "apple" in a text (the target of the annotation) to the concept of an apple, perhaps represented as WordNet (Fellbaum 1998a) synset "apple#1" (the body of the annotation).

Figure 1 shows the base model defined in the OAC model. The model, following linked data principles, assumes that each element of an annotation is a web-addressable entity that can be referenced with a URI.

Annotations can be augmented with meta-data, e.g. the author or creation time of the annotation. The model allows for each element of the annotation – the annotation itself, the target, and the body – to have different associated meta-data, such as different authors. Other features of the OAC model are that it can accommodate annotations over not only textual documents, but any media type including images or videos (for details, see the OAC model[8]). Text fragments are typically referred to using character positions.

4.2 Graph Annotations

The initial use cases for Open Annotation focused on single target-concept relationships, formalized as an expectation that the body of an Annotation be a single web resource. Recently, an extension that supports representation of collections of statements as the body of an annotation has been proposed (Livingston et al. 2011). In a revision of that extension (Livingston, personal communication), a *GraphAnnotation* is connected to a Body which is not a single web resource, but a set of RDF statements captured in a construct known as a *named graph* (Carroll et al. 2005). The named graph as a whole has a URI.

This extension enables complex semantics to be associated with a resource, as well as supporting fine-grained tracking of the provenance of compositional annotations. These developments make possible the integration of linguistic annotation with the scholarly annotation models.

5 Adapting LAF to Open Annotation

The Linguistic Annotation Framework, or LAF, (ISO 2008) defines an abstract data model for annotations which consists of nodes and edges. Both nodes and edges can be elaborated with arbitrary feature structures, consisting of feature-value pairs. Nodes can link via edges to other nodes, or directly to regions in the primary data being annotated. An example of a LAF annotation is shown in Figure 2.

While LAF has made significant progress towards unified, unambiguous annotation representations, adopting some representation decisions of the Open Annotation models will not only facilitate interoperability with those models, but also resolve some ambiguities and limitations inherent to the LAF model.

5.1 High-level representation compatibility

At a high level, the LAF model aligns well with the Open Annotation RDF models. Fundamentally, the LAF model is based on directed graphs, as is RDF. The abstract data model in LAF consists of a referential structure for associating annotations with primary data, and a feature structure for the annotation content. These are similar to the Open Annotation notions of target and body.

Importantly, these models agree that the source material being annotated is separate from the annotations. In other words, stand-off annotation is assumed. In a web context, this is particularly significant as it is often not possible to directly manipulate the underlying resource. It also facilitates collaborations and distribution, as

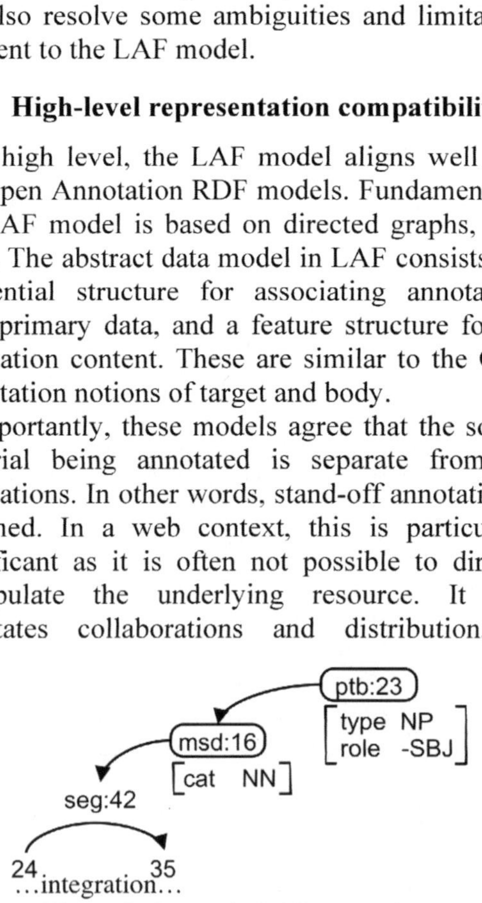

Figure 2: A sample LAF annotation, based on (Ide & Suderman 2007)

[8] http://www.openannotation.org/spec/beta/

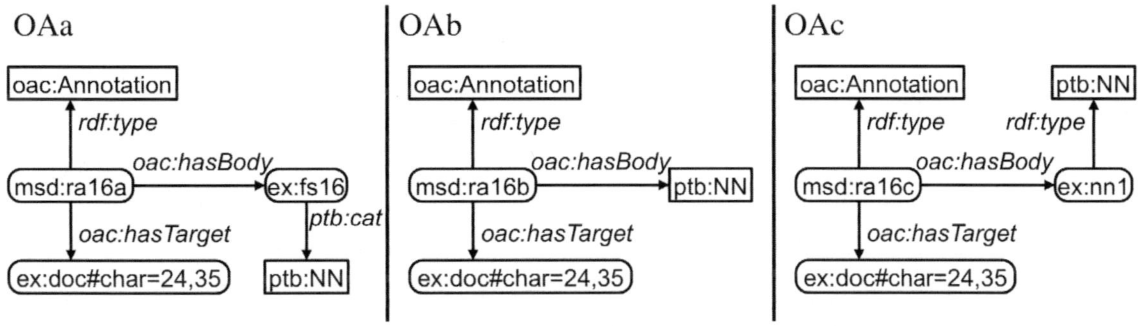

Figure 3: Options for an Open Annotation-compatible representation of the annotation msd:16 of Figure 2. Ovals represent instances, classes are boxed, and relations are italic labels on directed edges from subject to object.

annotations can be individually distributed and sets of annotations from different sources can be collected and used simultaneously.

5.2 Changes to LAF for Open Annotation

In order to facilitate integration of LAF with the Open Annotation models currently under development, a few changes would be required. A key difference is the separation in the Open Annotation models of three distinct elements: a target, a body, and the annotation itself, relating the previous two. These distinctions allow relations between any two elements to be made explicit and unambiguous, and further allow more detailed provenance tracking (Livingston et al. 2011).

5.2.1 Annotation content

In the LAF model, feature structures can be added to any node in the annotation graph. It has been shown that feature structures can be losslessly represented in RDF (Denecke 2002; Krieger & Schäfer 2010). In the XML serialization of LAF, GrAF (Ide & Suderman 2007), feature structures are represented within an annotation. An example of a LAF annotation from that paper is in Figure 2.

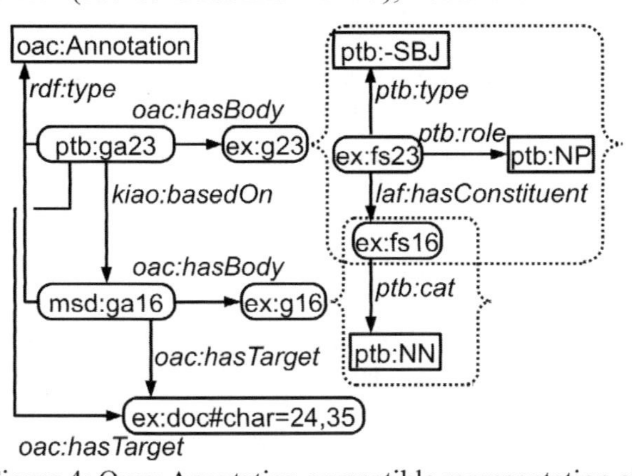

Figure 4: Open Annotation compatible representation of Figure 2 using GraphAnnotations. Graph contents are surrounded by dotted lines connected to their name.

In an Open Annotation model, the LAF feature structure corresponds to the body of the annotation. Figures 3 and 4 show several possibilities for representing the information in Figure 2 in a model compatible with the Open Annotation proposals. The most literal transformation for the part of speech annotation msd:16, Figure 3:OAa, utilizes an explicit feature structure representation in the body, consistent with automated feature structure transformations (Denecke 2002; Krieger & Schäfer 2010). Since RDF prefers URIs, concepts in the Open Annotation model are made explicit (pointing to an external definition for the Penn Treebank category of "NN", ptb:NN), in contrast to the LAF string representation of the feature and value. A named feature value pair is not necessarily needed and the concept could be annotated to directly, as is shown in Figure 3:OAb. This example, although much simpler, does lose the ability to refer to the specific instance. An instance could therefore be reified so that it could be referred to later, as is shown in Figure 3:OAc.

5.2.2 Named graphs

A GraphAnnotation explicitly separates the annotation from its content and provides a handle for the content as a whole, separate from the handle for the annotation, through reification of the content graph. The content of Figure 2 is represented as GraphAnnotations in Figure 4. The graph encapsulation clearly delineates which assertions are part of which annotation. For example, the hasConstituent relation from fs23 to fs16 in Figure 4 is part of the g23 graph, which is the body of the ga23 annotation, even though it shares concepts with the g16 graph.

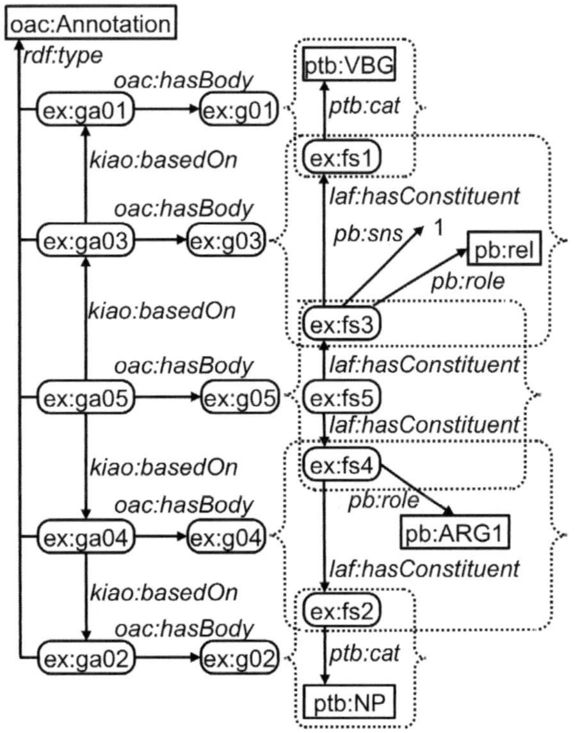

Figure 5: Literal RDF translation of a GrAF Propbank annotation representation from (Ide & Suderman 2007)

The separation of annotation and content also allows explicit provenance relations to be represented. For example, the relationship between the annotation for the NN part of speech (msd:ga16) and the annotation for the NP (ptb:ga23) as a kiao:basedOn relation (Livingston et al. 2011), indicating that the phrasal annotation is based on the part of speech annotation. This allows us to identify how analyses build on one another, and perform error attribution.

LAF annotations consist of feature structures, which have functional properties (restricted to only one object value per key), and a set of edges that connect nodes, which may have an unclear or ambiguous interpretation (see section 5.2.4). RDF-based graph annotations avoid these issues as they can directly contain any set of assertions in the annotation body that an annotator wishes to express. This includes capturing relations that are not functional, and information that might only be implicit in a LAF edge. This body representation is both more expressive and more explicit.

The greater expressivity and simpler structure of RDF based annotations can be clearly seen in contrasting Figure 5 with Figure 6. Both figures depict the same subset of information from a PropBank example in Section 3 of (Ide & Suderman 2007). Figure 5 represents a verbatim translation of the LAF following the feature structure in RDF conventions. In this figure, as in the original LAF figure, the proposition elements are distributed across 3 feature structures, for the relation (rel), arg1, and the proposition itself. In contrast, Figure 6 uses individual RDF triples in the annotation bodies; the representation is not only more succinct, it more naturally expresses the semantics of the information, with the relation and its argument within the same content graph. The pb:arg1 relation in Figure 6 alleviates the need for the entire ga04 annotation in Figure 5. Arguably it was an intentional choice by Ide and Suderman (2007) to use a LAF node/annotation instead of a LAF edge. However, this and other examples point to arbitrary selection of nodes and edges in LAF, with little surrounding semantics to ground them. While it is true that users must understand the semantics of any model to use it, the framework of RDF and the linked data best practices provide a structure for explicitly and formally defining the concepts and links, facilitating interoperability.

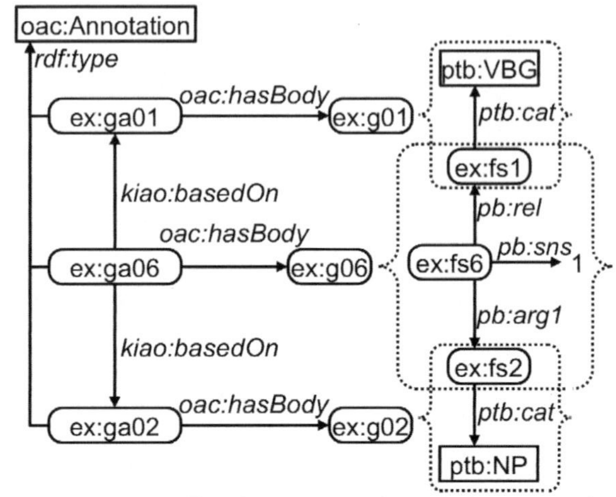

Figure 6: Streamlined representation of Figure 5, using a single feature structure for the core proposition (fs6).

5.2.3 Target objects

There are differences in how these models refer to specific region of a resource. LAF reifies structures to represent text spans but necessitates the use of a separate document enumerating (character-based) source text segmentation; subsequent annotations refer to those segments. The Open Annotation models have in common that they introduce a separate object (node in the graph) to point to the appropriate segment of the resource. OAC uses fragment URIs or *ConstrainedTargets*. The Annotation Ontology uses a construct called a *Selector*. While the details vary slightly, these constructs are encoding essentially equivalent information and attaching it to a reified entity.

LAF further encourages only creating non-overlapping spans at the segmentation level. This appears to be due to properties of the particular XML-based segmentation language chosen by LAF influencing the model. This characteristic impedes representation of annotations over other linguistic modalities, such as speech streams, as noted by Cassidy (2010). An additional segmentation document is unnecessary in the Open Annotation approaches; the models do not restrict the organization of different aspects of the annotations across documents or web resources.

The use of separate reified entities as the target of annotations also allows locations to be specified in any number of ways. As discussed above, the models employ various strategies for this and therefore can flexibly accommodate different requirements for different media sources.

In Figure 4, we show a proposed treatment of targets in the case of embedded linguistic objects, i.e. linguistic constructs that build on other constructs. We suggest that the target of a higher-order constituent such as a noun phrase consists of the target(s) of its constituent parts. In our example, it is a single target that is shared between the part of speech annotation and the NP annotation. For a more complex set of constituents, such as the elements of a dependency relation, the targets may refer to a collection of non-contiguous spans of the source document. For example, the annotation ga06 in Figure 6 would have multiple targets (not shown), one for each constituent piece.

5.2.4 Graph Edges

Edges between nodes in LAF do not always have a clear interpretation. Edges are often left untyped; in this case an unordered constituency relationship is assumed. For transparency, an edge type that specifically defines the semantics of the relationship would be preferable to avoid any potential ambiguity.

Furthermore, the LAF model allows feature structures to be added to edges, as well as nodes. We agree with Cassidy (Cassidy 2010) that the intended use of this is likely to produce typed edges, and not to produce unique instance data for each edge. However, this is another source of ambiguity in the LAF representation. For example, annotations are sometimes directly connected to edges in the segmentation document (Ide & Romary 2006).

In the LAF model, the body and the annotation itself can at times appear conflated. When an edge connects two nodes it is unclear if that edge contains information that relates to the body of the annotation or metadata about the annotation itself. In LAF it sometimes appears to be both. There is a single link in the LAF representation in Figure 2 from ptb:23 to msd:16. This link simultaneously encodes information about the target of the annotation, the representation of the body of the annotation, and the provenance of the annotation. The Open Annotation models provide for more explicit and detailed representations. This single ambiguous arc in LAF can be represented accurately as three triples. In Figure 4, these are the hasTarget link from ptb:ga23, the hasConstituent link relating parts of the annotation body, and the basedOn link recording provenance.

5.3 Web Linguistic Category representation

A challenge that must be addressed in moving LAF to the Web context is the need for resolvable and meaningful URIs as names for resources, per the Linked Data principles. LAF intentionally avoids defining or requiring the use of standard or semantically typed identifiers in its feature structures. However, to enable true interoperability as an exchange formalism, semantic standardization is important.

While there are many standard names and tagsets that are used in the NLP community, for instance the Penn Treebank tags (Marcus et al. 1993), and there are recent efforts to formally specify and standardize linguistic categories (e.g. ISOcat (Kemps-Snijders et al. 2008)) the use of URIs to capture such names is not widespread. Recent efforts (Windhouwer & Wright 2012) show the use of the ISOcat data category registry terms as URIs, e.g. the category of *verb* is represented as `http://www.isocat.org/datcat/DC-1424`. The OLiA reference model explicitly tackles mapping among existing terminology resources for linguistic annotation (Chiarcos 2010), e.g. ISOcat and GOLD (Farrar & Langendoen 2003). A specific example of mapping part of speech tags from an existing category system can be found in

(Schuurman & Windhouwer 2011). Such mappings will be necessary for any tag set used by annotations on the Semantic Web; while the work is not complete there is clear movement towards Linked Data compatibility for linguistic data.

Recent efforts to standardize of lexical representation in RDF, e.g. the W3C Ontology-Lexica Community Group[9] and the Working Group on Open Data in Linguistics[10], also will contribute to improved reuse and systematicity of annotations, and may in fact greatly simplify annotations at the lexical level. The *lemon* model (Buitelaar et al. 2011), for instance, provides for an ontology-based (RDF) representation of lexical information. Such lexical entries could be used directly as the content of an annotation, associating a word with its word form information, including all of the elements currently captured in, e.g., a LAF feature structure for a token.

5.4 DADA: LAF in RDF

The DADA annotation store (Cassidy 2010) provides an adaptation of LAF to RDF. We review it here for completeness; it is the only other work we are aware of that addresses the representation of LAF in RDF. However, this implementation does not conform entirely to the structure of the current scholarly annotation proposals.

Although the DADA model explicitly reifies anchors in a document, each anchor refers to only a single location in the document. A span of text that is the target of an annotation is captured by two or more such anchors and the span as a whole is not explicitly reified. Additional properties must be used to associate that structure with the annotation, in essence conflating the annotation with its target.

In some uses, the annotation in DADA appears conflated with its body. For instance, in Figure 3 of (Cassidy 2010) a type-specific relation (*biber*) is used to connect the annotation (*s1*) to the body, making it necessary to understand the annotation's content before that content can be located. That is, a system cannot know generically which relation to follow to access annotation content. Additionally, the model treats relations that could best be interpreted as existing between annotation content (e.g. a temporal relationship between two events) as a direct relationship between two annotations, instead of between their denoted content (the events). The proposed DADA representation of LAF is similar to the OAa subfigure of Figure 3. It therefore suffers from the same limitations with respect to attribution and provenance as the original LAF model.

6 Conclusions and Future Work

In this paper, we have examined linguistic annotation efforts from the perspective of the Semantic Web. We have identified several reasons to bring linguistic annotation practices in line with more general web-based standards for scholarly annotation, and specifically examined what would be required to make Linguistic Annotation Framework representations compatible with the Open Annotation model.

While the required changes are not trivial due to some variation in how LAF has been applied, they will result in several key benefits: (1) explicit, semantically typed concepts and relations for the content of annotations; (2) the opportunity for more expressivity in the content of annotations; (3) a representation which formally separates the construct of an annotation itself from both the content and the document targets of the annotation, enabling significantly richer source attribution and tracking; and (4) increased clarity and specificity – and hence, reusability – of the annotations produced based on the model.

In future work, we will refine our proposals for the representation of linguistic annotations in an Open Annotation-compatible model through discussion with the broader linguistic annotation community. We plan to release a version of the CRAFT Treebank (Verspoor et al. in press) in Open Annotation RDF based on those proposals.

Acknowledgments

We would like to thank Mike Bada for critiquing our proposals. We also thank Steve Cassidy for helpful discussions about DADA and LAF, and for providing examples to explore.

This work was supported by Award No. 2011-02048-05 from the Andrew W. Mellon Foundation to KV. Additional support came from NIH grant 3T15 LM00945103S1 to KL. KV receives funding through NICTA, which is supported by the Australian Government as represented by the

[9] http://www.w3.org/community/ontolex/

[10] http://wiki.okfn.org/Working_Groups/Linguistics

Department of Broadband, Communications and the Digital Economy and the Australian Research Council through the ICT Centre of Excellence program.

References

Alexander, K. & M. Hausenblas. 2009. Describing linked datasets-on the design and usage of void, the vocabulary of interlinked datasets, 2009.

Ankolekar, A., M. Krötzsch, T. Tran & D. Vrandecic. 2008. The two cultures: Mashing up Web 2.0 and the Semantic Web. Web Semantics: Science, Services and Agents on the World Wide Web 6.70-75.

Attwood, T. K., D. B. Kell, P. McDermott, J. Marsh, S. R. Pettifer & D. Thorne. 2010. Utopia documents: linking scholarly literature with research data. Bioinformatics 26.i568-i74.

Bizer, Christian, Tom Heath & Tim Berners-Lee. 2009. Linked Data—The Story So Far. International Journal on Semantic Web and Information Systems 5.1-22.

Buitelaar, Paul, Philipp Cimiano, John McCrae, Elena Montiel-Ponsoda & Thierry Declerck. 2011. Ontology Lexicalisation: The lemon Perspective. Paper presented at the 9th International Conference on Terminology and Artificial Intelligence, Paris.

Carroll, J.J., C. Bizer, P. Hayes & P. Stickler. 2005. Named graphs, provenance and trust, 2005.

Cassidy, Steve. 2010. Realisation of LAF in the DADA Annotation Server. Paper presented at the Fifth Joint ISO-ACL/SIGSEM Workshop on Interoperable Semantic Annotation (ISA-5), Hong Kong.

Chiarcos, Christian. 2010. Grounding an Ontology of Linguistic Annotations in the Data Category Registry. Paper presented at the Language Resource and Language Technology Standards workshop at LREC 2010, Malta.

Ciccarese, Paolo, Marco Ocana & Tim Clark. in press. Domeo: a web-based tool for semantic annotation of online documents. J Biomed Semantics.

Ciccarese, Paolo, Marco Ocana, Leyla Garcia Castro, Sudeshna Das & Tim Clark. 2011. An open annotation ontology for science on web 3.0. Journal of Biomedical Semantics 2.S4.

Denecke, Matthias. 2002. Signatures, Typed Feature Structures and RDFS. Paper presented at the Language, Resources and Evaluation Conference.

Farrar, Scott & Terry Langendoen. 2003. A linguistic ontology for the semantic web. GLOT International 7.1-4.

Fellbaum, C. 1998a. WordNet: An Electronic Lexical Database (Language, Speech, and Communication) Cambridge, Massachusetts: The MIT Press.

Hunter, J., T. Cole, R. Sanderson & H. Van de Sompel. 2011. The open annotation collaboration: A data model to support sharing and interoperability of scholarly annotations, 2011.

Hunter, J. & C. Yu. 2011. Assessing the Value of Semantic Annotation Services for 3D Museum Artefacts. Paper presented at the Sustainable Data from Digital Research Conference, Melbourne.

Ide, Nancy & Laurent Romary. 2006. Representing Linguistic Corpora and Their Annotations. Paper presented at the Proceedings of the Fifth Language Resources and Evaluation Conference.

Ide, Nancy & Keith Suderman. 2007. GrAF: A Graph-based Format for Linguistic Annotations. Paper presented at the Linguistic Annotation Workshop at ACL 2007, Prague.

ISO. 2008. ISO TC37 SC4 WG1. In *Language resource management -- Linguistic Annotation Framework*.

Kahan, J., M.R. Koivunen, E. Prud'Hommeaux & R.R. Swick. 2002. Annotea: An Open RDF Infrastructure for Shared Web Annotations. Computer Networks 39.589-608.

Kemps-Snijders, Marc, Menzo Windhouwer, Peter Wittenburg & Sue Ellen Wright. 2008. Corralling Data Categories in the Wild. Paper presented at the Sixth International Conference on Language Resources and Evaluation (LREC'08).

Krieger, HU & U Schäfer. 2010. DL Meet FL: A Bidirectional Mapping between Ontologies and Linguistic Knowledge. Paper presented at the 23rd International Conference on Computational Linguistics.

Kucera, H., and W. N. Francis. 1967. Computational analysis of present-day American English: Brown University Press.

Livingston, Kevin, Michael Bada, Lawrence Hunter & Karin M Verspoor. 2011. An Ontology of Annotation Content Structure and Provenance. Paper presented at the Proc Intelligent Systems in Molecular Biology: Bio-ontologies SIG.

Livingston, Kevin, Helen L. Johnson, Karin Verspoor & Lawrence E. Hunter. 2010. Leveraging Gene Ontology Annotations to Improve a Memory-Based Language Understanding System. Paper presented at the Fourth IEEE International

Conference on Semantic Computing (IEEE ICSC2010).
Marcus, Mitchell, Beatrice Santorini & Mary Ann Marcinkiewicz. 1993. Building a Large Annotated Corpus of English: The Penn Treebank. Computational Linguistics 19.313-30.
Sanderson, R., B. Albritton, R. Schwemmer & H. Van de Sompel. in press. Shared Canvas: A Collaborative Model for Medieval Manuscript Layout. International Journal of Digital Libraries.
Schuurman, Ineke & Menzo Windhouwer. 2011. Explicit Semantics for Enriched Documents. What Do ISOcat, RELcat and SCHEMAcat Have To Offer? Paper presented at the 2nd Supporting Digital Humanities conference (SDH 2011), Copenhagen.
Verspoor, Karin, K. Bretonnel Cohen, Arrick Lanfranchi, Colin Warner, Helen L. Johnson, Christophe Roeder, Jinho D. Choi, Christopher Funk, Yuriy Malenkiy, Miriam Eckert, Nianwen Xue, Jr. William A. Baumgartner, Michael Bada, Martha Palmer & Lawrence E. Hunter. in press. A corpus of full-text journal articles is a robust evaluation tool for revealing differences in performance of biomedical natural language processing tools. BMC Bioinformatics.
Windhouwer, Menzo & Sue Ellen Wright. 2012. Linking to Linguistic Data Categories in ISOcat. Linked Data in Linguistics, ed. by C. Chiarcos, S. Nordhoff & S. Hellmann, 99-107: Springer Berlin Heidelberg.

Intonosyntactic Data Structures: The Rhapsodie Treebank of Spoken French

Kim Gerdes

LPP, Sorbonne nouvelle & CNRS / NLPR, Institute of Automation, Chinese Academy of Sciences

kim@gerdes.fr

Sylvain Kahane
Anne Lacheret
Arthur Truong

Modyco, Université Paris Ouest Nanterre & CNRS

sylvain@kahane.fr
anne@lacheret.fr
arthur_truong@hotmail.com

Paola Pietrandrea

Modyco, Université Paris Ouest Nanterre & CNRS / Lattice, CNRS

paolapietrandrea@gmail.com

Abstract

In this work, we present the data structures that were developed for the Rhapsodie project, an intonosyntactic annotation project of spoken French. Phoneticians and syntacticians work on different base units: a time aligned sound file for the former, and a partially ordered list of tokens for the latter. The alignment between the sound-file and the tokens is partial and non-trivial. We propose to encode this data with a small set of interconnected structures: lists, constituent trees, and directed acyclic graphs (DAGs). Our query language remains simple, similar to the Annis Query language, as the precedence and including relations are handled in accordance with the requested objects and their type of alignment: The order between prosodic units is time-based, whereas the order between syntactic units is lexeme-based.

1 Introduction

Our work results from a corpus development project of Spoken French, Rhapsodie, set up for the study of the syntax-prosody interface. An intonosyntactic corpus has to allow corpus-based studies on the relation between prosody and syntax, which implies the recognition of prosodic structures, syntactic structures, and the relation between them. In spite of the abundance of work on treebanks, very few attempt to annotate spoken language, and even less spontaneous speech. We are aware of the Switchboard Corpus (Meteer et al. 1995), which is annotated with phrase structures, disfluencies, and illocutionary acts; the CHRISTINE Treebank (Rahman & Sampson 2000) is annotated with phrase structure, like the British component of the International Corpus of English (Nelson et al. 2002); the treebanks of English, German, and Japanese, created within the VERBMOBIL project (Hinrichs et al. 2000) have the Negra-style (Brants 2000) mixed annotation of functionally augmented constituent structures, the Venice Italian Treebank (Delmonte 2009) annotated with dependency and phrase structures, the Ester treebank for French (Cerisara et al. 2010, dependency annotation on radio transcripts), the CNG (Spoken Dutch Corpus; Schuurman et al. 2004, dependency annotation on spontaneous speech, skipping over disfluencies), the Hong Kong corpus (Cheng et al. 2008, prosodic annotation of prominence, tone, key and termination). We may add to this list the C-Oral Rom Corpus (Cresti and Moneglia 2005). The C-Oral Rom does not include an annotation of syntactic constituency or syntactic relations (what we call microsyntactic annotation), but is endowed with a rich macrosyntactic annotation (see below for the micro/macrosyntactic distinction).

1.1 Data-structures

The commonly used structures of spoken data annotation do not allow any complex syntactic annotation and inversely, syntactic formats are difficult to adapt or link to spoken data, because the nature of the data is profoundly different: Syntax is commonly based on a chain of lexemes and spoken data annotation consists of classifying time-aligned segments of the sound-file. Spontaneous spoken language has the additional twist that we have multiple tiers of partially overlapping speech. In this article we present the complete data structure of an intono-syntactic corpus of spontaneous spoken French. We show the complex relations that exist between prosodic and syntactic units and how we resolved multiple problems arising in the complex process of partial alignment. The goal is to obtain a non-redundant data-structure where the same syntactic or prosodic units can be part of different tree-structures, resulting in a highly complex acyclic graph structure as the common base structure of linguistic annotation. We describe the XML import and export format and the internal SQL representation of the data structure as well as the query language allowing for cross domain queries between syntax and prosody.

The Rhapsodie corpus is the result of a four-year project funded by the French National Research Agency (ANR). The corpus is made up of 57 samples of spoken French (5 minutes on average) mainly drawn from existing corpora of spoken French for a total of 3 hours and 33 000 words and distributed under a Creative Commons licence at http://www.projet-rhapsodie.fr. It synthesizes and formalizes various approaches to the syntactic and prosodic analysis of spoken French, in particular research stemming from the Aix school (Blanche-Benveniste et al. 1990, Deulofeu et al. 2010). The project provides a treebank endowed with both:

- a complete microsyntactic and macrosyntactic annotation (microsyntax: morpho-syntactic and functional (dependency) annotation; macrosyntactic: illocutionary groupings of maximal microsyntactic units, including discourse markers, dislocations, reported speech, parentheses, etc.)
- a rich prosodic annotation including perceptually identified phenomena such as prominences, breaks, disfluencies; phonetic alignments; detailed acoustic measurements; a large range of melodic contours; and annotation of prosodic macrostructures.

Moreover, a number of tools necessary to conduct a complete analysis at the interface of prosody, microsyntax and macrosyntax are provided.

1.2 Existing tools for the annotation of spoken language

The tools commonly used for editing prosodic transcription and aligning them to the signal (Praat (Boersma, Paul & Weenink 2012; Delais-Roussarie et al. 2003), WinPitch (Martin 2000), Exmeralda (Schmidt 2004)) allow for different segmentations of the same sample: different types of segments are stored in different independent tiers. This tier-based approach can simulate constituent structures by time-aligning bigger segments in one tier with smaller segments in another tier. Yet, this does not allow for an explicit encoding of constituent structure, because one segment cannot be linked to another segment. Therefore, neither constituency based nor dependency based syntactic structures can be described in the commonly used tools for prosodic annotation.

1.3 Treebank query tools

Inversely, the plenitude of tools that have been developed for tree-banking (visualization, annotation, correction, and search) are all token based. A well-known versatile tool is Annis (Zeldes et al. 2009) which allows for import, visualization, and search of various annotation formats and multiple annotations of the same text with segments, constituent trees, and dependency trees, all stored in a united XML format called Paula (Chiarcos et al. 2008). Annis is completely token based and although the tokens can be time-aligned, the Paula format is not well-adapted to spoken data, because we would have to choose the phonemic transcription as the base units and define the tokens (called *markables* in Paula) on this base transcription. This implies that all precedence relations are symbolic and not time-based and all order relations are based on the most fine-grained list of tokens. Moreover, as we will see, all lexemes cannot be decomposed into phonemes and the set of lexemes needs an independent (partial) order relation.

2 Linguistic annotation

2.1 Syntactic annotation

We have annotated two cohesive levels of syntax: microsyntax and macrosyntax.

Microsyntax describes the syntactic relations which are usually encoded through dependency trees or phrase structure trees. These relations are annotated in all the major syntactic treebanks such as the Penn Treebank, the Prague Treebank, the French Treebank, the Copenhagen Dependency Treebank, etc.

Macrosyntax can be regarded as an intermediate level between syntax and discourse. This level describes and classifies the sequences that make up one and only one illocutionary act as well as the relations holding between these sequences. We have identified the macrosyntactic structure of our corpus on purely discursive and syntactic arguments whereas in the C-Oral Rom corpus, macrosyntactic units are regarded as functional interpretations of prosodic units (Cresti 2005).

The annotation of macrosyntax is essential to account for a number of cohesion phenomena typical of spoken discourse and in particular of French spoken discourse, because of the high frequency of paratactic phenomena that characterize this language. See for example (1)

(1) moi < ma mère < le salon < c'est de la moquette //
me < my mother < the living room < it's carpet
'My mother's living room is carpeted'

The microsyntactic and macrosyntactic phenomena have been encoded independently from one another in a modular, partially computer-aided approach relying on collaborative online tools (Deulofeu et al. 2010). The annotation provides an analysis of all linguistic utterances of the samples and includes a complete annotation and a functional tagging of what we call *pile* structures: By piles we intend the multiple realization of the same structural position, which occurs in coordination (2), reformulation (3), disfluency (4), and correction (5) phenomena (Gerdes & Kahane 2009):

(2) nous avons été sous très gros bombardements { américains | **^puis** anglais } // (D003)
we have been under very heavy bombing { American | ^then English }

(3) tu arrives place aux Herbes avec { une | une } sorte **{ de halle | "quoi" { de |de |de } structure métallique }** // (M001)
you arrive Square of Herbs with {a | a } kind { of hall | "like" {of | of | of } metalic structure }

(4) alors < **{ { j'a~ | j'avais } beaucoup | j'avais beaucoup }** trop peur de m'installer (comme ça) seule **{ d~ | dans }** la brousse // (D204)
well < {{ I had | I had } too | I had too } much fear to settle (like that) alone {i~ | in } the jungle

(5) c'est la crise générale { { **des | des } Français** |} //+ {(**"enfin" des Français**//) | (pas simplement des Français "hein"//) | { { des | de } l'humanité | ^et de la lecture } } // (D004)
it's the general crisis {{ of | of } the Frenchmen|} //+ {("well" of the Frenchmen//) | (not simply of the Frenchmen "huh"//) | {{ of the | of } humanity | ^and of reading }}//

Albeit extremely frequent in spoken language, pile relations, which can be seen as a particular type of microsyntactic relation, are often disregarded in corpus annotation. By extensively annotating and tagging pile phenomena we could guarantee an exhaustive microsyntactic annotation of all our data, including disfluencies, repetitions, reformulations generally considered as performance errors and commonly not analyzed in spoken languages treebanks (see for instance the CNG).

In more general terms, we have provided a complete categorical and functional tagging for every word of the corpus, including discourse markers, which are integrated into the syntactic representation at the macrosyntactic level.

2.2 Prosodic annotation

As for prosody, we built on the theoretical hypothesis formulated by the Dutch-IPO school ('t Hart et al. 1990) stating that, out of the whole of information characterizing the acoustic domain, only some perceptual cues selected by the listener are relevant for linguistic communication. On this basis we decided to manually annotate only three perceptual phenomena characterizing real productions: prominences, pauses and disfluencies (Avanzi et al. 2010, Smith 2011).

We have annotated perceptual syllabic salience in speech context by using a gradual labeling distinguishing between strong, weak, and zero prominences. Strong prominences mark intonation packages and weak prominences mark rhythmic groups. Metrical feet are marked by prominences outside words.[1] Periods (Lacheret-Dujour & Victorri 2002) are ended by an occurrence of a pause of at least 300 ms, detection of an F0 pitch movement reaching a certain amplitude and of a "jump" and the absence of disfluency or a "uh" in the vicinity of the pause.

Various studies have shown the usefulness of seeing prosody as a tree structure (Tepperman & Narayanan 2008, Gibbon 2003) consisting of prosodic constituents of different levels. Building on the syllabic salience labeling, we were able to generate the totality of the prosodic tree structure made up of a hierarchy of prosodic segments characterized by more or less prominent frontiers. We

[1] Words are inflected forms of lexemes or amalgams of two lexemes (see section 3.2). A word has an orthographic, a phonetic, and a syllabized form. For example in *une extraordinaire aventure* 'an extraordinary adventure', the word *extraordinaire* has the phonetic form /ekstrordinEr/ and the syllabized form /nekstrordinE/, due to the liaisons between the words. Words are linked to two types of child nodes: the phonemes and the syllables, providing two, possibly different, time alignments. These links may not be one to one: In the example table 1, we see the word *il* 'it' and *y* 'there' sharing the same phoneme.

<table>
<tr><td>per</td><td colspan="30">do~ k@ ja a y n2 z9n Fi j@ a bi je tu ta~ nwaR</td></tr>
<tr><td>pkg</td><td colspan="15">do~ k@ ja a y n2 z9n Fi</td><td colspan="9">j@ a bi je tu</td><td colspan="6">ta~ nwaR</td></tr>
<tr><td>rhg</td><td colspan="4">do~ k@</td><td colspan="6">ja a y n2</td><td colspan="5">z9n Fi</td><td colspan="9">j@ a bi je tu</td><td colspan="6">ta~ nwaR</td></tr>
<tr><td>feet</td><td colspan="4">do~ k@</td><td colspan="6">ja a y n2</td><td colspan="5">z9n Fi</td><td colspan="3">j@ a</td><td colspan="6">bi je tu</td><td colspan="6">ta~ nwaR</td></tr>
<tr><td>pree</td><td colspan="2"></td><td colspan="2">W</td><td colspan="3"></td><td></td><td colspan="2">W</td><td colspan="3"></td><td colspan="2">S</td><td colspan="2"></td><td>W</td><td colspan="2"></td><td colspan="2"></td><td colspan="2">W</td><td colspan="2"></td><td colspan="4"></td></tr>
<tr><td>syl</td><td colspan="2">do~</td><td colspan="2">k@</td><td colspan="3">ja</td><td>y</td><td colspan="2">n2</td><td colspan="3">Z9n</td><td colspan="2">Fi</td><td colspan="2">j@</td><td>a</td><td colspan="2">bi</td><td colspan="2">je</td><td colspan="2">tu</td><td colspan="2">ta~</td><td colspan="4">nwaR</td></tr>
<tr><td>ph</td><td>d</td><td>o~</td><td>k</td><td>@</td><td colspan="2">j</td><td>a</td><td>y</td><td>n</td><td>2</td><td>Z</td><td>9</td><td>n</td><td>F</td><td>i</td><td>j</td><td>@</td><td>a</td><td>b</td><td>i</td><td>j</td><td>e</td><td>t</td><td>u</td><td>t</td><td>a~</td><td>n</td><td>w</td><td>a</td><td>R</td></tr>
<tr><td>w/ort</td><td colspan="3">donc</td><td>euh</td><td>il</td><td>y</td><td>a</td><td colspan="3">une</td><td colspan="3">jeune</td><td colspan="3">fille</td><td>euh</td><td colspan="5">habillée</td><td colspan="3">tout</td><td>en</td><td colspan="4">noir</td></tr>
<tr><td>w/ph</td><td colspan="3">do~k</td><td>@</td><td colspan="2">j</td><td>a</td><td colspan="3">yn2</td><td colspan="3">Z9n</td><td colspan="3">Fij</td><td>@</td><td colspan="5">abije</td><td colspan="3">tut</td><td>a~</td><td colspan="4">nwaR</td></tr>
<tr><td>w/syl</td><td colspan="3">do~</td><td>k@</td><td colspan="2"></td><td>ja</td><td colspan="3">yn2</td><td colspan="3">Z9n</td><td colspan="3">Fi</td><td>j@</td><td colspan="5">abije</td><td colspan="3">tu</td><td>ta~</td><td colspan="4">nwaR</td></tr>
<tr><td>english</td><td colspan="3">so</td><td>uh</td><td colspan="3">there is</td><td colspan="3">a</td><td colspan="3">young</td><td colspan="3">girl</td><td>uh</td><td colspan="5">dressed</td><td colspan="3">all</td><td>in</td><td colspan="4">black</td></tr>
</table>

Table 1: Structure of the phonetic and orthographic tiers:
per:period, pkg: packages, rhg: rhythmic groups, feet: metrical feet, pree: preeminences (on syllables), syl: syllables, ph: phonemes, w: word (with three forms: ort: orthographic, ph: phonetic, syl: syllabized)

identified global macro-prosodic units called periods, which are iteratively divided into intonational packages, rhythmic groups, feet, and syllables.

We generate prototypical-stylized melodic contours for all prosodic and syntactic units. The availability in the Rhapsodie Treebank of these various contours will allow the user to build various lexicons of intonational contours in an extremely flexible way according to his or her research goals. In more general terms, it should be highlighted that these annotation choices have allowed us on the one hand to identify the primitives of prosodic structure independently from any reference to syntax or pragmatics, and, on the other hand, to provide all the elements needed for a complete prosodic analysis of linguistic units.

3 Formal properties of the structure

3.1 Prosodic structure

Our prosodic structure consists of a hierarchy of segments of various levels: In the general case, a sample consists of speech turns that are segmented into periods. The periods are composed of prosodic packages that in turn are divided into intonational packages, which are divided into rhythmic groups. The rhythmic groups have two types of incompatible segmentations: feet and words. However, each foot and word is composed of syllables. The syllables are the smallest prosodic units, they are composed of phonemes and can combine to form (the syllabized form of) words.[2]

[2] In the example table, *fille* /Fij/ 'girl' is monosyllabic, but due to liaison with the following word, /j/ forms a syllable with the following vowel and is a child of the next word. In the same way, the words *il* and *y* corresponding to the phonetic form /j/ have an empty syllabized form, because /j/ forms a syllable with the vowel of the next word *a* /a/.

Table 1 shows the decomposition of a period in its prosodic components.
This structure corresponds to a non-recursive constituency-like representation of prosody (as the number of levels is predetermined in our prosodic model), however, the fact that feet and phonological words are segmentations of the same level implies that we have in fact two constituent trees, one including feet, the other including words. All other nodes are shared between the two constituent trees. Thus, our structure should be seen as a constituent DAG rather than a set of constituent trees.

The terminal nodes of those structures are generally phonemes, but the structures have terminal nodes at various levels, because pauses are not further developed, for example a pause between two rhythmic groups, is not developed all the way down to the foot level.

Another complication stems from the segmentation of the sound into speech turns, where in the case of overlaps (i.e. two people speaking at the same time), for technical reasons, a segmentation into units with a higher granularity is possible for at most one of the speakers. If one of the speakers is analyzable, this segment is handled just as any other non-overlapping part where the periods and subsequent segments are children of the analyzable speech turn. The unanalyzable parts of the overlaps have no further segmentation into finer grained segments. In case the sound of both speakers cannot be further analyzed, the unanalyzable segments of both speakers will share the same "overlap" node, which again gives a DAG structure and not a simple tree.

Each point of the time line is thus included in at most one element of each level (or is exactly at the border of two) with the exception of speech turns, where overlaps can occur.

L1: là par contre ça doit être | plus onéreux |
L2: | ouais il faut | faut compter autour de soixante soixante-dix
L1: *there on the contrary it must be* | *more onerous* |
L2: | *yeah you got* | *got to count around sixty seventy*

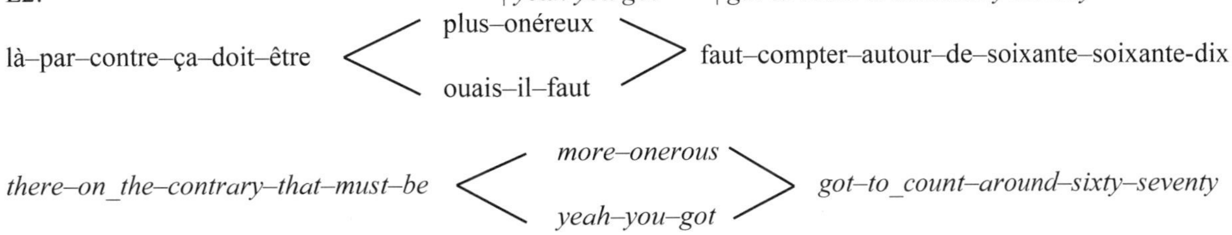

Figure 1: Transcription and lexical graph in case of overlap of speech turns

3.2 Syntactic structure

Just as phonemes are the base units of the prosodic structure, lexemes are the base units of syntax. All our syntactic structures are aligned on the lexemes. Most lexemes are time-aligned, i.e. we can determine the beginning and end of the utterance on the timeline because most lexemes correspond to words for which we have the time-alignment via the alignment of their phonemes. Some lexemes, however, are not time-aligned, for two different reasons:

Contrarily to the prosodic side of the data, generally, overlaps can be transcribed for all speakers. Nevertheless, the alignment of the words is not systematic and we do not access any time-alignment for lexemes contained in the overlap.

Secondly, we have lexemes that are not in a one-to-one relation with words. The most prominent case for French are porte-manteau words like *au* /o/ that are composed of two lexemes (À + LE, 'to + the') and contraction like *il y a* 'there is' pronounced /ja/ rather than /ilia/.[3]

This implies that the order of lexemes is nondeductible from the alignment of the lexemes on the time line and has to be provided independently. Contrarily, to the order of time-aligned prosodic structures, the order of the lexemes is a partial order, i.e. we do not have a precedence relation between any pair of lexemes. This is due to overlaps, where two speakers can produce lexemes at the same time.

The fact that a spoken corpus needs two orders for the annotation, a temporal order and a structural order, partially aligned, was anticipated and formalized by Bird & Liberman (2001). Their formalization was implemented for the AN.ANA.S corpus by Voghera & Cutugno 2009, however, without addressing our central problem of the duality of time-aligned and non time-aligned items. Contrarily to Bird & Liberman, we prefer to introduce an order on lexemes rather than to introduce abstract points with only structural order relations with the relevant time points (that is the start and end points of the time aligned units).

Figure 1 shows an extract from the Rhapsodie corpus containing a speech turn overlap: The transcription is followed by a lexical graph where some lexemes have been produced in parallel and thus have no mutual order, for example *onéreux* 'onerous' has no order relation with *ouais* 'yeah'.

The syntactic annotation consists of various constituent and dependency structures. The macrosyntactic structure is a constituent tree. The maximal macrosyntactic unit we consider is the illocutionary unit (IU), which is divided into one central component, the kernel, bearing the illocutionary force, and some peripheral components. The next examples are annotated following the conventions exposed in Deulofeu et al. (2010), which are equivalent to the associated constituent tree.

(6) là < par contre < ça doit être plus onéreux // (D005)
there < however < it got to be more onerous

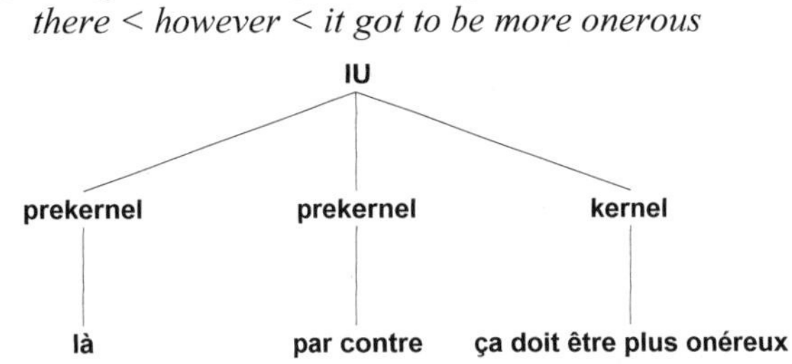

The macrosyntatctic tree is recursive because IUs can themselves contain other IUs, for instance in

[3] Due to technical reasons of our alignment process where lexemes were aligned to tokens, we encounter a similar situation when a token contains two lexemes due to elisions (*c'est* = CE + ÊTRE 'this + be' and *l'ami* = LE + AMI 'the + friend').

the following case of reported speech, *ça ce sont les anglais* forms an embedded illocutionary unit.

(7) ^et ^puis quand il a entendu le bombardement anglais { le de~ | le dernier soir } < il a dit [ça < ce sont les anglais //] //
^and ^then when he heard the English bombing { the la~ | the last evening } < he said [that < this are the English]

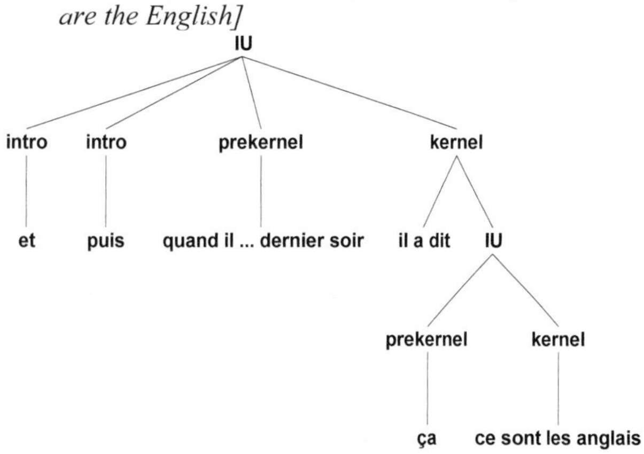

A dependency structure is commonly not a tree but a DAG (Tesnière 1959, Hudson 1990, Gerdes & Kahane 2011) because in some constructions, certain nodes are assigned multiple heads. For example, coordinations and other pile structures can have a symmetrical and an asymmetrical analysis. In the symmetrical analysis of (8) *dix-huit* and *dix-neuf* are coheads of the determiner phrase *dix-huit ou dix-neuf* and thus both dependent of *ans,* whereas in the asymmetrical analysis, *dix-huit* governs *ou*, which governs *dix-neuf.* We want a structure that subsumes both of these analyses which implies a graph (and not a tree) structure of our dependency analysis. We also add a paradigmatic link between the two conjuncts.

(8) enfin < j'avais l'air d'avoir {dix-huit | ^ou dix-neuf } ans (D201)
so < I had the appearance to have {18|^or 19} years
'Well, I looked like 18 or 19'

More precisely, we can type the two dependency links between *ans* 'years' and its determiners in a way to privilege one of the two links.[4]

The dependency analysis of Rhapsodie has no projectivity constraint, but we disallow directed cycles.[5] A dependency DAG canonically induces a

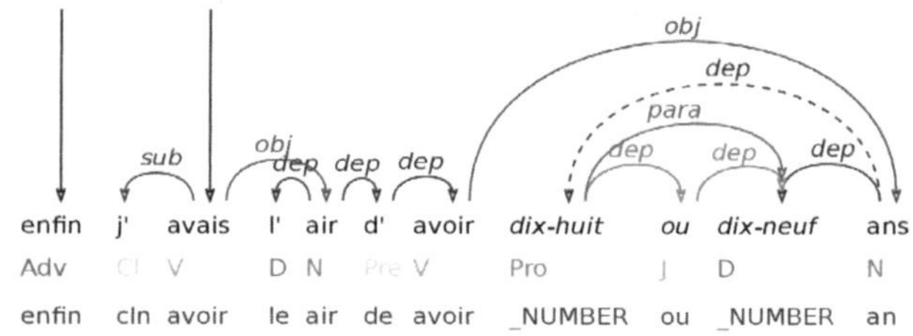

constituent tree, the tree of maximal projections of each lexeme. Note that in case of a node with multiple governors, the projection does not induce a partition of the lexemes, as the resulting constituents overlap and the projection of the node with governors appears (at least) twice in the resulting constituent tree. This constituent tree has discontinuous constituents if and only if the dependency DAG is non-projective (Lecerf 1961).

Note that, next to the macrosyntactic constituent tree and the constituency induced by dependency, we consider a third constituent structure, consisting of the piles with their layers, because many piles are not microsyntactic constituents (like for instance the disfluencies in (4)).

4 Implementation

4.1 Internal data exchange and export format

We developed an XML format for internal data exchange during the annotation process and for export of the final treebank. The format is well-adapted to our specific needs: It allows for time-aligned, partially time-aligned and only indirectly time-aligned DAGs of tokens, and two types of tree structures, dependency-like and constituency-like trees, on any of the token DAGs. For example, the syntactic annotation is based on the (incomplete, see above) time-alignment of the transcription. This is linked to another DAG of tokens where precedence relations are added based on the order of the transcription. This list is then linked to the lexemes. This linking is non trivial as it contains two-to-one relations (e.g *parce que* 'because') and one-to-two relations (e.g. *au* = À + LE 'to the').

The development of the format was guided by the Paula format and existing TEI norms. On the

[4] Some authors like Mel'čuk 1988 consider that the first conjoint is systematically the head. However, in the case of left headed coordinative structures we have good reasons to consider the second conjoint as preeminent because of closer prosodic and agreement ties between the latter conjoint and the head.

[5] For instance, some analyses of wh-words, like Tesnière (1959), see a double syntactic position of the relative pronoun, one as the complementizer and a second as the pronoun saturating a syntactic position inside of the relative clause. The dependency representation of this analysis causes a directed cycle.

one hand, the multiple token DAGs make the format slightly more complex than Paula, on the other hand, the single file structure and the limitation to the two types of tree-structure allowed us to slightly simplify Paula: A dependency graph is a simple list of relations on a token DAG, and constituency is encoded using directly the XML-inherent constituency structure (whereas in Paula, higher nodes have an explicitly encoded governor relations with the nodes it is composed of).

4.2 The structure of the database

Our treebank consists of three types of structures: different sets of segments on which hold precedence relations (partially induced from the time-alignment), constituent trees, and dependency graphs. We have decided to pre-compute and store in the Rhapsodie database the whole of acoustic correlates associated with each syntactic unit and each perceived prosodic event. It is therefore possible to search not only F0 tracks but also durations of segments, speech rates, temporal characteristics of a melodic contour, speech rate, intonational register, etc.

Each unit is stored in a "unit" table, with an attribute specifying its type ("syllable", "iu", ...). All the details of a unit (start time, end time, textual value, flow, particular attributes ...) are stored in an "attribute" table, with columns notably referring to the name of the attribute, its value, and the identifier of the corresponding unit. Relational tables store the different links between the units.[6]

[6]A first table refers to the "parent to child" relations, and includes two columns giving respectively the identifier of the parent and the identifier of the child. This table also provides two columns which indicate the place of the child unit among the other children of the parent, from the left and from the right. A second table stores the transitive closure of the "parent to child" table. We also have two tables storing the "direct" dependency relations between lexemes and their transitive closure (the "indirect" relations). The data base also provides tables to store the precedence and succession relations between units. In such tables, there are two columns corresponding to the identifiers of the left and right units. We also have to distinguish the temporal order (for the prosodic units) and the lexeme based order (for the syntactic units). Many segments of our annotation can thus appear twice with an identical span; once as a phonological group, once as a syntactic group. The database stores them separately, while keeping the identical time-alignment via the linking to the phoneme tier.

4.3 Rhapsodie QL

We developed the Rhapsodie Query Language based on the Annis Query Language (Zeldes et al. 2009). Our goal was to keep the full descriptive power of AnnisQL while adapting the language to the needs of intonosyntactic corpus searches. The differences are mainly caused by the multiple partial precedence relations that our trees are built upon and the rather numerical than symbolic character of the prosodic queries. Even queries crossing prosody and syntax are particularly simple as both annotations share the same constituency tree encoding. Moreover, we wanted to provide directly in the query language some simple mathematical functions for statistical studies of the corpus.

The Rhapsody QL covers the whole intono-syntactic structure of the corpus and allows to specify constraints on every level.

A query in RQL is composed of three parts:

- The **definition of variables** and their unit types:
  - $x1 = phone; $x2 = ui; ...
- The **constraints** to be applied on these variables. Such constraints correspond to "paths" through the structure to attain the nodes on which we want to define restrictions. To each level corresponds a unit type and a tree depth, where we want to define a restriction, or several restrictions with Boolean operators. A level is described between brackets.

  For example, we define a "group", and we want this group to be "rhythmic strong" or "rhythmic weak", or we want the group to be included in a period whose duration exceed 5 seconds:

  $gr = group; CONSTRAINT ([$gr.type = "rhythmic strong" | $gr.type = "rhythmic weak"] | [$gr] in [period.duration>5])*[7]
- The **results**: the specific attributes of the specific units we want to get.

  If we take the last example and we want to return the duration of the groups which satisfy the constraint, and also we want to take the textual value of the last phone of these groups

[7] We have defined a variable "$gr" whose type is "group", and we have two paths separated by the "OR" boolean: [$gr.-type="rhythmic strong" | $gr.type = "rhythmic weak"]. [$gr] in* [period.duration>5] consists in starting from the "group" level, to go up to the parent level "period" with the large child to parent relation "in*", and to restrict the level "period".

when this phone is not an "a", we continue the request by:*RETURN [$gr].duration; [$gr] in*(rl1) [phone.text!="a"].text;*
We asked for two results:
[$gr].duration: the duration of the selected groups
[$gr] ni(rl1) [phone.text="!a"].text*: for each group, we search the last phone child ("rl1": the first from right to left), we precise we do not want an "a", and we ask to return the attribute "text" (*ni* is the parent to child relation, the converse relation of *in*).

RhapsodieQL also provides functions, which will take as argument numbers, strings, queries, or recursive function calls. For instance, if we want the ratio between the mean of the duration of the rhythmic groups and the mean of the duration of all the groups, we will ask:

- *ratio(mean(RETURN[group.type="rhythmic %"].duration;!),mean(RETURN [group].duration;!))*

5 Conclusion

The development of both the prosodic and the syntactic annotation schemata was guided by the objective of modeling the interplay between prosody and syntax in discourse structuring. In order to achieve this goal we decided not to constrain the complexity of spontaneous speech productions within the limits of a given model of linguistic representation selected a priori. Rather we borrowed and formalized general representation principles from various compatible data-oriented models – such as the Dutch-IPO school for prosody, dependency grammars, and the macrosyntactic theory of syntax. Building on the difficulties we encountered in the annotation task, we induced and refined our formal models of syntactic and prosodic representations. We incrementally adapted our annotation to these emerging models. Traditional annotation schemata could not be applied due to our choice of not neglecting what is usually considered as "performance" phenomena: hesitations, disfluencies, incomplete utterances, dialogical completion of syntactic structures, parentheses, overlaps, grafts, etc.

The choice of giving a unified representation of prosodic and syntactic phenomena has raised a number of new theoretical and practical issues.

1. We found that whereas prosodic units are all time-aligned, syntactic constituents are aligned on lexemes, i.e., on units which are only partially time-aligned.
2. Our database considers therefore two types of orders for our structures: time on the one hand and partial order of lexemes on the other hand. These two orders are partially aligned to one another.
3. Several constituent structures are considered: two hierarchies for prosody (rhythmic groups can be independently partitioned into words or metric feet) and three hierarchies for macrosyntax, microsyntax, and piles.
4. Our dependency structure is represented through a directed acyclic graph rather than a tree. This representation has been chosen to account for the various possible analyses of the syntactic structures of a pile.

RhapsodieQL, the query language developed for parsing our data structures, extends previous query languages as it allows the user to simultaneously explore time-based and lexeme-based structures and to cross-search prosody and syntax.

This corpus allows to answer some important questions concerning spoken language in general and spoken French in particular:

- The hypothesis of the dependency connectivity of prosodic constituents (Mertens 1987)
- The prosodic structure of cleft sentences.
- The prosodic contours of left and right dislocated elements (pre- and post-kernels)
- The frequency in spoken language of non-canonical sentences, i.e. illocutionary units which are not realized by complete verbal dependency units.
- The study of prosodic differences between coordination and reformulation (Kahane & Pietrandrea 2012)

The free status of the Rhapsodie corpus and the corresponding tools as well as the existing prosodic and deep syntactic annotations provide a good basis for additional and competing levels of syntactic, prosodic, and semantic analyses. Further levels of annotation on the corpus could for instance include a complete discourse structure and coreference annotation, which will allow for a deeper study of the prosodic realizations of information packaging (the communicative structure).

References

Avanzi M., Simon A.-C., Goldman J.-Ph., Auchlin A. 2010. C-PROM. An annotated corpus for French prominence studies. Prosodic Prominence: Perceptual and Automatic Identification, Proc. Speech Prosody, Chicago.

Bird S., Liberman M. 2001. A formal framework for linguistic annotation. Speech Communication, 33(1,2), 23-60.

Boersma P., Weenink D. 2012. Praat: doing phonetics by computer [Computer program]. Version 5.3.10, http://www.praat.org/.

Brants Th. 2000. Inter-annotator agreement for a German newspaper corpus, Proc. LREC.

Cerisara C., Gardent C., Anderson C. 2010. Building and Exploiting a Dependency Treebank for French Radio Broadcast. Proc. 9th international workshop on Treebanks and Linguistic Theories (TLT9), Tartu : Estonie

Cheng W., Greaves C., Warren M. 2008. Discourse Intonation systems. A Corpus-driven Study of Discourse Intonation The Hong Kong Corpus of Spoken English (Prosodic). Benjamins.

Cresti E. 2005. Notes on lexical strategy, structural strategies and surface clause indexes in the C-ORAL-ROM spoken corpora. In E. Cresti, M. Moneglia (2005), 209-256.

Cresti E., Moneglia M. (eds.) 2005. C-ORAL-ROM. Integrated reference corpora for spoken romance languages, DVD + vol., Benjamins.

Chiarcos C., Dipper S., Götze M., Leser U., Lüdeling A., Ritz J., Stede M. 2008. A Flexible Framework for Integrating Annotations from Different Tools and Tag Sets. Traitement Automatique des Langues, 49.

Delais-Roussarie E., Meqqori A., Tarrier J.-M. 2003. Annoter et segmenter des données sous Praat. In E. Delais-Roussarie, J. Durand (eds.). Corpus et Variation en Phonologie. Presses Universitaires du Mirail.

Delmonte R. 2009. Treebanking in VIT: from Phrase Structure to Dependency Representation, in S. Nirenburg (ed.), Language Engineering for Lesser-Studied Languages, IOS Press, Amsterdam, The Netherlands, 51-80.

Deulofeu J., Dufort L., Gerdes K., Kahane S., Pietrandrea P. 2010. Depends on what the French say: Spoken corpus annotation with and beyond syntactic function, The Fourth Linguistic Annotation Workshop (LAW IV), 8 p.

Gerdes K., Kahane S. 2009. Speaking in Piles. Paradigmatic Annotation of a Spoken French Corpus. Proc. Corpus Linguistics Conference, Liverpool.

Gerdes K., Kahane S. 2011, Defining dependencies (and constituents), Proceedings of Depling, Barcelona.

Gibbon D. .2003. Corpus-based syntax-prosody tree matching. Proc. Eurospeech 2003, Geneva.

Hinrichs E. W., Bartels J., Kawata Y., Kordoni V., Telljohann H. (2000) The VERBMOBIL Treebanks. In W. Zuehlke, E. G. Schukat-Talamazzini (eds.), Proc. KONVENS 2000 Sprachkommunikation, ITG-Fachbericht 161, 107-112. VDE Verlag.

Hudson R. 1990. English Word Grammar. Oxford: Blackwell.

Kahane S., Pietrandrea P. 2012. Les parenthétiques comme « Unités Illocutoires Associées » : un approche macrosyntaxique, in M. Avanzi & J. Glikman (éd.), Les Verbes Parenthétiques : Hypotaxe, Parataxe ou Parenthèse ?, Linx, 61, 19 p.

Lacheret-Dujour A., Victorri B. 2002. La période intonative comme unité d'analyse pour l'étude du français parlé : modélisation prosodique et enjeux linguistiques. Verbum, M. Charolles (ed), Nancy, 55-72

Lacheret A., Obin N., Avanzi M. 2010. Design and evaluation of shared prosodic annotation for spontaneous French speech: from expert knowledge to non-expert annotation", Proc. 4th Linguistic Annotation Workshop (LAWIV), Uppsala, 265-273.

Lecerf Y. 1961. Une représentation algébrique de la structure des phrases dans diverses langues naturelles", C. R. Acad. Sc., Paris.

Martin Ph. 2000. WinPitch 2000: a tool for experimental phonology and intonation research, Proc. Prosody 2000 Workshop, Kraków, Pologne.

Mel'čuk I. 1988. Dependency Syntax: Theory and Practice. The SUNY Press, Albany, N.Y.

Mertens, P. 1987. L'intonation du français. De la description linguistique à la reconnaissance automatique. Unpublished Ph.D., Univ. Leuven, Belgium.

Meteer M. et al. rev. by A. Taylor. 1995. Dysfluency Annotation Stylebook for the Switchboard Corpus.

Nelson G., Wallis S., Aarts B. (eds.) 2002. Exploring Natural Language: Working with the British Component of the International Corpus of English, John Benjamins Publishing Company, Varieties of English Around the World G29.

Pulgram E. 1970. Syllable, Word, Nexus, Cursus. La Haye: Mouton.

Rahman A., Sampson G. R. 2000. Extending grammar annotation standards to spontaneous speech. In J.M. Kirk (ed.), Corpora Galore: Analyses and Techniques in Describing English, Amsterdam: Rodopi, 295-311.

Schmidt T. 2004. Transcribing and annotating spoken language with EXMARaLDA. Proc. LREC-Workshop on XML-based richly annotated corpora.

Schuurman I., Goedertier W., Hoekstra H., N. Oostdijk, R. Piepenbrock, Schouppe M. 2004. Linguistic annotation of the Spoken Dutch Corpus: If we had to do it all over again ..., Proc. LREC, Lisbon, 57-60.

Silverman K., Beckman M., Pitrelli J., Ostendorf M., Wightman C., Price P., Pierrehumbert J., Hirschberg, J. 1992. TOBI: a standard for labeling English prosody", Proc. ICSLP-1992, 867-870.

Smith, C. 2011. Naïve Listeners' Perceptions of French Prosody Compared to the Predictions of Theoretical Models. Proc. 3rd IDP conference, 349-335

't Hart J., Collier R., Cohen A. 2006. A perceptual study of intonation, an experimental phonetic approach to speech melody, Cambridge University Press.

Tepperman J., Narayanan S. 2008. Using articulatory representations to detect segmental errors in nonnative pronunciation. IEEE Transactions on Speech, Audio and Language Processing, 16(1):8-22.

Tesnière L. 1959, Éléments de syntaxe structurale, Klincksieck, Paris 1959

Voghera M., Cutugno F. AN.ANA.S.: aligning text to temporal syntagmatic progression in Treebanks. In Proceedings of the fifth Corpus Linguistics Conference, Liverpool 20-23 July. 2009

Zeldes A., Ritz J., Lüdeling A., Chiarcos C. 2009. ANNIS: A Search Tool for Multi-Layer Annotated Corpora. Proc. Corpus Linguistics 2009, Liverpool, UK.

Annotation Schemes to Encode Domain Knowledge in Medical Narratives

Wilson McCoy
Dept. of Interactive Games and Media
wgm4143@rit.edu

Cecilia Ovesdotter Alm
Dept. of English
coagla@rit.edu

Cara Calvelli
College of Health Sciences and Technology
cfcscl@rit.edu

Rui Li
Computing and Information Sciences
rxl5604@rit.edu

Jeff B. Pelz
Center for Imaging Science
pelz@cis.rit.edu

Pengcheng Shi
Computing and Information Sciences
spcast@rit.edu

Anne Haake
Computing and Information Sciences
arhics@rit.edu

Rochester Institute of Technology

Abstract

The broad goal of this study is to further the understanding of doctors' diagnostic styles and reasoning processes. We analyze and validate methods for annotating verbal diagnostic narratives collected together with eye-movement data. The long-term goal is to understand the cognitive reasoning and decision-making processes of medical experts, which could be useful for clinical information systems. The linguistic data set consists of transcribed recordings. Dermatologists were shown images of cutaneous conditions and asked to explain their observations aloud as they proceeded towards a diagnosis. We report on two linked annotation studies. In the first study, a subset of narratives were annotated by experts using a unique annotation scheme developed specifically for capturing decision-making components in the *diagnostic process* of dermatologists. We analyze annotator agreement as well as compare this annotation scheme to *semantic types* of the Unified Medical Language System as validation. In the second study, we explore the annotation of *diagnostic correctness* in the narratives at three relevant diagnostic steps, and we also explore the relationship between the two annotation schemes.

1 Introduction

From a scientific perspective, it is important to understand the cognitive decision-making processes of physicians. This knowledge can be useful for natural language processing systems and user-centered decision support in the medical field. Annotation schemes can be used to encode such information. With the growth of electronic medical records, reliable and robust annotation schemes can potentially also make the retrieval and use of archived medical information more effective. This research analyzes two annotation schemes in the context of dermatology for transcribed verbal medical narratives. One scheme is additionally compared to semantic types in the MetaMap semantic network contained in the Unified Medical Language System or *UMLS* (Aronson, 2006) as external validation. This study furthers research in linguistically annotated corpora by creating and validating schemes with future potential applications in the medical industry.

2 Data Set

For clarity, we begin by outlining the original data collection experiment (McCoy et al., 2012). The experiment included 16 physicians with dermatological expertise. Of these, 12 were attending physicians and 4 were residents (i.e., dermatologists in training). The experts were shown a series of 50 images of dermatological conditions.[1] The experts' verbal narratives were recorded, as were their eye-movements. 707 narratives were used in this study.

The participating physicians were instructed to narrate their thoughts and observations about each image to a silent student, while arriving at a differential diagnosis and possible final diagnosis. This data elicitation approach is a modified version of the Master-Apprentice interaction scenario (Beyer and Holtzblatt, 1997). The verbal data were later

[1] Some images courtesy of Logical Images, Inc.

time-aligned using the speech processing tool Praat[2] (Boersma, 2001) and stored as Praat TextGrid files. Disfluencies and pauses were also transcribed (e.g. Womack et al. (2012) analyzes certain disfluencies in this data set). The average length of a narrative is 55.6 seconds with an average of 105 words. There is an average of 15.4 pauses across narratives and an average total silent time of 19.7 seconds per narrative.

For methodological reasons, clean text transcripts were distributed to annotators in the two studies. These were cleaned of most disfluencies and agrammatical characteristics that otherwise could distract the annotator while reading.

3 Annotation Study 1: Diagnostic Thought Units

An annotation scheme was created to reveal the cognitive decision-making processes of physicians. This scheme divides the narratives into diagnostic units known henceforth as *thought units*. A thought unit is a single word or sequence of words to receive a descriptive label based on its part in the diagnostic process. With input from dermatologist and co-author Cara Calvelli, referred to below as MD 1, we defined a set of nine basic thought units. The creation of this scheme was separate from the annotation procedure. The tags and abbreviations are in Table 1.

Thought Unit Label	Tag Abbr.	Example
Patient Demographics	DEM	young
Body Location	LOC	arm
Configuration	CON	linear
Distribution	DIS	acral
Primary Morphology	PRI	papule
Secondary Morphology	SEC	scale
Differential Diagnosis	DIF	*X*, *Y* or *Z*
Final Diagnosis	DX	this is *X*
Recommendations	REC	*P* should *Q*

Table 1: Thought unit tags, their abbreviations given to experts in annotation study 1, and hypothetical examples. Thought units can span multiple words in the transcripts. For clarity, thought unit tags are in capital letters.

Of the narratives, 60 were chosen to be annotated in the first study. These represented transcripts of 10 images, selected because of their differing medical lesion morphologies. For each of the chosen images, the three longest and three shortest transcripts were included, thus comprising examples with potentially larger vs. smaller numbers of thought unit tokens (e.g. to understand which thought units were likely to be skipped).

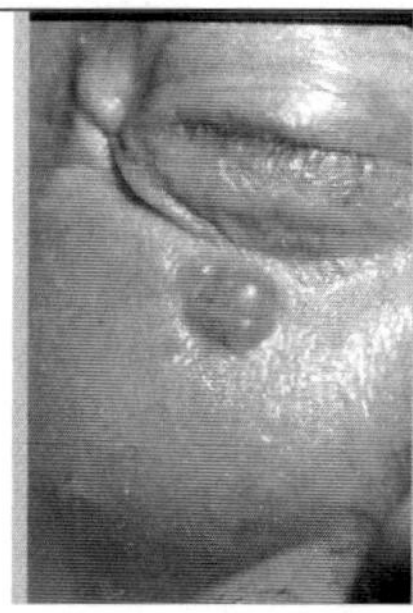

Involving an [older patient's]$_{DEM}$ [infraorbital area]$_{LOC}$ is a [pearly papule]$_{PRI}$ with [overlying telangiectasia]$_{SEC}$ suggestive of a [basal cell carcinoma]$_{DX}$.

Figure 1: An example annotated narrative. Annotated text is shown inside of brackets followed by the annotated thought unit tag abbreviation subscript.

Printed and shuffled transcripts of the 60 narratives were independently provided to two physicians, referred to below as MD 1 and MD 2, who did not take part in the original data elicitation experiment. The expert annotators were instructed to mark sequences of words which they believed comprised the provided thought units. A short example narrative as annotated by one expert and the associated image is shown in Figure 1.

MD 2 expanded the tag set with an additional subset of thought unit tags, however, they are largely not considered in this analysis.[3] This is because of their inability to be compared to thought unit tags used by MD 1 as well as their generally low frequency (9 of the 15 new thought units each account for less than 1% of MD 2's thought unit tokens).

[2]See: http://www.fon.hum.uva.nl/praat/.

[3]MD 2 added the tags *Color* (COL), *Adjective* (ADJ), *Disease Category* (CAT), *Associated Skin Condition* (ASX), *Vague Skin Impression* (VSI), *Skin Morphologic Diagnosis* (SDX), *General Description* (GD), *Size* (SIZE), *Descriptive Classifier* (CLASS), *Temporal Description* (TEMP), *Underlying Diagnosis* (UDX), *Associated History* (AHX), *Underlying Medical Description* (UMD), and *Severity* (SEV).

After these annotations were completed, and after sufficient time had passed, the same set of 60 transcripts, reshuffled, were given to MD 1 again to re-annotate. MD 1 was aware that this was a re-annotation. MD 1's original annotation is referred to as MD 1a and the re-annotation as MD 1b. With the completion of this annotation set, inter-annotator and intra-annotator agreement could be analyzed.

Thought unit annotations were then time-aligned as tiers below a word tier in Praat. This allowed us to compare thought unit tokens directly along a temporal scale visually as well as automatically. It also allows the comparison of both local and global speech phenomena. Figure 2 shows a slice of a diagnostic narrative in Praat with thought unit annotations that have perfect overlap between MD 1a and MD 1b. It also shows that there was partial disagreement by MD 2 regarding the SEC token. The MD 1a and MD 1b annotations included "surrounding" as part of the secondary lesion morphology and the MD 2 annotation did not. In this example, MD 2 also partially agreed with MD 1's PRI tokens but not on the complete word sequence; "violaceous" is marked as COL, one of MD 2's added tags.

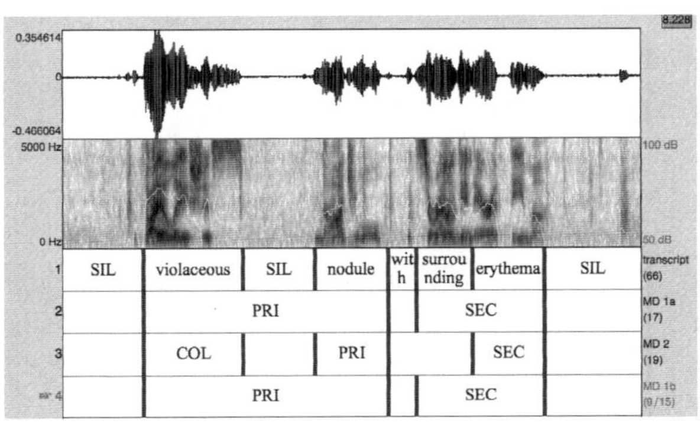

Figure 2: A screenshot of the annotation data entry.

Wordle[4] was used to visualize the prominence of concepts by thought units, given frequencies. The word clouds for *body location* (LOC) and *primary morphology* (PRI) are shown in Figure 3 and Figure 4, respectively. In Figure 3, as expected, words relating to body parts are most prominent. In Figure 4, the most prominent words, *plaque, papule, and patch*, are important primary morphology types.

[4]See http://www.wordle.net. In Figures 3 and 4, concepts with multiple word forms were lemmatized.

Figure 3: A word cloud generated from all words marked as *body location*.

Figure 4: A word cloud generated from all words marked as *primary morphology*.

3.1 Analysis of Thought Units' Distributions

Occurrences of each thought unit were tabulated. Raw counts as well as their percentages of the total thought unit tokens are shown in Tables 2 and 3. The percent of narratives in which a thought unit tag appeared was also calculated. A tag was considered *present* in a narrative if any annotation (MD 1a, MD 2, or MD 1b) used it at least once in said narrative.

In regards to intra-annotation variation, the MD 1a annotation used a similar number of tokens as the MD 1b re-annotation. In fact, the tags themselves are also similarly distributed, varying by at most 5% of the total tokens. In regards to inter-annotation variation, the MD 2 annotation used roughly 144% and 143% the number of tag tokens that were used by the MD 1a and MD 1b annotations, respectively. This is largely because of the additional tags that MD 2 created.

In analyzing the presence of tags, we found that every annotated narrative contained the *primary morphology* (PRI) tag type. All but two of the nine

Tag	MD 1a	% of MD 1a tags	MD 2	% of MD 2 tags	MD 1b	% of MD 1b tags	% Present
PRI	106	23	98	15	117	25	100
LOC	39	8	97	14	58	12	88
DX	42	9	71	11	32	7	86
SEC	81	17	69	10	91	19	85
DIS	51	11	9	1	29	6	66
CON	47	10	29	4	54	12	64
DIF	73	16	35	5	64	14	61
DEM	25	5	25	4	22	5	34
REC	2	<1	3	<1	2	<1	3
Total	466	100	436	65	469	100	

Table 2: Provided thought unit tags used by each annotator, the percent of all tokens with that tag, and the percent of narratives in which tags were present. 35% of MD 2's tags were self-created, see Table 3.

Tag	MD 2	% of MD 2 tags	% Present
COL	65	10	64
ADJ	62	9	64
CAT	28	4	29
ASX	26	4	36
VSI	16	2	24
SDX	6	1	10
GD	9	1	8
SIZE	6	1	8
CLASS	6	1	7
TEMP	3	<1	5
UDX	4	1	3
AHX	3	<1	3
UMD	2	<1	3
SEV	1	<1	2
Total	237	35	

Table 3: Thought unit abbreviations created by MD 2, the percent of MD 2's tokens assigned to tags, and the percent of narratives in which tags were present (see Table 2).

provided tags appeared in more than 60% of the annotated narratives. These two tags were *patient demographics* (DEM) and *recommendations* (REC).

3.2 Temporal Distribution of Thought Units in the Diagnostic Process

The positions of thought unit tokens in the narratives combining MD 1a, MD 2, and MD 1b were also calculated and are shown in Figure 5 on the next page, excluding additional thought unit tags created by MD 2. Because tokens could span several words, the time at the center of the token was used to calculate its position. This number was then normalized to a number from 0 to 1 with 0 being the beginning of the narrative and 1 being the end. Positions were rounded down to the nearest .05.

The overall temporal reasoning trajectory found seems intuitive. Doctors tend to follow a cognitive path with most DIS, DEM, CON, and LOC tokens occurring toward the beginning, followed by PRI, SEC, and DIF tokens, and concluded with DX tokens. The REC tokens appear infrequently but mostly occur at the end alongside DIF and DX tokens.

Doctors largely follow the same descriptive path of stating medical morphologies and other observable information, creating a differential diagnosis, and then choosing a final diagnosis, thus the analysis confirmed our expectations. The observed trend could also relate to traditions and training in dermatology. MD 1 and MD 2 did not know each other and received their dermatology training in different areas of the United States. We recognize that the analysis is biased towards MD 1 as that expert annotated twice.

We performed the temporal analysis on the new thought units created by MD 2, however the results were less conclusive and are therefore not included here. The created tags *Color* (COL) and *Adjective* (ADJ) largely appear near the beginning of the narrative similarly to PRI. This, and the fact that most new thought units were rare, indicate that the new thought units seemed to represent an unnecessarily

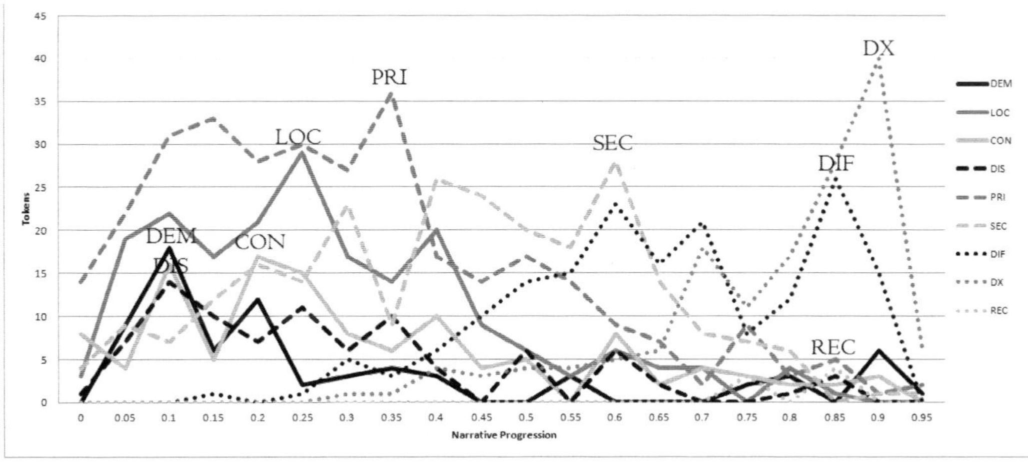

Figure 5: Distributions of provided thought unit tokens over narrative length, expressed as a ratio from 0 to 1 with 0 being the beginning and 1 being the end of the narrative. The frequency peak of each thought unit is marked.

fine granularity as a similar behavior was already captured by the provided thought units.

3.3 Agreement Metrics

Confusion matrices were created for each annotator pair. As a unit of agreement analysis, we compared overlap of tokens by individual words (including silences and disfluencies) because tokens could span and overlap in a variety of ways as shown in Figure 2. The intra-annotation matrix (MD 1a/MD 1b) is shown as a heat-map in Figure 6 with darker cells showing tags that were more often annotated together. Inter-annotation matrices were also created between MD 1a/MD 2 and MD 2/MD 1b but are not shown here. In figure 6, as a general trend, the diagonal shows that there was strong agreement on most tags. In this inter-annotation matrix, some of the most confused thought units are DIS and LOC which both refer to spatial phenomena as well as DIF and DX which both refer to diagnostic conclusions. We maintain each of these as separate labels, however, because it is good practice in dermatology to specifically assess each one.

The annotator agreement measures of observed agreement and Cohen (1960) kappa were also calculated from the data set. For the results shown in Table 4, thought units created by MD 2 were reassigned to one of the 9 provided tags based on the created confusion matrices. This was done only for this metric because MD 2 often used a created tag but in the same place as both MD 1 annotations as shown in the case of COL and PRI tokens in Figure 2. With this, these metrics better represent the agreement regarding positions of tokens instead of the disagreement between the tags used. The calculations of these metrics showed moderate to good agreement between all annotation pairs.

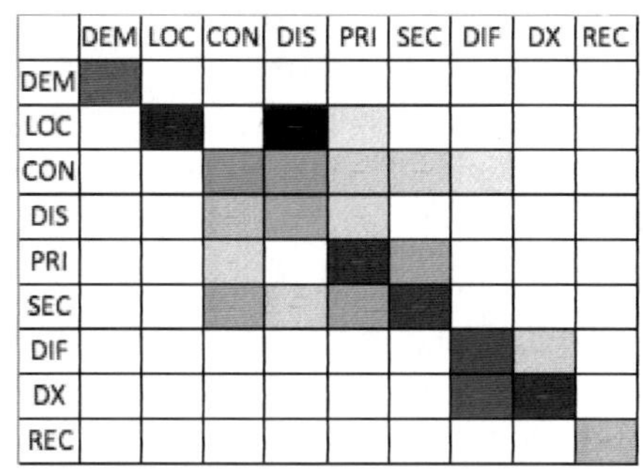

Figure 6: A heat-map of MD 1a's (columns) and MD 1b's (rows) confusion matrix. Darker cells indicate greater token overlap.

MD	1a - 2	2 - 1b	1a - 1b
% Agreement	80.69	77.72	80.98
Kappa	.56	.54	.62

Table 4: Agreement metrics for thought unit annotations. Calculations are performed pairwise for MD 1a, MD 2, and MD 1b. 1a - 1b is an intra-annotation measure.

3.4 External Validation with UMLS MetaMap

To externally validate the annotation scheme, it was compared to the semantic types used in the Unified Medical Language System (UMLS) (Bodenreider, 2004). With its 133 types, many of which are abstractions (such as "Conceptual Entity" and "Laboratory Procedure"), the UMLS ontology contains much fine-grained information. Our annotation scheme focuses on the cognitive process of dermatologists during a diagnostic procedure; we are not proposing a replacement for UMLS. Although UMLS and our annotation scheme are for different purposes (i.e., overall medicine vs. dermatology diagnostics), we regard a comparison between the two valid.

The text of each thought unit annotation was used as a query to the MetaMap semantic network. This returned a list of MetaMap entries and their semantic types. MetaMap was configured to only return the most likely match, or matches in the case of a tie. The semantic type or types of each result were counted towards the relationship to the thought unit tag the word sequence corresponded to. These relationships were then analyzed. We found that for most thought units, the most frequently occurring semantic types were often similar to the definitions of our thought units. Some examples are the LOC tag having "Spatial Concept" and "Body Part, Organ, or Organ Component" as its two most common semantic types and the DEM tag having "Age Group" and "Population Group" as its two most common semantic types.

A network density graph was created of all of these relationships with edge lengths inversely proportional to the strength of the relationship. It was too large and complex to show in this paper; instead, only the 40 strongest relationships were used to create a smaller network density graph shown in Figure 7. This also reduced noise from false positives returned by MetaMap.[5]

Based on Figure 7, a few conclusions can be drawn. PRI and SEC tags share many of the same semantic types. Eight of PRI's eleven shown relationships include semantic types that are shared among SEC's ten shown relationships. DIF has seven shown relationships compared to three of DX. Both of these thought units, however, are strongly related to "Neoplastic Process" and "Disease or Syndrome". Semantic types are also shared among DIS, LOC, and CON. These findings correspond to the confusion among these tags noted in Section 3.3 and Figure 6. Among the 40 strongest relationships, only one is not from the set of nine provided tags. This validates the tag set and indicates that perhaps *color* (COL) should be re-considered for inclusion in future work.

[5]Some noise, however, is still present. For example, the relationship between "Medical Device" and two of our created tags exists because the word 'scale' exists in a dermatological sense and as the item to weigh objects.

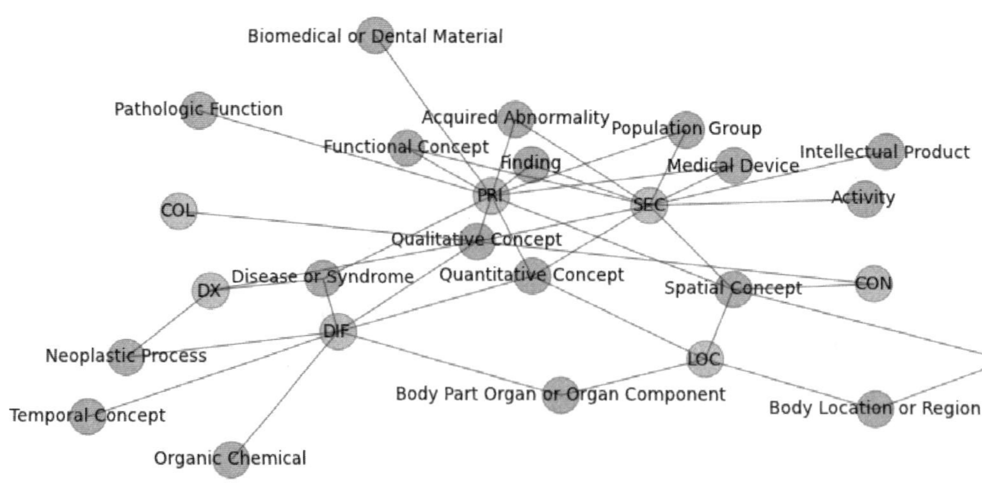

Figure 7: A network density graph of the 40 strongest relationships between text marked with thought unit tags and UMLS semantic types. The included thought units are *differential diagnosis* (DIF), *final diagnosis* (DX), *secondary morphology* (SEC), *primary morphology* (PRI), *configuration* (CON), *distribution* (DIS), *body location* (LOC), and *color* (COL) which was added by MD 2. Less strong relationships were filtered out (e.g., removing DEM, REC)

4 Annotation Study 2: Diagnostic Correctness

Cleaned transcripts were sent to three expert dermatologists referred to as MD A, MD B, and MD C to evaluate each narratives' correctness. Co-author Dr. Calvelli took part in this study as well due to limited resources and is referred to as MD A. Narratives were evaluated on three categories: correctness of the *medical lesion morphology* (*Mlm*), inclusion of the correct answer in the *differential diagnosis* (*Ddx*), and correctness of the final diagnosis (*Fdx*). Annotators were asked to use tags provided in Table 5. Inter-annotator agreements were calculated by annotator pair and are shown in Table 6. There is very good agreement between the annotators in most metrics. The lowest scores were all regarding *Mlm* most likely because of its subjectivity and greater number of class labels.

We were interested in determining how the thought units analyzed in Section 3 related to correctness annotations. To do this, we first calculated three accuracy scores for each narrative (one score for each diagnostic step scored by the annotators). The formula for correctness is shown below using Final Diagnosis (*Fdx*) as an example. Let t be a thought unit in the set T, n be a narrative in set N, and a be an annotator in set A.

$$n_{score} = \frac{\sum_{i=1}^{|A|} n(a_i(Fdx)) = \text{`Correct'} \{ \begin{smallmatrix} 1 : \text{True} \\ 0 : \text{False} \end{smallmatrix}}{|A|}$$

We then calculated the correctness based on thought unit presence using the following formula.

Class of label	Possible labels
Medical Lesion Morphology (Mlm)	*Correct* *Incorrect* *None Given* *Incomplete*
Differential Diagnosis (Ddx)	*Yes* *No* *No Differential*
Final Diagnosis (Fdx)	*Correct* *Incorrect* *None Given*

Table 5: Labels for correctness annotations. To not confuse these labels with thought unit labels (Section 3), they are written with an initial capital letter and italics.[7]

Diagnostic step	Metric	A - B	B - C	C - A
Mlm	% Agr.	67.75	72.40	71.52
Ddx	% Agr.	91.84	88.46	88.71
Fdx	% Agr.	88.21	91.97	83.56
Mlm	Kappa	0.24	0.22	0.39
Ddx	Kappa	0.85	0.79	0.79
Fdx	Kappa	0.79	0.84	0.70

Table 6: Pairwise agreement metrics between MD A, MD B, and MD C performed on correctness annotations at three levels. Annotators assigned three labels to each narrative (one at each diagnostic step). See Table 5.

$$t_{score} = \frac{\sum_{i=1}^{|N|} t \text{ in } n_i \{ \begin{smallmatrix} n_{score} : \text{True} \\ 0 : \text{False} \end{smallmatrix}}{\sum_{i=1}^{|N|} t \text{ in } n_i \{ \begin{smallmatrix} 1 : \text{True} \\ 0 : \text{False} \end{smallmatrix}}$$

These scores were computed with the nine provided thought units and are shown in Table 7.

As expected, when a DX token was present, a narrative was more often marked *'Correct'* for *Fdx*. Contrary to this general finding, the appearance of a DIF token decreased the ratio of *'Correct'* tags for *Fdx*. This could be because we did not ask for a differential diagnosis in the elicitation experiment and experts generally gave differentials, so perhaps experts were more likely to give a differential if they were unsure of their diagnosis. Another interesting finding was that DEM tokens also slightly decreased the ratio of *'Correct' Fdx*. We suspect that this is because the observers were more likely to mention demographics when presented cases with which they are not as familiar.

5 Previous Work

Woods et al. (2006) performed a study to compare the UMLS vocabulary to terms used by doctors to describe images. They found that between 94% and 99% of concepts returned by the UMLS metathesaurus were regarded as exact matches by their dermatologists. The authors conclude that the UMLS metathesaurus is a reliable tool for indexing images by keywords. This provides evidence that the UMLS metathesaurus is useful as a form of validation. Hahn and Wermter (2004) have discussed the difficulties with applying natural language concepts to medical domains because of the complexity and domain-specific knowledge. Because of this we work together with expert physicians. Derma-

		Fdx		*Ddx*		*Mlm*	
Thought Unit	% Present	Present	Absent	Present	Absent	Present	Absent
PRI	100	.61	NaN	.26	NaN	.66	NaN
LOC	88	.60	.71	.29	0	.64	.81
DX	86	.66	.29	.24	.42	.67	.58
SEC	85	.67	.30	.27	.07	.70	.44
DIS	66	.69	.45	.26	.25	.63	.72
CON	64	.67	.51	.28	.16	.71	.54
DIF	61	.44	.87	.43	0	.60	.75
DEM	36	.59	.62	.38	.19	.54	.73
REC	3	.50	.61	.83	.24	.67	.66

Table 7: Ratios of correctness of the three diagnostic steps when individual thought units are present vs. when they are absent (a tag is present in a narrative if at least one annotator used it at least once in thought unit annotation). Also included are the percent of narratives in which each thought unit appeared in.

tologists were instrumental in creating schemes for annotation and several dermatologists were involved in annotating the data set. By modeling our annotation scheme after the decision-making process of a trained physician, we can better capture the domain-specific knowledge and how it is being used. Niu and Hirst (2004) have done work with annotations of clinical texts. These contain much information but do not give us insight into the cognitive process. The data set reported on in this study shows diagnostic cognitive processes through narrations spoken impromptu. Because of this, the data set captures cognitive associations, including speculative reasoning elements. Such information could be useful in a decision-support system, for instance to alert physicians to commonly confused diagnostic alternatives. Other work has been done in annotating medical texts. For example, Mowery et al. (2008) focused on finding temporal aspects of clinical texts, whereas we attempt to show the steps of the cognitive processes used by physicians during decision-making. Marciniak and Mykowiecka (2011) also report on annotating medical texts. They verified an automatic system against manual annotation of hospital discharge reports for linguistic morphologies.

Importantly, this study responds to the need identified by Kokkinakis and Gronostaj (2010) for better methods for parsing scientific and medical data. The presented annotations schemes and the annotated data set we report upon will be useful for developing and evaluating relevant systems for processing clinical dermatology texts. This research is also a starting point for empirically exploring the theoretical division of physicians' decision-making systems by Croskerry (2009) into "intuitive" and "analytical" (p. 1022). We plan to investigate the relationship between thought units and Croskerry's hypothesized differences in medical reasoning situations further.

6 Conclusion

This study investigates two annotation schemes that capture cognitive reasoning processes of dermatologists. Our work contributes to the understanding the linguistic expression of cognitive decision-making in a clinical domain and appropriate annotation processes that capture such phenomena. With this information, intuitive decision support systems and new electronic medical records storage and retrieval methods can be developed to help the growing field of medical technology. In future work, integration of gaze data will allow us to map eye-movement patterns to thought units; the multimodal approach will elucidate the link between visual perceptual and verbally expressed conceptual cognition.

Acknowledgements

This research was supported by NIH 1 R21 LM010039-01A1, NSF IIS-0941452, RIT GC-CIS Seed Funding, and RIT Research Computing (http://rc.rit.edu). We thank Lowell A. Goldsmith, M.D., anonymous reviewers, Preethi Vaidyanathan, and transcribers.

References

Alan R. Aronson. 2006. MetaMap: Mapping Text to the UMLS Metathesaurus. July.

Hugh Beyer and Karen Holtzblatt. 1997. *Contextual Design: Defining Customer-Centered Systems*. Morgan Kaufmann.

Olivier Bodenreider. 2004. The Unified Medical Language System (UMLS): integrating biomedical terminology. *Nucleic Acids Research*, pages D267–D270.

Paul Boersma. 2001. Praat, a system for doing phonetics by computer. *Glot International*, pages 341–345.

Jacob Cohen. 1960. A Coefficient of Agreement for Nominal Scales. *Educational and Psychological Measurement*, 20:37–46.

Pat Croskerry. 2009. A Universal Model of Diagnostic Reasoning. *Academic Medicine*, pages 1022–1028.

Udo Hahn and Joachim Wermter. 2004. High-Performance Tagging on Medical Texts. *Proceedings of the 20th international conference on Computational Linguistics*, pages 973–979.

Dimitrios Kokkinakis and Maria Toporowska Gronostaj. 2010. Linking SweFN++ with Medical Resources, towards a MedFrameNet for Swedish. *Proceedings of the NAACL HLT 2010 Second Louhi Workshop on Text and Data Mining of Health Documents*, pages 68–71.

Malgorzata Marciniak and Agnieszka Mykowiecka. 2011. Towards Morphologically Annotated Corpus of Hospital Discharge Reports in Polish. *Proceedings of the 2011 Workshop on Biomedical Natural Language Procesing, ACL-HLT*, pages 92–100.

Wilson McCoy, Cecilia Ovesdotter Alm, Cara Calvelli, Jeff Pelz, Pengcheng Shi, and Anne Haake. 2012. Linking Uncertainty in Physicians' Narratives to Diagnostic Correctness. *Proceedings of the ExProM 2012 Workshop*.

Danielle L. Mowery, Henk Harkema, and Wendy W. Chapman. 2008. Temporal Annotation of Clinical Text. *BioNLP 2008: Current Trends in Biomedical Natural Language Processing*, pages 106–107.

Yun Niu and Graeme Hirst. 2004. Analysis of Semantic Classes in Medical Text for Question Answering. *ACL 2004 Workshop on Question Answering in Restricted Domains*.

Kathryn Womack, Wilson McCoy, Cecilia Ovesdotter Alm, Cara Calvelli, Jeff Pelz, Pengcheng Shi, and Anne Haake. 2012. Disfluencies as Extra-Propositional Indicators of Cognitive Processing. *Proceedings of the ExProM 2012 Workshop*.

James Woods, Charles Sneiderman, Karam Hameed, Michael Ackerman, and Charlie Hatton. 2006. Using UMLS Metathesaurus Concepts to Describe Medical Images: dermatology vocabulary. *Computers in Biology and Medicine 36*, pages 89–100.

Usability Recommendations for Annotation Tools

Manuel Burghardt
Media Informatics Group
University of Regensburg
manuel.burghardt@ur.de

Abstract

In this paper we present the results of a heuristic usability evaluation of three annotation tools (GATE, MMAX2 and UAM CorpusTool). We describe typical usability problems from two categories: (1) general problems, which arise from a disregard of established best practices and guidelines for user interface (UI) design, and (2) more specific problems, which are closely related to the domain of linguistic annotation. By discussing the domain-specific problems we hope to raise tool developers' awareness for potential problem areas. A set of 28 design recommendations, which describe generic solutions for the identified problems, points toward a structured and systematic collection of usability patterns for linguistic annotation tools.

1 Introduction

To find valuable clues about annotation tools and the role of usability, we have reviewed the LAW proceedings from 2007-2011[1] (altogether 140 articles) systematically with regard to their main topics. As expected, most articles are concerned with linguistic corpus annotation scenarios, which are oftentimes realized by deploying automatic tools. However, articles which use a manual or semi-automatic annotation approach are just as frequent. Most manual annotation projects rely on annotation tools, which are either selected from the wide range of freely available tools, or crafted for the very project. Although the usability of such tools, which is oftentimes paraphrased as *ease-of-use* or *user-friendliness*, is generally understood as an important factor to reduce time and effort for laborious annotation projects (Dandapat et al., 2009; Santos and Frankenberg-Garcia, 2007), a serious account on how to systematically test and engineer usability for annotation tools is largely missing. Dipper et al. (2004) are amongst the few who evaluate the usability of a selection of tools in order to choose an adequate candidate for their annotation project. In other respects, usability is only mentioned as a rather vague requirement that is (if at all) implemented according to the developer's personal assumption of what makes a usable tool (cf. e.g. Eryigit, 2007).

The rest of the paper is structured as follows: in chapter 2 we show that usability is not some vague postulation, but actually a criterion that can be measured and systematically engineered. Chapter 3 describes the testing method that has been applied to evaluate three annotation tools (GATE, MMAX2 and UAM CorpusTool) in order to reveal typical usability problems. We discuss the results of the evaluation in chapter 4 and present usability recommendations for annotation tools in chapter 5. These recommendations will help developers to design tools which are more usable than current implementations. They can also be used as a basic usability checklist for annotators who have to choose from the wide variety of available tools. Finally, the set of recommendations will serve as a starting point for further research concerning the usability of annotation tools, with the ultimate goal being to provide a wholesome collection of usability patterns for this

[1] http://www.cs.vassar.edu/sigann/previous_workshops.html

very domain. Chapter 6 provides an outlook to the wider context of this particular study.

2 Usability fundamentals

2.1 Defining usability

According to Nielsen (1993), usability can not be described as a one-dimensional criterion, but must rather be seen as a concept that consists of multiple components such as *learnability*, *efficiency*, *memorability*, *error rate* and *satisfaction*. Each of these usability components can be measured individually, thus making the hitherto vague concept of usability more concrete. There are also more formal definitions, e.g. the ISO 9241-11 standard (1999), which characterizes usability as

> "the extent to which a product can be used by specified users to achieve specified goals with effectiveness, efficiency, and satisfaction in a specified context of use."

Barnum (2011) emphasizes the use of the term *specified* in this definition, which indicates that usability has to be engineered for a specific user with specific goals in a specific context.

2.2 Usability engineering

Usability engineering can be seen as a set of activities, which describe a systematic way to create usability for a system throughout its development life-cycle. Hence, there are several suggestions for usability engineering life-cycles, which show similarities and parallels to existing software engineering and development processes. The ISO standard for *human-centered design of software* (ISO 9241-210, 2010) describes four elementary stages: (1) understand and specify context of use, (2) specify user requirements, (3) produce design solutions, (4) evaluate designs and iterate the previous steps if necessary.

2.3 Usability testing

Usability testing is an important activity throughout the usability engineering life-cycle (cf. stage 4 of the ISO 9241-210 process), but it may also be used as a stand-alone-method, to achieve one of the following goals:

(I) To find out which system is better (comparison)

(II) To judge how well a system works (summative judgment)

(III) To find out why a system is bad (reveal usability problems)

The annotation tools evaluated in this paper are neither compared to each other, so as to find out which one is best, nor are they tested against some predefined set of criteria. The goal of our evaluation is to reveal usability problems for existing annotation tools (cf. goal III).

There is a huge collection of different usability testing methods, which can be used to conduct a usability evaluation. Basically, they can be divided into two main categories (Rosson and Carroll, 2002): *Empirical methods*, which collect information about the usability of a system by observing and interviewing actual users, and *analytic methods*, which rely on usability-experts who try to put themselves in the position of actual users. Usually, analytic methods are used early in the design process because they are less laborious than empirical methods. Empirical methods however are by nature more demanding, as they require real users, and the data has to be interpreted by usability experts afterwards. Among the analytic methods are the so-called *inspection methods*, which include e.g. the *cognitive walkthrough* (CW) and the *heuristic evaluation* (HE).

Cognitive walkthrough — During a CW the evaluator tries to put himself in the position of an actual user in order to explore and experience the system from the user's point of view. It is important to know the basic characteristics of the actual user (e.g. by observing real users) and to make use of four control questions (Wharton et al., 1994) (cf. Table 1).

The CW method can be described as being very structured and task-oriented: the evaluator explores and tests the system as he tries to solve some predefined tasks step by step. These tasks have to be designed in such a way as to ensure that the evaluator will experience the most important features of the system. The evaluator documents every step, either positive or negative, on his way to solving the task.

Q1	Will users know what they need to do next to accomplish their task?
Q2	Will users notice that there is a control available that will allow them to accomplish the next part of their task?
Q3	Once users find the control, will they know how to use it?
Q4	If users perform the correct action, will they see that progress is being made toward completing the task?

Table 1: Control questions to support empathy with the actual user.

Heuristic evaluation — Basically, the HE is a rather unstructured expert evaluation, where a collection of usability principles (the heuristics) serves as a basic guideline for the usability-experienced evaluator. The heuristics are formulated in a generic way and are meant to provide some basic structure for the evaluation process. Among the most widely-known sets of usability heuristics are Nielsen's (1994) ten heuristics[2] (cf. Table 2).

H1	Visibility of system status
H2	Match between system and the real world
H3	User control and freedom
H4	Consistency and standards
H5	Error prevention
H6	Recognition rather than recall
H7	Flexibility and efficiency of use
H8	Aesthetic and minimalist design
H9	Help users recognize, diagnose, and recover from errors
H10	Help and documentation

Table 2: Nielsen's heuristics for user interface design.

These heuristics are intended to facilitate the discovery of actual usability problems, as the evaluator relates identified usability problems to one or more heuristics and ranks the severity of the problem. Once the evaluation is finished, the heuristics make it easy to cluster usability problems and to identify those problematic areas where the system needs to be improved.

A HE can be conducted by multiple evaluators. For the ideal cost-benefit ratio, Nielsen (1994) recommends 3-5 evaluators, as this number of evaluators on average discovers about 60-75% of all potential usability problems of a system. The ideal evaluator is a double-expert, i.e. he is both a domain expert and a usability expert (Nielsen, 1992).

Heuristic walkthrough — Sears (1997) describes the heuristic walkthrough (HW) as a method which sorts out some of the problems of existing inspection methods. Among the problems of the HE is its lack of structure and its strong focus on abstract heuristics. As a result, the heuristic evaluator is prone to find only problems that are captured by the heuristics, or if still unexperienced, he might even find false usability problems by misinterpreting the heuristics. While conducting a HE it is important to know that not every violation of a heuristic results in a usability problem. Sometimes the violation of one heuristic can be interpreted as an intentional compromise for not violating three other heuristics. The CW on the other hand has too much structure by relying on a list of user tasks and a guided set of questions. The CW approach discourages the discovery of usability problems that are not covered by the tasks or the questions.

The HW method borrows ideas from both, HE and CW: from HE it takes the free-form evaluation and the list of usability heuristics, from CW it takes the idea of user tasks and the check-questions, which emphasize the most important steps during a dialog. The HW also incorporates ideas from the usability walkthrough method (Karat et al., 1992), which is a two-way process consisting of a heuristics-based, free-form evaluation, and a more structured, task-based phase.

3 Usability evaluation of annotation tools

This study applies the HW method to demonstrate that the usability of annotation tools can be tested even with scarce resources. Another goal is to provide some exemplary proof that existing tools suffer from considerable usability problems, which di-

[2]Nielsen's ten heuristics (accompanied by short, explanatory decriptions) are also freely available online: http://www.useit.com/papers/heuristic/heuristic_list.html

rectly influence the benefit-to-cost ratio of annotation projects (Dandapat et al., 2009). A third goal is to collect typical usability problems from the annotation domain, which can serve as a starting point to generate a collection of best practices and usability recommendations for the design of annotation tools.

3.1 Evaluation design

This subsection describes how the HW has been adopted to evaluate annotation tools.

Evaluators and prearrangements — For the evaluation of three exemplary annotation tools we chose three evaluators, with each of them testing each tool. One of the three evaluators was a double-expert[3], i.e. the evaluator is not only experienced in usability-testing, but also has experience in linguistic annotation and the use of annotation tools. The other two evaluators are usability experts, with a basic background in linguistic annotation. The double-expert thus had the additional function of making the usability experts aware of domain- and user-specific problems and requirements (cf. Reidsma et al., 2004). A brief introductory text, which contained the essential contextual information, was provided for the other evaluators before they conducted the actual tests. Additionally, the double-expert could be addressed during the first phase (CW) if any domain-specific problems kept the evaluators from solving their tasks. The tasks were designed by the double-expert and pretested by two additional test persons before the actual HW session. Although the tasks were slightly modified for each of the three tested tools, they included the following basic constituents:

(I) Import a text document into the tool

(II) Create an annotation scheme with two annotation layers, one for parts of speech, and one for phrases

(III) Create some basic tags in each of the created annotation layers

(IV) Annotate the first sentence of the imported text

(V) Delete an annotation

[3]Note: the double-expert is also the author of this paper.

Limitations of this study — Further requirements for annotation tools, like e.g. the search and querying for annotations within the tool, or the export of annotated data for further processing, have not been studied in this evaluation, as the tasks would have become to complex for a HW session. For means of feasibility we did not consider the special needs of multi-user annotation scenarios in this evaluation study. We also simplified our test scenario by assuming that the schema designer and the actual annotator are the same person. Large annotation projects, which involve many different annotators and schema designers at different skill levels, however imply additional requirements for annotation tools. Such multi-user requirements are hard to test with expert-based evaluation approaches, but should be rather addressed by using empirical test methods (e.g. user observation or interviews).

System exploration (CW) — During the first phase of the evaluation the main steps and user comments were recorded as a screen capture with the corresponding audio track. The main steps and important remarks were also written down by the double-expert, who acted as a passive observer. After the evaluators had finished the first phase of the HW, the documented steps were quickly recapitulated by the observer.

Documentation of problems (HE) — In the second phase, the evaluators wrote down usability problems which they had discovered while solving the tasks from the first phase. During this phase, they were still allowed to use and explore the annotation tool. The evaluators used a template for problem documentation, which provides fields for the name of the problem, the severity of the problem, and the violated heuristic(s). The scale for the severity rating ranges from 1 (cosmetic problem) to 4 (usability catastrophe).

Data analysis and clustering — At the end of the test sessions, all usability problems were analyzed by the double-expert. The problems were aggregated if several evaluators described the same problem for one tool. The problems were also clustered into thematic categories, which emerged during the analysis of the problems, and which are described in more detail in the results section.

3.2 Selection of tools

Elementary differences between the vast number of existing annotation tools can be found with respect to the type of software as well as to the modality of annotation. Software types reach from simple, proprietary stand-alone programs to complex, standardized annotation and text processing frameworks. Tools also differ in the modality of annotation (images, spoken or written text, audio or video files). We chose to evaluate three freely available tools for the annotation of written texts. The selected tools represent different software types and showed quite different implementation approaches in earlier pretests (Burghardt and Wolff, 2009).

The first subject of evaluation was GATE[4] (*General Architecture for Text Engineering*), a widely used text annotation framework, which has been developed since 1997. GATE was last updated in 02/2012[5] and claims to have around 35.000 downloads p.a. (GATE, 2009). GATE is actually more than just an annotation tool, as it allows to integrate many automatic processing modules. However, for this evaluation, only the manual annotation features were tested and judged. Furthermore, we decided to evaluate MMAX2[6] (*Multi-Modal Annotation in XML*) and UAM[7] (*Universidad Autonoma de Madrid*) CorpusTool. Both tools are stand-alone annotation tools and therefore cannot be extended as easily as the GATE framework, but both implement interesting annotation features in very distinct and unique ways. Although the last update for MMAX2 dates back to 07/2010, and the number of downloads is at a moderate 4.700, we chose the tool, as it occurs frequently in literature and annotation projects. UAM CorpusTool was updated in 12/2011, and so far has 10.200 downloads[8].

4 Evaluation results

This section describes the results of the HW. The first part views the results with focus on the violated heuristics, and the second part focuses on more generic problem categories, which will be discussed in more detail in the next chapter.

4.1 Heuristic violations

There seems to be a trend toward the violation of H5 in each of the tools (cf. Figure 1), indicating that *error prevention* is a usability problem category that should be considered by annotation tool developers with particular attention. There are also numerous problems which violate H1 (*visibility of system status*), H2 (*match between system and the real world*), H4 (*consistency and standards*) and H6 (*recognition rather than recall*), and fewer records for the violation of H8 (*aesthetic and minimalistic design*) and H10 (*help and documentation*). In general, none of the tools does exceptionally well or bad with regard to these heuristics when compared to each other. At the same time, H3 (*user control and freedom*), H7 (*flexibility and efficiency of use*) and H9 (*help users recognize, diagnose, and recover from errors*) on average are not violated very often. This implies that the three evaluated tools contain many positive examples for implementing features which fall into the described heuristic categories.

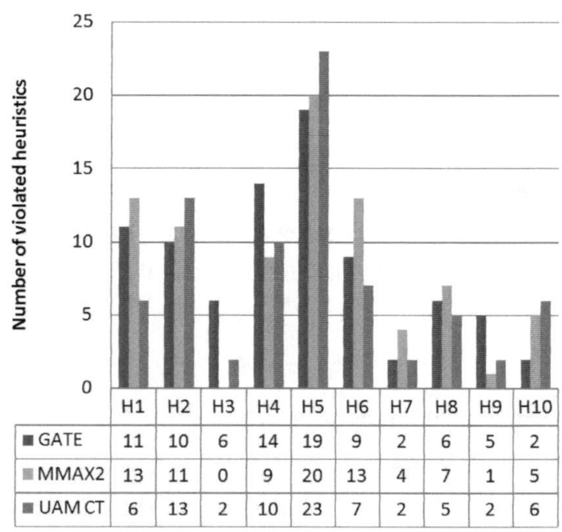

	H1	H2	H3	H4	H5	H6	H7	H8	H9	H10
■ GATE	11	10	6	14	19	9	2	6	5	2
■ MMAX2	13	11	0	9	20	13	4	7	1	5
■ UAM CT	6	13	2	10	23	7	2	5	2	6

Figure 1: Number of violated heuristics per tool.

Strikingly positive or negative counts of violated heuristics for individual tools will not be discussed in detail here, but are rather captured in the recommendations chapter. Nevertheless, the specific numbers display that there are tool-specific strengths and

[4] http://gate.ac.uk/
[5] Note: the evaluation was conducted with GATE 6.1.
[6] http://mmax2.sourceforge.net/
[7] http://www.wagsoft.com/CorpusTool/
[8] Both, MMAX2's and UAM CorpusTool's download numbers describe the state of February 2012.

weaknesses, which consequently means that recommendations and best practices will have to be gathered from different tools, and that none of the tested tools can without further ado be used as the *gold standard* for a perfectly usable annotation tool.

4.2 Problem counts and categories

The test results of the three evaluators for the annotation tools GATE, MMAX2 and UAM CorpusTool reveal a total of 143 usability problems, of which 81 can be identified as unique usability problems. The number of unique problems per tool is quite balanced, with 23 problems for MMAX2, and 29 problems for both GATE and UAM CorpusTool (cf. Table 3). The counts for unique problems together with the average problem severity of each tool show that neither of the tools outperforms the others with regard to usability. Although the average severity (scale: 1.0 - 4.0) of the problems found for each tool is not very meaningful by itself, the values (2.8 - 2.9) indicate that the majority of problems are more than just cosmetic problems or nice to have features, but rather serious issues that need to be addressed by tool developers.

Tool	All problems	Unique problems	Average severity
GATE	51	29	2.8
MMAX2	41	23	2.9
UAM CT	51	29	2.8

Table 3: Number of identified usability problems per tool.

By looking at the identified problems in more detail, it becomes obvious that most of them are very tool specific, which proves the previous claim that different tools have individual positive and negative features. During the process of sorting and aggregating the identified usability problems to meaningful clusters, two main categories with a total of seven subcategories emerged. The first main category can be subsumed as "general usability problems", i.e. problems in this category are not specifically related to the field of annotation tools, but could be traced in any other kind of software. The second category contains problems which are closely connected to the field of linguistic annotation.

4.3 General usability problems

The evaluation revealed a total of 30 general usability problems, which can be further distinguished as belonging to one of the following two subcategories (cf. Table 4):

Cat.	Description	G	M	U	Total
A	Feedback and user guidance, error messages	2	6	7	15
B	UI elements and design	4	3	8	15

Table 4: Number of general usability problems per tool (G=GATE, M=MMAX2, U=UAM CorpusTool).

Typical examples for such problems reach from cryptic error messages or unclear system prompts (category A) to badly designed buttons and menus (category B). As the treatment of such general problems is extensively described in numerous guidelines and best practice collections (cf. e.g. Johnson, 2007; Apple, 1992), these problems and their solutions will not be further discussed in this paper.

4.4 Domain-specific annotation usability problems

The second main category contains a total of 51 domain-specific annotation usability problems, which are aggregated to form another five subcategories (cf. Table 5).

Cat.	Description	G	M	U	Total
C	Wording and metaphors	4	1	2	7
D	Import / edit primary data	4	2	3	9
E	Import / create / edit annotation scheme	7	5	5	17
F	Apply / edit / delete annotations	6	3	2	11
G	Visualize annotations	2	3	2	7

Table 5: Number of domain-specific annotation usability problems per tool (G=GATE, M=MMAX2, U=UAM CorpusTool).

The problems in these subcategories are very interesting for tool designers, as they are closely connected to the specific domain of annotation tools. They are summed up as design recommendations in the next chapter.

5 Design recommendations for usable annotation tools

This section subsumes the insights gathered from positively evaluated tool features and the lessons learned from problematic features in the form of general design recommendations for annotation tools. These recommendations provide solutions for the most severe usability problems found in our evaluation study.

5.1 Wording and metaphors

The wording and the use of metaphors (category C) within an annotation tool are crucial for the basic understanding, the learnability and the memorability of the tool. Most problems occurred when the wording or the metaphors for basic functions deviated from conventions established by similar kinds of software, like e.g. text processing software. The wording for more domain-specific functions often seems to be very technical or theory-driven, i.e. it is not easily understood by the "plain annotator" (Reidsma et al., 2004).

R1 Do not invent new metaphors for fundamental interaction paradigms that are known from numerous other tools, but rather stick to conventionalized wording for basic actions like e.g. importing or saving a file

R2 Refrain from using technical wording, although it might seem obvious from a developer's point of view, but rather try to rephrase technical concepts in the domain-specific language

R3 Make sure that metaphors are understood by users from the domain of linguistic annotation; if using a set of metaphors, make sure they are consistent and easy to differentiate

R4 The help function should use wording that describes a problem from the user's perspective

5.2 Primary data

In order to import a document (category D) into an annotation tool, the user usually has to set all kinds of importing and preprocessing parameters. In many cases, the plain annotator is unable to cope with all these settings and options, besides he does not realize which effects the settings will have on the later annotation process. Another potential problem with imported text occurs with the possibility of editing the primary data.

R5 Guide the user through the import process and make clear which parameters have to be set by providing default values and a list of options rather than free text fields

R6 Automatize preprocessing parameters as far as possible and provide standard users with meaningful default values; offer optional advanced settings for more experienced users

R7 Provide a preview of the imported text, but make sure the user realizes it is only a preview and not the actual document

R8 Allow users to optionally customize and style the appearance of the primary text (color, size, fonts, etc.)

R9 Provide an adequate visual separation of primary data and annotation base markers

R10 Provide a mechanism to import and organize multiple documents within an annotation project (basic corpus management features)

R11 Make sure that the primary text cannot be edited accidentally; also make sure to inform the user about possible consequences of changes in the primary text

5.3 Annotation scheme

Before a user can start to annotate, he needs to be able to import or define a new annotation scheme (category E). The definition and editing of annotation schemes is realized very differently in the three tools, each with specific problems.

R12 Allow the import of existing schemes and make clear which formal requirements will have to be met

R13 Allow the creation and editing of an annotation scheme from within the tool; hide technical details by providing a graphical scheme-editor and offer an optional XML-mode for advanced users

R14 Make clear which annotation scheme is associated with the imported text

R15 For most users, the creation of an annotation layer, which has the function of a container, and the creation of tags for this layer, are closely connected:

provide a mechanism that does not separate the creation of a layer and the creation of the actual tags; at the same time, allow to edit the layer as a whole (delete, rename, change order, etc.) but also allow to edit individual tags on a layer

R16 Provide an easy mechanism to move tags from one layer to another

R17 As in many annotation projects the scheme gradually evolves with the actual annotation process allow the ad hoc modification of the scheme; make sure the user is aware of potential inconsistencies and provide a basic validation mechanism

5.4 Annotation process

In order to apply an annotation (category F), some user-defined unit of the original text has to be selected via mouse or keyboard, functioning as the "base of the annotation" (Fogli et al., 2004). Depending on whether the annotation base is a single word, or some specific phrase in a complex syntactic construction, the selection process itself can be fairly challenging for the human annotator already. Applying or deleting an annotation to or from a selected text-unit bears the most problem potential for interaction design. The interaction becomes even more demanding when multi-level annotations have to be applied, i.e. an annotation base is annotated with multiple, parallel annotations.

R18 Provide conventionalized interaction mechanisms which are familiar from existing text editors such as single click, double click and click-drag-release

R19 Provide an option for automatic segmenting tools such as tokenizers or sentence splitters; also allow for easy overwriting of those automatically generated segments if necessary

R20 Allow easy modification (expand or shrink the range) and deletion of existing annotation bases

R21 Display the annotation scheme of a specific layer of annotation at any time in order to simplify the application of the appropriate annotation

R22 Provide a quick and easy annotation mechanism, with a minimum number of steps (=mouse-clicks / key-strokes): select an annotation base (step 1), select an appropriate annotation from the scheme (step 2), apply the annotation (step 3)

R23 Provide an easy mechanism to select tags from different annotation layers

5.5 Annotation visualization

The recommendations for the last problem category are concerned with the adequate visualization of the annotated data (category G). The main challenge here is to integrate the annotations into the primary text in a way the user can distinct not only different annotations from the primary text, but also parallel annotations from each other.

R24 Display an annotation when clicking on or hovering over an annotated text-unit

R25 Provide filtering of visible annotations by single tags (e.g. show all nouns) and by the whole annotation layer (e.g. hide all part of speech annotations)

R26 Allow the user to customize and style his annotation and the annotation base by using different colors or markers

R27 Provide an adequate visualization of parallel annotations for one annotation base, e.g. by using the layer- or stack-metaphor

R28 Provide an optional XML-view of the annotated data for advanced users

6 Outlook and future work

While human-computer interaction has been and still is the subject of extensive research, the subgenre of *humanist-computer interaction* has been treated with significantly less attention. Fortunately, usability is increasingly perceived as a key factor in the entire corpus creation process (Santos and Frankenberg-Garcia, 2007), which besides annotation includes the digitization of primary data and the querying and visualization of the annotated data (Culy and Lyding, 2009).

The recommendations derived from the usability evaluation of three existing annotation tools may serve as a starting point for subsequent studies which point toward a more structured and validated set of usability patterns for the design of annotation tools[9]. Such a collection of patterns (Borchers, 2001) can help tool developers to systematically engineer usability for future tools, or to refactor the usability (Garrido et al., 2011) of existing tools.

[9] The evaluation study described in this paper accompanies an ongoing dissertation project on usability patterns for annotation tools.

Acknowledgments

I would like to thank Isabella Hastreiter and Florian Meier for taking part in the HW study, and Tim Schneidermeier and Prof. Christian Wolff for feedback and helpful advice throughout the project.

References

Apple Computer. 1992. Macintosh human interface guidelines. Addison-Wesley.

Carol M. Barnum. 2011. Usability Testing Essentials: Ready, Set...Test . Morgan Kaufmann Publishers.

Jan Borchers. 2001. A pattern approach to interaction design. Wiley & Sons.

Manuel Burghardt and Christian Wolff. 2009. Werkzeuge zur Annotation diachroner Korpora. In: *Proc. GSCL-Symposium Sprachtechnologie und eHumanities*, 21–31.

Chris Culy and Verena Lyding. 2009. Corpus clouds - facilitating text analysis by means of visualizations. In: *LTC'09 Proceedings of the 4th conference on Human language technology: challenges for computer science and linguistics*, Springer-Verlag, 351–360.

Sandipan Dandapat, Priyanka Biswas, Monojit Choudhury, and Kalika Bali 2009. Complex linguistic annotation - no easy way out! A case from Bangla and Hindi POS labeling tasks. In: *Proceedings of the Third Linguistic Annotation Workshop, Morristown, NJ*, 10–18.

Stefanie Dipper, Michael Götze, and Manfred Stede. 2004. Simple annotation tools for complex annotation tasks: an evaluation. In: *Proceedings of the LREC Workshop on XML-based Richly Annotated Corpora*, 54–62.

Gülsen Eryigit. 2007. ITU treebank annotation tool. In: *Proceedings of the First Linguistic Annotation Workshop, Prague*, 117–120.

Daniela Fogli, Giuseppe Fresta, and Piero Mussio. 2004. On electronic annotation and its implementation. In: *Proceedings of the working conference on Advanced visual interfaces - AVI '04*, 98–102.

Alejandra Garrido, Gustavo Rossi, and Damiano Distante. 2011. Refactoring for usability in web applications. In: *IEEE Software* vol. 28, 60–67.

GATE. 2009. GATE online brochure http://gate.ac.uk/sale/gate-flyer/2009/gate-flyer-4-page.pdf, accessed in February 2012.

ISO 9241-11. 1999. Ergonomic requirements for office work with visual display terminals – Part 11: Guidance on usability. ISO.

ISO 9241-210. 2010. Ergonomics of human-system interaction – Part 210: human-centred design process for interactive systems. ISO.

Jeff Johnson. 2007. GUI Bloopers 2.0: common user interface design don'ts and dos. Morgan Kaufmann Publishers.

Claire-Marie Karat, Robert Campbell, and Tarra Fiegel. 1992. Comparison of empirical testing and walkthrough methods in user interface evaluation. In: *CHI '92 Proceedings of the SIGCHI conference on Human factors in computing systems*, ACM Press, 397–404.

Jakob Nielsen. 1992. Finding usability problems through heuristic evaluation. In: *Proceedings of the ACM CHI'92 Conference*, 373–380.

Jakob Nielsen. 1993. Usability Engineering. Morgan Kaufmann Publishers.

Jakob Nielsen. 1994. Heuristic evaluation. In: Jakob Nielsen and Robert Mack (eds.): *Usability Inspection Methods.* John Wiley & Sons, 25–62

Dennis Reidsma, Natasa Jovanovic, and Dennis Hofs. 2004. Designing annotation tools based on properties of annotation problems. *Report for the Centre for Telematics and Information Technology. University of Twente: Dept. of Computer Science, HMI Group.*

Mary Beth Rosson and John M. Carroll. 2002. Usability Engineering. Scenario-based development of human-computer interaction. Morgan Kaufmann Publishers.

Diana Santos and Ana Frankenberg-Garcia. 2007. The corpus, its users and their needs: a user-oriented evaluation of COMPARA. In: *International Journal of Corpus Linguistics*, 12(3), 335–374.

Andrew Sears. 1997. Heuristic walkthroughs: finding the problems without the noise. In: *International Journal of Human-Computer Interaction*, 9(3), 213–234.

Cathleen Wharton, John Rieman, Clayton Lewis, and Peter Polson. 1994. The cognitive walkthrough method: a practitioner's guide. In: Jakob Nielsen and Robert Mack (eds.): *Usability Inspection Methods.* John Wiley & Sons, 105–140.

Search Result Diversification Methods to Assist Lexicographers

Lars Borin Markus Forsberg Karin Friberg Heppin
Richard Johansson Annika Kjellandsson
Språkbanken, Department of Swedish, University of Gothenburg
Box 100, SE-40530 Gothenburg, Sweden
first.last@svenska.gu.se

Abstract

We show how the lexicographic task of finding informative and diverse example sentences can be cast as a search result diversification problem, where an objective based on relevance and diversity is maximized. This problem has been studied intensively in the information retrieval community during recent years, and efficient algorithms have been devised. We finally show how the approach has been implemented in a lexicographic project, and describe the relevance and diversity functions used in that context.

1 Introduction

Modern lexicography is empirical: the lexicographer describing a word, phrase, or construction needs to understand its variations in patterns of usage by searching in large and diverse set of corpora to see the contexts in which it appears (Atkins and Rundell, 2008). Unless studying very rare phenomena, it is then important that the lexicographer has access to usable tools that are able to search in a corpus and quickly aggregate the results in a way that is meaningful for the lexicographic task at hand. The results of this aggregation can then be used when selecting example sentences for inclusion in dictionary entries.

What kind of aggregation would a lexicographer need? As we have hinted above, the goals are twofold: 1) selection of representative and relevant prototypes; 2) giving a good overview of the diversity of the full search result. There are a number of automatic methods for selection of examples for lexicographers, most of which have focused on the first of these goals. One well-known method is GDEX (Kilgarriff et al., 2008), which has been used in conjunction with the Sketch Engine (Kilgarriff et al., 2004) in several lexicographic tasks. GDEX uses a set of rules of thumb designed to address the relevance issue for lexicographers: example sentences should be medium-short (but not too short) and avoid rare words and syntactic constructions, and the search term should preferably be in the main clause.

In this paper, we argue that the two goals of representativeness and diversity can be cast as a *search result diversification* problem. The task of diversification has seen much recent interest in the information retrieval community (Gollapudi and Sharma, 2009; Drosou and Pitoura, 2010). While diversification is computationally intractable in most cases, fast approximation algorithms exist (Drosou and Pitoura, 2009; Minack et al., 2011) and have facilitated the development of practical systems for the diversification of search results for searches on the web, for documents as well as images (Hare et al., 2009; Krestel and Dokoohaki, 2011). Note that the purpose of diversification in information retrieval is typically different from that in lexicography: increasing the probability of finding a particular piece of information that the user is looking for.

2 Diversification of Search Result Sets

We will now formally define the problem of set diversification (Drosou and Pitoura, 2010). We assume that we are given a *relevance function* $r(i)$ that assigns a "suitability" score to an item i, and a *distance function* $d(i, j)$ that measures how different the two items i and j are. These functions should be tailored to suit the task at hand.

Assuming we are looking for a subset of size k of a full set $\boldsymbol{U}$ of search results. Then for given relevance and distance functions r and d, we define the diversification task as an optimization problem where we find the subset $\boldsymbol{S}_k^*$ that maximizes some objective f:

$$\boldsymbol{S}_k^* = \underset{\substack{\boldsymbol{S}_k \subseteq \boldsymbol{U} \\ |\boldsymbol{S}_k| = k}}{\arg\max} f(\boldsymbol{S}_k, r, d)$$

How should we then choose the objective f in terms of the relevance r and distance d? One obvious way is to sum all relevance and pairwise internal distance scores. This objective is called the SUM function.

$$f_{\text{SUM}}(\boldsymbol{S}_k, r, d) = (k-1) \sum_{i \in \boldsymbol{S}_k} r(i) + \lambda \sum_{\substack{i,j \in \boldsymbol{S}_k \\ i \neq j}} d(i,j)$$

Here λ is a weight controlling the tradeoff between relevance and distance.

Another possible objective, the MIN function, uses the minimum relevance and internal distance:

$$f_{\text{MIN}}(\boldsymbol{S}_k, r, d) = \min_{i \in \boldsymbol{S}_k} r(i) + \lambda \min_{\substack{i,j \in \boldsymbol{S}_k \\ i \neq j}} d(i,j)$$

The problems of finding the sets maximizing these objectives are referred to as MAXSUM and MAXMIN, and they are both NP-hard and need approximations to be usable in practice.

2.1 Approximate Diversification of Search Result Streams

There are a number algorithms to solve the MAXSUM and MAXMIN optimization problems approximately (Drosou and Pitoura, 2009). In this paper, we will make use of the online diversification algorithm presented by Minack et al. (2011). This algorithm is completely incremental, which leads to several advantages: 1) the processing time is linear in the number of search hits, as opposed to other algorithms that have higher computational complexity; 2) we do not have to know the size of the full result set beforehand; 3) we do not have to keep the full set in memory; 4) intermediate results are meaningful and can be presented to the user, which improves the feeling of responsiveness of the user interface. Minack et al. (2011) found that the greedy approximation algorithm produced diverse subsets of a quality comparable to that of more complex algorithms. However, one question they did not address is how the efficacy of the greedy algorithm is affected by the properties of the relevance and distance functions.

The incremental diversification algorithm is very simple. A diverse set $\boldsymbol{S}$ is maintained at each step, and when we encounter a new item i, find the item j in the current instance of $\boldsymbol{S}$ that leads to the maximal increase in f when adding i and removing j. This means that we enforce the size constraint of $\boldsymbol{S}$ at all times. Algorithm 1 shows the pseudocode.

Algorithm 1 Diversification of a stream of search results (Minack et al., 2011).

```
input Search result iterator I
      Maximum size k of the output set
      Optimization objective function f
  S ← ∅
  while I has another item i
    if |S| < k
      S ← S ∪ i
    else
      S_max ← S
      for j in S
        S' ← S ∪ {i} \ {j}
        if f(S', r, d) > f(S_max, r, d)
          S_max ← S'
      S ← S_max
  return S
```

We omit the description of further implementation details. In particular, the f_{SUM} and f_{MIN} objectives can be computed by incremental updates, which speeds up their evaluation greatly.

3 A Case Study: Diversity and Relevance in a Lexicographic Project

We applied the search result diversification method in a new annotation user interface used in the Swedish FrameNet (SweFN) project. This is a lexical resource under development (Borin et al., 2010; Friberg Heppin and Toporowska Gronostaj, 2012) that is based on the English version of FrameNet constructed by the Berkeley research group (Baker et al., 1998). It is found on the SweFN website[1], and is available as a free resource. All lexical resources

[1] `http://spraakbanken.gu.se/eng/swefn`

used for constructing SweFN are freely available for downloading.

The lexicographers working in this project typically define frames that are fairly close in meaning to their counterparts in the Berkeley FrameNet. When a frame has been defined, lexical units are added. For each lexical unit, a set of example sentences are then selected from KORP, a collection of corpora of different types (Borin et al., 2012). Finally, the lexicographers annotate the frame element (semantic role) structure on the example sentences.

We now proceed to describe the relevance and distance measures used in the FrameNet lexicographic task.

3.1 GDEX-inspired Relevance Measure

As mentioned above, GDEX (Kilgarriff et al., 2004) is a method for extracting example sentences from corpora. The stated purpose is that the selected examples should be

- typical, exhibiting frequent and well-dispersed patterns of usage;
- informative, helping to elucidate the definition;
- intelligible to learners, avoiding complex syntax and rare words.

These goals are of course hard to quantify, but GDEX includes a number of rules of thumb intended to capture these properties. We defined a relevance measure based on a simplified subset of the rules used in GDEX.

Sentence length: if the sentence was shorter than 10 or longer than 25 words, five relevance points were subtracted.

Rare words: one relevance point was subtracted for each infrequent word.

Main clause: since we didn't want to parse the sentence, we just subtracted one relevance point if the search term occurred after the tenth position in the sentece.

3.2 Contextual Distances

To compute distances between the two examples i and j, we used a standard Euclidean distance between feature vector representations of i and j:

$$d(i,j) = \sqrt{\|\phi(i)\|^2 + \|\phi(j)\|^2 - 2\phi(i)\phi(j)}$$

We developed two different feature extraction functions ϕ, based on based on the syntactic and lexical contexts, respectively.

The purpose of the *syntactic* context representation is to distinguish grammatical constructions and subcategorization frames, which is central to the FrameNet lexicographic task. When building the syntactic context representation ϕ_{syn}, we used dependency parse trees provided by MaltParser (Nivre et al., 2007). The trees are pre-computed and stored in the corpus database, so this does not significantly affect the computational performance. The feature vector consists of one feature for each incoming and outgoing dependency relation of each word in the search hit. Direct objects needed some special consideration to take care of reflexives.

The *lexical* context representation uses a standard bag-of-words representation of a window around the search hit. In the future, we aim to compress the feature space by using dimensionality reduction techniques such as random indexing (Kanerva et al., 2000).

3.3 Implementation

Figure 1 shows a screenshot of the user interface for the selection of example sentences for the Swedish FrameNet. The user interface includes an implemenation of the diversification functionality. The implementation proved to be very fast: compared to the time spent iterating through the search result, the diversification added just 14%.

The screenshot shows an example of a diversified result set. We searched for the Swedish word *slag*, and applied the diversification algorithm to produce a set of size 50; we used the GDEX-inspired relevance function and the syntactic context distance measure, and the SUM objective function with a λ of 1. The word *slag* is quite polysemous, with 8 senses listed in the SALDO lexicon (Borin and Forsberg, 2009). In most general Swedish corpora, the completely dominant sense of this word is that corresponding to the English word *type* or *kind*. In the diversified set, we observed 6 of the 8 senses, which shows that the diversification method has worked quite well for this word.

Figure 1: Screenshot of the Swedish FrameNet example selection and annotation user interface.

4 Discussion

We have argued that the recent developments in search result diversification in the information retrieval community are relevant for lexicographers. The work described in this paper builds on previous work in two separate communities that we think may benefit from a cross-fertilization. This has not been very common until now; the most related approach is probably that described by de Melo and Weikum (2009), which similarly defined an optimization problem to build a useful set of example sentences. Although similar in spirit to our method, there are some differences: first, our method does not rely on parallel corpora; second, we maintain a clear separation between relevance and diversity.

We see several obvious ways to proceed. The relevance and distance measures described here are our first attempts, and we believe that more sophisticated measures can be devised. Another necessary next step would to carry out an usability and quality evaluation where annotators are asked whether the presence of the diversified set leads to a better overview of usage and a higher quality of the end result. However, the protocol of this type of evaluation is non-trivial to define.

Acknowledgements

The research presented here was supported by the Swedish Research Council (the project *Swedish Framenet++*, VR dnr 2010-6013) and by the University of Gothenburg through its support of the Centre for Language Technology and Språkbanken (the Swedish Language Bank).

References

B. T. Sue Atkins and Michael Rundell. 2008. *Oxford Guide to Practical Lexicography*. The Oxford University Press.

Collin Baker, Charles Fillmore, and John Lowe. 1998. The Berkeley FrameNet project. In *Proc. of Coling/ACL*.

Lars Borin and Markus Forsberg. 2009. All in the family: A comparison of SALDO and WordNet. In *Proceedings of the Nodalida 2009 Workshop on WordNets and other Lexical Semantic Resources – between Lexical Semantics, Lexicography, Terminology and Formal Ontologies*, Odense, Denmark.

Lars Borin, Dana Dannélls, Markus Forsberg, Maria Toporowska Gronostaj, and Dimitrios Kokkinakis. 2010. The past meets the present in the Swedish FrameNet++. In *Proc. of EURALEX*.

Lars Borin, Markus Forsberg, and Johan Roxendal. 2012. Korp – the corpus infrastructure of Språkbanken. In *Proceedings of LREC-2012 (to appear)*.

Gerard de Melo and Gerhard Weikum. 2009. Extracting sense-disambiguated example sentences from parallel corpora. In *Proceedings of the First Workshop on Definition Extraction in conjunction with RANLP 2009*, pages 40–46, Shoumen, Bulgaria.

Marina Drosou and Evaggelia Pitoura. 2009. Diversity over continuous data. *IEEE Data Eng. Bull.*, 32(4):49–56.

Marina Drosou and Evaggelia Pitoura. 2010. Search result diversification. *SIGMOD Record*, 39(1):41–47.

Karin Friberg Heppin and Maria Toporowska Gronostaj. 2012. The rocky road towards a Swedish FrameNet. In *Proceedings of LREC-2012 (to appear)*.

Sreenivas Gollapudi and Aneesh Sharma. 2009. An axiomatic approach for result diversification. In *Proceedings of the 18th international conference on World wide web*, WWW '09, pages 381–390, New York, United States.

Jonathon Hare, David Dupplaw, and Paul Lewis. 2009. IAM@ImageCLEFphoto 2009: Experiments on maximising diversity using image features. In *Proceedings of the CLEF 2009 Workshop*, page 42.

Pentti Kanerva, Jan Kristoffersson, and Anders Holst. 2000. Random indexing of text samples for latent semantic analysis. In *Proceedings of the 22nd annual conference of the cognitive science society*.

Adam Kilgarriff, Pavel Rychlý, Pavel Smrz, and David Tugwell. 2004. The Sketch engine. In *Proceedings of Euralex*, pages 105–116, Lorient, France.

Adam Kilgarriff, Miloš Husák, Katy McAdam, Michael Rundell, and Pavel Rychlý. 2008. GDEX: Automatically finding good dictionary examples in a corpus. In *Proceedings of the XIII Euralex international congress*.

Ralf Krestel and Nima Dokoohaki. 2011. Diversifying product review rankings: Getting the full picture. In *Web Intelligence*, pages 138–145.

Enrico Minack, Wolf Siberski, and Wolfgang Nejdl. 2011. Incremental diversification for very large sets: a streaming-based approach. In *Proceedings of the 34th international ACM SIGIR conference on Research and development in Information Retrieval*, SIGIR '11, pages 585–594, New York, NY, USA. ACM.

Joakim Nivre, Johan Hall, Jens Nilsson, Atanas Chanev, Gülşen Eryiğit, Sandra Kübler, Svetoslav Marinov, and Erwin Marsi. 2007. MaltParser: A language-independent system for data-driven dependency parsing. *Natural Language Engineering*, 13(2).

Simultaneous error detection at two levels of syntactic annotation

Adam Przepiórkowski
Institute of Computer Science
Polish Academy of Sciences
ul. Jana Kazimierza 5
01-248 Warszawa, Poland
adamp@ipipan.waw.pl

Michał Lenart
Institute of Computer Science
Polish Academy of Sciences
ul. Jana Kazimierza 5
01-248 Warszawa, Poland
michal.lenart@ipipan.waw.pl

Abstract

The paper describes a method for measuring compatibility between two levels of manual corpus annotation: shallow and deep. The proposed measures translate into a procedure for finding annotation errors at either level.

1 Introduction

Syntactic parsers are typically evaluated against manually or semi-automatically developed treebanks. Although, in evaluation tasks, such hand-produced resources are treated as if they were error-free, it is well known that even the most carefully annotated corpora contain errors. Some attention has been given to this problem within the last decade, and statistical techniques have been proposed to locate untypical – and, hence, possibly erroneous – annotations.

In this paper we examine a related issue, namely, the possibility of finding annotation errors by comparing two independently annotated levels of syntactic annotation: shallow (roughly: chunking) and deep (fully connected syntactic trees spanning the whole sentence).

2 Related Work

There are two strands of work relevant to the current enterprise. First, there is a line of work on discovering errors in manually annotated corpora (van Halteren 2000, Eskin 2000, Dickinson and Meurers 2003a), including treebanks (Dickinson and Meurers 2003b, Boyd et al. 2008, Dickinson and Lee 2008, Kato and Matsubara 2010). These methods concentrate on finding inconsistencies in linguistic annotations: if similar (in some well-defined way) inputs receive different annotations, the less frequent of these annotations is suspected of being erroneous. Experiments (reported elsewhere) performed on a Polish treebank show that such methods reach reasonable precision but lack in recall.

The second relevant line of research is concerned with the evaluation of syntactic parsers. The standard measure is the so-called Parseval measure (Black et al. 1991), used in the eponymous series of competitions. It calculates precision and recall on the set of (perhaps labelled, Magerman 1995) spans of words, i.e., on brackets identified in parse results and in the gold standard. Unfortunately, this measure – regardless of the fact that it has been repeatedly criticised on various grounds (Briscoe and Carroll 1996, Sampson and Babarczy 2003, Rehbein and van Genabith 2007, Kübler et al. 2008) – is not applicable to the current problem, as spans of discovered constituents are very different *by design*.

A more promising measure, older than Parseval (cf. Sampson et al. 1989), but gaining prominence only recently, is Leaf-Ancestor (LA; Sampson 2000, Sampson and Babarczy 2003), which compares trees word-by-word. For each word, the similarity of the path from this word to the root of the tree in both trees is calculated as a number in $\langle 0, 1 \rangle$, and the mean of these similarities over all words in a sentence is the score for this sentence.[1] While also not

[1] The very lenient IOB (Ramshaw and Marcus 1995, Tjong Kim Sang and Veenstra 1999) accuracy measure, used sometimes in chunking, can be considered as an extreme case of the LA measure.

directly applicable to the current scenario, this measure is much more flexible, as path similarity may be defined in various ways. The method proposed in section 4 has been inspired by this measure. Another general source of inspiration have been evaluation measures used in dependency parsing, where the notion of head is of paramount importance.

3 Levels of Syntactic Annotation

Among the various levels of linguistic annotation in the National Corpus of Polish (`http://nkjp.pl/`; NKJP; Przepiórkowski et al. 2010), two are immediately relevant here: morphosyntax (roughly, parts of speech and values of grammatical categories such as case or gender) and shallow syntactic groups. A 1-million-word subcorpus of NKJP was semi-automatically annotated at these levels: first relevant tools (morphological analyser, shallow grammar) were used to automatically add mark-up and then human annotators carefully (2 annotators per sentence plus a referee) selected the right interpretation, often correcting the automatic outcome.

In a related project (Woliński et al. 2011), the morphosyntactic level was used as a basis for constructing the level of deep syntax. Again, sentences were run through a deep parser and human annotators carefully selected the right parse.

The two syntactic annotation layers, illustrated in Figure 1, are described in more detail below.

3.1 Shallow Syntax

By shallow syntactic annotation we understand here a little more than chunking (Abney 1991): various types of basic groups are found (nominal, prepositional, adverbial, sentential), each marked with a syntactic head and a semantic head, and some hierarchical structure is allowed to the extent that sentential groups may contain smaller groups (including sentential ones). On the other hand, the general chunking principle of not resolving attachment ambiguities is preserved, so, e.g., instead of the nested structure $[\text{P}\ [\text{NP}\ [\text{P NP}]_{\text{PP}}]_{\text{NP}}]_{\text{PP}}$ for *w kolejce do kasy* in the right-hand tree in Fig. 1, two smaller $[\text{P N}]_{\text{PP}}$ constituents are marked at the shallow level (cf. the tree on the left).[2]

3.2 Deep Syntax

Complete constituent trees are assigned to sentences at the deep syntactic level. Labels of pre-terminals reflect parts of speech (e.g., *przyimek* 'preposition' or *formarzecz* 'nominal form'), higher non-terminal labels mostly correspond to standard labels such as PP (*fpm*), NP (*fno*), VP (*fwe*, understood here rather as a verbal group) or S (*zdanie*), with an additional level containing information about argument (*fw*) or non-argument (*fl*) status of phrases. No further dependency-like information is provided, i.e., there is no special marking of subjects, direct objects, etc.

4 Comparing Annotation Levels

Let us first note that all measures mentioned above are symmetrical in the sense that the evaluation of tree T_1 against tree T_2 gives the same results – perhaps after swapping precision and recall – as the evaluation of T_2 against T_1. In the current scenario, the two annotation schemata are rather different, with the shallow level containing – by design – fewer and smaller constituents. Hence, two different measures of precision are needed for the two levels (each measure having the dual role of measuring recall of the other level).

Second, since both annotation schemata assume the existence of syntactic heads for all constituents (see the thick lines in Fig. 1), and – together with dependency grammarians, practitioners of HPSG (Pollard and Sag 1994), etc. – we take headedness to be a crucial property of constituents, the proposed measures will build on this notion.

Let us first start with the types of shallow groups that cannot be nested, i.e., nominal, prepositional, etc., but not sentential. We define shallow precision, P_s, as the percentage of those segments contained in such groups which are annotated consistently with deep syntax:

$$P_s = \frac{|\{w : \exists G\ w \in \mathit{yield}(G) \wedge c(w, G)\}|}{|\{w : \exists G\ w \in \mathit{yield}(G)\}|}, \quad (1)$$

where w ranges over words, G ranges over (non-sentential) groups, and $c(w, G)$ is the compatibility predicate, which is true if and only if the annotation

[2]Note that non-terminal labels used in the figure differ from the ones used in text, and that in particular the deep tree uses Polish mnemonic names such as *fno* (*fraza nominalna*, nominal phrase). We hope that – given explanations in text – this does not lead to much confusion.

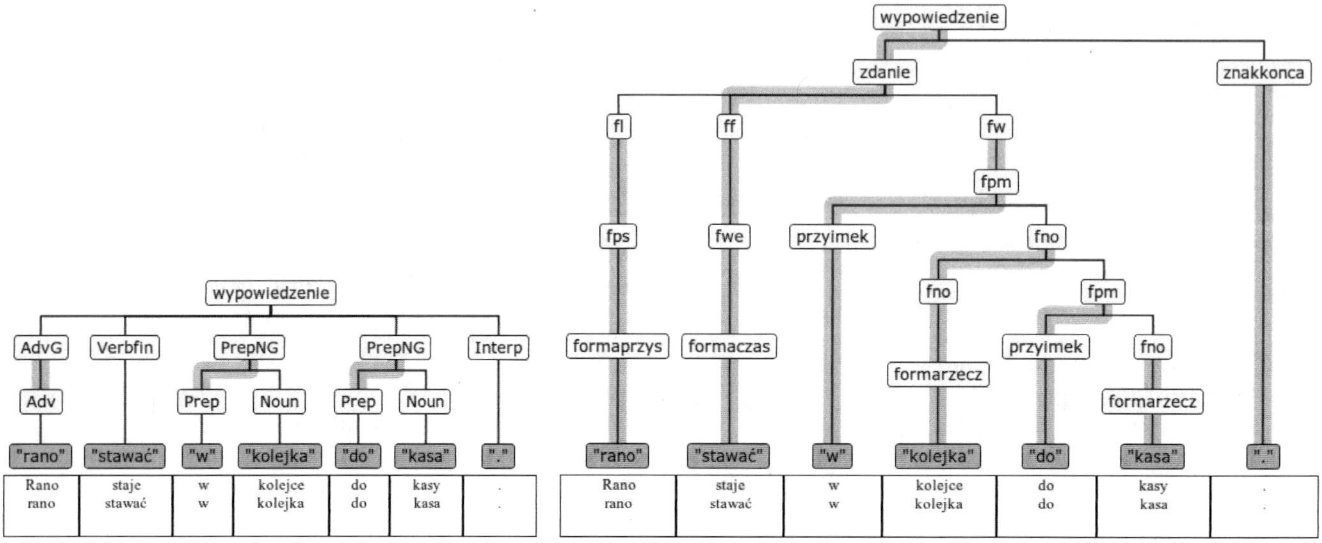

Figure 1: An example of shallow (on the left) and deep (on the right) syntactic annotation of *Rano staje w kolejce do kasy.* 'In the morning, (s)he queues to the cash desk.', lit. 'morning stands in queue to cash-desk'. In the shallow annotation, an artificial root (*wypowiedzenie* 'utterance') is added to connect all words and groups.

of w is compatible across the two levels. More precisely, $c(w, G)$ is true iff there exists a phrase F at the deep annotation of the same sentence such that $w \in yield(F)$, and also G and F have the same lexical heads. These conditions imply that w has the same headedness status with respect to G and F, i.e., it is either the head of both or of neither.

A labelled version of P_s, marked as lP_s, additionally requires that labels of G and F are compatible, in the sense of a manually defined mapping that relates – to give examples based on Fig. 1 – *PrepNG* to *fpm*, *AdvG* to *fps*, etc.

Applying this measure to Fig. 1 we note that there are 5 words belonging to some shallow group (*Rano*, *w*, *kolejce*, *do*, *kasy*). All these words, together with their respective groups, satisfy $c(w, G)$ and the condition on labels, so both P_s and lP_s are 1.0. For example, for w = *kolejce*, G is the *PrepNG* yielding *w kolejce*, whose head is the preposition *w*. Consequently, F is the *fpm* yielding *w kolejce do kasy*.

Deep precision, P_d, is defined in a similar way, but we are only interested in words w which are *more or less directly* contained in a phrase of a type corresponding to the types of groups considered here (i.e., nominal, prepositional, etc.). We say that w is *more or less directly* contained in F iff the path from w to F does not contain any sentential labels.[3] For every such word w we require that for one of its *more or less directly* dominating phrases, F, there is a corresponding shallow group G with the same head as F and also containing w; in case of labelled deep precision, lP_d, the labels of F and G should also match. For the deep annotation in Fig. 1, both unlabelled and labelled precision is again 1.0. This means that the two trees in this figure match perfectly, given the differing annotation schemata.

Recall that above measures do not take into account sentential constituents. This is due to the fact that finding clauses is not typically part of shallow parsing, and also in the current setup it is limited to complementiser clauses (*CG*) and embedded questions (*KG*). Although, given these constraints, it is not clear how to measure recall in this task, we can measure precision by checking that for each constituent *CG* and *KG* there is a corresponding sentential node at deep syntax. However, aware of the criticisms directed at Parseval, we do not want to excessively punish annotations for having slightly different spans of clauses, so we define the proximity of a clause in shallow syntax to a sentential constituent

[3]The reason for this requirement is that we cannot expect shallow nominal, prepositional, etc., groups to contain sentential clauses.

in the deep syntax as the F-measure over the words they contain.[4] The final clausal precision of the shallow level is defined as the mean over all clauses.

5 Experiments and Evaluation

The measures defined above were applied to a 7600-sentence subcorpus annotated at both syntactic levels. For the whole corpus, the mean (micro-average) unlabelled precisions were: $P_s = 98.7\%$ and $P_d = 93.4\%$. This shows that, while the two levels of annotation are largely compatible, there are differences in the extents of some constituents. Also, the fact that $P_d < P_s$ shows that it is more common for the shallow level to miss (parts of) deep-level constituents, than the other way round.

We manually examined 50 sentences containing words on which the two annotations do not agree according to the unlabelled measures; there were 104 such word-level disagreements.

Discrepancies discovered this way may be divided into those 1. resulting from the insufficient subtlety of the measure, 2. reflecting controversial design decisions at the shallow level, 3. showing real differences, i.e., possible errors.

The biggest subset of class 1. results from the fact that not only syntactic groups are marked at the shallow level, but also some multi-token syntactic words, e.g., some adverbial groups resembling prepositional constructions. If such a syntactic word is the head of a group, a mismatch with the corresponding deep phrase is over-zealously reported. Around 35% of all differences belong to this group. Additionally, 16% of mismatches reflect differences in the treatment of adjectival participles. Hence, over 50% of reported differencies can be avoided by making the measures sensitive to such special cases.

Another 15% of differences, belonging to class 2., are caused by the controversial design decision to split larger coordinate structures at the shallow level into separate constituents, with only the final two conjuncts forming a coordinated group.

Finally, the remaining 1/3 of mismatches reflect real differences, often corresponding to errors at one of the levels. The most interesting subclass of these are discontinuities, currently handled only at the shallow level, e.g., cases of sentential conjunctions incorporated into NPs or discontinuous numeral phrases. Other differences include: some particles analysed as parts of NPs at one level, but not at the other, some adverbs or participles not analysed as adverbial groups at the shallow level, incorrect analysis of the highly ambiguous *to* as a noun (instead of a particle) at the deep level, etc.

Labelled measures have significantly lower values than the the unlabelled equivalents: $lP_s = 95.1\%$ and $lP_d = 91.1\%$. This is somewhat surprising, as at both levels constituents are marked for their lexical heads and it would seem that the morphosyntactic properties of the head should determine the label of the constituent. It turns out that the two main reasons for label mismatches are different approaches to some relative pronouns, and to some apparently prepositional constructions (analysed as adverbial at the shallow level).

Let us also note that the overall clausal precision of the shallow level is 0.996. Out of 691 sentences containing *CG* and *KG* groups, 670 match the deep level perfectly. In the remaining sentences, the usual problem is that *CG* or *KG* extends too far to the right (in 1 case it is too short), although in some cases it is the deep phrase that is too long or that is wrongly analysed, and in other cases two different spans reflect a genuine semantic ambiguity in the sentence.

6 Conclusion

It is not always easy to ascertain whether a mismatch between two syntactic annotation levels is a real error, but – on the basis of the manual examination of 50 sentences containing such mismatches – we estimate that between 12 and 15 of them contained errors at one or the other level. Since in the whole corpus 1882 non-matching (in the strong sense of unlabelled precision measures) sentences were found, this gives us the estimate of between 450 and 565 sentences containing real errors, thus complementing other methods currently used for Polish, which are estimated to find around 185 mismorfmed trees at the deep syntax level. Once these measures are made more subtle along the lines proposed above, the precision of such error reports should increase twofold from the current 20–30%, making human inspection of these reports worthwhile.

[4] Obviously, for any shallow-level clause we select a deep-level sentential constituent that maximises this F-measure.

References

Steven Abney. Parsing by chunks. In Robert Berwick, Steve Abney, and Carol Tenny, editors, *Principle-Based Parsing*, pages 257–278. Kluwer, 1991.

Ezra Black, Steve Abney, Dan Flickinger, Claudia Gdaniec, Ralph Grishman, Phil Harrison, Don Hindle, Robert Ingria, Frederick Jelinek, Judith L. Klavans, Mark Liberman, Mitchell P. Marcus, Salim Roukos, Beatrice Santorini, and Tomek Strzałkowski. A procedure for quantitatively comparing the syntactic coverage of English grammars. In *Proceedings of the DARPA Speech and Natural Language Workshop*, pages 306–311, Pacific Grove, 1991.

Adriane Boyd, Markus Dickinson, and Detmar Meurers. On detecting errors in dependency treebanks. *Research on Language and Computation*, 6(2):113–137, 2008. URL `http://jones.ling.indiana.edu/~mdickinson/papers/boyd-et-al-08.html`.

Ted Briscoe and John Carroll. A probabilistic LR parser of part-of-speech and punctuation labels. In Jenny Thomas and Mick Short, editors, *Using Corpora for Language Research, London*, pages 135–150. Longman, London, 1996.

Markus Dickinson and Chong Min Lee. Detecting errors in semantic annotation. In LREC. URL `{http://jones.ling.indiana.edu/~mdickinson/papers/dickinson-lee08.html}`.

Markus Dickinson and W. Detmar Meurers. Detecting errors in part-of-speech annotation. In *Proceedings of the 10th Conference of the European Chapter of the Association for Computational Linguistics (EACL 2003)*, pages 107–114, Budapest, 2003a.

Markus Dickinson and W. Detmar Meurers. Detecting inconsistencies in treebanks. In Joakim Nivre and Erhard Hinrichs, editors, *Proceedings of the Second Workshop on Treebanks and Linguistic Theories (TLT 2003)*, pages 45–56, Växjö, Norway, 2003b. URL `http://jones.ling.indiana.edu/~mdickinson/papers/dickinson-meurers-tlt03.html`.

LREC. *Proceedings of the Sixth International Conference on Language Resources and Evaluation, LREC 2008*, Marrakech, 2008. ELRA.

Eleazar Eskin. Automatic corpus correction with anomaly detection. In *Proceedings of the 1st Meeting of the North American Chapter of the Association for Computational Linguistics (NAACL 2000)*, pages 148–153, Seattle, WA, 2000.

Yoshihide Kato and Shigeki Matsubara. Correcting errors in a treebank based on synchronous tree substitution grammar. In *Proceedings of the ACL 2010 Conference Short Papers*, pages 74–79, Stroudsburg, PA, 2010. URL `http://dl.acm.org/citation.cfm?id=1858842.1858856`.

Sandra Kübler, Wolfgang Maier, Ines Rehbein, and Yannick Versley. How to compare treebanks. In LREC.

David M. Magerman. Statistical decision-tree models for parsing. In *Proceedings of the 33rd Annual Meeting of the Association for Computational Linguistics*, pages 276–283, Cambridge, MA, 1995. doi: 10.3115/981658.981695. URL `http://www.aclweb.org/anthology/P95-1037`.

Carl Pollard and Ivan A. Sag. *Head-driven Phrase Structure Grammar*. Chicago University Press / CSLI Publications, Chicago, IL, 1994.

Adam Przepiórkowski, Rafał L. Górski, Marek Łaziński, and Piotr Pęzik. Recent developments in the National Corpus of Polish. In *Proceedings of the Seventh International Conference on Language Resources and Evaluation, LREC 2010*, Valletta, Malta, 2010. ELRA.

Lance A. Ramshaw and Mitchell P. Marcus. Text chunking using transformation-based learning. In *Proceedings of the Third Workshop on Very Large Corpora*, pages 82–94, Cambridge, MA, 1995. ACL.

Ines Rehbein and Josef van Genabith. Treebank annotation schemes and parser evaluation for German. In *Proceedings of the 2007 Joint Conference on Empirical Methods in Natural Language Processing and Computational Natural Language Learning (EMNLP-CoNLL)*, pages 630–639, 2007. URL `http://www.aclweb.org/anthology/D/D07/D07-1066`.

Geoffrey Sampson. A proposal for improving

the measurement of parse accuracy. *International Journal of Corpus Linguistics*, 5:53–68, 2000. URL http://www.grsampson.net/APfi.html.

Geoffrey Sampson and Anna Babarczy. A test of the leaf-ancestor metric for parse accuracy. *Natural Language Engineering*, 9:365–380, 2003. URL http://www.grsampson.net/ATot.html.

Geoffrey Sampson, Robin Haigh, and Eric S. Atwell. Natural language analysis by stochastic optimization: a progress report on Project APRIL. *Journal of Experimental and Theoretical Artificial Intelligence*, 1:271–287, 1989.

Erik F. Tjong Kim Sang and Jorn Veenstra. Representing text chunks. In *Proceedings of the 9th Conference of the European Chapter of the Association for Computational Linguistics (EACL 1999)*, pages 173–179, Bergen, 1999.

Hans van Halteren. The detection of inconsistency in manually tagged text. In *Proceedings of the 2nd Workshop on Linguistically Interpreted Corpora (LINC 2000)*, 2000.

Marcin Woliński, Katarzyna Głowińska, and Marek Świdziński. A preliminary version of Składnica—a treebank of Polish. In Zygmunt Vetulani, editor, *Proceedings of the 5th Language & Technology Conference: Human Language Technologies as a Challenge for Computer Science and Linguistics*, pages 299–303, Poznań, Poland, 2011.

Exploring Temporal Vagueness with Mechanical Turk

Yuping Zhou
Computer Science Department
Brandeis University
Waltham, MA 02452
yzhou@brandeis.edu

Nianwen Xue
Computer Science Department
Brandeis University
Waltham, MA 02452
xuen@brandeis.edu

Abstract

This paper proposes schematic changes to the TempEval framework that target the temporal vagueness problem. Specifically, two elements of vagueness are singled out for special treatment: vague time expressions, and explicit/implicit temporal modification of events. As proof of concept, an annotation experiment on explicit/implicit modification is conducted on Amazon's Mechanical Turk. Results show that the quality of a considerable segment of the annotation is comparable to annotation obtained in the traditional double-blind setting, only with higher coverage. This approach offers additional flexibility in how the temporal annotation data can be used.

1 Introduction

Event-based temporal inference aims at determining temporal anchoring and relative ordering of events in text. It is a fundamental natural language technology that supports a wide range of natural language applications, such as Information Extraction (Ji, 2010), Question Answering (Harabagiu and Bejan, 2005; Harabagiu and Bejan, 2006) and Text Summarization (Lin and Hovy, 2001; Barzilay et al., 2002). Crucial to developing this technology is consistently annotated, domain-independent data sufficient to train automatic systems, but this has proven to be challenging.

The difficulty has mainly been attributed to rampant temporal vagueness in natural language, affecting all high-level annotation tasks (Verhagen et al., 2009). Focusing on one of the tasks, Zhou and Xue (2011) show that by pairing up discourse-related events and by making the classification scheme paying more attention to vagueness in natural language, inter-annotator agreement increases from 65% to the low 80%. Despite the significant improvement, problems identified by Zhou and Xue (2011) towards the end of their paper suggest that how temporal modification is handled in the TempEval annotation scheme needs to be revised to further keep vagueness in line. This paper is an attempt in that direction.

The rest of the paper is organized as follows: In Section 2, we first offer arguments for changing the way temporal modification is handled in temporal annotation, then lay out an outline for the change and motivate the experiment being carried out on Amazon's Mechanical Turk. We then describe the design of the experiment in detail in Section 3, and present experiment results in Section 4. And finally in Section 5, we conclude the paper.

2 Motivation

2.1 Treatment of temporal modification in the TempEval framework

In the TempEval framework (Verhagen et al., 2009; Verhagen et al., 2010), the part of temporal modification to be annotated is time expressions, i.e. those bearing the <TIMEX3> tag following the definition in the TimeML (Pustejovsky et al., 2003). Simply put, they are elements that express time, date, duration etc., for example, *7 o'clock*, *June 19, 2008*, and *ten years*. In this framework, time expressions in text are identified and subjected to the following kinds of annotation:

- their type is classified: {*time, date, duration, set*};
- their value is specified in a normalized form (e.g. "2008/6/19" for *June 19, 2008*);
- their temporal relation to some selected events is classified: {*before, overlap, after, before-or-overlap, overlap-or-after, vague*}.

2.2 Problems concerning "temporal vagueness"

2.2.1 Do all time expressions fit into the same mold?

In the current scheme, all time expressions have a VALUE attribute and the TimeML specifies how to standardize it (Pustejovsky et al., 2003). However, a subgroup of time expressions are noticeably ignored by the specifications: those whose value is hard to pinpoint, for example, *now*, *soon*, *several years* etc. These vague expressions constitute a large part of the vagueness problem in temporal annotation. Although their values are hard to pinpoint, they are an important part of temporal specification in natural language, and can provide information useful in temporal inference if they are adequately characterized in a way communicable with those having a definite value.

2.2.2 Should time expressions participate in temporal relation with events?

How useful a temporal relation classification is between an event and a time expression in certain types of temporal modifier is highly questionable. Let us take *from June 6 to August 14* as an example. According to the TimeML, there are two time expressions in this phrase: *June 6* and *August 14*, but suppose it is used to specify the temporal location of an event *e1* in a sentence, to specify that *e1* OVERLAPs *June 6* and that *e1* OVERLAPs *August 14* does not capture the exact relation between *from June 6 to August 14* and *e1*.[1] In other words, temporal vagueness is artificially introduced into annotation by the scheme when the text itself is perfectly clear in this respect. Other types of temporal modifiers that share this problem include *since [1990]*, *[three years] ago*, *until [now]* etc. (square brackets delimit time expressions).

2.2.3 How to choose time$\sim$event pairs for annotation?

How to find annotation targets for different types of temporal relation has been a long-standing problem in temporal annotation, and the normal solution is to annotate all pairs that satisfy some technical constraints specified in syntactic, semantic and/or discourse terms (Verhagen et al., 2009; Xue and Zhou, 2010; Zhou and Xue, 2011). In the case of temporal relation between time and event, Xue and Zhou (2010) proposed to let annotators judge which event(s) a given time expression is intended to modify. There are at least three problems with this proposal as it stood.

First, as alluded to in Section 2.2.2, time expressions usually do not modify predicates by themselves, unless they can stand alone as a temporal modifier (e.g. *now*, *tomorrow*, *this week*). To use the temporal modifier *from June 6 to August 14* as an example again, neither *June 6* nor *August 14*, but the whole prepositional phrase, has an intended modification target.

Second, the modification relation is construed in terms of syntactic scope, hence the range of choice is restricted to the same sentence. This is of course understandable: Given the double-blind setup and inherently greater uncertainty associated with modification relation across sentence boundaries, it makes sense to minimize uncertainty for higher agreement. On the other hand though, this restriction can potentially result in significant information loss since a temporal expression can have (semantic/discourse) scope over several sentences or even paragraphs. So who should decide precision or recall should take precedence? And at what point?

The third problem is the directionality of it: to find events given a time or the other way around? This may seem a trivial point–and it is with the "same sentence" restriction in place–but operationally it makes quite a difference if the restriction is abandoned. Suppose we are to find all time$\sim$event pairs in an article containing 10 temporal modifiers and 60 events. In a simplified version, to find events

[1]It is possible to capture this temporal relation with the full-blown TimeML apparatus, however, there is a reason why the TempEval framework is a simplified version of the TimeML (Verhagen et al., 2009).

given a temporal modifier amounts to 10 searches to find an uncertain number of hits out of 60 candidates, whereas to find the temporal modifier for a given event amounts to 60 searches to find 1 hit out of 10 candidates. Clearly the latter way presents an easier individual task than the former, but presents it more times, so the overall quality of the results is probably better. Furthermore, if we consider the problem in a more realistic scenario where temporal modification only happens to events in the same sentence and below, to find the temporal modifier of a given event can be done in the (relatively) normal flow of one careful reading because the candidates for selection are already in the familiar territory. To find events being modified by a given temporal modifier means doing the search and paying attention to new material at the same time, which can be highly distracting.

2.3 Outline of a solution

Two levels should be distinguished in annotation with respect to temporal modification: The first level is time expressions (as defined in the TimeML) and the second is temporal modifiers, the predicate-modifying units, usually (but not always) time expressions along with prepositions/postpositions associated with them.

These two levels are obviously related, but play different roles in temporal annotation. Time expressions should be divided into two subgroups: *definite* and *indefinite*, each associated with a different value-characterizing scheme. Annotation of time expressions serves as a building block to interpretation of temporal modifiers, and temporal modifiers are linked directly to events that they modify, explicitly or implicitly. In other words, it is temporal modifiers, not time expressions, that have a relation with events; furthermore, it is a modification relation that should be identified according to speakers' interpretation of the text.

Two parts of this solution are challenging, if not impossible, for the traditional double-blind annotation: characterization of indefinite time expressions, and linking events with modifying temporal expressions without distance restrictions. Both would involve a healthy amount of variability and would rely on a distribution for usable data. This leads us to Amazon's Mechanical Turk (MT). In this paper, we only describe the experiment that deals with linking temporal modifiers with events.

3 HIT design

We make use of data from two sources. The first source is Chinese annotation data prepared for the TempEval-2 campaign (Verhagen et al., 2010), from which we use the time expressions and verbal events. The second source is the Chinese TreeBank (CTB) (Xue et al., 2005), in which temporal-related nodes (close to our notion of "temporal modifier") are suffixed with the "-TMP" function tag, so we use it to expand time expressions (taken directly from TempEval-2 data) into temporal modifiers as follows: Without passing an S node, find the nearest ancestor of the time expression that bears the "-TMP" suffix and then use all the terminal nodes within as the corresponding temporal modifier.

Verbal events (taken directly from TempEval-2 data) are split into groups so that each HIT deals with fewer than 20 events. A non-event is chosen randomly as a decoy to help weed out irresponsible Tukers. In each HIT, the article is presented in the one-sentence-per-line format, with temporal expressions underlined and events in boldface (see Figure 1 for a screenshot). Next to each event is a drop-down list, presenting three types of choice:

1. <temporal modifiers in quotes>
2. *not in the list*
3. *not the main element of a predicate*

The *not the main element of a predicate* option is for the decoys and the *not in the list* option is for atemporal events, events that do not have a temporal modifier, or events that have a temporal modifier outside the given list. Temporal expressions appearing in the text up to the event anchor are presented in quotation marks in the reverse order of their occurrence, with the newer instance of the same lexical item replacing the old one as it emerges. In Figure 1, each type of choice has a representative.

4 Results

The distribution of all annotations and those representing a time∼event link with respect to the majority MT-internal agreement is shown in Table 1.

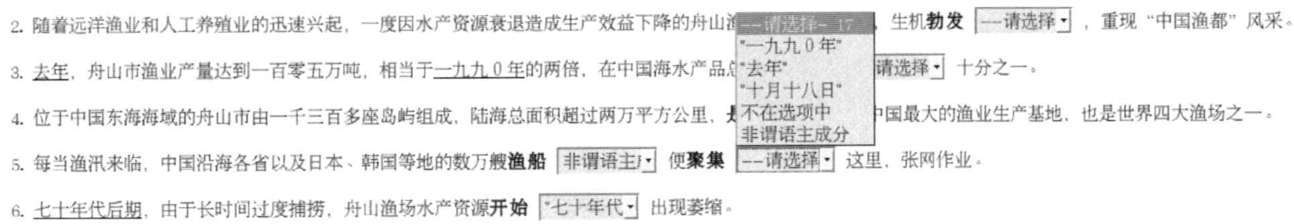

Figure 1: Part of a HIT from the experiment

Range	No. tkn (percent)	Links	
		Total (percent)	No. intraS
0.2-0.5	153(6.3)	83(3.4)	17
0.5-0.6	449(18.6)	244(10.1)	57
0.6-0.7	245(10.1)	143(5.9)	59
0.7-0.8	138(5.7)	84(3.5)	57
0.8-0.9	353(14.6)	235(9.7)	158
0.9-1.0	1082(44.7)	922(38.1)	864
Total:	2420(100)	1711(70.7)	1212

Table 1: Distribution of all annotations and time∼event links. *No. intraS*: number of intra-sentential links.

65% of all tokens fall within the 0.7-1 MT-internal agreement range, 70.7% of all majority annotations produce a link between a temporal modifier and an event, and 72.5% of links created have an MT-internal agreement of 0.7 or higher. Intra-sentential links are very concentrated in the top MT-internal agreement range, and their concentration for the most part correlates with both the MT-internal agreement and agreement with expert annotation, as shown in Table 2 below. Also, the decline of agreement with expert annotation by and large keeps pace with the MT-internal agreement. These trends are consistent with what one expects from annotation of this sort and the assumption that the uncertainty level increases as annotation goes across sentence boundaries.

Within the high-agreement range, the quality of the MT annotation is comparable to that produced in a double-blind setting with trained annotators (Xue and Zhou, 2010), as shown in Table 3. With comparable levels of agreement, the MT annotation has a coverage 11-15 percentage points greater than the previously reported double-blind annotation of the same data, presumably because the "same sentence"

Range	***Agreement*** (%)	***Concentration intraS*** (%)
0.2≤ A <0.5	48.2	20.5
0.5≤ A <0.6	59.5	23.4
0.6≤ A <0.7	71.7	41.3
0.7≤ A <0.8	74.9	67.9
0.8≤ A <0.9	83.2	67.2
0.9≤ A ≤1.0	91.5	93.7
Total:	78.0	70.8

Table 2: Agreement with expert annotation

restriction is lifted. It should be noted that the maximum value of coverage is not 100% (i.e. not all events have a temporal modifier), and with the problem of vagueness, is probably unknowable.

MT annotation			***Double-blind***	
Range	*Agr*	*Coverage*	*Agr*	*Coverage*
≥0.8	88.6	47.8%	86	36.4%*
≥0.7	86.1	51.3%		

Table 3: Comparison with double-blind annotation of the same data. *Coverage*: no. of events in a link/total no. of events; *: this number is directly based on the TempEval-2 Chinese data.

With this distribution of data, the MT annotation offers greater flexibility in using the annotation: Depending on demands on different levels of data reliability, one can take a section of the data by choosing different cutoffs. So this choice is left to the user of the annotation data, not the creator.

5 Conclusions

Three takeaways: i) To tackle the vagueness problem, elements of vagueness need to be identified and treated with care; ii) vagueness can be characterized with a distribution of different annotations and MT makes it feasible; iii) this approach, when implemented successfully, not only provides high-quality data, but also offers additional flexibility in data use with respect to information quantity vs. certainty.

Acknowledgments

This work is supported by the National Science Foundation via Grant No. 0855184 entitled "Building a community resource for temporal inference in Chinese". All views expressed in this paper are those of the authors and do not necessarily represent the view of the National Science Foundation.

References

Regina Barzilay, Noemie Elhadad, and Kathleen McKeown. 2002. Inferring strategies for sentence ordering in multidocument news summarization. *Journal of Artificial Intelligence Research*, 17:35–55.

Sanda Harabagiu and Cosmin Adrian Bejan. 2005. Question Answering Based on Temporal Inference. In *Proceedings of the AAAI-2005 Workshop on Inference for Textual Question Answering*, Pittsburgh, Pennsylvania.

Sanda Harabagiu and Cosmin Adrian Bejan. 2006. An Answer Bank for Temporal Inference. In *Proceedings of LREC 2006*, Genoa, Italy.

Heng Ji. 2010. Challenges from information extraction to information fusion. In *Proceedings of COLING 2010*, pages 507–515, Beijing, China, August.

Chin-Yew Lin and Eduard Hovy. 2001. Neats: A multidocument summarizer. In *Proceedings of the Document Understanding Workshop*.

James Pustejovsky, Jose Castano, Roser Sauri, Robert Gaizauskas, Andrea Setzer, and Graham Katz. 2003. Timeml: Robust specification of event and temporal expressions in text. In *Proceedings of the 5th International Workshop on Computational Semantics (IWCS-5)*, Tilburg, July.

Marc Verhagen, Robert Gaizauskas, Frank Schilder, Mark Hepple, Jessica Moszkowicz, and James Pustejovsky. 2009. The TempEval Challenge: Identifying Temporal Relation in Text. *Language Resources and Evaluation*, 43(1):161–179.

Marc Verhagen, Roser Sauri, Tommaso Caselli, and James Pustejovsky. 2010. Semeval-2010 task 13: Tempeval-2. In *Proceedings of the 5th International Workshop on Semantic Evaluation*, pages 57–62, Uppsala, Sweden, July. Association for Computational Linguistics.

Nianwen Xue and Yuping Zhou. 2010. Applying Syntactic, Semantic and Discourse Constraints to Chinese Temporal Annotation. In *Proceedings of COLING 2010*, pages 1363–1372, Beijing, China, August.

Nianwen Xue, Fei Xia, Fu dong Chiou, and Martha Palmer. 2005. The Penn Chinese TreeBank: Phrase Structure Annotation of a Large Corpus. *Natural Language Engineering*, 11(2):207–238.

Yuping Zhou and Nianwen Xue. 2011. Discourse-constrained temporal annotation. In *Linguistic Annotation Workshop 2011*, pages 161–169.

Developing Learner Corpus Annotation for Korean Particle Errors

Sun-Hee Lee
Wellesley College
slee6@wellesley.edu

Markus Dickinson
Indiana University
md7@indiana.edu

Ross Israel
Indiana University
raisrael@indiana.edu

Abstract

We aim to sufficiently define annotation for post-positional particle errors in L2 Korean writing, so that future work on automatic particle error detection can make progress. To achieve this goal, we outline the linguistic properties of Korean particles in learner data. Given the agglutinative nature of Korean and the range of functions of particles, this annotation effort involves issues such as defining the tokens and target forms.

1 Introduction and Motivation

One area of analyzing second language learner data is that of detecting errors in function words, e.g. prepositions, articles, and particles (e.g., Tetreault and Chodorow, 2008; De Felice and Pulman, 2008; de Ilarraza et al., 2008; Dickinson et al., 2011; Tetreault et al., 2010; Han et al., 2006), as these tend to be problematic for learners. This work has developed much, but it has mostly been for English. We thus aim to further the development of methods for detecting errors in functional elements across languages, by developing annotation for post-positional particles in Korean, a significant source of error for learners (Ko et al., 2004; Lee et al., 2009) and an area of interest for computer-assisted language learning (CALL) (Dickinson et al., 2008). As there is at present very little work on annotated learner corpora for morphologically-rich languages, this represents a significant step forward.

There have been some efforts for annotating particle errors in Korean, but they have not directly linked to automatic error detection. The corpus in Lee et al. (2009) is made up of college student essays; is divided according to student level (beginner, intermediate) and student background (heritage, non-heritage);[1] and is hand-annotated for particle errors. This corpus, however, does not contain gold standard segmentation, requiring users to semi-automatically determine particle boundaries. In addition to segmentation, to make particle error detection a widespread task where real systems are developed, we need to outline the scope of particle errors (e.g., error types, influence of other errors) and incorporate insights into an annotation scheme.

Selecting the correct particle in Korean is complicated by many factors. First, particles combine with preceding words in written Korean, as opposed to being set apart by white space, as in English. Thus, segmentation plays an integrated role. Secondly, selecting a particle for annotation is not a simple question, as they are sometimes optional, influenced by surrounding errors, and can be interchangeable. Thirdly, Korean particles have a wide range of functions, including modification and case-marking. Annotation, and by extension the task of particle error detection, must account for these issues.

We focus on the utility of annotation in evaluating particle error detection systems, ensuring that it can support the automatic task of predicting the correct particle (or no particle) in a given context. Given that other languages, such as Japanese and Arabic, face some of the same issues (e.g., Hanaoka et al., 2010; Abuhakema et al., 2008), fleshing them out for error annotation and detection is useful beyond this one situation and help in the overall process of "developing best practices for annotation and evalu-

[1] Heritage learners have had exposure to Korean at a young age, such as growing up with Korean spoken at home.

ation" of learner data (Tetreault et al., 2010).

2 Korean particles

Korean postpositional particles are morphemes[2] that appear after a nominal to indicate a range of linguistic functions, including grammatical functions, e.g., subject and object; semantic roles; and discourse functions. In (1), for instance, *ka* marks the subject (function) and agent (semantic role).

(1) Sumi-**ka** John-**uy** cip-**eyse** ku-**lul** twu
Sumi-SBJ John-GEN house-LOC he-OBJ two
sikan-**ul** kitaly-ess-ta.
hours-OBJ wait-PAST-END
'Sumi waited for John for (the whole) two hours in his house.'

Similar to English prepositions, particles can have modifier functions, adding meanings of time, location, instrument, possession, etc., also as in (1). Note here that *ul/lul* has multiple uses.[3]

Particles are one of the most frequent error types for Korean language learners (Ko et al., 2004).

3 Defining particle error annotation

3.1 Defining the tokens

Korean is agglutinative: words are generally formed by attaching suffixes to a stem. Particles are written without spaces, making token definitions non-trivial. In the next three sections, we discuss a three-layered annotation, where the output of one layer is used as the input for the next.

Spacing errors Given the differences in word formation and spacing conventions (e.g., compounds are often written without spaces), spacing errors are common for learners of Korean (Lee et al., 2009). As particles are word-final entities, correcting spacing errors is necessary to define where a particle can be predicted. This is similar to predicting a preposition between two words when those words have been merged. Consider (2). To see where the particle *-lul* is to be inserted, as in (2b), the original merged form in (2a) must be split.[4]

(2) a. O: yey-tul-myen
example-take-if
'if (we) take an example'

b. C: yey-lul tul-myen
example-OBJ take-if

We also correct words which have incorrectly been split, often arising when learners treat particles as separate entities. Additionally, we perform standard tokenization on this layer, such as splitting words separated by hyphens or slashes, making the tokens compatible with POS taggers.

Spelling errors Following the idea that a full system will handle spacing, punctuation, or spelling errors (e.g., Tetreault and Chodorow, 2008), we correct spelling errors, in a second tier of annotation. As with spacing errors, when spelling errors are not corrected, the correct particle cannot always be defined. Correct particles rely on correct segmentation (section 3.1), which misspellings can mask. In (3), for instance, *ki* makes it hard to determine the boundary between the stem and suffix.

(3) a. O: kalpi mas**ki**lonun
rib ???

b. C: kalpi mas-ulo-nun
rib taste-AUX-TOP
'as for rib taste'

Segmentation To know whether a particle should be used, we have to define the *position* where it could be, leading to the correct segmentation of particle-bearing words (i.e., nominals). This annotation layer builds upon the previous two: we segment corrected forms since we cannot reliably segment learner forms (cf. (3)). With segmentation, one can propose evaluating: 1) against the full correct form, or 2) against the correct particle. Note also that the important segmentation is of nominals, as we are interested in particle error detection.

3.2 Defining the target form(s)

We annotate three different categories of errors from Lee et al. (2009)—omission, replacement and addition—and one new category of errors, ordering. What we need is clarity on assigning the correct particle, i.e., the *target form*.

[2]The exact linguistic status of particles—e.g., as affixes or clitics—is a matter of some debate (see, e.g., Yoon, 2005), but is not crucial for our annotation.

[3]*Ul/lul*, *un/nun*, etc. differ phonologically.

[4]We use *O* to refer to a original form and *C* to its correction.

Defining grammaticality We follow the principle of "minimal interaction," (e.g., Hana et al., 2010): the corrected text does not have to be perfect; it is enough to be grammatical (at least for particles). One complication for defining the target particle is that particles can be dropped in spoken and even written Korean. As we focus on beginning learners who, by and large, are required to use particles, the corrected forms we annotate are obligatory within a very specific definition of *grammaticality*: they are particles which beginning learners are taught to use. Our decision captures the minimum needed for particle prediction systems and is consistent with the fact that particles are usually not dropped in formal Korean (Lee and Song, 2011).

Determining the correct particle As with English prepositions and articles, there are situations where more than one particle could be correct. In these cases, we list all reasonable alternates, allowing for a system to evaluate against a set of correct particles. There are no clear criteria for selecting one best particle out of multiple candidates, and we find low interannotator agreement in a pilot experiment, whereas we do find high agreement for a set of particles (section 4.2).

The influence of surrounding errors While many learner errors do not affect particle errors, some are relevant. For example, in (4), the verb (*uycihanta*, 'lean on') is wrong, because it requires an animate object and *sihem* ('exam') is inanimate. If we correct the verb to *tallyeissta* ('depend'), as in (4b), the correct particle is *ey*. If we do not correct the verb, the learner's particle is, in a syntactic sense, appropriate for the verb, even if the verb's selectional restrictions are not followed.

(4) a. O: nay insayng-i i sihem-**ul** <u>uycihanta</u>
my life-SBJ this exam-**OBJ** lean-on

b. C: nay insayng-i i sihem-**ey** <u>tallyeissta</u>
my life-SBJ this exam-**ON** depend

'My life depends on this exam'

It is important to clearly designate *at what point* in the process the particle is correct. Our current annotation does not deal with word choice and related semantic issues, and we thus annotate the particle at the point before any such errors are corrected. In (4), we do not correct it to (4b). Previous work has corrected sets of errors (Rozovskaya and Roth, 2010), eliminated sentences with nested or adjacent errors (Gamon, 2010), or built multiple layers of annotation (Hana et al., 2010; Boyd, 2010). Our decision makes the particle-selection task for machine learning more attainable and is easily extendible with multi-layered annotation (section 4.1).

3.3 Classifying particles

For every particle in the learner corpus, error or not, we mark its specific category, e.g., GOAL. This categorization helps because learners can make different kinds of mistakes with different kinds of particles, and systems can be developed, evaluated, or optimized with respect to a particular kind of particle.

4 Putting it together

The previous discussion outlines the type of annotation needed for evaluating Korean particle errors made by learners. As the purpose is at present to demonstrate what annotation is needed for particle error detection evaluation, we have added annotation to a small corpus. An example of full annotation is given in figure 1, for the sentence in example (5).

In the figure, positions 12 and 13 are merged to correct the spelling, as the particle (*pakkey*) was originally written as a separate token. There is a substitution error ('2' on the *Error Type* layer), with both original and correct particles noted and encoded as auxiliary particles ('A').

4.1 Annotating a corpus

We have obtained 100 learner essays from American universities, composed of 25 heritage beginners, 25 heritage intermediates, 25 foreign beginners, and 25 foreign intermediates.[5] While this is a small amount of data, it allows us to properly define the annotation scheme and show how it helps evaluation.

Table 1 provides information about the 100 essays.[6] Following previous multi-layer annotation for learner language (Lüdeling et al., 2005;

[5]The data and annotation will be available for research purposes at: `http://cl.indiana.edu/~particles/`

[6]*Raw* denotes the numbers of phenomena in the learner corpus before annotation, and *Corrected* in the fully corrected corpus., *Ecels* refer to whitespace-delimited "words".

		8	9	10	11	12	13	14	15	16	17
Token		물론	뉴욕에서	태어났기	때문에	영어	밖에	할	수	있겠죠	.
Spacing		물론	뉴욕에서	태어났기	때문에	영어밖에		할	수	있겠죠	.
Correct Spelling		물론	뉴욕에서	태어났기	때문에	영어밖에		할	수	있겠죠	.
Answer		물론	뉴욕에서	태어났기	때문에	영어만		할	수	있겠죠	.
Segmentation		물론	뉴욕+에서	태어났기	때문+에	영어+만		할	수	있겠죠	.
Error Type			0		0	2					
Original Particle			에서		에	밖에					
Correct Particle			에서		에	만					
Original Particle Type			BL		A	A					
Correct Particle Type			BL		A	A					

Figure 1: Corpus annotation for (5), using the PartiturEditor of EXMARaLDA (Schmidt, 2010)

(5) a. O: New York-eyse thayenass-ki ttaymwun-ey **yenge** **pakkey** hal swu iss-keyss-cyo.
New York-IN born-NML reason-FOR English ONLY speak be able to-FUT-END
'Since (I) was born in New York, I was able to speak only in English. '

b. C: ttaymwun-ey **yenge-man** hal ...
reason-FOR English-ONLY speak ...

Boyd, 2010), we use EXMARaLDA for encoding (Schmidt, 2010).

	Beginner		Intermediate	
	F	H	F	H
Sentences	360	376	373	297
Raw ecels	1601	2278	3483	2676
Corrected ecels	1582	2245	3392	2613
Nominals	647	949	1404	1127
Raw particles	612	808	1163	923
Corrected particles	647	887	1207	979
Omission	43	45	57	61
Substitution	60	29	47	41
Extraneous	8	8	13	5
Ordering	0	2	1	0

Table 1: Corpus Statistics (*F* = foreign, *H* = heritage)

4.2 Interannotator agreement

To gauge the reliability of the annotation, we had two experienced annotators annotate the correct particle and the error type on the heritage intermediate subcorpus, and we report the agreement on both tasks. Given the high number of times they both gave no particle to a word (in 1774 ecels), we removed these cases when calculating agreement, so as not to overly inflate the values. When either annotator used more than one particle for an instance (occurring 9 times), we only count full agreement.

The agreement rate was 94.0% for the error type (Cohen's kappa=79.1%), and 92.9% (kappa=92.3%) for specific particles. The high values can be explained by the fact that these annotators were highly-trained and were using a relatively stable set of guidelines under development for over a year (based on Lee et al. (2009)). Kappa for particle agreement is high because of the fact that there are over 30 particles, with no overwhelming majority categories, so it is unlikely for annotators to agree by chance. Previous work (Lee et al. (2009)), which did not allow multiple particles per position, had a lower agreement rate (e.g., kappa for particle value = 62%), likely due to less well-articulated guidelines.

Multiple particles To gauge how difficult it is to assign more than one particle, we selected 30 verbs that license more than two particles for a nominal argument. Using these verbs, we presented hand-constructed sentences with missing particles and asked two annotators to fill in the missing particles in the order of preference. Although the agreement rate of sets of particles was 87.8%, the agreement of the "best" particle was only 60%. This supports our decision in section 3.2 to annotate sets of particles.

References

Ghazi Abuhakema, Reem Farajand, Anna Feldman, and Eileen Fitzpatrick. 2008. Annotating an Arabic learner corpus for error. In *Proceedings of LREC 2008*. Marrakech.

Adriane Boyd. 2010. EAGLE: an error-annotated corpus of beginning learner German. In *Proceedings of LREC-10*. Malta.

Rachele De Felice and Stephen Pulman. 2008. A classifier-baed approach to preposition and determiner error correction in L2 English. In *Proceedings of COLING-08*. Manchester.

Arantza Díaz de Ilarraza, Koldo Gojenola, and Maite Oronoz. 2008. Detecting erroneous uses of complex postpositions in an agglutinative language. In *Proceedings of COLING-08*. Manchester.

Markus Dickinson, Soojeong Eom, Yunkyoung Kang, Chong Min Lee, and Rebecca Sachs. 2008. A balancing act: How can intelligent computer-generated feedback be provided in learner-to-learner interactions. *Computer Assisted Language Learning*, 21(5):369–382.

Markus Dickinson, Ross Israel, and Sun-Hee Lee. 2011. Developing methodology for Korean particle error detection. In *Proceedings of the 6th Workshop on Innovative Use of NLP for Building Educational Applications*. Portland, OR.

Michael Gamon. 2010. Using mostly native data to correct errors in learners' writing. In *Proceedings of HLT-NAACL-10*, pages 163–171. Los Angeles, California.

Na-Rae Han, Martin Chodorow, and Claudia Leacock. 2006. Detecting errors in English article usage by non-native speakers. *Natural Language Engineering*, 12(2).

Jirka Hana, Alexandr Rosen, Svatava Škodová, and Barbora Štindlová. 2010. Error-tagged learner corpus of Czech. In *Proceedings of the Fourth Linguistic Annotation Workshop*, pages 11–19. Uppsala, Sweden.

Hiroki Hanaoka, Hideki Mima, and Jun'ichi Tsujii. 2010. A Japanese particle corpus built by example-based annotation. In *Proceedings of LREC 2010*. Valletta, Malta.

S. Ko, M. Kim, J. Kim, S. Seo, H. Chung, and S. Han. 2004. *An analysis of Korean learner corpora and errors*. Hanguk Publishing Co.

Sun-Hee Lee, Seok Bae Jang, and Sang-Kyu Seo. 2009. Annotation of Korean learner corpora for particle error detection. *CALICO Journal*, 26(3).

Sun-Hee Lee and Jae-Young Song. 2011. Particle ellipsis in korean corpora. In *The 10th Conference for the American Association for Corpus Linguistics*. Atlanta, GA.

Anke Lüdeling, Maik Walter, Emil Kroymann, and Peter Adolphs. 2005. Multi-level error annotation in learner corpora. In *Proceedings of Corpus Linguistics 2005*. Birmingham.

Alla Rozovskaya and Dan Roth. 2010. Annotating ESL errors: Challenges and rewards. In *Proceedings of the Workshop on Innovative Use of NLP for Building Educational Applications*, pages 28–36. Los Angeles.

Thomas Schmidt. 2010. Linguistic tool development between community practices and technology standards. In *Proceedings of the Workshop on Language Resource and Language Technology Standards*. Malta.

Joel Tetreault and Martin Chodorow. 2008. The ups and downs of preposition error detection in ESL writing. In *Proceedings of COLING-08*. Manchester.

Joel Tetreault, Elena Filatova, and Martin Chodorow. 2010. Rethinking grammatical error annotation and evaluation with the Amazon Mechanical Turk. In *Proceedings of the Workshop on Innovative Use of NLP for Building Educational Applications*, pages 45–48. Los Angeles.

James H. Yoon. 2005. Non-morphological determination of nominal particle ordering in Korean. In L. Heggie and F. Ordonez, editors, *Clitic and Affix Combinations: Theoretical Perspectives*, pages 239–282. John Benjamins.

Annotating Archaeological Texts: An Example of Domain-Specific Annotation in the Humanities

Francesca Bonin
SCSS and CLCS,
Trinity College Dublin,
Ireland

Fabio Cavulli
University of Trento,
Italy

Aronne Noriller
University of Trento,
Italy

Massimo Poesio
University of Essex, UK,
University of Trento,
Italy

Egon W. Stemle
EURAC,
Italy

Abstract

Developing content extraction methods for Humanities domains raises a number of challenges, from the abundance of non-standard entity types to their complexity to the scarcity of data. Close collaboration with Humanities scholars is essential to address these challenges. We discuss an annotation schema for Archaeological texts developed in collaboration with domain experts. Its development required a number of iterations to make sure all the most important entity types were included, as well as addressing challenges including a domain-specific handling of temporal expressions, and the existence of many systematic types of ambiguity.

1 Introduction

Content extraction techniques – so far, mainly used to analyse news and scientific publications – will play an important role in digital libraries for the humanities as well: for instance, certain types of browsing that content extraction is meant to support, such as entity, spatial and temporal browsing, could sensibly improve the quality of repositories and their browsing. However, applying content extraction to the Humanities requires addressing a number of problems: first of all, the lack of large quantities of data; then, the fact that entities in these domains, additionally to adhering to well established standards, also include very domain-specific ones.

Archaeological texts are a very good example of the challenges inherent in humanities domains, and at the same time, they deepen the understanding of possible improvements content extraction yields for these domains. For instance, archaeological texts could benefit of temporal browsing on the basis of the temporal metadata extracted from the content of the publication (as opposed to temporal browsing based on the date of publication), more than biological publications or general news. In this paper, we discuss the development of a new annotation schema: it has been designed specifically for use in the archaeology domain to support spatial and temporal browsing. To our knowledge this schema is one of only a very few schemata for the annotation of archaeological texts (Byrne et al., 2010), and Humanities domains in general (Martinez-Carrillo et al., 2012) (Agosti and Orio, 2011). The paper is structured as follows. In Section 2 we give a brief description of the corpus and the framework in which the annotation has been developed; in Section 3, we describe a first annotation schema, analysing its performance and its weaknesses; in Section 4 we propose a revised version of the annotation schema, building upon the first experience and, in Section 5, we evaluate the performance of the new schema, describing a pilot annotation test and the results of the inter-annotator agreement evaluation.

2 Framework and Corpus Description

The annotation process at hand takes place in the framework of the development of the Portale della Ricerca Umanistica / Humanities Research Portal (PRU), (Poesio et al., 2011a), a one-stop search facility for repositories of research articles and other types of publications in the Humanities. The portal uses content extraction techniques for extracting, from the uploaded publications, citations and metadata, together with temporal, spatial, and entity references (Poesio et al., 2011b). It provides access to the Archaeological articles in the APSAT / ALPINET repository, and therefore, dedicated content extraction resources needed to be created, tuned on the specificities of the domain. The corpus of articles in the repository consists of a complete collection of the journal Preistoria Alpina published by the Museo Tridentino di Scienze Naturali. In order to make those articles accessible through the portal, they are tokenized, PoS tagged and Named Entity (NE) annotated by the TEXTPRO[1] pipeline (Pianta et al., 2008). The first version of the pipeline included the default TEXTPRO NE tagger, EntityPro, trained to recognize the standard ACE entity types. However, the final version of the portal is based on an improved version of the NEtagger capable of recognising all relevant entities in the APSAT/ALPINET collection (Poesio et al., 2011b; Ekbal et al., 2012)

3 Annotation Schema for the Archaeological Domain

A close collaboration with the University of Trento's "B. Bagolini" Laboratory, resulted in the development of an annotation schema, particularly suited for the Archaeological domain, (Table 1). Differently from (Byrne et al., 2010), the work has been particularly focused on the definition of specific archaeological named entities, in order to create very fined grained description of the documents. In fact, we can distinguish two general types of entities: *contextual entities*, those that are part of the content of the article (as `PERSON`s, `SITE`s, `CULTURE`s, `ARTEFACT`s), and *bibliographical entities*, those that refer to bibliographical information (as `PubYEAR`s, etc.) (Poesio et al., 2011a).

In total, domain experts predefined 13 entities, and also added an *underspecification* tag for dealing with ambiguity. In fact, the archaeological domain is rich of polysemous cases: for instance, the term 'Fiorano' refers to a `CULTURE`, from the Ancient Neolithic, that takes its name from the `SITE`, 'Fiorano', which in turn is named from Fiorano Modenese; during the first annotation, those references were decided to be marked as underspecified.

[1] `http://textpro.fbk.eu/`

NE type	Details
Culture	Artefact assemblage characterizing a group of people in a specific time and place
Site	Place where the remains of human activity are found (settlements, infrastructures)
Artefact	Objects created or modified by men (tools, vessels, ornaments)
Ecofact	Biological and environmental remains different from artefacts but culturally relevant
Feature	Remains of construction or maintenance of an area related with dwelling activities (fire places, post-holes, pits, channels, walls, ...)
Location	Geographical reference
Time	Historical periods
Organization	Association (no publications)
Person	Human being discussed in the text (Otzi the Iceman, Pliny the Elder, Caesar)
Pubauthor	Author in bibliographic references
Publoc	Publication location
Puborg	Publisher
Pubyear	Publication year

Table 1: Annotation schema for Named Entities in the Archaeology Domain

3.1 Annotation with the First Annotation Schema and Error Analysis

A manual annotation, using the described schema, was carried out on a small subset of 11 articles of Preistoria Alpina (in English and Italian) and was used as training set for the NE tagger; the latter was trained with a novel active annotation technique (Vlachos, 2006), (Settles, 2009). Quality of the initial manual annotation was estimated using qualitative analyses for assessing the representativeness of the annotation schema, and quantitative analyses for measuring the inter-annotator agreement. Qualitative analyses revealed lack of specificity of the entity `TIME` and of the entity `PERSON`. In fact, the annotation schema only provided a general `TIME` entity used for marking historical periods (as *Mesolitic, Neolithic*) as well as specific dates (as *1200 A.D.*) and proposed dates(as *from 50-100 B.C.*), although all these instances need to be clearly distinguished in the archaeological domain. Similarly, `PERSON` had been used for indicating general persons belonging to the document's contents and scientists working on the same topic (but not addressed as bibliographical references). For the inter-annotator agreement on the initial manual annotation, we calculated a kappa value of 0.8, which suggest a very good agreement. Finally, we carried out quantitative analyses of the

NE Type	Details
Culture	Artefact assemblage characterizing a group of people in a specific time and place
Site	Place where the remains of human activity are found (settlements, infrastructures)
Location	Geographical reference
Artefact	Objects created or modified by men (tools, vessels, ornaments, ...)
Material	Found materials (steel)
AnimalEcofact	Animal remains different from artefacts but culturally relevant
BotanicEcofact	Botanical remains as trees and plants
Feature	Remains of construction or maintenance related with dwelling activities (fire places, post-holes)
ProposedTime	Dates that refer to a range of years hypothesized from remains
AbsTime	Exact date, given by a C-14 analysis
HistoricalTime	Macro period of time referring to time ranges in a particular area
Pubyear	Publication year
Person	Human being, discussed in the text (Otzi the Iceman, Pliny the Elder, Caesar)
Pubauthor	Author in bibliographic references
Researcher	Scientist working on similar topics or persons involved in a finding
Publoc	Publication location
Puborg	Publisher
Organization	Association (no publications)

Table 2: New Annotation Schema for Named Entities in the Archaeology Domain

automatic annotation. Considering the specificity of the domain the NE tagger reached high performances, but low accuracy resulted on the domain specific entities, such as `SITE`, `CULTURE`, `TIME` (F-measures ranging from 34% to 70%) In particular `SITE`, `LOCATION`, and `CULTURE`, `TIME`, turned out to be mostly confused by the system. This result may be explained by the existence of many polysemous cases in the domain, that annotators used to mark as underspecified.

This cross-error analysis revealed two main problems of the adopted annotation schema for Archaeological texts: *1)* the lack of representativeness of the entity `TIME` and `PERSON`, used for marking concurrent concepts, *2)* the accuracy problems due to the existence of underspecified entities.

4 A Revised Annotation Schema and Coding Instructions

Taking these analyses into consideration, we developed a new annotation schema (Table 2): the aforementioned problems of the previous section were solved and the first schema's results were outperformed in terms of accuracy and representativeness.

The main improvements of the schema are:

1. New `TIME` and `PERSON` entities
2. New decision trees, aimed at overcoming underspecification and helping annotators in ambiguous cases.
3. New domain specific NE such as: material
4. Fine grained specification of `ECOFACT`: `AninmalEcofact` and `BotanicEcofact`.

Similarly to (Byrne, 2006), we defined more fine grained entities, in order to better represent the specificity of the domain; however, on the other hand, we also could find correlations with he CIDOC Conceptual Reference Model (Crofts et al., 2011). [2]

4.1 TIME and PERSON Entities

Archaeological domain is characterized by a very interesting representation of time. Domain experts need to distinguish different kinds of `TIME` annotations.

In some cases, C-14 analysis, on remains and artefacts, allow to detected very exact dating; those cases has been annotated as `AbsTIME`. On the other hand, there are cases in which different clues, given by the analysis of the settlements (technical skills, used materials, presence of particular species), allow archaeologists to detect a time frame of a possible dating. Those cases have been annotated as *ProposedTime* (eg. *from 50-100 B.C*).

Finally, macro time period, such as *Neolithic, Mesolithic*, are annotated as `HistoricalTIME`: interestingly, those macro periods do not refer to an exact range of years, but their collocation in time depends on cultural and geographical factors.

4.2 Coding Schema for Underspecified Cases

In order to reduce ambiguity, and helping coders with underspecified cases, we developed the following decision trees:

[2] The repertoire of entity types in the new annotation scheme overlaps in part with those in the CIDOC CRM: for instance, AbsTime and PubYears are subtypes of E50 (Date), Historical-Time is related to E4 (Period), Artefact to E22 (Man Made Object), etc.

SITE vs LOCATION: coders are suggested to mark as LOCATION only those mentions that are clearly geographical references (eg. *Mar Mediterraneo*, Mediterranean Sea); SITE has to be used in all other cases (similar approach to the GPE markable in ACE); CULTURE vs TIME:

a) coders are first asked to mark as HistoricalTIME those cases in which the mention belongs to a given list of macro period (such as Neolithic, Mesolithic):

- *eg.: nelle societa' Neolitiche (in Neolithic societies).*

b) If the modifier does not belong to that list, coders are asked to try an insertion test: *della cultura + ADJ, (of the ADJ culture)* :

- *lo Spondylus e' un simbolo del Neolitico Danubiano = lo Spondylus e' un simbolo della cultura Neolitica Danubiana (the Spondylus is a symbol of the Danubian Neolithic = the Spondylus is a symbol of the Danubian Neolithic culture).*
- *la guerra fenicia != la guerra della cultura dei fenici (Phoenician war != war of the Phoenician culture).*

Finally, cases in which tests *a)* and *b)* fail, coders are asked to mark and discuss the case individually.

5 Inter-Annotator Agreement and Evaluation

To evaluate the quality of the new annotation schema, we measured the inter-annotator agreement (IAA) achieved during a first pilot annotation of two articles from Preistoria Alpina. The IAA was calculated using the kappa metric applied on the entities detected by both annotators, and the new schema reached an overall agreement of 0.85. In Table 3, we report the results of the IAA for each NE class. Interestingly, we notice a significant increment on problematic classes on SITE and LOCATION, as well as on CULTURE. [3]

Annotators performed consistently demonstrating the reliability of the annotation schema. The new entities regarding coordinates and time seem also to be well defined and representative.

[3]Five classes are not represented by this pilot annotation test; however future studies will be carried out on a significantly larger amount of data.

NE Type	Total	Kappa
Site	50	1.0
Location	13	0.76
Animalecofact	3	0.66
Botanicecofact	6	-0.01
Culture	4	1.0
Artefact	18	0.88
Material	11	0.35
Historicaltime	6	1.0
Proposedtime	0	NaN
Absolutetime	0	NaN
Pubauthor	48	0.95
Pubyear	32	1.0
Person	2	-0.003
Organization	7	0.85
Puborg	0	NaN
Feature	36	1.0
Publoc	2	-0.0038
Coordalt	0	NaN
Geosistem	0	NaN
Datum	2	1.0

Table 3: IAA per NE type: we report the total number of NE and the kappa agreement.

6 Conclusions

In this study, we discuss the annotation of a very specific and interesting domain namely, Archaeology: it deals with problems and challenges common to many other domains in the Humanities. We have described the development of a fine grained annotation schema, realized in close cooperation with domain experts in order to account for the domain's peculiarities, and to address its very specific needs. We propose the final annotation schema for annotation of texts in the archaeological domain. Further work will focus on the annotation of a larger amount of articles, and on the development of domain specific tools.

Acknowledgments

This study is a follow up of the research supported by the LiveMemories project, funded by the Autonomous Province of Trento under the Major Projects 2006 research program, and it has been partially supported by the 'Innovation Bursary' program in Trinity College Dublin.

References

M. Agosti and N. Orio. 2011. The cultura project: Cultivating understanding and research through adaptivity. In Maristella Agosti, Floriana Esposito, Carlo Meghini, and Nicola Orio, editors, *Digital Libraries and Archives*, volume 249 of *Communications in Computer and Information Science*, pages 111–114. Springer Berlin Heidelberg.

E. J. Briscoe. 2011. Intelligent information access from scientific papers. In J. Tait et al, editor, *Current Challenges in Patent Information Retrieval*. Springer.

P. Buitelaar. 1998. CoreLex: Systematic Polysemy and Underspecification. Ph.D. thesis, Brandeis University.

K. Byrne and E. Klein, 2010. Automatic extraction of archaeological events from text. In *Proceedings of Computer Applications and Quantitative Methods in Archaeology*, Williamsburg, VA

K. Byrne, 2006. Proposed Annotation for Entities and Relations in RCAHMS Data.

N. Crofts, M. Doerr, T. Gill, S. Stead, and M. Stiff. 2011. Definition of the CIDOC Conceptual Reference Model. ICOM/CIDOC CRM Special Interest Group, 2009.

A. Ekbal, F. Bonin, S. Saha, E. Stemle, E. Barbu, F. Cavulli, C. Girardi, M. Poesio, 2012. Rapid Adaptation of NE Resolvers for Humanities Domains using Active Annotation. In *Journal for Language Technology and Computational Linguistics (JLCL) 26 (2)*:39–51.

A. Herbelot and A. Copestake. 2011. Formalising and specifying underquantification. In *Proceedings of the Ninth International Conference on Computational Semantics*, IWCS '11, pages 165–174, Stroudsburg, PA, USA.

A. Herbelot and A. Copestake 2010. Underquantification: an application to mass terms. In *Proceedings of Empirical, Theoretical and Computational Approaches to Countability in Natural Language*, Bochum, Germany, 2010.

B. Magnini, E. Pianta, C. Girardi, M. Negri, L. Romano, M. Speranza, V. Bartalesi Lenzi, and R. Sprugnoli. I-CAB: the Italian Content Annotation Bank: pages 963–968.

A.L. Martinez Carrillo, A. Ruiz, M.J. Lucena, and J.M. Fuertes. 2012. Computer tools for archaeological reference collections: The case of the ceramics of the iberian period from andalusia (Spain). In *Multimedia for Cultural Heritage*, volume 247 of *Communications in Computer and Information Science*, Costantino Grana and Rita Cucchiara, editors, pages 51–62. Springer Berlin Heidelberg.

M. Palmer, H. T. Dang, and C. Fellbaum. 2007. Making fine-grained and coarse-grained sense distinctions, both manually and automatically. *Natural Language Engineering*, 13(02):137–163.

E. Pianta, C. Girardi, and R. Zanoli. 2008. The textpro tool suite. In *Proceedings of 6th LREC*, Marrakech.

M. Poesio, P. Sturt, R. Artstein, and R. Filik. 2006. Underspecification and Anaphora: Theoretical Issues and Preliminary Evidence. In *Discourse Processes* 42(2): 157-175, 2006.

M. Poesio, E. Barbu, F. Bonin, F. Cavulli, A. Ekbal, C. Girardi, F. Nardelli, S. Saha, and E. Stemle. 2011a. The humanities research portal: Human language technology meets humanities publication repositories. In *Proceedings of Supporting Digital Humanitites (SDH)*, Copenhagen.

M. Poesio, E. Barbu, E. Stemle, and C. Girardi. 2011b. Structure-preserving pipelines for digital libraries. In *Proceedings of LaTeCH*, Portland, OR.

J. Pustejovsky. 1998. The semantics of lexical underspecification. *Folia Linguistica*, 32(3-4):323?348.

J. Pustejovsky and M. Verhagen. 2010. Semeval-2010 task 13 : Evaluating events, time expressions, and temporal relations. *Computational Linguistics*, (June 2009):112–116.

B. Settles. 2009. Active learning literature survey. *Computer Sciences Technical Report 1648*, University of Wisconsin–Madison.

A. Vlachos. 2006. Active annotation. In *Proceedings EACL 2006 Workshop on Adaptive Text Extraction and Mining*, Trento.

Annotating Preferences in Chats for Strategic Games

Anaïs Cadilhac, Nicholas Asher and Farah Benamara
IRIT, CNRS and University of Toulouse
118, route de Narbonne
31062 Toulouse, France
{cadilhac, asher, benamara}@irit.fr

Abstract

This paper describes an annotation scheme for expressions of preferences in on-line chats concerning bargaining negotiations in the online version of the competitive game *Settlers of Catan*.

1 Introduction

Information about preferences is an important part of what is communicated in dialogue. A knowledge of ones own preferences and those of other agents are crucial to decision-making (Arora and Allenby, 1999), strategic interactions between agents (Brainov, 2000) (Hausman, 2000) (Meyer and Foo, 2004). Modeling preferences divides into three subtasks (Brafman and Domshlak, 2009): *preference acquisition*, which extracts preferences from users, *preference modeling* where a model of users' preferences is built using a preference representation language and *preference reasoning* which aims at computing the set of optimal outcomes.

We focus in this paper on a particular instantiation of the first task, extracting preferences from chat turns of actual conversation; and we propose an annotation scheme that is general enough to cover several domains. We extend the annotation scheme of (Cadilhac et al., 2012), which investigates preferences within negotiation dialogues with a common goal like fixing a meeting time (`Verbmobil` (C_V)) or making a hotel or plane reservation (`Booking` (C_B)) to a more complex domain provided by a corpus of on line chats concerning the game *Settlers of Catan*. In *Settlers*, players with opposing strategic interests bargain over scarce resources. Our results show that preferences can be easily annotated by humans and that our scheme adapts relatively easily to different domains.

2 Preferences in game theory

A preference is traditionally a complete ordering by an agent over outcomes. In traditional game theory (Osborne and Rubinstein, 1994), preferences or utilities over outcomes drive rational, strategic decision. They are the terminal states of the game, the end states of complete strategies, which are functions from the set of players $\mathcal{P}$ to the set of actions $\mathcal{A}$; by assigning end states a utility, strategies are thereby also assigned a preference. Game theory postulates that agents calculate their actions based on a common knowledge of all the players' preferences.

In real life, strategic interactions almost always occur under the handicap of various forms of imperfect information. People don't know what other relevant actors are going to do, because they typically don't know what they believe and what they want. In addition, the underlying game is so large that agents with limited computational power can't hope to compute in analytical fashion the optimal actions they should perform.

Because a knowledge of preferences is crucial to informed strategic action, people try to extract information about the preferences of other agents and often provide information about their own preferences when they talk. Almost always this information provides an ordinal definition of preferences, which consists in imposing a ranking over relevant possible outcomes and not a cardinal definition based on numerical values. A *preference relation*, written $\succeq$, is a reflexive and transitive binary relation over elements of Ω. The preference orderings are not necessarily complete, since some candidates may not be comparable for a given agent. Let $o_1, o_2 \in \Omega$, $o_1 \succeq o_2$ means that outcome o_1 is equally or more preferred to the decision maker than o_2. *Strict preference* $o_1 \succ o_2$ holds iff $o_1 \succeq o_2$ and not $o_2 \succeq o_1$. The associated *indifference relation* is $o_1 \sim o_2$ if $o_1 \succeq o_2$ and $o_2 \succeq o_1$. Among elements of Ω, some outcomes are acceptable for the agent, i.e. the agent is ready to act in such a way as to realize them, and some outcomes are not. Among the acceptable outcomes, the agent will typically prefer some to others.

3 Data

Settlers of Catan is a competitive win-lose game that involves negotiations. The game is played online, and the state of the game is recorded and aligned with players' conversations. Each player acquires resources, hidden to the other players (of 5 types: ore, wood, wheat, clay, sheep), which they use in different combinations to build roads, settlements and cities, which in turn give them points towards winning. They can get these resources from rolls of the dice or through trades with the other players. *Settlers* is a positional game with a combinatorial number of possible states. Agents often forget information, with the result that they are uncertain about the resources opponents have as well as about the scoring function other players are using. We have modified the online version of the game so that agents have to converse to carry out trades, using a chat interface. So far we have twenty pilot games involving mostly casual players; each game transcript contains 30 or more self-contained bargaining conversations, for a total of around 2000 dialogue turns.

The data in *Settlers* is more complex than that in C_V or C_B because the dialogues typically involve three or more agents, each with incompatible overall goals. The need to trade requires players to form coalitions in which the participants negotiate the bargain over resources. Thus, there are preferences over which coalition to form, as well as over actions like giving or receiving resources.

Most of the turns in the chats involve negotiation and represent offers, counteroffers, and acceptances or rejections of offers. The example from our corpus in Table 1 involves some creative vocabulary (*alt tab* as a lexical verb) or V ellipsis without a surface antecedent (*I can wheat for clay*) with imperfect knowledge/recall amply evident (Euan's *what's up?*). There are also strategic comments, a persuasion move (49), and underspecified bargaining moves that get specified as more information becomes common knowledge.

While in this paper we concentrate on the annotation of preferences of chat turns, our annotated example shows that our corpus incorporates four layers of annotations: (1) the pre-annotation involves a segmentation of the dialogue into chat lines and the author of each chat line is automatically given, (2) the addressee of the turn, (3) the discourse structure and (4) the players' preferences. The discourse structure of most of the dialogues in *Settlers*, established by consensus, is relatively straightforward. The discourse structure is needed to specify the underspecified elements in our preference annotation.

4 Preference annotation layer

As for C_V and C_B (Cadilhac et al., 2012), our annotation of expressed preferences in each turn involves two steps: identify the set Ω of outcomes, on which the agent's preferences are expressed, and then identify the dependencies between the elements of Ω by using a set of specific non-boolean operators. Preferences in *Settlers* can be atomic preferences or complex preferences.

Atomic preference statements are of the form "I prefer X" where X paradigmatically is identified with a verb phrase ("to trade" or "to give wheat for sheep") or an entire clause describing an action. Sometimes X is identified by a definite noun phrase ("some of your sheep"). The action in question is determined by taking into account of the verb to which X is an argument to specify the action and the full outcome. Agents may also express preferences using questions. That is, in "Do you want to trade?", the agent implicates a preference for trading with the addressee. For negative and wh-interrogatives, the implication is even stronger. A negative preference expresses an unacceptable outcome, i.e. what the agent does not prefer. It can be explicitly expressed ("I have no wood") or inferred from the con-

Speaker	Id	Turn	addressee	Rhet. function
Euan	47	And I alt tab back from the tutorial. What's up?	ALL	
Joel	48	do you want <to trade>_1 ** 1	EUAN	Q-elab(47, 48)
Card.	49	<joel>_1 fancies <a bit of your clay>_2 ** receive(1, Euan, <2,?>)	EUAN	Expl*(48, 49)
Joel	50	yes <>_1 ** 1	CARD	Ackn(49, 50)
Joel	51	!	EUAN	Comment(50, 51)
Euan	52	Whatcha got? <>_1 ** 1	JOEL	Q-elab([48-50], 52)
Joel	53	<wheat>_1 or <wood>_2 ** offer(Joel, Euan, <1,?> $\triangledown$ <2,?>)	EUAN	QAP(52, 53)
Euan	54	I can <wheat>_1 for <1 clay>_2. ** receive(Euan, Joel, <1,?>) $\mapsto$ offer(Euan, Joel, <2,1>	JOEL	Elab([52,53], 54)
Joel	55	awesome <>_1 ** 1	EUAN	Ackn(54, 55)

Table 1: Example negotiation with discourse annotation

text ("no"), which means that the player rejects an offer and thus does not want to trade.

Complex preference statements express dependencies between outcomes (Boutilier et al., 2004)). Among the possible combinations, we find conjunctions, disjunctions and conditionals. We examine operations over outcomes and suppose a language with non-boolean operators &, $\triangledown$ and $\mapsto$ respectively, taking outcome expressions as arguments. With conjunctions of preferences, as in "Can I have one sheep and one ore?", the agent expresses two preferences (respectively over the acceptable outcomes of his getting one sheep and his getting one ore) that he wants to satisfy and he prefers to have one of them if he cannot have both. The semantics of a disjunctive preference is a free choice one. For example in "I can give wheat or sheep", the agent states that giving sheep or wheat is an acceptable outcome and he is indifferent between the choice of the outcomes. Finally, some turns express conditional among preferences. In our corpus, all offers and counteroffers express conditional preferences; "I can wheat for sheep", there are two preferences: one for receiving sheep, and, given the preference for receiving sheep, one for the giving of wheat.

In *Settlers*, an outcome X can play a role in several actions: a preference for the speaker's receiving or offering the resource X, a preference for a trade, a preference for performing the action X, etc. To specify these different actions, we use, in addition to the vocabulary of our previous annotation language, two functions: *receive(o, a, <r,q>)* and *offer(o, a, <r,q>)* such that: o is the preference owner, a is the addressee, r is the resource and q is the quantity of the resource needed (or offered). If some of these arguments are underspecified, we put *?*. Outcomes, which are closed under our non-boolean operators, can specify one or more arguments of our new predicates, or range over an action description. In addition, we have decided to annotate anaphoric and unspecified bargaining moves using an empty outcome (50). Table1 shows how the example is annotated (*<outcome>*_i indicates outcome number i in the turn; preference annotation is given after **).

5 Inter-annotator agreements

Two judges manually annotated two games from our corpus of 20 *Settlers* dialogues using the previously described annotation scheme. The two games contain 74 bargaining conversations for a total of 980 turns with 632 outcomes, 147 of which are unacceptable (*not* operator). There are 20 instances of &, 27 of $\triangledown$ and 80 of $\mapsto$. We computed four inter-annotator agreements on: (a) outcome identification, (b) outcome acceptance, (c) outcome attachment and (d) operator identification.

For (a), we compute a *lenient* match between annotations using Cohen's Kappa (i.e. there is an overlap between their text spans as in "sheep" and "some sheep"). We obtain a Kappa of 0.92 for *Settlers* while for both C_V and C_B we obtained a Kappa of 0.85. As in C_V and C_B, the main case of disagreement concerns redundant preferences which we decided not to keep in the gold standard because the player just wants to insist by repeating already stated preferences. In *Settlers*, we observed four additional cases of disagreement: (1) sometimes judges do not annotate underspecified preferences which are often used to introduce new, to make current preferences more precise or to accept preferences. Hence, we decided to annotate them in the gold standard. (2)

annotators sometimes forget to annotate a resource when it is lexicalized by a synonym (as "dolly" and "sheep"), (3) annotators often fail to decide if the action is about receiving or offering a resource (as in "ore for clay") mainly because the same lexicalizations do not always lead to the same actions, (4) judges do not always annotate preferences that are not directly related to the action of trading, offering or receiving a resource.

For (b), the aim is to compute the agreement on the *not* operator, that is if an outcome is acceptable, as in Dave: "I will give <you>_1 <wheat>_2", or unacceptable, as in Tomm: "No <ore>_1, sorry". We get a Kappa of 0.97 for *Settlers* while we obtained a Kappa of 0.90 for C_V and 0.95 for C_B. As in C_V and C_B, the main case of disagreement concerns negations that are inferred from the context.

For (c), since the structure of the bargaining packages outcomes in a very predictable way, it is quite intuitive, and simpler than for C_V and C_B, to decide how options are integrated in the preference annotation in *Settlers* which includes functions (offer and receive). We computed annotator agreement using the F-score measure because this task involves structure building as in "Joel wants to trade wheat for clay, or wheat for ore", which gives us: *(receive(Joel,?,<clay,?>)* $\mapsto$ *offer(Joel,?,<wheat,?>))* $\triangledown$ *(receive(Joel,?,<ore,?>)* $\mapsto$ *offer(Joel,?,<wheat,?>))*. The agreement concerns turns that contain at least three outcomes and was computed on the previously built gold standard once annotators discussed cases of outcome identification disagreements. We obtain an agreement of 93% for C_V, 82% for C_B and perfect agreement for *Settlers*.

Finally, in our *Settlers* corpus, the most frequent operators are not and $\mapsto$ because the main purpose of the players in this corpus is to propose, accept or reject a trade. The other two operators & and $\triangledown$ are equally split. The most frequently used binary operators were $\mapsto$ in C_V and & and $\mapsto$ in C_B. The Cohen's Kappa for (d), averaged over all the operators, is 0.93 for C_V, 0.75 for C_V and 0.95 for *Settlers*. In C_V and C_B, we observed two main cases of disagreement: between $\triangledown$ and &, and between & and $\mapsto$. These cases were more frequent for C_B, accounting for the lower Kappa there than for C_V. In *Settlers*, the main case of disagreement concerns the confusion between $\triangledown$ and &. The high agreement on $\mapsto$ reflects the fact that $\mapsto$ occurs in the description of an offer which is easy to annotators to spot.

The same linguistic realizations do not always lead to the same annotations. The coordinating conjunction "or" is a strong predictor for recognizing a disjunction of preferences, at least when "or" is clearly outside of the scope of a negation. In C_V and C_B, the coordinating conjunction "and" can also give a disjunction, especially when it is used to link two acceptable outcomes that are both of a single type (e.g., day, type of room) between which an agent wants to choose a single realization. In *Settlers*, the connector "and" generally links two outcomes that the agent wants to satisfy simultaneously and involves a conjunction of preferences, as in Dave: "I can give <you>_1 <one wheat>_2 and <ore>_3 for <wood>_4" where we have: *receive(Dave, 1, <4, ?>)* $\mapsto$ *offer(Dave, 1, <2, 1> & <3, ?>)*. When "and" links two outcomes and one at least is unacceptable, it gives a conjunction of preferences, as in Dave: "I dont have <any ore>_1, but i do have <plenty clay>_2" where we have: *not offer(Dave, ?, <1, ?>) & offer(Dave, ?, <2, ?>)*.

6 Conclusion and Future Work

We have proposed a linguistic approach to preference acquisition that aims to infer preferences from chats concerning bargaining negotiations in an online version of the game *Settlers of Catan*. The described annotation scheme extends the scheme of (Cadilhac et al., 2012), which investigated preferences within negotiation dialogues with a common goal like fixing a meeting time or making a hotel or plane reservation to the more complex domain of *Settlers*, where the types of actions were more diverse. The next step is to automate the process of preference extraction from turns or elementary discourse units using NLP methods, while at the same time pursuing the annotation and automation of the discourse parsing process. We also plan to study the evolution of these preferences *vis à vis* strategies of the underlying game, giving us an insight into how humans strategize within complex games like *Settlers* or real life situations, for which standard game theoretic solution concepts are not feasible for limited agents like us.

References

Neeraj Arora and Greg M. Allenby. 1999. Measuring the influence of individual preference structures in group decision making. *Journal of Marketing Research*, 36:476–487.

Craig Boutilier, Craig Brafman, Carmel Domshlak, Holger H. Hoos, and David Poole. 2004. Cp-nets: A tool for representing and reasoning with conditional *ceteris paribus* preference statements. *Journal of Artificial Intelligence Research*, 21:135–191.

Ronen I. Brafman and Carmel Domshlak. 2009. Preference handling - an introductory tutorial. *AI Magazine*, 30(1):58–86.

Sviatoslav Brainov. 2000. The role and the impact of preferences on multiagent interaction. In *Proceedings of ATAL*, pages 349–363. Springer-Verlag.

Anaïs Cadilhac, Nicholas Asher, and Farah Benamara. 2012. Annotating preferences in negotiation dialogues. In *Proceedings of *SEM*.

Daniel M. Hausman. 2000. Revealed preference, belief, and game theory. *Economics and Philosophy*, 16(01):99–115.

Thomas Meyer and Norman Foo. 2004. Logical foundations of negotiation: Strategies and preferences. In *In Proceedings of the Ninth International Conference on Principles of Knowledge Representation and Reasoning (KR04*, pages 311–318.

Martin Osborne and Ariel Rubinstein. 1994. *A Course in Game Theory*. MIT Press.

Morpheme Segmentation in the METU-Sabancı Turkish Treebank

Ruket Çakıcı
Computer Engineering Department
Middle East Technical University
Ankara, Turkey
ruken@ceng.metu.edu.tr

Abstract

Morphological segmentation data for the METU-Sabancı Turkish Treebank is provided in this paper. The generalized lexical forms of the morphemes which the treebank previously lacked are added to the treebank. This data maybe used to train POS-taggers that use stemmer outputs to map these lexical forms to morphological tags.

1 Introduction

METU-Sabancı Treebank is a dependency treebank of about 5600 modern day Turkish sentences annotated with surface dependency graphs (Atalay et al., 2003; Oflazer et al., 2003). The words in the treebank are annotated with their morphological structure. However, only the tag information is used in the annotations. These tags are combined to create what was called inflectional groups (IG). An IG field contains one or more inflectional morpheme tag groups separated by derivational boundaries. An example IG with two inflectional groups from Figure 1 is *IG='[(1,"dayan+Verb+Pos")(2,"Adv+AfterDoingSo")]'*. A derivational boundary marking a part-of-speech change (from Verb in the first IG to Adverb in the second IG) is seen here.

The lexical forms of the morphemes and the lemma information were initially planned to be included in the annotated data. Thus the annotation files have fields MORPH and LEM that are empty in the current version. With this study, we aim to include this missing information and provide the treebank data in a more complete form for further studies. The sentence in (1) is taken from the treebank and is shown with the intended representation given in Figure 1. The LEM field contains the lemma information whereas the MORPH field contains the lexical representations of the morphemes involved in forming the word. For the explanations of the rest of the fields the reader is referred to Atalay et al. (2003) and Oflazer et al. (2003).

(1)

Kapının	kenarındaki	duvara	dayanıp
door	**side**	**wall**	**lean**
bize	baktı	bir	an.
us	**looked**	**one**	**moment**

(He) looked at us leaning on the wall next to the door, for a moment.

Part-of-speech (POS) tagging with simple tags such as *Verb, Adverb* etc. is not appropiate and sufficient for agglutinative languages like Turkish. This is especially obvious in the Turkish dependency treebank. A derived word may have arguments (dependents) of its root but it may have different dependencies regarding its role in the sentence. Most of the voice changes, relativisation and other syntactic phenomena is handled through morphology in Turkish (Çakıcı, 2008). Therefore morphological taggers for agglutinative languages are usually preferred over simple part-of-speech taggers since there is not a simple part-of-speech tagset for Turkish. METU-Sabancı treebank is the only available syntactically annotated data for Turkish. Providing the morphological segmentation of the words in the treebank will make it easier to map the morphological structure in the IG fields to the wordforms.

```
<S No="3">
<W IX="1" LEM="kapı" MORPH="kapı+nHn" IG='[(1,"kapı+Noun+A3sg+Pnon+Gen")]' REL="[2,1,(POSSESSOR)]"> Kapının </W>
<W IX="2" LEM="kenar" MORPH="kenar+nHn+DA+ki" IG='[(1,"kenar+Noun+A3sg+P3sg+Loc")(2,"Adj+Rel")]' REL="[3,1,(MODIFIER)]"> kenarındaki </W>
<W IX="3" LEM="duvar"MORPH="duvar+yA" IG='[(1,"duvar+Noun+A3sg+Pnon+Dat")]' REL="[4,1,(OBJECT)]">duvara </W>
<W IX="4" LEM="dayanmak" MORPH="dayan+Hp" IG='[(1,"dayan+Verb+Pos")(2,"Adv+AfterDoingSo")]' REL="[6,1,(MODIFIER)]"> dayanıp </W >
<W IX="5" LEM="bize" MORPH="biz+yA" IG='[(1,"biz+Pron+PersP +A1pl+Pnon+Dat")]' REL="[6,1,(OBJECT)]"> bize </W>
<W IX="6" LEM="bakmak" MORPH="bak+DH" IG='[(1,"bak+Verb+Pos +Past+A3sg")]' REL="[9,1,(SENTENCE)]">baktı </W>
<W IX="7" LEM="bir" MORPH="bir" IG='[(1,"bir+Det")]' REL="[8,1,(DETERMINER)]"> bir </W>
<W IX="8" LEM="an" MORPH="an" IG='[(1,"an+Noun+A3sg+Pnon+Nom")]' REL="[6,1,(MODIFIER)]"> an </W>
<W IX="9" LEM="." MORPH="." IG='[(1,".+Punc")]' REL="[,()]"> . </W>
</S>
```


Figure 1: The encoding of the sentence in (1) in the dependency treebank

The segmentation data provided here is universal unlike the tag mapping in IGs, thus it may also be applied to morphological information decodings in alternative formats which may prove more useful for parsing Turkish dependency treebank sentences with structures other than the one in use at the moment.

The example in (2) shows a not-so-complicated Turkish word from the treebank *düşünmediklerim – the ones that I did not think of.* The lexical segmentation of this word is as shown in (2b), and the corresponding morpheme functions are shown with the tags in (2c). Here, *Neg* represents the negative morpheme for verbs, *Rel* represents the nominalization morpheme that is also used for relative clause formation in Turkish (PastPart in d) and *Agr1sg* is used for aggreement (Poss1sg in d). (2d) shows the IG field for this word in the treebank.

(2) a). düşünmediklerim
b). düşün+me+dik+ler+im
c). think+Neg+Rel+Plural+Agr1sg
d). (1, "düşün+Verb+Neg")
(2,"Noun+PastPart+Plu+Poss1sg+Nom")

The MORPH information to be added in the case of (2) will be *düşün+mA+dHk+lAr+Hm*. Generalization is aimed when adding this information to the treebank. Therefore we will not use the surface realizations or allomorphs as in (2b) but the lexical forms of the morphemes instead. The meaning of the capital letters in these lexical forms are given in Section 2.

There are approximately 60000 words in the treebank. Reliable POS tagging requires morphological analysis and disambiguation of the words used. However, a full part of speech tagger that assigns morphological structures like the ones adopted in the treebank is not currently available freely. The reason for that partly is the fact that the tag information in the treebank is too long and this causes sparse data problems when training classifiers with the full tag sequences as in (2d). The morphological tags include all kinds of derivational and inflectional morphemes. Moreover, they include some tags that do not correspond to any surface form such as the *Nom* tag in (2d). We believe morphological segmentation information included will make training and developing POS taggers for the Turkish treebank possible by providing the mapping between the lexical/surface morphemes/allomorphs to the tags or tag groups in the treebank data.

In the next section the lexical forms of the morphemes are described and are related to the data in the treebank. In Section 3 a brief history of part-of-speech tagging in Turkish is covered. The annotation method is then described in Section 4 and conclusion and future work section follows.

2 The Morpheme Set and the Mapping

Oflazer et al. (1994) give a list of all the morphemes in Turkish morpheme dictionary. These contain some compositional derivational morphemes as well. What we mean by that is that the derivation is productive and the semantics of it can be guessed with compositional semantics principles. Moreover, most morphosyntactic phenomena such as relativization and voice changes are marked on the verb as derivational morphology in the Turkish treebank.

Case	+DA, +nHn, +yA, +DAn, yH, ylA, +nA, +nH, +ndA, +ndAn
Agreement	+lAr, +sH, +m, +n, +lArH, +mHz, +nHz
Person	+sHnHz, +yHm, +sHn,+yHz,+sHnHz,+lAr, 0, +m, +n, +k,+nHz +z, +zsHn, +zsHnHz, +zlAr
Voice	+Hş, +n, +Hl, +DHr, +t, +Hr,
Possessive	+sH, +lArH, +Hm, +Hn,+HmHz, +HnHz
Derivation	+cA, +lHk, +cH, +cHk, +lAş, +lA, +lAn, +lH, +sHz, +cAsHnA, +yken, +yArAk, +yAdur, +yHver, +Akal, +yHver, +yAgel, +yAgör ,+yAbil+, yAyaz, +yAkoy, +yHp, +yAlH, +DHkçA, +yHncA, +yHcH, +mAksHzHn, +mAdAn, +yHş, +mAzlHk
Rel/Nom	+ki, +yAn, +AsH, +mAz, +dHk, +AcAK, +mA, +mAk
Tense	+ydH, +ysA, +DH,+ymHş, +yAcAk, +yor, +mAktA, +Hr
Negative	+mA, +yAmA
Mood	+yA, +sA, +mAlH, 0(imperative)

Table 1: Morpheme list

The list of morphemes in Oflazer et al. (1994) is given in Table 1. The capital letters in the lexical forms of these morphemes represent generalization over allomorphs of the morpheme. *H* in the morpheme representations designates a high vowel (*i,ı, u, ü*) whereas *D* can be instantiated as one of *d,t* and *A* as one of *a,e*. These abstactions are necessary for representing the allomorphs of these morphemes in the lexical forms in a compact manner. The surface representations for the morphemes conform to certain voice changes such as vowel harmony present in Turkish and these capital letters are instantiated as one of the surface letters they represent.

Some morphemes in the list are shown as 0 such as the 3rd person singular. This means that these morphemes are not realized in the surface form. Moreover, some morphemes are ambiguous in the surface form and, furthermore, in grammatical functions such as *+AcAk*, the future tense morpheme and *+AcAk* , the relativization morpheme. Another example to this is *+lAr*, the plural marker of nominal morphology and the third person plural marker in verbal morphology. Agreement class contains the plural marker *+lAr* and also the agreement morphemes attached to nominalizations and relativization. We have separated these in this list because of their functional/grammatical differences with the possessive markers on nouns although they have the same lexical and surface forms.

In this study, we use the two modes of the Turkish morphological analyser built for the Turkish dependency treebank (Atalay et al., 2003) using Xerox Research Centre Finite State Toolkit (Karttunen and Beesley, 2003). The *lexmorph* mode creates morphological tag analyses similar to IGs used in the treebank and the *lexical* mode creates the generalized lexical forms consisting of the morphemes in Table 1.

A1pl	NotState	A1sg	Noun
A2pl	Num	A2sg	Opt
A3pl	Ord	A3sg	P1pl
Abl	P1sg	Able	P2pl
Acc	P2sg	Acquire	P3pl
Adj	P3sg	Adv	Pass
Agt	Past	AfterDoingSo	PastPart
Aor	PCAbl	As	PCAcc
AsIf	PCDat	Become	PCGen
ByDoingSo	PCIns	Card	PCNom
Caus	PersP	Cond	Pnon
Conj	Pos	Cop	Postp
Dat	Pres	Demons	PresPart
DemonsP	Prog1	Desr	Prog2
Det	Pron	Distrib	Prop
Dup	Punc	Equ	Ques
FitFor	QuesP	Fut	Range
FutPart	Real	Gen	Recip
Hastily	Reflex	Imp	ReflexP
InBetween	Rel	Inf	Related
Ins	Since	SinceDoingSo	Interj
JustLike	Stay	Loc	Time
Ly	Verb	Nar	When
Neces	While	Neg	With
Without	Ness	WithoutHavingDoneSo	Nom
Zero			

Table 2: Morphological tags in the METU-Sabancı Turkish treebank data.

3 Morphological tagging of Turkish

The first attempt in automatically recognizing Turkish morphology is a two-level system of finite state transducers. Oflazer (1994) implements the morphotactic rules of Turkish that are explained in Oflazer et al. (1994) by using PC-KIMMO which is a two level morphological analyser system developed by Antworth (1990). A Xerox FST implementation of this morphological analyser was also used for morphological analysis in METU-Sabancı Treebank (Atalay et al., 2003; Oflazer et al., 2003).

When the level of morphological ambiguity is considered in Turkish, morphological disambiguators that choose between different analyses are vital for practical NLP systems with a morphological processing component.Oflazer and Tür (1996) and Oflazer and Tür (1997) are two of the early disambiguators that use hybrid models of hand crafted rules and voting constraints modelling the context of the word to be tagged. A purely statistical model is created by Hakkani-Tür et al. (2002).

Yüret and Türe (2006) use decision trees and train a separate model for each of the morphological features/tags the morphological analyser creates. These features are the 126 morphological tags that Oflazer (1994)'s morphological analyser creates. They report a tagging result of 96% when a separate classifier is trained for each tag and 91% when decision lists are used to tag the data without the help of a morphological analyser. The training data was a semi-automatically disambiguated corpus of 1 million words and test data is a manually created set of 958 instances. Sak et al. (2011) reports 96.45 on the same dataset of 958 manually disambiguated tokens with the use of perceptron algorithm. They also provide a morphological analyser. However, none of these studies report results on METU-Sabancı Turkish treebank data.

4 Method

The annotation of the MORPH fields in the treebank are done by applying a matching algorithm for matching the lexical forms and the tag sequences. We run the morphological analyser in two different modes as described before. Then, among the parses with tags and the lexical form output of the morphological parser, we compare the morphological tag sequence and choose the lexical form that matches the morphological tag sequence in the corresponding analysis. A lexical form may be represented with different tag sequences but this is not important since we only take the matching lexical form. We assume the morphological tag sequences are gold-standart altough as Çakıcı (2008) notes the treebank may have annotation errors in morphological disambiguation as well. For instance the first word of the example sentence in Figure 1 has a different morphological analysis assigned to it in the original treebank annotation which is corrected here. The words that could not be parsed were annotated by hand. However, the data that is created automatically by the matching algorithm need to be checked for errors caused by IG errors possibly inherent in the treebank.

Lemma field in the treebank is annotated with the stems extracted from the IGs (morphological tag sequence) for the words except verbs. The lemma for verbs are created by attaching to the extracted stem the infinitive marker *-mek* or *-mak*. The choice of the allomorph is determined by the last vowel of the extracted stem because of the vowel harmony rule in Turkish.

5 Conclusion and Future Work

In this study, we provide a treebank with complete morphological annotation. This information can be used to train systems for accurate and easier POS tagging. This can be done by various methods. One is to use a stemmer which is much more abundant in variety than morphological analysers and match the segmented data to the tags. This requires a lot less data and effort than training POS taggers that can assign the more complicated tags of the treebank directly. The use of lexical forms instead of different allomorphs or surface representation allows generalization and will prevent the sparse data problem when training these POS taggers to an extent.

None of the studies in Section 3 have reported on Turkish dependency treebank data. We aim to train automatic part of speech taggers using the segmentation data and the mapping of this segmentation to the tags in IGs using the new annotations introduced in this paper.

References

Ewan L. Antworth. 1990. *PC-KIMMO: A two-level Processor for Morphological Analysis*. Summer Institure of Linguistics, Dallas.

Nart B. Atalay, Kemal Oflazer, and Bilge Say. 2003. The annotation process in the Turkish Treebank. In *Proceedings of the EACL Workshop on Linguistically Interpreted Corpora*, Budapest, Hungary.

Ruket Çakıcı. 2008. *Wide-Coverage Parsing for Turkish*. Ph.D. thesis, University of Edinburgh.

Dilek Hakkani-Tür, Kemal Oflazer, and Gökhan Tür. 2002. Statistical morphological disambiguation for agglutinative languages. *Computers and the Humanities*, 36(4):381–410.

Lauri Karttunen and Kenneth R. Beesley. 2003. *Finite-State Morphology: Xerox Tools And Techniques*. CSLI Publications. Stanford University.

Kemal Oflazer and Gökhan Tür. 1996. Combining hand-crafted rules and unsupervised learning in constraint-based morphological disambiguation. In *Proceedings of the Conference on Empirical Methods in Natural Language Processing*, pages 69–81.

Kemal Oflazer and Gökhan Tür. 1997. Morphological disambiguation by voting constraints. In *Proceedings of the 35th Annual Meeting of the ACL*, pages 222–229.

Kemal Oflazer, Elvan Göçmen, and Cem Bozşahin. 1994. An outline of Turkish morphology. Technical Report TU-LANGUAGE, NATO Science Division SfS III, Brussels.

Kemal Oflazer, Bilge Say, Dilek Zeynep Hakkani-Tür, and Gökhan Tür. 2003. Building a Turkish treebank. In Anne Abeillé and Nancy Ide, editors, *Treebanks*, volume 20 of *Text, Speech and Language Technology*, pages 261–277. Springer Netherlands.

Kemal Oflazer. 1994. Two-level description of Turkish morphology. *Literary and Linguistic Computing*, 6(2).

Hasim Sak, Tunga Güngör, and Murat Saraclar. 2011. Resources for turkish morphological processing. *Language Resources and Evaluation*, 45(2):249–261.

Deniz Yüret and Ferhan Türe. 2006. Learning morphological disambiguation rules for Turkish. In *Proceedings of the Human Language Technology Conference (HLT-NAACL'06)*, pages 328–334, New York City, USA, June. Association for Computational Linguistics.

AlvisAE: a collaborative Web text annotation editor for knowledge acquisition

Frédéric Papazian **Robert Bossy** **Claire Nédellec**
Mathématique, Informatique et Génome, Institut National de la Recherche Agronomique
INRA UR1077 – F78352 Jouy-en-Josas
{forename.lastname}@jouy.inra.fr

Abstract

AlvisAE is a text annotation editor aimed at knowledge acquisition projects. An expressive annotation data model allows AlvisAE to support various knowledge acquisition tasks like construction gold standard corpus, ontology population and assisted reading. Collaboration is achieved through a workflow of tasks that emulates common practices (*e.g.* automatic pre-annotation, adjudication). It is implemented as a Web application requiring no installation by the end-user, thus facilitating the participation of domain experts. AlvisAE is used in several knowledge acquisition projects in the domains of biology and crop science.

1 Introduction

Text annotation editors have become key tools in various fields of research like Computational Linguistics, Information Extraction, Text Mining or Semantic Web. The requirements of each specific community drive the implementation of annotation editors developed in the past ten years. We advance AlvisAE, an annotation editor that focuses on semantic annotation for the purpose of knowledge acquisition and formal modeling in specific domains. There are several uses for text annotations in knowledge acquisition among which three are enumerated in the following:

1. Machine Learning-based Information Extraction systems capture the knowledge contained in a domain speech. But they require training sets; annotation editors are essential tools to build gold standards from corpus, but, provided they have the appropriate facilities, they can also assist the design of the annotation guidelines and the supervision of the annotation quality (*e.g.* Inter-Annotator Agreement scores, adjudication features).

2. Annotation editors are powerful companion tools for ontology population and terminology design. Indeed, they allow annotators to access and select domain terms and concepts in their speech context and to establish explicit relationships between the lexical level and the conceptual level. Thus, by providing a user-friendly interface, annotation editors help to choose more relevant terms and concept labels together with their definition and to discover semantic relations between concepts.

3. In the context of Information Retrieval, the Annotation Editor can provide reading assistance by highlighting relevant concepts and relationships within the text. The annotation editor can also empower the users to give feedback about the Information Retrieval results and then about the domain model.

AlvisAE is an annotation editor and framework implemented with these goals. It supports an expressive annotation schema language that allows to specify a wide variety of annotation tasks including: automatic supporting linguistic annotations (*e.g.* tokenization, POS tagging, NER, parsing, anaphora), text-bound annotation (*e.g.* named-entities, terms), semantic relations and events and ontology population. AlvisAE also supports collaborative annotation through the definition of a workflow that specifies a sequence of tasks. By breaking an annotation project into tasks, AlvisAE facilitates the division of work among annotators according to their skills. Finally the AlvisAE client is a full Web application that requires only a modern browser to operate, in this way it targets any domain expert regardless of their workstation device.

In section 2 we discuss related work, then we describe AlvisAE principles and implementation in section 3. Finally, we present ongoing projects using AlvisAE and our plans for the future in section 4.

2 Related work

Semantic annotation of text requires that annotators can express complex bits of knowledge through the editor data model. The benefit of allowing the annotation of relations is attested, although most annotations editors are limited to text span annotations. A major challenge of the annotation of relations is the representation on screen. Indeed, the most natural way to display relations is graphically, by a line between the relation arguments. However lines can disrupt the reading flow if they cross or hide the text and thus can hinder the annotator productivity. Some tools like Glozz (Widlöcher and Mathet, 2009) and BRAT (Stenetorp et al., 2012) have proposed original and non-intrusive displays for relational data, like improved line routing algorithms or a tabular display next to the text.

Collaborative annotation has been a vibrant topic in the recent years because (1) the Web application technologies are becoming mature enough to deal with large collaborative projects, and (2) virtual markets like Amazon's Mechanical Turk raise the expectations of available workforce and offer a new reward scheme for annotators. The most basic collaboration form is the Optimistic Concurrency Control, where concurrent commits are considered to be independent. Knowledge acquisition requires more elaborate collaboration schemes because knowledge models are often the result of a consensus between annotators. A few frameworks go a step beyond by providing a finer control over concurrency as well as a true model of collaboration. For example, GATE Teamwork (Kalina et al., 2010) includes a workflow engine in order to specify the sequence of tasks that will ensure a complete annotation of each document. This work is particularly interesting because the authors advance general types of tasks specific to text annotation projects: automatic annotation tasks by the GATE pipeline, manual annotation tasks and adjudication tasks.

Finally, the most recently developed editors are Web applications like Serengeti (Stührenberg et al., 2007), BRAT (Stenetorp et al., 2012) or ODIN (Rinaldi et al., 2010). As stated above, the libraries for building browser-based clients have reached a level of stability that allows their extensive use. Moreover, Web applications have very low system requirements for the end user thus ensuring a wider community of annotators, in particular domain experts.

3 Description of AlvisAE

The AlvisAE architecture consists of a RESTful server and a Web application client. The server has the responsibility for the storage of documents and annotations, for authentication and authorization of the annotators, and for workflow enforcement. The client is a Web application that allows the user to log in, to request documents and tasks and to visualize and to edit annotations. Figure 1 illustrates the interaction of the user with AlvisAE.

3.1 Annotation Model

The AlvisAE annotation model has been designed to encompass the requirements of knowledge acquisition projects. An AlvisAE project must specify an annotation schema that enumerates a set of annotation types. These types usually represent operational categories of annotations (*e.g.* named-entity types, relations). The schema also specifies that each type of annotation belongs to one of the three kinds described in the following:

Text-bound annotations are directly linked to the text of the document by their character position. AlvisAE supports enclosing, overlapping and discontinuous text-bound annotations. Discontinuous annotations are bound to a set of fragments of the document text; they allow to represent entities that are spread in different locations of a sentence, such as coordinated modifiers with the same head (*e.g.*

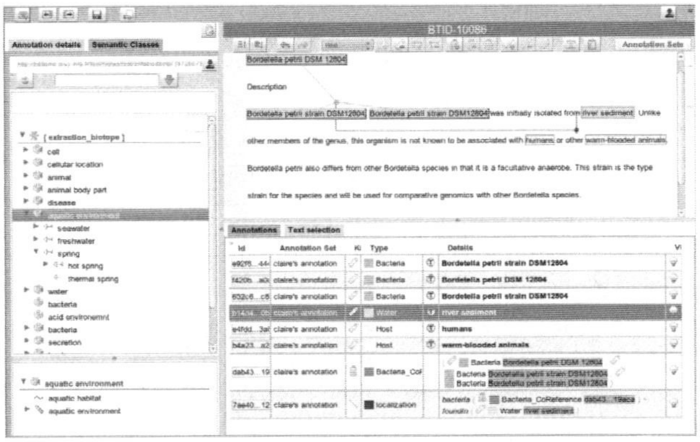

Figure 1: **AlvisAE client screen capture.** The upper-right panel displays the text and the annotations: text-bound annotations are highlighted, relations are lines connected with a lozenge, and groups are lines connected with a circle. The lower-right panel is a tabular representation of all annotations in the current document; the user can select and navigate by using either panels. The left panel shows an ontology that is being collaboratively designed; users can drag and drop text-bound annotations to create new concept labels and synonyms.

"North and South America"). A type of text-bound annotations can be constrained to token boundaries.

Relations Relation annotations are tuples of annotations; each argument is labelled with a role. The annotation schema can specify the types of annotations allowed for each role. AlvisAE is not restricted to text-bound relation arguments, meaning that there can be higher-order relations (*e.g.* relations of relations). Even though most relations are binary, AlvisAE supports relations of arbitrary arity. Relations are displayed either in the table layout, or as lines connecting arguments, nevertheless they can be hidden to improve the readability.

Groups Group annotations are collections of annotations; group elements are neither labelled or ordered. Groups are useful to connect an arbitrary number of annotations, for instance to represent coreference chains. In the same way as relations, groups can contain annotations of any kind.

Additionally all annotations have properties in the form of key-value pairs. The schema can express standard constraints on property values (*e.g.* closed value set, numeric range). Furthermore, property values can be bound to an external resource like an ontology or a terminology. In the screen capture (figure 1), the left layout shows a shared termino-ontology managed by the TyDI software (Nedellec et al., 2010). Text-bound annotations can be added as new terms or synonyms in the terminology (left layout) or as new concept labels with a simple simple drag-and-drop operation.

3.2 Annotation Task Workflow

Collaborative annotation with AlvisAE is supported through the definition of a workflow in a similar way as with Teamware (Kalina et al., 2010). The workflow is a set of tasks; each task is an atomic unit of annotation work that covers a subset of annotation types of the schema. Different tasks for the same document can be assigned to different annotators. In this way, the tasks can be dispatched according to the skill of each annotator. For example, junior domain experts can be assigned to the named-entities annotation task, natural language experts can be assigned to the coreference annotation task, and senior domain experts can be assigned to domain-specific relation annotation task. AlvisAE supports pre-annotation by an automatic corpus processing as a task to be assigned to a software agent instead of a human annotator. For example, AlvisAE can easily call the AlvisNLP (Nédellec et al., 2009) corpus processing engine that includes the most common NLP tasks.

AlvisAE workflow also specifies for each task a *cardinality* that is the number of annotators that must perform this task for each document. A cardinality of one means that the task is carried out by a single annotator. A cardinality of two emulates the common practice of double annotation.

Finally, a workflow may specify *review* tasks. A review task is bound to a regular annotation task and covers the same annotation types. The annotator assigned to a review is required to go through the annotations created within the scope of the preceding tasks, and to correct them according to the guidelines. If the preceding task has cardinality greater than one, then the annotator has to review all the concurrent annotations and pull out a consensus. In other words review tasks are adjudication tasks where the cardinality is greater than one.

The order in which tasks are performed on a document is constrained by both the schema and the required reviews. Tasks that cover compound annotations types (relations and groups) depend on the the tasks that cover the annotation types of their arguments and elements. Reviews depend on the tasks to which they are bound by definition. AlvisAE checks the consistency of the workflow against straightforward rules (*e.g.* all annotation types must be covered by a task, circular workflows are invalid, tasks with cardinality greater than one must be reviewed). More importantly, the characterization of the workflow ensures a full traceability of knowledge model produced collectively by the annotators.

4 Applications and Future Work

AlvisAE is currently used in several funded projects in the domains of biology and crop science, although it is not restricted to these domains:

OntoBiotope aims at building an ontology of bacteria habitats and tropisms as well as the annotation of a training corpus for Information Extraction systems.

FSOV SAM gathers knowledge about the relationships between phenotypes, genes and markers in a corpus of wheat genetics literature.

Bacteria Gene Interactions designs training corpus for Information Extraction systems about genic interactions in bacteria. This project is a follow-up of the BioNLP Bacteria Gene Interaction shared task (Bossy et al., 2012).

Our future efforts will concentrate in the development of adjudication tools and interface. The main challenge lies on the simultaneous alignment of several kinds of annotations. Indeed, the adjudication of compound annotations (relations and groups) depends on the prior adjudication of their arguments.

Currently, the specification of a schema and a workflow rely on two configuration files in XML, and the set up of an AlvisAE project is done by a command-line interface. We plan to develop a Web client dedicated to project management including its creation, definition and supervision.

References

Robert Bossy, Julien Jourde, Alain-Pierre Manine, Philippe Veber, Erick Alphonse, Maarten Van De Guchte, Philippe Bessières, and Claire Nédellec. 2012. BioNLP 2011 Shared Task - The Bacteria Track. *BMC Bioinformatics*, 13(suppl. 8):S3.

Bontcheva Kalina, H. Cunningham, I. Roberts, and V. Tablan. 2010. Web-based collaborative corpus annotation: Requirements and a framework implementation. In *New Challenges for NLP Frameworks (LREC)*, Malta, May.

Claire Nedellec, Wiktoria Golik, Sophie Aubin, and Robert Bossy. 2010. Building large lexicalized ontologies from text: A use case in automatic indexing of biotechnology patents. In *EKAW*, pages 514–523.

Claire Nédellec, Adeline Nazarenko, and Robert Bossy. 2009. Information extraction. In Peter Bernus, Jacek Blazewicz, Günter J. Schmidt, Michael J. Shaw, Steffen Staab, and Rudi Studer, editors, *Handbook on Ontologies*, International Handbooks on Information Systems, pages 663–685. Springer, Berlin Heidelberg.

Fabio Rinaldi, Simon Clematide, Gerold Schneider, Martin Romacker, and Thérèse Vachon. 2010. Odin: An advanced interface for the curation of biomedical literature. In *Fourth International Biocuration Conference*.

Pontus Stenetorp, Sampo Pyysalo, Goran Topić, Tomoko Ohta, Sophia Ananiadou, and Jun'ichi Tsujii. 2012. brat: a web-based tool for nlp-assisted text annotation. In *Proceedings of the Demonstrations at the 13th Conference of the European Chapter of the Association for Computational Linguistics*, pages 102–107, Avignon, France, April. Association for Computational Linguistics.

Maik Stührenberg, Daniela Goecke, Nils Diewald, Irene Cramer, and Alexander Mehler. 2007. Web-based annotation of anaphoric relations and lexical chains. In Branimir Boguraev, Nancy M. Ide, Adam Meyers, Shigeko Nariyama, Manfred Stede, Janyce Wiebe, and Graham Wilcock, editors, *Proceedings of the Linguistic Annotation Workshop*, pages 140–147, Prague. Association for Computational Linguistics.

Antoine Widlöcher and Yann Mathet. 2009. La plate-forme glozz : environnement d'annotation et d'exploration de corpus. TALN, Senlis, France.

CSAF - a community-sourcing annotation framework

Jin-Dong Kim and **Yue Wang**
Database Center for Life Science (DBCLS),
Research Organization of Information and Systems (ROIS),
2-11-16, Yayoi, Bunkyo-ku, Tokyo, 113-0032, Japan
{jdkim|wang}@dbcls.rois.ac.jp

Abstract

This paper presents a community-sourcing annotation framework, which is designed to implement a "marketplace model" of annotation tasks and annotators, with an emphasis on efficient management of community of potential annotators. As a position paper, it explains the motivation and the design concept of the framework, with a prototype implementation.

1 Introduction

Corpus annotation is regarded indispensable for the development of language-processing software and technology, e.g., natural language processing (NLP) and text mining. Nevertheless, the high cost required for finding and maintaining human annotators often hinders the development of various corpus annotation. For an annotation project, annotators, e.g., domain experts, need to be recruited, trained, then deployed for actual annotation. After the annotation project is over, usually they are dismissed. The same cycle then needs to be repeated for a new annotation project. In this setup, the recruitment and training of annotators actually take non-trivial cost.

Recently, crowdsourcing, e.g., Amazon Mechanical Turk (MTurk, hereafter), is gaining a big attention as a source of finding intelligent human labor. For corpus annotation also, the usability of MTurk has been explored (Callison-Burch and Dredze, 2010; Buzek et al., 2010; Little et al., 2009). There are also other efforts to achieve a large-scale annotation based on community-wide efforts (Ide et al., 2010), which shows current trends toward systematic incorporation of contributions from a community rather than from a small group.

In this work, we propose a community-sourcing annotation framework (CSAF, hereafter) which defines the components and protocol of a computer system to enable community-sourcing annotation. It is similar to MTurk to some extent in its concept, but it is more specifically designed for corpus annotation tasks, particularly for those which require special expertise from annotators, e.g., domain knowledge. With "community", it means a group of people who are regarded as qualified potential annotators for a specific type of annotation tasks. For example, for semantic annotation of biological literature, e.g., PubMed, graduate students of biology may be regarded qualified, and will be expected to form a community of potential annotators. The goal of CSAF is to provide a framework of computer system to enable an effective and efficient maintenance of such communities, so that when an annotation project is launched, available annotators in a community can be immediately found and deployed. It is also expected that the effect of training can be accumulated in the community.

With the background, in this position paper, the the core design concept (section 2) and the specifications and a prototype implementation (section 3) of CSAF is discussed.

2 Community-sourcing annotation framework (CSAF)

CSAF consists of four components: annotation editor (AE), task server (TS), task manager (TM), and community manager (CM). Among them, the first three, which are shown in figure 1, are actually required for any usual annotation project, no matter how explicitly they are implemented. The last one, CM, being integrated with the others, enables community-sourcing annotation.

2.1 Components for usual annotation

An AE provides annotators with a user interface (UI) for creation or revision of annotations. This component is often the most explicitly required software for an annotation project.

A TS takes the role of assigning annotation targets, e.g., documents, to annotators. Often, the assignment is performed manually by the organizers, particularly when the annotation projects are in a small scale. However by automating it, the assignment could be achieved in a more systematic and error-free way. A possible implementation may include a sequential assignment with a periodic overlap of some documents over the annotators for quality control, e.g., inter-annotator agreement rate. A TS may be regarded as manifestation of an assignment policy while an AE as manifestation of an annotation scheme.

A TM is to manage the progress of annotations performed by an individual annotator. Also, the management is often performed manually, but provision of a proper tool should enhance the management substantially. Together with an AE, it provides annotators with an annotation environment. As usually annotators are not experts of computer systems, provision of a convenient annotation environment is closely related to the productivity of annotation practice.

Although the three components do not include any notion of community-sourcing, separation of the three eases incorporation of an additional component, community manager which will be explained in next section.

Figure 1 illustrates how the three components work with together over the standard HTTP protocol in CSAF. An annotator on an annotation task will work with a TM and AE. The annotator may begin the annotation by requesting a document to the TS (1). On request, the identifier of the annotator needs to be notified to the TS, so that the TS can perform an assignment considering the annotators. The annotator then can open the document in the AE (2), and work on annotation. after a session of annotation, the resulting annotation will be downloaded to TM (3). The steps (2) and (3) may be repeated until the annotation is completed. When complete, the final annotation will be uploaded to the TS (4).

2.2 A component for community-sourcing

Figure 2 illustrates how an additional component, CM, enables community-sourcing of annotation. A CM plays like a job market where annotators and annotation tasks are registered, and associations, e.g., recruitment, between them are made. A possible scenario would be as follows: whenever a new task is registered, it is notified to the registered annotators; available annotators will apply to working on the task; and on approval of the task organizer, the association will be made. For each association, a TM is created for the management of the progress of the annotation by the annotator on the task. Once a TM is created, annotation by an individual annotator is carried over in the way described in the previous section

3 Specifications and implementations

In CSAF, all the four components are designed to be web services that will communicate with each other over the standard HTTP protocol.

3.1 Annotation Editor

An AE is supposed to take parameters (by HTTP POST) for two objects, a document and a set of pre-annotations, to enable production of a new set of annotations (by annotators), and to allow download (by HTTP GET) of the newly produced annotations. For the parameters, the document and the pre-annotations themselves may be passed over in an XML or JSON format. Alternatively, the URLs of them may be passed so that they can be read by the AE, when they are accessible from the network. The IO interface is intended to be minimal and flexible so that many existing web-based annotation editors can be integrated in the framework at a minimal cost. As a reference implementation, a simple AE that supports a named entity-style annotation is implemented. Figure 3 shows a screen-shot of it.

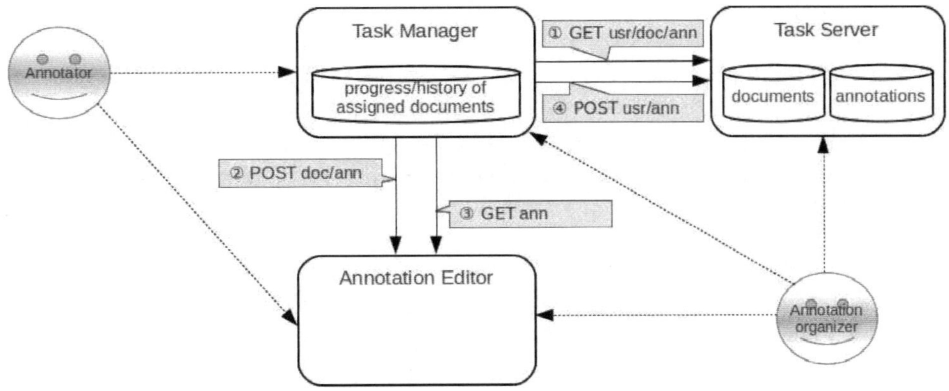

Figure 1: Components for usual annotation tasks

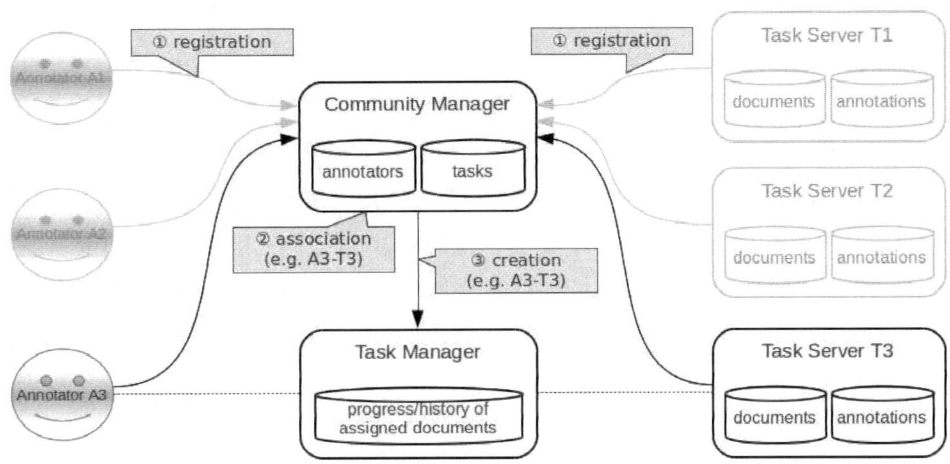

Figure 2: The role of community manager for community sourcing

3.2 Task Server

A TS is supposed to provide (1) annotation guidelines and (2) a document dispatcher, and to take back a new set of annotations (by HTTP POST). Annotators will access the guidelines (by HTTP GET) for reference before application and during annotation. The document dispatcher is an implementation of the organizer's strategy on how to assign documents to the annotators. On request from TM (by HTTP GET), a document is assigned to the annotator, optionally with a set of pre-annotations.

3.3 Task Manager

A TM is created for each association of an annotator and a task, based on the information supplied by the task organizer. It communicates with a TS to get a document to annotate, and with an AE to produce a set of new annotations. It is the responsibility of a TM to maintain the progress of annotation, e.g., the documents that have been or to be annotated.

3.4 Community Manager

As a community manager, account management, e.g., registration or unsubscription, is a fundamental function of CM. The users of a CM are either *annotators* or *task organizers*[1]. The task organizers can register annotation tasks to the CM. Figure 4 shows an example of task registration. Note that URLs given for the *job request* and *editor* specify how the required parameters, `annotator_id`, `document_url`, and `annotation_url` can be passed to the TM and AE.

[1]There is also a superuser who has all the privilege to modify or delete all the other accounts.

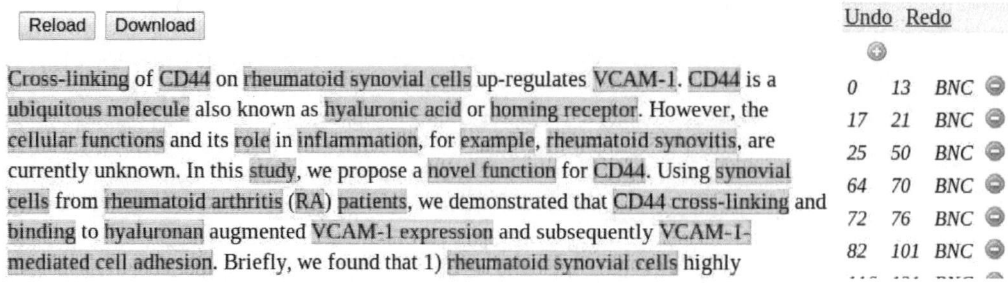

Figure 3: An annotation editor with base-noun-phrase annotations

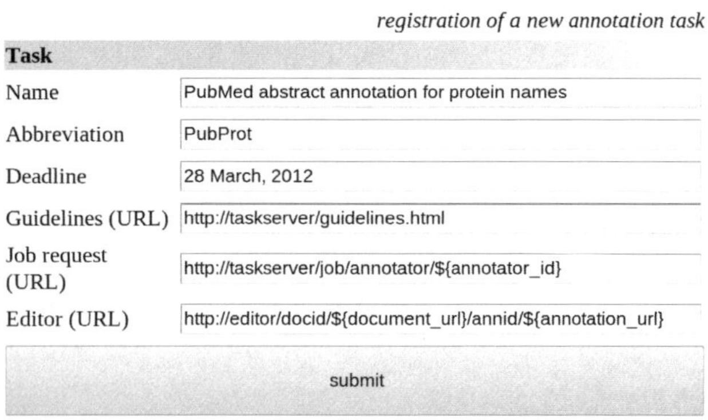

Figure 4: Registration of a new task to the prototype community manager

On registration of a new task, more than one annotators can be associated with the task through a negotiation. For each association of an annotator and a task, an instance of TM is created based on the information shown in Figure 4.

4 Discussions and conclusions

While the importance of corpus annotation is widely accepted, the low productivity of annotation often discourage production of new annotation. In this work, we present a community-sourcing annotation framework (CSAF) with the goal to reduce the cost for recruitment and also training of annotators. A prototype system of CSAF is implemented as a testbed, with a simple annotation editor as a reference implementation. The prototype system will be released to the public.

There is a much room for improvement in the framework and the prototype system. For example, the format of annotation is not yet specified, and it is currently the organizers responsibility to prepare a pair of TS and AE that can work with each other. The way of negotiation for recruitment and the rewarding system are also not yet specified. We plan to keep developing CSAF, and hope this position paper to facilitate discussions and collaborations.

Acknowledgments

This work was supported by the "Integrated Database Project" funded by the Ministry of Education, Culture, Sports, Science and Technology of Japan.

References

Olivia Buzek, Philip Resnik, and Benjamin B. Bederson. 2010. Error driven paraphrase annotation using mechanical turk. In *Proceedings of the NAACL HLT 2010 Workshop on Creating Speech and Language Data with Amazon's Mechanical Turk*, CSLDAMT '10, pages 217–221, Stroudsburg, PA, USA. Association for Computational Linguistics.

Chris Callison-Burch and Mark Dredze. 2010. Creating speech and language data with amazon's mechanical turk. In *Proceedings of the NAACL HLT 2010 Workshop on Creating Speech and Language Data with Amazon's Mechanical Turk*, CSLDAMT '10, pages 1–12, Stroudsburg, PA, USA. Association for Computational Linguistics.

Nancy Ide, Collin Baker, Christiane Fellbaum, and Rebecca Passonneau. 2010. The manually annotated sub-corpus: A community resource for and by the people. In *Proceedings of the ACL 2010 Conference Short Papers*.

Greg Little, Lydia B. Chilton, Max Goldman, and Robert C. Miller. 2009. Turkit: tools for iterative tasks on mechanical turk. In *Proceedings of the ACM SIGKDD Workshop on Human Computation*, HCOMP '09, pages 29–30, New York, NY, USA. ACM.

A Dependency Treebank of Urdu and its Evaluation

Riyaz Ahmad Bhat
LTRC, IIIT Hyderabad
riyaz.bhat@research.iiit.ac.in

Dipti Misra Sharma
LTRC, IIIT Hyderabad
dipti@iiit.ac.in

Abstract

In this paper we describe a currently underway treebanking effort for Urdu-a South Asian language. The treebank is built from a newspaper corpus and uses a Karaka based grammatical framework inspired by Paninian grammatical theory. Thus far 3366 sentences (0.1M words) have been annotated with the linguistic information at morpho-syntactic (morphological, part-of-speech and chunk information) and syntactico-semantic (dependency) levels. This work also aims to evaluate the correctness or reliability of this manual annotated dependency treebank. Evaluation is done by measuring the inter-annotator agreement on a manually annotated data set of 196 sentences (5600 words) annotated by two annotators. We present the qualitative analysis of the agreement statistics and identify the possible reasons for the disagreement between the annotators. We also show the syntactic annotation of some constructions specific to Urdu like $Ezafe$ and discuss the problem of word segmentation (tokenization).

1 Introduction

Hindi and Urdu[1] are often socially considered distinct language varieties, but linguistically the division between the two varieties is not well-founded. (Masica, 1993, p. 27) explains that while they are different languages officially, they are not even different dialects or sub-dialects in a linguistic sense; rather, they are different literary styles based on the same linguistically defined sub-dialect. He further explains that at colloquial level, Hindi and Urdu are nearly identical, both in terms of core vocabulary and grammar. However, at formal and literary levels, vocabulary differences begin to loom much larger (Hindi drawing its higher lexicon from Sanskrit and Urdu from Persian and Arabic) to the point where the two styles/languages become mutually unintelligible. In written form not only lexical items but the way Urdu and Hindi is written makes one believe that they are two separate languages. They are written in separate orthographies, Hindi being written in Devanagari, and Urdu in a modified Perso-Arabic script. Under the treebanking effort for Indian languages, two separate treebanks are being built for both Hindi and Urdu. Among the two, however, Hindi treebank has matured and grown considerably (Bhatt et al., 2009), (Palmer et al., 2009).

The paper is arranged as follows, next Section gives a brief overview of the related works on syntactic treebanking. Section 3 describes the grammatical formalism chosen for the annotation. In Section 4 we discuss treebanking pipeline of Urdu followed by some of the Urdu specific issues in Section 5. In Section 6 we discuss the empirical results of inter-annotator agreement. Section 7, concludes the paper.

2 Related Work

A treebank is a text corpus annotated with syntactic, semantic and sometimes even inter sentential relations (Hajičová et al., 2010). Treebanks are of multifold importance, they are an invaluable resource for testing linguistic theories on which they are built

[1] Hindi-Urdu is an Indo-Aryan language spoken mainly in North India and Pakistan.

and are used for a number of NLP tasks like training and testing syntactic parsers. Owing to their great importance, a number of syntactic treebanking projects have been initiated for many different languages. Among the treebanks include Penn treebank (PTB) (Marcus et al., 1993), Prague Dependency treebank (PDT) (Hajicová, 1998) for Czech, (Rambow et al., 2002) for English, Alpino (Van der Beek et al., 2002) for Dutch, TUT (Bosco and Lombardo, 2004) for Italian, TIGER (Brants et al., 2002) for German and many others. Currently existing treebanks mainly differ in the grammatical formalism adopted. Dependency based formalism compared with the constituency based formalism is assumed to suit better for representing syntactic structures of free word order languages, its representation does not crucially rely on the position of a syntactic unit in a sentence thus easily handles the scrambling of arguments in such languages (Shieber, 1985), (Bharati et al., 1995), (Hajič, 1998), (Hajicová, 1998), (Oflazer et al., 2003). Not only are dependency-based representations suitable for less configurational languages, they are also favorable for a number of natural language processing applications (Culotta and Sorensen, 2004), (Reichartz et al., 2009).

Structural relations like subject and direct object are believed to be less relevant for the grammatical description of Indian languages (ILs) because of the less configurational nature of these languages (Bhat, 1991). Indian languages are morphologically rich and have a relatively free constituent order. (Begum et al., 2008) have argued in favor of using Karaka relations instead of structural relations for the syntactic analysis of ILs. They proposed an annotation scheme for the syntactic treebanking of ILs based on the Computational Paninian Grammar (CPG), a formalism inspired by Paninian grammatical theory. Currently dependency treebanks of four ILs, namely Hindi, Urdu, Bangla and Telegu, are under development following this annotation scheme. The dependency structures in all the four treebanks are, under this annotation scheme, annotated with the Karaka relations. Although English does not belong to the free word order languages, a number of attempts have been made to study the applicability of CPG based syntactic analysis to it as well (Bharati et al., 1996), (Vaidya et al., 2009), (Chaudhry and Sharma, 2011).

3 CPG Formalism

The CPG formalism, inspired by the grammatical theory of Panini, the fifth century B.C. grammarian of Sanskrit, is a dependency grammar. As in other dependency grammars, the syntactic structures in this formalism essentially consists of a set of binary, asymmetric relations between words of a sentence. A dependency relation is defined between a dependent, a syntactically subordinate word and a head word on which it depends. In this formalism verb is treated as the primary modified (the root of the dependency tree) and the elements (nominals) modifying the verb participate in the activity specified by it. The relation that holds between a verb and its modifier is called a *karaka* relation. There are six basic *karakas* defined by Panini namely (i) *karta* 'agent', (ii) *karma* 'theme', (iii) *karana* 'instrument', (iv) *sampradaan* 'recipient', (v) *apaadaan* 'source', and (vi) *adhikarana* 'location'. Besides *karaka* relations that hold between a verb and the participants of the action specified by the verb, dependency relations also exist between nouns (genitives), between nouns and their modifiers (adjectival modification, relativization), between verbs and their modifiers (adverbial modification including clausal subordination). A detailed tag-set containing all these different kinds of dependency relations has been defined in the annotation scheme based on the CPG formalism (Bharati et al., 2009). Examples (1) and (2) depict some of the *karaka* relations (*k1 'karta', k2 'karma', k3 'karana'*) of verbs کھایا *'eat'* and کاٹا *'cut'* respectively while example (3) shows a genitive relation between two nouns, یاسین *'Yasin'* and قلم *'pen'*.

(1) یاسین نے سیب کھایا

yAsIn-ne	*saeb*	*khAyA*
Yasin-ERG	apple-NOM	eat-PST+PERF

'Yasin ate an apple.'

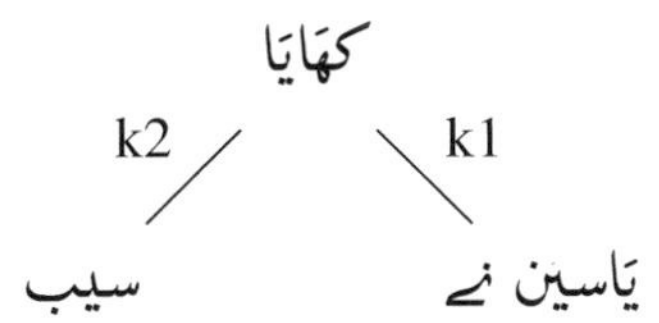

(2) یاسین نے چاکو سے سیب کاٹا

yAsIn-ne *chAku-se* *saeb*
Yasin-ERG knife-INST apple-NOM
kAtA
eat-PST+PERF
'Yasin cut the apple with a knife.'

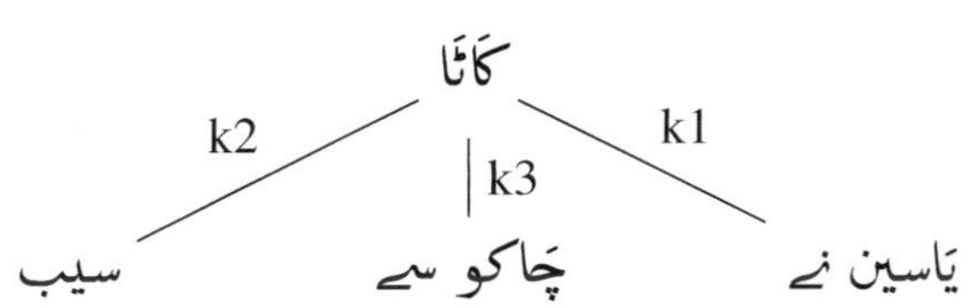

(3) یاسین کا قلم

yAsIn-kA *qalam*
Yasin-GEN pen
'Yasin's pen.'

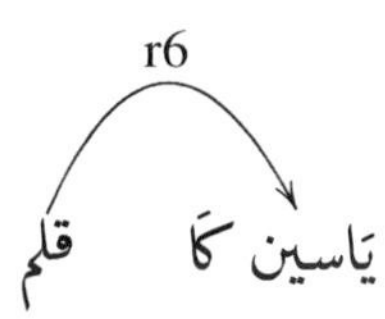

4 Annotation Pipeline

The dependency treebanks for Indian languages based on CPG formalism are developed following a generic pipeline. The process of treebank development under the pipeline consists of a series of steps namely (i) Tokenization, (ii) Morph-Analysis, (iii) POS-tagging, (iv) Chunking, and (v) Dependency annotation. Annotation process begins with the tokenization of raw text. The tokens obtained during tokenization are, in the next steps, annotated with morphological and POS tag information. After morph-analysis and POS-tagging correlated, inseparable words are grouped into chunks. The processing at the steps mentioned thus far are automated by highly accurate tools built in-house (tokenizer, morph analyzer, POS-tagger and chunker). The output of each tool is, however, manually corrected and validated by the human annotators. The final step in the pipeline is the manual dependency annotation. Only the inter-chunk dependencies are marked leaving the dependencies between words in a chunk unspecified because the intra-chunk dependencies are observed to be highly predictive given the head of a chunk and can be easily generated by a set of rules at a later stage.

UDT is steadily being developed following this treebanking pipeline by annotating the newspaper articles by a team of annotators with expertise in linguistics. The tool being used for the annotation is a part of Sanchay[2] (Singh, 2006). The annotations are represented in Shakti Standard Format (SSF) (Bharati et al., 2007). Hitherto, 3226 sentences (around 0.1M words) have been annotated with dependency structure. Each sentence contains an average of 29 words and an average of 13.7 chunks of average length 2.0.

5 Languages Specific Issues

5.1 Word segmentation

Urdu is written in a *Nastaliq style cursive Arabic script*. In this script an individual letter acquires different shapes upon joining with the adjacent letters. There are four possible shapes a letter can acquire namely $initial, medial, final$ form in a connected sequence of letters or an $isolated$ form. The letters acquiring all these four shapes depending on the context of their occurrence are called as $joiners$. An another set of letters, however, called as $non-joiners$ do not adhere to this four-way shaping. They only join with the letters before them and have only $final$ and $isolated$ forms. An example of a joiner is Arabic Letter 'Teh' ت and a non-joiner is Arabic letter '$waaw$' و.

The concept of space as a word boundary marker is not present in Urdu writing (Durrani and Hussain, 2010), (Lehal, 2010). Space character is primarily required to generate correct shaping of words. For example a space is necessary within the word ضَرُورَت مَند "needy" to generate the visually correct and acceptable form of this word. Without

[2]http://apps.sanchay.co.in/latest-builds/

space it appears as ضَرُورَتمَند which is visually incorrect. In contrast to this, writers of Urdu find it unnecessary to insert a space between the two words اردُو مَرکز "Urdu Center", because the correct shaping is produced automatically as the first word ends with a non-joiner. Therefore اردُو مَرکز and اردُومَرکز look identical. Although space character is primarily used to generate correct shapes of words, it is now being used as a word separator as well. This two-way function of space character in Urdu makes it an unreliable cue for word boundary which poses challenges to the process of tokenization. In UDT pipeline raw text is tokenized into individual tokens using a tokenizer which uses space as word boundary. The generation of erroneous tokens (single words broken into multiple fragments) is obvious, since, as mentioned above, space not only marks word boundary it is also used to generate correct shaping of a word. To ensure that only valid tokens are processed in the further stages of the pipeline, tokenization is followed by human post-editing. The fragments of a word are joined using an underscore '_'. This ensures that such words retain their visually correct shape. For example two fragments ضَرُورَت and مَند of a single word ضَرُورَت مَند generated by the tokenizer will be joined into single word with an '_' as ضَرُورَت_مَند.

5.2 Ezafe

Ezafe is an enclitic short vowel e which joins two nouns, a noun and an adjective or an adposition and a noun into a possessive relationship. In Urdu ezafe is a loan construction from Persian, it originated from an Old Iranian relative pronoun $-hya$, which in Middle Iranian changed into y/i a device for nominal attribution (Bögel et al., 2008). The Urdu ezafe construction functions similarly to that of its Persian counter part. In both the languages the ezafe construction is head-initial which is different from the typical head-final nature of these languages. As in Persian the Urdu ezafe lacks prosodic independence, it is attached to a word to its left which is the head of the ezafe construction. It is pronounced as a unit with the head and licenses a modifier to its right. This is in contrast to the Urdu genitive construction, which conforms to the head-final pattern typical for Urdu. The genitive marker leans on the modifier of the genitive construction not on the head and is pronounced as a unit with it. Example (4) is a typical genitive construction in Urdu while (5) shows an ezafe construction.

(4) یَاسین کَا قلم

yAsIn-kA *qalam*
Yasin-GEN pen
'Yasin's pen.'

(5) حکومتِ پَاکستَان

hukummat-e *Pakistan*
government-Ez Pakistan
'Government of Pakistan.'

The ezafe construction in Urdu can also indicate relationships other than possession. In current Urdu treebank when an ezafe construction is used to show possessive relationship, it is annotated similar to genitive constructions indicating possession with an *"r6"* label as shown in example (6), the head noun سَاحب *'owner'* *'possesses'* the modifying noun تَکهت *'throne'*. However, in example (7) ezafe does not indicate a possessive meaning, in such cases *"NMOD"* (noun modifier) is used instead of *"r6"*, the adjective روشن *'bright'* does not stand in a possession relation to the روزِ *'day'*, but simply modifies the head noun in an attributive manner.

(6) سَاحبِ تَکهت

sahb-e *takht*
owner-Ez throne
'The owner of the throne.'

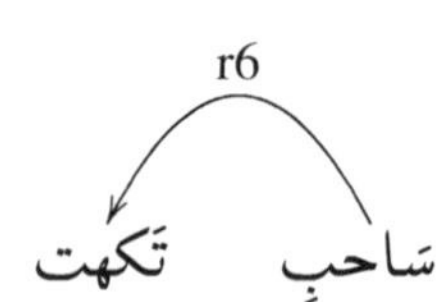

(7) روزِ روشن

rooz-e *rooshan*
day-Ez bright
'Bright day.'

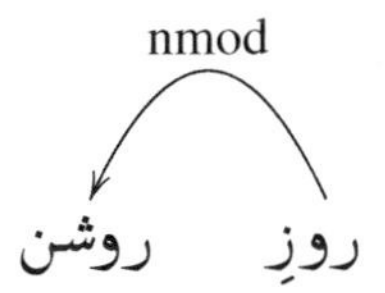

6 Agreement Analysis

In order to ensure the reliability of manual dependency annotations in UDT, we did an agreement analysis using a data set of 5600 words annotated by two annotators, without either annotator knowing other's decisions. A good agreement on the data set will assure that the annotations in UDT are reliable. The data set used contains 2595 head-dependent dependency chains marked with dependency relations belonging to a tag-set of 39 tags. The agreement measured is chunk based; for each chunk in a sentence agreement was measured with regard to its relation with the head it modifies.

Inter-annotator agreement was measured using Cohen's kappa (Cohen and others, 1960) which is the mostly used agreement coefficient for annotation tasks with categorical data. Kappa was introduced to the field of computational linguistics by (Carletta et al., 1997) and since then many linguistics resources have been evaluated using the matrix such as (Uria et al., 2009), (Bond et al., 2008), (Yong and Foo, 1999). The kappa statistics show the agreement between the annotators and the reproducibility of their annotated data sets. Similar results produced by the annotators on a given data set proves the similarity in their understanding of the annotation guidelines. However, a good agreement does not necessarily ensure validity, since annotators can make similar kind of mistakes and errors.

The kappa coefficient κ is calculated as:

$$\kappa = \frac{Pr(a) - Pr(e)}{1 - Pr(e)} \tag{8}$$

$Pr(a)$ is the observed agreement among the coders, and $Pr(e)$ is the expected agreement, that is, $Pr(e)$ represents the probability that the coders agree by chance.

Based on the interpretation matrix of kappa value proposed by Landis and Koch (Landis and Koch, 1977) as presented in Table 1, we consider that the agreement as presented in Table 2, between the annotators on the data set used for the evaluation, is reliable. There is a substantial amount of agreement

Kappa Statistic	Strength of agreement
<0.00	Poor
0.0-0.20	Slight
0.21-0.40	Fair
0.41-0.60	Moderate
0.61-0.80	Substantial
0.81-1.00	Almost perfect

Table 1: Coefficients for the agreement-rate based on (Landis and Koch, 1977).

No. of Annotations	Agreement	Pr(a)	Pr(e)	Kappa
2595	1921	0.74	0.097	0.71

Table 2: Kappa statistics

between the annotators which implies their similar understanding of the annotation guidelines and of the linguistic phenomenon present in the language.

Urdu as discussed earlier is a morphologically rich language, information concerning the arrangement of words into syntactic units or cues to syntactic relations, is expressed at word level through case clitics (Mohanan, 1990). Because information about the relations between syntactic elements is expressed at word level, the prediction of the syntactic relations becomes easier for an annotator. However, as mentioned in Table 3 case markers and case roles don not have a one to one mapping, each case marker is distributed over a number of case roles, this phenomenon is called as **case syncretism**. Among the 6 case markers viz نے *(ergative)*, کو *(dative)*, کو *(accusative)*, سے *(instrumental)*, سے *(ablative)*, کا *(genitive)* and پر, مے *(locative)* only نے *(ergative)* is unambiguous, all others are ambiguous between different roles. This syncretism is one of the reason for the disagreement between the annotators. Out of 965 case marked nominals 735 are agreed upon by both the annotators and for 230 nominals both disagreed. Examples below show syncretism in case marker کو 'ko'. کو marks the 'recipient', 'theme' and the 'experiencer' of the main verbs in sentences (9), (10) and (11) respectively.

	نے (ne)	کو (ko)	کا (kA)	سے (se)	مے (mem)	پر (par)
$k1$	100	22	1	0	0	0
$k2$	0	46	1	15	0	0
$k3$	0	0	0	2	0	0
$k4$	0	17	0	19	0	0
$k4a$	0	2	0	0	0	0
$k5$	0	0	0	14	0	0
$k7$	0	0	1	1	60	70
$k7t$	0	5	2	11	6	0
$k7p$	0	0	0	0	19	10
$r6$	0	0	89	0	0	0
rh	0	0	0	5	0	0

Table 3: Agreement among the Annotators on Karaka roles given a Case Marker.

The nominals carrying کو in these sentences will be labeled in UDT as *k4 'recipient'*, *k2 'theme'* and *k4a 'experiencer'* respectively.

(9) نادیا نے یاسین کو کتاب دی

Nadiya-ne Yasin-ko kitab
Nadya-ERG Yasin-DAT book-NOM
di.
give-PST+PRF
'Nadiya gave Yasin a book.'

(10) نادیا نے یاسین کو بُلایا

Nadiya-ne Yasin-ko bhulaayaa.
Nadya-ERG Yasin-ACC call-PST+PRF
'Nadiya called Yasin.'

(11) یاسین کو کہانی یاد آی

Yasin-ko kahani yaad
Yasin-Dat story-NOM memory
aayi.
come-PST+PRF
'Yasin remembered the story.'

Table 5 shows the statistics of the annotation-the number of labels used by each annotator and the frequency of agreement and disagreement per label. Statistics in Table 4 and 5 show that a considerable amount of confusion is between *'k1' (agent) and 'k2' (theme)*; *'k1' (agent) and 'pof' (part of)*; *'k1s' (noun complement) and 'pof' (part of)* and *'k2' (theme) and 'pof' (part of)*. Out of 110 disagreements for label *'pof'*, the annotators differ 81 (74%) times in marking a given dependency structure either with a *'pof'* relation or with *'k1, 'k1s' or 'k2'*. Similarly for *'k1'* 38% disagreements are between *'k2' and 'pof'* and for *'k2'* 49% disagreements are between *'k1' and 'pof'*. The high number of disagreements among the members of this small subset of labels $(k1, k2, k1s, pof)$ suggest the validity of the disagreement that is to say that the disagreements are not random or by chance and can be attributed to the ambiguity or some complex phenomenon in the language. All the disagreements involving *'pof'* relation occur due to the complexity of identifying the complex predicates in Urdu. The challenges in the identification of complex predicates (Begum et al., 2011) coupled with similar syntactic distribution of these Karaka roles explain the differences among the annotators for these relations. Take for example the case of sentences (12) and (13) both مدد *'help'* and چابی *'key'* have similar syntactic context, but in (12) مدد *'help'* is part of the complex predicate and has a *'pof'* (part of complex predicate) relation with the light verb لی *'take'* while in (13) چابی *'key'* is the 'theme' of the main verb لی *'take'* and will be marked as its *'k2'*. Similarly in (14) and (15) دھمکی *'threat'* and کتاب *'book'* have similar context, similar to مدد *'help'* in (12), دھمکی *'threat'* has a *'pof'* relation with the verb دی *'give'* and کتاب *'book'* in (15) is its 'theme' marked with the label *'k2'*.

(12) نادیا نے یاسین سے مدد لی

Nadiya-ne Yasin-se madad
Nadya-ERG Yasin-ABL help
li.
take-PST+PRF
'Nadiya took help from yasin.'

(13) نادیا نے یاسین سے چابی لی

Nadiya-ne *Yasin-se* *chaabi*
Nadya-ERG Yasin-ABL key-NOM
li.
take-PST+PRF
'Nadiya took key from Yasin.'

(14) نادیا نے یاسین کو دھمکی دی

Nadiya-ne *Yasin-ko* *dhamki*
Nadya-ERG Yasin-ACC threaten
di.
give-PST+PRF
'Nadiya threatened Yasin.'

(15) نادیا نے یاسین کو کتاب دی

Nadiya-ne *Yasin-ko* *kitab*
Nadya-ERG Yasin-DAT book-NOM
di.
give-PST+PRF
'Nadiya gave Yasin a book.'

	k1	**k1s**	**k2**	**k2s**	**k3**	**k4**	**k4a**	**k5**	**k7**	**k7p**	**k7t**	**pof**
k1	0	1	5	0	1	5	1	0	2	1	0	**11**
k1s	2	0	2	0	0	0	0	0	0	0	0	**16**
k2	**43**	2	0	1	0	1	0	3	2	0	1	**38**
k2s	0	1	8	0	0	0	0	0	0	0	0	2
k3	0	0	1	0	0	0	0	0	0	0	0	0
k4	2	0	6	0	0	0	1	0	0	0	0	0
k4a	1	0	0	0	0	0	0	0	0	0	0	0
k5	0	0	1	0	1	2	0	0	0	3	0	0
k7	0	0	0	0	0	0	0	0	0	3	3	1
k7p	0	0	0	0	0	0	0	0	8	0	0	0
k7t	0	0	0	0	0	0	0	0	2	0	0	0
pof	1	**9**	6	1	0	0	0	0	2	0	0	0

Table 4: Confusion Matrix between the Annotators.

7 Conclusion

In this paper we have discussed an ongoing effort of building a dependency treebank for Urdu based on CPG framework. We discussed some of the Urdu specific issues like $Ezafe$ construction and word segmentation encountered during the treebank development. We also discussed the evaluation of dependency level annotation by measuring the inter-annotator agreement using the Kappa statistics. The

	Relations	**Ann.1**	**Ann.2**	**Agr.**	**Disagr.**
1	$ras-k4$	0	1	0	1
2	$ras-k1$	4	6	3	4
3	$ras-k2$	1	3	0	4
4	$pof\_\_idiom$	1	0	0	1
5	$r6-k1$	10	8	4	10
6	$r6-k2$	63	50	43	27
7	$rbmod$	2	0	0	2
8	pof	325	271	243	110
9	rt	43	48	38	15
10	$k3$	11	8	6	7
11	rs	1	8	1	7
12	$k2s$	21	30	17	17
13	$k2p$	4	3	2	3
14	$k1$	346	320	254	158
15	rd	13	3	2	12
16	$k2$	249	298	179	189
17	$nmod\_\_relc$	27	30	13	31
18	$k7$	160	156	123	70
19	$jjmod$	23	8	8	15
20	$k5$	15	28	12	19
21	$k4$	46	50	34	28
22	$nmod\_\_k2inv$	2	3	2	1
23	rh	21	15	7	22
24	$k4a$	10	12	7	8
25	$k7a$	5	6	4	3
26	adv	47	45	30	32
27	$nmod\_\_k1inv$	0	1	0	1
28	$fragof$	6	7	5	3
29	$k7p$	46	44	29	32
30	$k7t$	67	71	53	32
31	$nmod\_\_emph$	1	2	0	3
32	$k1s$	62	70	41	50
33	$r6$	297	335	258	116
34	$k1u$	0	1	0	1
35	$vmod$	102	98	63	74
36	$nmod$	91	96	48	91
37	$ccof$	436	486	389	144
38	$sent-adv$	1	0	0	1
39	$r6v$	5	5	3	4

Table 5: Agreement and Disagreement between the Annotators.

agreement as presented in this work is considered to be reliable and substantial ensuring that the syntactic annotations in the treebank are consistent and are annotated by the annotators with a substantial clarity of the annotation guidelines.

8 Acknowledgement

We would like to thank Anjum Parveen for annotating the data set used for the experiments of inter-annotator agreement. The work reported in this paper is supported by the NSF grant (Award Number: CNS 0751202; CFDA Number: 47.070). Any opinions, findings, and conclusions or recommendations expressed in this material are those of the author(s) and do not necessarily reflect the views of the National Science Foundation.

References

R. Begum, S. Husain, A. Dhwaj, D.M. Sharma, L. Bai, and R. Sangal. 2008. Dependency annotation scheme for indian languages. In *Proceedings of IJCNLP*. Citeseer.

R. Begum, K. Jindal, A. Jain, S. Husain, and D. Misra Sharma. 2011. Identification of conjunct verbs in hindi and its effect on parsing accuracy. *Computational Linguistics and Intelligent Text Processing*, pages 29–40.

A. Bharati, V. Chaitanya, R. Sangal, and KV Ramakrishnamacharyulu. 1995. *Natural Language Processing: A Paninian Perspective*. Prentice-Hall of India.

A. Bharati, M. Bhatia, V. Chaitanya, and R. Sangal. 1996. Paninian grammar framework applied to english. Technical report, Technical Report TRCS-96-238, CSE, IIT Kanpur.

A. Bharati, R. Sangal, and D.M. Sharma. 2007. Ssf: Shakti standard format guide. Technical report, Technical report, IIIT Hyderabad.

A. Bharati, D.M. Sharma, S. Husain, L. Bai, R. Begum, and R. Sangal. 2009. Anncorra: Treebanks for indian languages guidelines for annotating hindi treebank (version–2.0).

D.N.S. Bhat. 1991. *Grammatical relations: the evidence against their necessity and universality*. Psychology Press.

R. Bhatt, B. Narasimhan, M. Palmer, O. Rambow, D.M. Sharma, and F. Xia. 2009. A multi-representational and multi-layered treebank for hindi/urdu. In *Proceedings of the Third Linguistic Annotation Workshop*, pages 186–189. Association for Computational Linguistics.

T. Bögel, M. Butt, and S. Sulger. 2008. Urdu ezafe and the morphology-syntax interface. *Proceedings of LFG08*.

F. Bond, S. Fujita, and T. Tanaka. 2008. The hinoki syntactic and semantic treebank of japanese. *Language Resources and Evaluation*, 42(2):243–251.

C. Bosco and V. Lombardo. 2004. Dependency and relational structure in treebank annotation. In *Proceedings of Workshop on Recent Advances in Dependency Grammar at COLING'04*.

S. Brants, S. Dipper, S. Hansen, W. Lezius, and G. Smith. 2002. The tiger treebank. In *Proceedings of the workshop on treebanks and linguistic theories*, pages 24–41.

J. Carletta, S. Isard, G. Doherty-Sneddon, A. Isard, J.C. Kowtko, and A.H. Anderson. 1997. The reliability of a dialogue structure coding scheme. *Computational linguistics*, 23(1):13–31.

H. Chaudhry and D.M. Sharma. 2011. Annotation and issues in building an english dependency treebank.

J. Cohen et al. 1960. A coefficient of agreement for nominal scales. *Educational and psychological measurement*, 20(1):37–46.

A. Culotta and J. Sorensen. 2004. Dependency tree kernels for relation extraction. In *Proceedings of the 42nd Annual Meeting on Association for Computational Linguistics*, page 423. Association for Computational Linguistics.

N. Durrani and S. Hussain. 2010. Urdu word segmentation. In *Human Language Technologies: The 2010 Annual Conference of the North American Chapter of the Association for Computational Linguistics*, pages 528–536. Association for Computational Linguistics.

E. Hajicová. 1998. Prague dependency treebank: From analytic to tectogrammatical annotation. *Proceedings of TSD98*, pages 45–50.

J. Hajič. 1998. Building a syntactically annotated corpus: The prague dependency treebank. *Issues of valency and meaning*, pages 106–132.

E. Hajičová, A. Abeillé, J. Hajič, J. Mírovský, and Z. Urešová. 2010. Treebank annotation. In Nitin Indurkhya and Fred J. Damerau, editors, *Handbook of Natural Language Processing, Second Edition*. CRC Press, Taylor and Francis Group, Boca Raton, FL. ISBN 978-1420085921.

J.R. Landis and G.G. Koch. 1977. The measurement of observer agreement for categorical data. *Biometrics*, pages 159–174.

G.S. Lehal. 2010. A word segmentation system for handling space omission problem in urdu script. In *23rd International Conference on Computational Linguistics*, page 43.

M.P. Marcus, M.A. Marcinkiewicz, and B. Santorini. 1993. Building a large annotated corpus of english: The penn treebank. *Computational linguistics*, 19(2):313–330.

C.P. Masica. 1993. *The Indo-Aryan Languages*. Cambridge Univ Pr, May.

T.W. Mohanan. 1990. *Arguments in Hindi*. Ph.D. thesis, Stanford University.

K. Oflazer, B. Say, D.Z. Hakkani-Tür, and G. Tür. 2003. Building a turkish treebank. *Abeillé (Abeillé, 2003)*, pages 261–277.

M. Palmer, R. Bhatt, B. Narasimhan, O. Rambow, D.M. Sharma, and F. Xia. 2009. Hindi syntax: Annotating dependency, lexical predicate-argument structure, and phrase structure. In *The 7th International Conference on Natural Language Processing*, pages 14–17.

O. Rambow, C. Creswell, R. Szekely, H. Taber, and M. Walker. 2002. A dependency treebank for english. In *Proceedings of LREC*, volume 2.

F. Reichartz, H. Korte, and G. Paass. 2009. Dependency tree kernels for relation extraction from natural language text. *Machine Learning and Knowledge Discovery in Databases*, pages 270–285.

S.M. Shieber. 1985. Evidence against the context-freeness of natural language. *Linguistics and Philosophy*, 8(3):333–343.

L. Uria, A. Estarrona, I. Aldezabal, M. Aranzabe, A. Díaz de Ilarraza, and M. Iruskieta. 2009. Evaluation of the syntactic annotation in epec, the reference corpus for the processing of basque. *Computational Linguistics and Intelligent Text Processing*, pages 72–85.

A. Vaidya, S. Husain, P. Mannem, and D. Sharma. 2009. A karaka based annotation scheme for english. *Computational Linguistics and Intelligent Text Processing*, pages 41–52.

L. Van der Beek, G. Bouma, R. Malouf, and G. Van Noord. 2002. The alpino dependency treebank. *Language and Computers*, 45(1):8–22.

C. Yong and S.K. Foo. 1999. A case study on inter-annotator agreement for word sense disambiguation.

Annotating Coordination in the Penn Treebank

Wolfgang Maier
Universität Düsseldorf
Institut für Sprache und Information
maierw@hhu.de

Sandra Kübler
Indiana University
Department of Linguistics
skuebler@indiana.edu

Erhard Hinrichs
Universität Tübingen
Seminar für Sprachwissenschaft
eh@sfs.uni-tuebingen.de

Julia Krivanek
Universität Tübingen
Seminar für Sprachwissenschaft
julia.krivanek@student.uni-tuebingen.de

Abstract

Finding coordinations provides useful information for many NLP endeavors. However, the task has not received much attention in the literature. A major reason for that is that the annotation of major treebanks does not reliably annotate coordination. This makes it virtually impossible to detect coordinations in which two conjuncts are separated by punctuation rather than by a coordinating conjunction. In this paper, we present an annotation scheme for the Penn Treebank which introduces a distinction between coordinating from non-coordinating punctuation. We discuss the general annotation guidelines as well as problematic cases. Eventually, we show that this additional annotation allows the retrieval of a considerable number of coordinate structures beyond the ones having a coordinating conjunction.

1 Introduction

1.1 Motivation

Coordination is a difficult topic, in terms of linguistic description and analysis as well as for NLP approaches. Most linguistic frameworks still struggle with finding an account for coordination that is descriptively fully adequate (Hartmann, 2000). This is also the reason why coordination is not adequately encoded in the annotation of major treebanks. From an NLP perspective, coordination is one of the major sources for errors in parsing (Hogan, 2007). If parsing of coordinate structures can be improved, overall parsing quality also benefits (Kübler et al., 2009). And consequently, downstream NLP applications, such as question answering or machine translation, would benefit as well.

However, since linguistic frameworks in general are challenged by the diverse phenomena of coordination, a consistent annotation of coordinate structures, clearly marking the phenomenon as such as well as its scope, is a difficult enterprise. Consequently, this makes the detection of conjuncts and their boundaries a highly non-trivial task. Nevertheless, an exact detection of coordination scopes is necessary for improving parsing approaches to this phenomenon.

A first step in the detection of the single conjuncts of a coordinate structure is a reliable detection of the presence of a coordinate structure as such and of the boundaries between its conjuncts. One highly predictive marker for the detection of coordinate structures is the presence of a coordinating conjunction such as `and`, `or`, `neither...nor`, and `but`. In treebanks, coordinating conjunctions are generally easy to identify by a specialized part of speech (POS) tag, for instance `CC` in the Penn Treebank (PTB) (Marcus et al., 1993) and `KON` in the Stuttgart-Tübingen tagset (STTS) (Thielen and Schiller, 1994). However, if the coordinate structure has more than 2 conjuncts, or if it is on the clause level, the conjuncts are separated by punctuation signs such as commas rather than by overt coordinating conjunctions. In the PTB, they are annotated with the POS tag `,`; in the German treebanks, TIGER (Brants et al., 2002), Negra (Skut et al., 1998), TüBa-D/S (Hinrichs et al., 2000), and TüBa-D/Z (Telljohann et al., 2004) using the STTS, they are annotated with the POS tags `$,` and `$:`, like all other punctuation without coordinating function.

Automatically identifying coordinate structures and the scope of their conjuncts in the Penn Treebank is challenging since coordinate structures as a whole and their conjuncts are not explicitly marked in the annotation by special phrasal or lexical nodes. Figure 1 shows an example sentence with two coordinate structures, the inside one a coordinate noun phrase (NP) with 3 conjuncts, and the outside one a coordinate verb phrase (VP) with two complex conjuncts. These coordinate structures are labeled by ordinary phrasal categories such as VP and NP and can thus not be distinguished at the phrasal level from VPs and NP that do not involve coordination.

There are approaches to improving parsing for coordinations, but most of these approaches are restricted to very narrow definitions such as coordinations of noun compounds such as "oil and gas resources" (Nakov and Hearst, 2005), coordinations of symmetrical NPs (Hogan, 2007; Shimbo and Hara, 2007), or coordinations of "A CC B" where A and B are conjuncts, and CC is an overt conjunction (Kübler et al., 2009). To our knowledge, there is no attempt at covering all coordination types.

One goal of this paper is to demonstrate a wide range of coordination phenomena that have to be taken into account in a thorough treatment of coordinations. We additionally present a proposal for an enhanced annotation of coordination for the Penn Treebank. The annotation is focused on punctuation and allows for an in-depth investigation of coordinations, for example for linguistic treatments, but also for work on coordination detection, from which many NLP applications can profit.

The structure of this paper is as follows. In section 2, we look at syntactic treatments of coordination, and we have a look at the Penn Treebank guidelines. Section 3 is dedicated to the presentation of a "stylebook" for the enhanced annotation of coordination that we advocate in the present paper. We outline our annotation decisions and the issues that we encountered. Section 4 contains an empirical analysis of the coordinations in the PTB, made possible by the new annotation. Finally, section 5 concludes the paper.

2 Related Work

2.1 Coordination in Linguistics

Coordinations are complex syntactic structures that consist of two or more elements (conjuncts), with one or more conjuncts typically, but not always preceded by a coordinating conjunction such as `and`, `or`, `neither...nor`, and `but`. However, see section 3 for examples of coordinations that lack coordinating conjunctions altogether. Coordinate structures can conjoin lexical and phrasal material of any kind and typically exhibit syntactic parallelism in the sense that each conjunct belongs to the same lexical or phrasal category. However, coordinations of unlike categories such as `Loch Ness is a lake in Scotland and famous for its monster` are also possible. The conjuncts are typically syntactic constituents; in fact, coordinate structures are among the classic constructions used to test for constituency. However, there are well-known cases of non-constituent conjunctions such as `Sandy gave a record to Sue and a book to Leslie` and gapping structures with one or more elliptical conjuncts such as `Leslie likes bagels and Sandy donuts`. Incidentally, the coordinate structure in Figure 1 consitutes an example of non-constituent conjunction since the second conjunct `lower in Zurich` does not form a single constituent. The PTB treats this conjunct as a VP. However, note that the conjunct is not headed by a verb; rather the verb is elided.

It is precisely the wide range of distinct subcases of constituent structures that makes their linguistic analysis challenging and that makes it hard to construct adequate language models for the computational processing of coordinate structures. The purpose of the present paper is not to refine existing theoretical accounts of coordinate structures such as those proposed in Generative Grammar, Generalized Phrase Structure Grammar, Head-Driven Phrase Structure Grammar, Tree Adjoining Grammar, or Dependency Grammar. Rather, our goal is a much more modest one and focuses on written language only, where punctuation is among the reliable cues for predicting cases of coordinate structures and for identifying the boundaries of individual conjuncts, especially for coordinate structures with

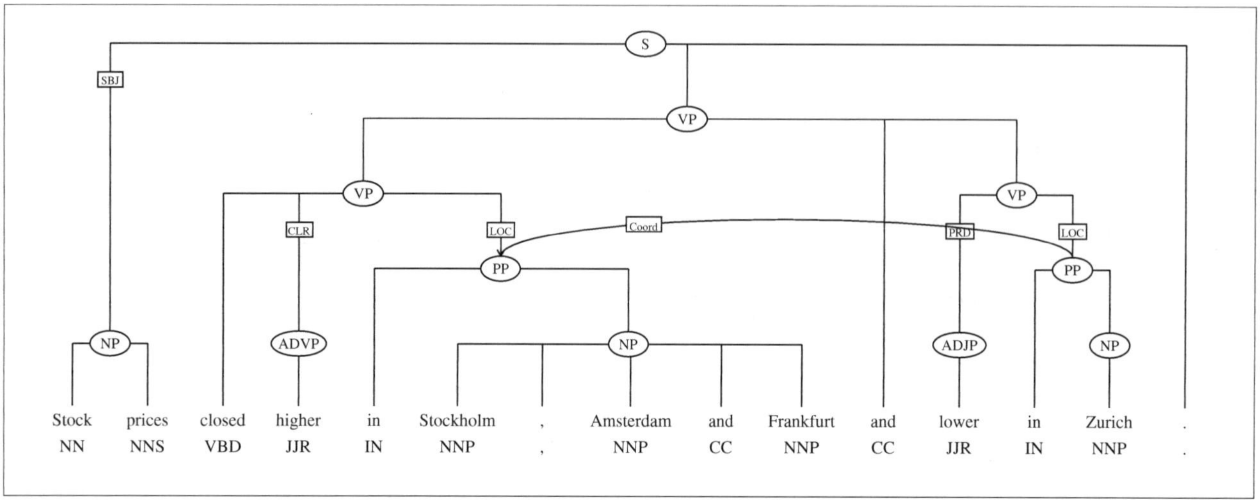

Figure 1: An example with two embedded coordinations.

more than two conjuncts, which have been largely ignored in computational modeling of language thus far.

Since supervised models for statistical parsing require annotated training material, we will propose a more fine-grained annotation scheme for punctuation than has thus far been incorporated into existing treebanks. The present paper focuses on English only and will use the Penn Treebank Bracketing Guidelines as the annotation scheme for which such more fine-grained annotations will be proposed. However, the proposed modifications can be easily imported to other treebanks for English such as CCGBank or treebanks for other language, and we conjecture that they would lead to improved language models for coordinate structures for those treebanks as well.

In order to properly ground the discussion, we will now review Penn Treebank Bracketing Guidelines.

2.2 Penn Treebank Guidelines

The Penn Treebank Bracketing Guidelines (Bies et al., 1995, sec. 7) describe extensively how to treat coordination in terms of bracketing. The guidelines state that coordinate structures are annotated on the lowest level possible. One word conjuncts are coordinated on the word level. An example for this is shown in Figure 1 in the coordinated NP `Stockholm , Amsterdam and Frankfurt`. In gapped structures, symmetrical elements in the conjuncts are marked using gap-coindexation. In the example in Figure 1, the coindexation is shown as a secondary edge from the prepositional phrase (PP) in the second conjunct to the PP in the first one.

The guidelines also discuss multi-word coordinating conjunctions such as `as well as` or `instead of` and discontinuous conjunctions such as `not only ...but` or `not ...but instead`. Multi-word coordinating conjunctions, including discontinuous ones, are grouped into `CONJP` constituents. Single word portions of discontinuous conjunctions are not marked as such. Figure 2 shows an example of a discontinous coordinating conjunction in which the first part is projected to a `CONJP` while the second part is a single word and thus not projected.

The manual does not mention coordinate structures with more than 2 conjuncts or without overt conjunctions, and the only examples in which the comma takes over the role of a coordinating conjunction refer to "difficult cases" such as the sentence in Figure 3, in which symmetry is enforced by anti-placeholders `*NOT*`.

3 Annotation of Coordinating Punctuation

We annotate all intra-sentential punctuation in the Penn Treebank and determine for each punctuation sign whether it is part of a coordination or not. As far as possible, decisions are based on the syntactic

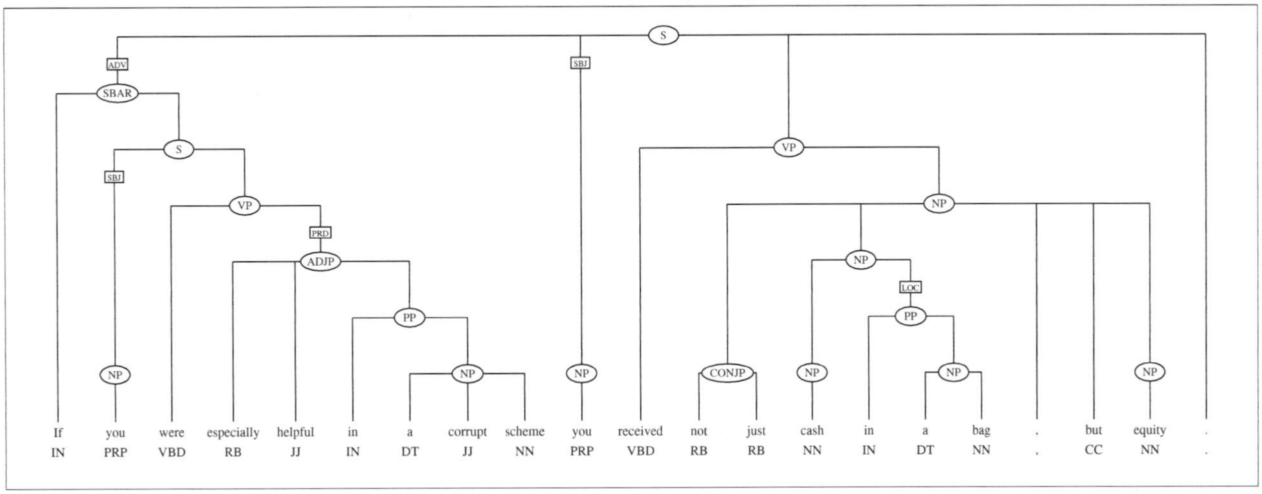

Figure 2: An example with a multi-word conjunction.

annotations in the treebank.

3.1 Annotation principles

The principal guidelines for the enhanced annotation of coordination are as follows. Let t be a punctuation token and let t_l and t_r be the tokens immediately on the left and the right of t (disregarding coordinating conjunctions). We annotate t as coordinating iff

1. t is attached to the lowest node t_c which dominates both t_l and t_r, and

2a. in the symmetrical case: the non-terminals directly dominated by t_c which also dominate t_l, resp. t_r, have the same label;

2b. in the asymmetrical case: t_c is labeled UCP (coordination of unlike constituents) – or t_c is S, and the two non-terminals dominating t_l and t_r are different (since coordination of unlike clausal constituents is grouped under an S rather than a UCP).

In cases where there are no nodes between t and t_c, we check the POS tags of t_l and t_R for equality. In theory, these two rules, given the syntactic annotation, should be sufficient to find all cases of coordination. However, in practice, the situation is more complicated, as shown in the next subsection.

For example, in Figure 1, the comma is labeled as coordination since the two words to the left and right are directly dominated by an NP, and they both have the same POS tag, NNP, and thus follow rule 2a. The comma in Figure 2 is also annotated as a coordination following 2a since the words to the left and right are both dominated by NPs, as is the node dominating all words in question. We present examples for symmetrical coordinations on the clausal and phrasal level in (1).

(1)
a. Richard Stoltzman has taken a [$_{JJR}$ gentler] , [$_{ADJP}$ more audience-friendly approach] . (PTB 3968)
b. The two leaders are expected to discuss [$_{NP}$ changes sweeping the East bloc] as well as [$_{NP}$[$_{NP}$ human-rights issues] , [$_{NP}$ regional disputes] and [$_{NP}$ economic cooperation]] . (PTB 6798)
c. These critics are backed by several academic studies showing that the adoption of poison pills reduces shareholder values not merely [$_{PP}$ in the short run] , but also [$_{PP}$ over longer periods] . (PTB 5056)
d. Our pilot simply [$_{VP}$ laughed] , [$_{VP}$ fired up the burner] and [$_{VP}$ with another blast of flame lifted us , oh , a good 12-inches above the water level] . (PTB 4465)
e. [$_S$ He believes in what he plays] , and [$_S$ he plays superbly] . (PTB 3973)
f. [$_S$ Dow Jones industrials 2596.72 , off 17.01] ; [$_S$ transportation 1190.43 , off 14.76] ; [$_S$ utilities 215.86 , up 0.19] .

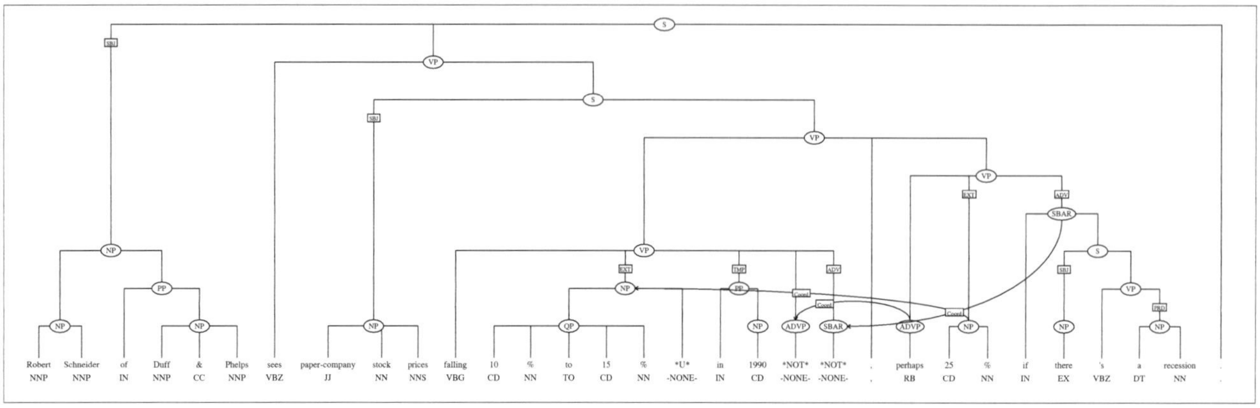

Figure 3: A difficult coordination example.

(PTB 13082)

The examples in (2) show cases of coordination of unlike constituents. These cases are covered by the rule 2b described above; in the first two sentences, all conjuncts are dominated by `UCP`, and the last sentence is an example of a clausal coordination, that is projected to an `S` node.

(2) a. Assuming final enactment this month , the prohibition will take effect [$_{ADVP}$ 96 days later] , or [$_{PP}$ in early February] . (PTB 6499)

b. My wife and I will stay [$_{PP}$ through the skiing season] , or [$_{SBAR}$ until the money runs out] – whichever comes first . (PTB 15255)

c. This perhaps was perceived as [$_{NP}$ a " bold " stance] , and thus [$_{ADJP}$ suspicious] . (PTB 18051)

d. [$_{S}$ Mr. Trotter 's painting showed a wall of wood boards with painted ribbons tacked down in a rectangle] ; [$_{SINV}$ tucked behind the ribbons were envelopes , folded , faded and crumpled papers and currency] . (PTB 8698)

The example in (3) shows a comma that has two different functions: The comma before `and` delimits the relative clause modifying `oral orders`, and at the same time marks the coordination. Since we are interested in all cases of coordination, such multi-functional punctuation marks are annotated as coordinations if that is one of their functions.

(3) The affected practices include [$_{NP}$ the placing of oral orders , which is the way most public customer orders are placed] , and [$_{NP}$ trading between affiliated brokers] , even though in some cases trading with affiliates may be the only way to obtain the best execution for a client . (PTB 15541)

3.2 Problematic Cases

Coordination vs. apposition In many cases, appositions show the same characteristics as the rules above. An apposition is not restricted to be of the same category as the constituent it modifies, but in many cases, it is. These cases are the main reason for the manual annotation since they cannot be distinguished automatically. Thus, if the second phrase defines or modifies the first one, we do not annotate the intervening commas as coordination. An example for an apposition that follows the rules above is given in (4).

(4) The last two months have been the whole ball game , " says [$_{NP}$ Steven Norwitz] , [$_{NP}$ a vice president] . (PTB 15034)

The same holds for cases in which a temporal NP modifies another NP, such as in example (5). Here, the NP `Tass` is modified by the temporal NP `June 10 , 1988`.

(5) – : Letter from Eduard Shevardnadze to U.N. Secretary-General Perez de Cuellar , reported in [$_{NP}$ Tass] , [$_{NP-TMP}$ June 10 , 1988] . (PTB 21148)

There are cases, especially ones in which the second phrase is negated, for which it is difficult to decide between coordination and apposition. The sentence in (6) shows an example. For these cases, we decided to treat them as coordination.

(6) He is [$_{NP}$ a mechanical engineer] , [$_{NP}$ not an atmospheric chemist] . (PTB 7158)

Ambiguous punctuation Commas before coordinating conjunctions are typically signs of coordination. Note that the usage of commas in the Penn Treebank is not very regular, and cases of "A, B, and C" can be found along with cases of "A, B and C" and cases of "A, and B", as shown in the examples in (7). All these cases are covered by rule 2a.

(7) a. Describing itself as " asset rich , " Sea Containers said it will move immediately to sell [$_{NP}$ two ports] , [$_{NP}$ various ferries] , [$_{NP}$ ferry services] , [$_{NP}$ containers] , and [$_{NP}$ other investments] . (PTB 6105)

b. Stocks closed higher in [$_{NP}$ Hong Kong] , [$_{NP}$ Manila] , [$_{NP}$ Singapore] , [$_{NP}$ Sydney] and [$_{NP}$ Wellington] , but were lower in Seoul . (PTB 4369)

c. [$_{NP}$ Sidley & Austin , a leading Chicago-based law firm] , and [$_{NP}$ Ashurst Morris Crisp , a midsized London firm of solicitors] , are scheduled today to announce plans to open a joint office in Tokyo . (PTB 5367)

However, there are also cases in which the comma before a coordinating conjunction is clearly not part of the coordination, but rather belongs to the preceding constituent, such as in the examples in (8). In these cases, the syntactic annotation shows that the comma is not a coordination comma by attaching it low to the preceding constituent; we do not annotate these commas as coordination phenomena.

(8) a. Berthold [$_{VP}$ is based in Wildbad , West Germany ,] and [$_{VP}$ also has operations in Belgium] . (PTB 4988)

b. Under the plan , Gillette South Africa will sell [$_{NP}$ manufacturing facilities in Springs , South Africa ,] and [$_{NP}$ its business in toiletries and plastic bags] to Twins Pharmaceuticals Ltd. , an affiliate of Anglo American Corp. , a South African company . (PTB 6154)

c. [$_{S}$ Last week 's uncertainty in the stock market and a weaker dollar triggered a flight to safety] [$_{PRN}$, he said ,] [$_{S}$ but yesterday the market lacked such stimuli] . (PTB 8252)

d. [$_{S}$ I want white America to talk about it , too ,] but [$_{S}$ I 'm convinced that the grapevine is what 's happening] . " (PTB 10130)

Another ambiguous case can be found in coordinate structures on the clausal level, which often does not use overt coordinating conjunctions, but rather commas or semicolons. These cases of coordination are difficult to distinguish automatically from other types of parataxis. The examples in (9) we regard as coordinations while the examples in (10) are not since the relation between them is elaborative.

(9) a. [$_{S}$ In 1980 , 18 % of federal prosecutions concluded at trial] ; [$_{S}$ in 1987 , only 9 % did] . (PTB 12113)

b. [$_{S}$ Various ministries decided the products businessmen could produce and how much] ; and [$_{S}$ government-owned banks controlled the financing of projects and monitored whether companies came through on promised plans] . (PTB 12355)

(10) a. [$_{S}$ This does n't necessarily mean larger firms have an advantage] ; [$_{S}$ Mr. Pearce said GM works with a number of smaller firms it regards highly] . (PTB 12108)

b. [$_{S}$ Senator Sasser of Tennessee is chairman of the Appropriations subcommittee on military construction] ; [$_{S}$ Mr. Bush 's $ 87 million request for Tennessee increased to $ 109 million] . (PTB 12223)

Non-coordinative use of conjunctions There are sentences that involve coordinating conjunctions in structures that are not coordinations but rather appositions. While the first example in (11) cannot be distinguished from coordination based on our annotation guidelines (cf. sec. 3.1) and the syntactic annotation, the syntactic annotation for the other two sentences shows that these are not considered cases of coordination, either by grouping the coordinating conjunction under a parenthetical node (PRN) or under a fragment (FRAG).

(11) a. The NASD , which operates the Nasdaq computer system on which 5,200 OTC issues trade , compiles short interest data in $[_{NP}$ $[_{NP}$ two categories$]$: $[_{NP}$ the approximately two-thirds , and generally biggest , Nasdaq stocks that trade on the National Market System ; and the one-third , and generally smaller , Nasdaq stocks that are n't a part of the system$]]$. (PTB 21080)

b. Martha was $[_{ADJP}$ pleased , $[_{PRN}$ but nowhere near as much as Mr. Engelken$]]$. (PTB 14598)

c. The HUD scandals will simply $[_{VP}$ continue , $[_{FRAG}$ but under new mismanagement$]]$. (PTB 15629)

Coordination in NP premodification The Penn Treebank Bracketing Guidelines (Marcus et al., 1993) state that generally conjuncts are projected to the phrase level before they are coordinated. There is one exception: premodifiers in NPs, which are only projected if they consist of more than one word. In such cases, it is not obvious from the tree that there is a coordination. But even if there is no explicit marking of coordination in the syntactic analysis, we do annotate the coordination. Examples are shown in (12).

(12) a. Yesterday , it received a $[_{ADJP}$ \$ 15 million$]$, $[_{JJ}$ three-year$]$ contract from Drexel Burnham Lambert . (PTB 6485)

b. There 's nothing in the least contradictory in all this , and it would be nice to think that Washington could tolerate a $[_{ADJP}$ reasonably sophisticated$]$, $[_{JJ}$ complex$]$ view . (PTB 8018)

c. Perhaps the shock would have been less if they 'd fixed to another $[_{NN}$ low-tax$]$, $[_{VBN}$ deregulated$]$, $[_{JJ}$ supply-side$]$ economy . (PTB 10463)

	full		av. per sent.	
	total	coord.	total	coord.
,	28 853	3 924	1.22	0.17
;	684	547	0.03	0.02
CCs	14 267		0.60	

Table 1: Annotation of punctuation

4 Properties of the Annotation

For the empirical analysis presented here, we use approximately half the Penn Treebank. The data set has a size of 23 678 sentences and 605 064 words in total, with an average length of 25.6 words per sentence.

Table 1 shows some basic statistics, more specfically:

1. the numbers of annotated commas, semicolons, and coordinating conjunctions (CC) and their total numbers over the entire data set, and

2. the average numbers of annotated commas, semicolons, and coordinating conjunctions (CC) and their average number per sentence.

The numbers show that approximately 14% of all commas and 80% of all semicolons are used in coordinate structures. CCs constitute only 2.36% of all words. If we count CCs as well as the punctuation signs that are annotated as being part of a coordination, the number rises to 3.10% of all words. These numbers show that we cannot assume that all sentence-internal punctuation is related to coordination, but that the use of commas and semicolons to separate conjuncts is not a marginal phenomenon.

Table 2 offers a first look at the distribution of the number of conjuncts that occur in coordinate structures. Our present investigation focuses exclusively on noun phrase coordination. Given that, in principle, our annotation marks all conjunctions, and given that our annotation guidelines state that all conjuncts must be sisters, it is rather straightforward to determine the number of conjuncts of a coordination: We simply count the separators between conjuncts, i.e. CCs and conjunction punctuation, below a given non-terminal while counting

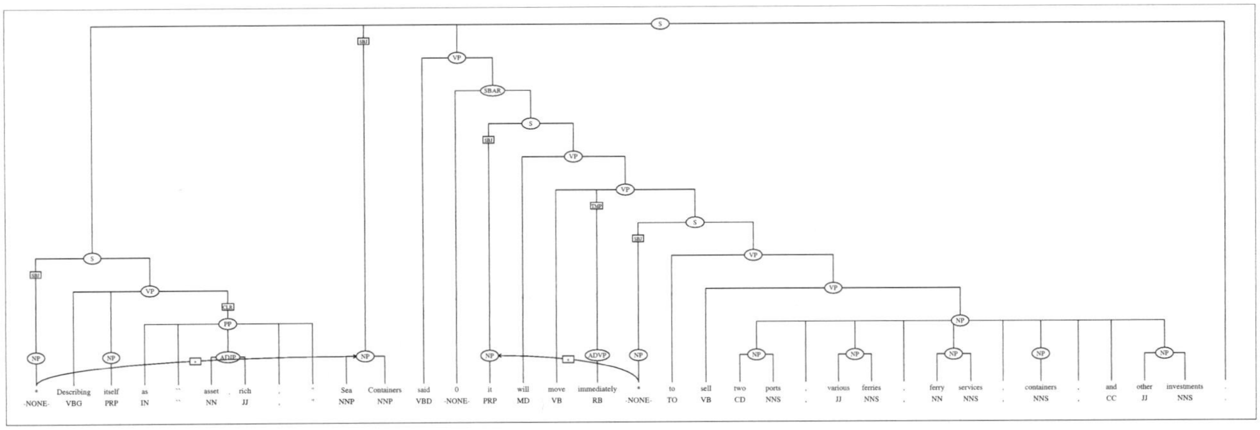

Figure 4: An example with more than two conjuncts.

No. of conj.	w/ annot.	w/o annot.
2	12 689	13 917
3	2 243	1 195
4	653	220
5	234	35
6	90	18
≥ 7	94	0

Table 2: Number of conjuncts below NX/NP

adjacent separators as singles (in order to count sequences of "A, and B" as single separator). The number of conjuncts is then the number of separators plus one. Without annotation, i.e. when only considering CC, we find that 2 882 sentences (12% out of the total of 23 678 sentences) have coordinations consisting of more than two conjuncts. If we additionally consider the coordination punctuation, this number rises significantly to 4 764 (20%). When looking at noun phrase coordination, more precisely, at coordination below NX and NP, the added value of our enhanced coordination annotation is especially apparent: It is clear from the numbers in Table 2 that we would miss a high number of coordinations, especially multi-conjunct structures, without the annotation and that this additional number of coordinations can be found reliably using our enhanced annotation.

As an example for a coordination that would be difficult to identify correctly, consider sentence (7-a). The syntactic annotation is shown in Fig. 4. While the CC tag on the last `and` would allow for the identification of the coordination of `containers, and other investments`, all NPs which are in front of those two could not be recognized as part of the coordination. A more detailed investigation of coordinate structures beyond noun phrases that would also include an assessment of the scope of coordinations is left for future work.

5 Conclusion

In this paper, we have listed a wide range of coordination phenomena that have to be taken into consideration for an exhaustive treatment of coordination. We have presented a new annotation layer for the Penn Treebank which allows for a thorough treatment of coordination by clarifying the status of punctuation. Furthermore, in an empirical analysis, we have demonstrated the utility of our annotation, showing that it allows for the detection of a large number of coordinations which cannot be detected when only coordinating conjunctions are considered.

The annotation opens the way for interesting future research. We are pursuing two different paths. On the one hand, we are investigating possibilites for the identification of coordination scope, also beyond phrasal coordination. For the first time, this is now possible using supervised methods. On the other hand, we are working on improving parser performance on coordinations on the basis of our new annotation, beyond the restricted types of coordination considered in previous works.

References

Ann Bies, Mark Ferguson, Karen Katz, and Robert MacIntyre, 1995. *Bracketing Guidelines for Treebank II Style Penn Treebank Project*. University of Pennsylvania.

Sabine Brants, Stefanie Dipper, Silvia Hansen, Wolfgang Lezius, and George Smith. 2002. The TIGER treebank. In Erhard Hinrichs and Kiril Simov, editors, *Proceedings of the First Workshop on Treebanks and Linguistic Theories (TLT 2002)*, pages 24–41, Sozopol, Bulgaria.

Katharina Hartmann. 2000. *Right Node Raising and Gapping*. John Benjamins, Amsterdam, The Netherlands.

Erhard W. Hinrichs, Julia Bartels, Yasuhiro Kawata, Valia Kordoni, and Heike Telljohann. 2000. The Verbmobil treebanks. In *Proceedings of KONVENS 2000, 5. Konferenz zur Verarbeitung natürlicher Sprache*, pages 107–112, Ilmenau, Germany.

Deirdre Hogan. 2007. Coordinate noun phrase disambiguation in a generative parsing model. In *Proceedings of the 45th Annual Meeting of the Association of Computational Linguistics*, pages 680–687, Prague, Czech Republic.

Sandra Kübler, Erhard W. Hinrichs, Wolfgang Maier, and Eva Klett. 2009. Parsing coordinations. In *Proceedings of the 12th Conference of the European Chapter of the ACL (EACL)*, pages 406–414, Athens, Greece.

Mitchell P. Marcus, Beatrice Santorini, and Mary Ann Marcinkiewicz. 1993. Building a large annotated corpus of English: The Penn Treebank. *Computational Linguistics*, 19(2):313–330. Special Issue on Using Large Corpora: II.

Preslav Nakov and Marti Hearst. 2005. Using the web as an implicit training set: Application to structural ambiguity resolution. In *Proceedings of Human Language Technology Conference and Conference on Empirical Methods in Natural Language Processing*, pages 835–842, Vancouver, Canada.

Masashi Shimbo and Kazuo Hara. 2007. A discriminative learning model for coordinate conjunctions. In *Proceedings of the 2007 Joint Conference on Empirical Methods in Natural Language Processing and Computational Natural Language Learning (EMNLP-CoNLL)*, pages 610–619, Prague, Czech Republic.

Wojciech Skut, Thorsten Brants, Brigitte Krenn, and Hans Uszkoreit. 1998. A linguistically interpreted corpus of German newspaper texts. In *ESSLLI Workshop on Recent Advances in Corpus Annotation*, Saarbrücken, Germany.

Heike Telljohann, Erhard Hinrichs, and Sandra Kübler. 2004. The TüBa-D/Z treebank: Annotating German with a context-free backbone. In *Proceedings of the Fourth International Conference on Language Resources and Evaluation (LREC)*, pages 2229–2235, Lisbon, Portugal.

Christine Thielen and Anne Schiller. 1994. Ein kleines und erweitertes Tagset fürs Deutsche. In Helmut Feldweg and Erhard Hinrichs, editors, *Lexikon & Text*, pages 215–226. Niemeyer, Tübingen.

Annotating Particle Realization and Ellipsis in Korean

Sun-Hee Lee
Wellesley College
Wellesley, MA 02481, U.S.A.
slee6@wellesley.edu

Jae-young Song
Yonsei University
Seoul, Korea
jysong@yonsei.ac.kr

Abstract

We present a novel scheme for annotating the realization and ellipsis of Korean particles. Annotated data include 100,128 *Ecel* (a space-based word unit) in spoken and written corpora composed of four different genres in order to evaluate how register variation contributes to Korean particle ellipsis. Identifying the grammatical functions of particles and zero particles is critical for deriving a valid linguistic analysis of argument realization, semantic and discourse analysis, and computational processes of parsing. The primary challenge is to design a reliable scheme for classifying particles while making a clear distinction between ellipsis and non-occurrences. We determine in detail issues involving particle annotation and present solutions. In addition to providing a statistical analysis and outcomes, we briefly discuss linguistic factors involving particle ellipsis.

1 Introduction

In Korean, the grammatical function of a nominal is represented by a morphologically-attached postpositional particle. Particles involve a wide range of linguistic information such as grammatical relations (subject, object), semantic roles (Agent, Patient, Location, Instrument, etc.), discourse/pragmatic properties, such as topic markers, delimiters and auxiliary particles, as well as conjunctions. Due to their complex linguistic functions, particles are one of the most rigorously investigated topics in Korean linguistics.

In example (1), the particle *ka* indicates subjecthood and *ul* refers to objecthood.[1]

(1) onul-**un** Mina-**ka** kyosil-**eyse** cemsim-**ul** mek-e.
today-**TOP** M-**SUBJ** classroom-**in** lunch-**OBJ** eat-ENG
'Mina eats lunch in the classroom.'

The subject particle *ka* also marks Agent (semantic role); the locative particle *eyse* combines with a nominal referring to Location; *un* marks topichood in the given discourse, etc.

In spite of their linguistic function (representing the grammatical relations of subject and object), these particles frequently disappear, particularly in spoken Korean (Hong et al., 1998; Kim and Kwon, 2004; Lee and Thompson, 1985; Lee 2006, 2008). Previous studies have mainly focused on case particles and suggested that register variation is the key factor in particle ellipsis. However, few studies have comprehensively examined both spoken and written data with specific annotation features and guidelines. By using balanced spoken and written data, this paper explores the realization of all particles and ellipsis of case particles including subject and object case. In order to test the effect of register variation on particle realization, we designed a balanced corpora to include four different styles. The spoken corpora include everyday conversations, informal monologues (story-telling), TV debates, and lectures/speeches; the written corpora include personal essays, novels, news articles, and academic papers.

Categorizing particles requires a well-articulated classification. Particles have complex grammatical

[1] The subject and object particles have the phonological variants *i* and *lul*, respectively.

functions, and it is difficult to determine if a missing particle is a case of ellipsis or non-occurrence. We discuss these challenges in the context of developing a novel annotation scheme and guidelines. We examine particle ellipsis patterns across registers, as well as semantic and pragmatic factors triggering particle ellipsis.

2 Relevant Background

Within theoretical linguistics, Korean particles have been classified according to three distinct linguistic functions: case particles, auxiliary particles, and conjunctive particles (Nam, 2000; Lee, 2006)[2]. A case particle combines with an argument or adjunct nominal and specifies the grammatical relation and semantic role of the nominal within the argument structure of a predicate. In contrast to case particles, auxiliary particles are not based on the grammatical relation of a nominal and a predicate; they introduce extra semantic and discourse interpretations. This category includes topic markers and delimiters, as well as other particles with diverse lexical meanings. In addition, there are conjunctive particles that attach to nominals and connect them to the following ones.

Identifying the diverse functions of particles is important for syntactic, semantic, and discourse analyses in Korean. When a particle is elided, recovering the information behind a missing particle is essential for determining accurate grammatical relations, which is a prerequisite for computational processes of parsing, discourse analysis, machine translation, etc. However, the recovery process for missing particles does not include auxiliary particles as candidates due to their unpredictable distributions; auxiliary particles have their own discourse and pragmatic meanings, and their distributions over nominals are not restricted by grammatical relations with predicates.

On the one hand, the validity of recovering a missing particle into its original form itself can be questionable; it has been argued in the literature that zero marking is the unmarked option and there is no ellipsis or deletion of particles (Lee and Thompson, 1989; Fujii and Ono, 2000 inter alia). However, whether a particle is deleted or originates as a zero form, it is important that a missing particle corresponds to a particular case particle and identification of it is crucial for determining the grammatical and semantic function of the bare nominal.

With respect to particle ellipsis in Korean and also Japanese, most previous research has focused on subject and object particles. There have been contradictory reports on the dropping rates of these particles. Whereas Kwon (1989) and Hong et al. (1998) report a higher dropping rate for subject particles, Kim and Kwon (2004) and Lee (2006) argue for a higher dropping rate for object case markers in colloquial Korean. Among these studies, Hong et al. (1998) analyzes different radio shows with a total time span of 60 minutes and Lee (2006) analyzes the Call Friend Korean (CFK) corpus of telephone speech. Even disregarding the small data size (the former with fewer than 2000 noun phrases and the latter with 1956 overtly expressed subject and object NPs), the statistical results are less than convincing given the lack of a specific annotation scheme and guidelines. For example, Hong et al. (1998) include nominals with some topic markers or delimiters as tokens of case marker ellipsis. However, as mentioned in Lee (2008), these cases need to be excluded from the list of case ellipsis because the subject or object particles are morphologically restricted from co-occurring with auxiliary particles in Korean. Although Lee (2008) excludes optional occurrences of object particles in light verb constructions, it is not quite clear how non-occurrences of particles are separated from ellipsis of particles in the corpus study without specific guidelines. In order to develop a more comprehensive analysis of case ellipsis, it is necessary to employ large data sets with different registers across spoken and written Korean and a well-established annotation scheme and guidelines.

3 The Data and Annotation Scheme

3.1 Data

We extracted 100,128 *Ecel* with morphological tagging from the Sejong Corpora to create spoken and written balanced corpora composed of four different registers with different degrees of formality. Approximately 2000 *Ecel* were each

[2] Although particles combine with nominals, they sometimes follow a verbal phrase or a sentence adding semantic and pragmatic meanings of honorification, focus, etc. Some researchers assign these particles to a special category (Nam, 2000). In this study, we only examine particles combining with nominals and not with phrasal or sentential categories.

selected from 49 files to build balanced corpora. Table 1 summarizes the composition of the data.

Type	Registers		# of Files	Size
Spoken	Private	Everyday Conversations (E)	7	12,504
		Monologues (M)	6	12,502
	Public	TV Debates & Discussions (D)	6	12, 547
		Lectures & Speeches (L)	6	12, 526
Written	Personal Essays (PE)		6	12, 510
	Novels (N)		6	12, 505
	Newspaper Articles (P)		6	12, 511
	Academic Textbooks (A)		6	12, 505

Table 1. Composition of Balanced Corpora

3.2 Annotation Scheme

In agglutinative languages like Korean, particles are attached to preceding nominals without spaces, and identifying the position of a particle requires accurate segmentation. Although we extracted data with morphological tags, the tags sometimes reflected errors in spacing, morpheme identification, segmentation, etc. Therefore, we manually corrected relevant errors in segmentation and morpheme tags before performing annotation. Using morpheme tags, we identified all the nominal categories in the corpora that can combine with particles, including all the nominals with and without particles. We annotated realized particles and determined their categories using the tag set in Figure 1. In addition, we selected four annotation features to mark up particle realization and ellipsis. The given tag set has been used to annotate both realized particles and missing particles. However, annotating missing particles presents challenges and requires a new annotation scheme. Elided particles are recovered using the case particles based upon grammatical relations between a nominal and a predicate. The details are presented in the next section.

- **Tag Set of Particles**
  - o **Case Particles**[3]**:**

Subject (S): *ka/i* Subject Honorific (SH): *keyse*
Object (O): *ul/lul* Genitive (G): *uy*
Dative (D): *ey/eykey* ('to'), *hanthey* ('to')
Dative Honorific (DH): *kkey* ('to')
Complement (C): *ka/i*
Adverbial Case (B):
  Time (BT): *ey* ('in, at')
  Location (BL): *ey* ('to'), *eyse* ('from')
  Instrument (BI): *lo/ulo* ('with')
  Direction (BD): *lo/ulo* ('to, as')
  Source (BS): eyse ('from'), *eykey(se)* ('from'), *hanthey(se)* ('from') , *pwuthe* ('from'), *ulopwuthe* ('from'), *eysepwuthe* ('from'),
  Goal (BG): *ey* ('to'), kkaci ('to')
  Accompany (BA): *wa/kwa* ('with'), *hako* ('with'), *ilang/lang* ('with')
Vocative (V): *a/ya*
Comparative (R): *pota* ('than'), *mankhum* ('as~as'), etc.

  - o **Discourse/Modal**:

Topic (T): *un/nun/n*
Auxiliary (A): *to* ('also'), *man* ('only'), *mata* ('each'), *pakkey* ('only'), chelem ('like'), *mankhum* ('as much as'), etc.

  - o **Conjunction** (J): *wa/kwa* ('and'), *hako* ('and'), *ina/na* ('or'), *itunci/tunci* ('or'), *ilang/lang* ('and'), etc.

- **Annotation Features**
  Realized Particle, Realized Particle Type
  Missing Particle, Missing Particle Type

Figure 1. Annotation Scheme of Particles

3.3. Ellipsis vs. Non-Occurrence of Particles

As defined in Fry (2001), ellipsis is the phenomenon whereby a speaker omits an obligatory element of syntactic structure. However, there are at least three morpho-syntactic constructions in Korean where a particle does not need to be recovered because it is not obligatory in the given position. Our annotation distinguishes these optional non-occurrences from the particle ellipsis phenomenon and marks them separately.

First, the occurrence of the genitive case *uy* is optional depending on various syntactic and semantic relation between two nominals in Korean. For example, the genitive *uy* tends to disappear after a complement nominal of a verbal noun, e.g., *yenghwa-uy/Ø chwalyeng* (movie-GEN + filming) 'filming of a movie', whereas it appears after a subject nominal of a verbal noun, e.g., John-uy/$*^{?}$Ø *wusung* (John-GEN + winning) 'John's winning'. Due to complex linguistic factors, there is still controversy regarding how to predict occurrences of the genitive case in Korean (Lee, 2005; Hong,

[3] We focused on particles that directly follow nominals. Thus, particles that appear after verb phrases or sentences have been excluded from our tag set, including the direct quotation particle *lako* and *hako*.

2009), and native speakers' intuitions on the positions of the dropped genitive particle and its recoverability vary.[4] Therefore, we chose not to annotate the genitive particle *uy* when it does not occur and we do not count particle ellipsis within a nominal phrase.

Second, particles are optional in light verb constructions, as mentioned in previous research (e.g., Lee and Thompson, 1989; Lee and Park, 2008). In Korean, the morphological formation of a Sino-Korean (or foreign-borrowed) verbal noun and the light verbs (LV) *hata* 'do', *toyta* 'become', and *sikhita* 'make' is very frequent, e.g., *silhyen* (accomplishment)+*hata/toyta/sikhita*to 'accomplish /to be accomplished/to make it accomplish', *stheti* (study) +*hata*, 'to study' etc. In these light verb constructions, the subject particle *i/ka* or the object particle *ul/lul* can appear after the verbal nouns as in *silhyen-**ul** hata* (accomplishment-OBJ do), *silhyen-**i** toyta* (accomplishment-SBJ become), *silhyen-**ul** sikhita* (accomplishment-OBJ make), *stheti-**lul** hata* (study-OBJ do), etc. Realization of these case particles, however, is not mandatory and even unnatural when the argument of a verbal noun appears in the same sentence, as in the following example.

(3) ?*John-i kkum-**ul** silhyen-**ul** hayssta.
J-nom dream-**OBJ** accomplishment-**OBJ** did
'John accomplished his dream.'

In considering the morpho-syntactic unity of N+LV combinations as single predicates and the awkwardness of a realized particle after a verbal noun, we conclude that N + LV combinations do not involve case ellipsis.[5] However, when these LV combinations include negation, the negative adverb intervenes between a verbal noun and the LV, and the particle *i/ka* or *ul/lul* follows the verbal noun. In those constructions, we exceptionally assume particle ellipsis. This decision affects the result of our corpus analysis due to the high frequency of LV combinations, particularly with respect to object particle ellipsis. In contrast, Lee and Thompson (1989) assume particle ellipsis in N+LV combinations unless there is another nominal with an object particle licensed in front of the verbal noun. Although we exclude particle ellipsis in light verb constructions, we separately mark up possible case realizations of LV combinations in order to measure the extent to which they affect the statistical results.

Third, optional particles frequently appear with bound nouns (or defective nouns) in Korean. Bound nouns refer to nominals that do not occur without being preceded by a demonstrative, an adnoun clause, or another noun, which includes *tey* 'place', *ttay* 'time' *swu* 'way', *ke(s)* 'thing', *cwul* 'way', *check* 'pretense', etc.

(4) hakkyo-eyse kongpwuha-l swu(-**ka**) issta.
school-at study-REL way (-**NOM**) exist
'It is possible to go to study at school.'

Bound nouns are functionally limited with respect to neighboring constituents. For instance, a bound noun *ttay* 'time' only combines with a clause ending with the adnominal ending *-(u)l*, whereas *hwu* 'after' combines with a clause ending with *-(u)n*.[6] In addition to morpho-syntactic reliance on the preceding clause, many bound nouns form formulaic expressions with the following predicates (i.e., the bound noun *swu* 'way' only combines with existential predicates, *issta* 'exist' and *epsta* 'do not exist'). Considering that particles in bound nouns are frequently dropped and do not represent grammatical relations of bound nouns with respect to the predicate, we also exclude them as cases of ellipsis.[7]

[4] Although semantic change and lexical insertion can be used for identifying morphological compounds, it is still very difficult to distinguish nominal compounds and syntactic nominal complexes. Therefore, school grammars present some inconsistent distinctions. For example, *wuli nala* (we country) 'our country' is considered a single lexical word, a compound nominal, whereas the similar combination, *wuli kacok* (we family) 'our family' is a complex NP composed of two separate nouns.

[5] It is also arguable whether the realization of a particle after a verbal noun is based on the subcategorization feature of the light verb *hata* or *toyta*. Through personal conversations, some scholars suggest that the realization of a particle after a verbal noun may be a case of insertion. When adopting this argument, particle omission is not even possible for the LV constructions. This needs to be more thoroughly investigated through examining historical corpus data.

[6] For bound nouns in Korean, refer to Sohn (1999).

[7] Classifiers belonging to bound nouns show interesting patterns of case particle realization in Korean; classifiers form morphosyntactic combinations such as [Noun + Number + Classifier], e.g., *sakwa han kay* (apple one thing) 'one apple'. Normally, a case particle appears on the initial content noun or the final classifier (e.g. [sakwa-**ka/lul** han kay][[sakwa han kay-**ka/lul**]) or there is a copy of the case particle from the content noun (e.g.[sakwa-**ka/lul** han kay-**ka/lul**]). In this study,

Spoken Corpora		E	M	D	L	Total
Particle Realization		**2081**	**2853**	**3334**	**3672**	**11940**
Predicate Nominals (P)		741	590	742	757	2830
Zero Particles	Ellipsis	**843**	**395**	**237**	**185**	**1660**
	Compounds (N)	320	297	350	411	1378
	Optional (E)	796	735	841	802	3174
	Light Verb (L)	308	190	482	410	1390
	Vocative (V)	24	3	6	20	53
Errors		82	36	41	43	202
Written Corpora		PE	N	P	A	Total
Particle Realization		**4707**	**4715**	**4603**	**4928**	**18953**
Predicate Nominals (P)		593	600	393	612	2197
Zero Particles	Ellipsis	**98**	**86**	**165**	**12**	**361**
	Compounds (N)	406	104	1941	728	3179
	Optional (E)	996	1125	1492	712	4325
	Light Verb (L)	361	437	965	917	2680

Table 2. Grammatical Realization of the Nominal Category[8]

In addition to optional particles, we also note that some constructions mandatorily require non-occurrence of particles. We have already seen that the genitive particle is not allowed within nominal compounds, e.g. [*palcen+Ø(*-uy) keyhwoyk+Ø(*-uy) pokose*] 'development plan report'. In addition, some bound nouns form formulaic (or idiomatic) expressions with their neighboring words and do not combine with particles, e.g., *kes-(*kwa)+ kathta* (thing-(*with) + similar) 'seem', *ke-Ø* + *aniya* (thing + isn't) 'isn't it?', N-Ø + *ttaymwun* (N + reason), etc.

Also, particle omission is required by the lexical properties of nominals. For example, numbers belonging to the nominal category combine with subject or object particles as well as with other auxiliary and discourse particles (e.g., *tases-**un/-i/-ul*** 'five-**TOP/SBJ/OBJ**'). However, they cannot take any particle when followed by count bound nouns, e.g., *tases-**Ø*** + *kay/salam/pen/kacil...* (five + items/people/sorts, etc.). Similarly, time nominals such as *onul* 'today', *ecey* 'yesterday', *nayil* 'tomorrow' stand alone without particles as adverbial phrases even though they combine with other particles in different syntactic positions. In contrast, time nominals such as *onul achim* 'this morning' and *2000 nyen* 'year 2000' can stand alone but also combine with the time particle *ey*. These temporal *ey*s are considered to be optional.

In summary, optional and mandatory non-occurrence of particles restricted by morpho-syntactic and lexical constraints needs to be distinguished from the omission of obligatory particles. Therefore, we include the following features to annotate bare nominals that do not mandate recovery of particles.

E - Non-occurrence of a particle based upon lexical or morpho-syntactic constraints.

N - Non-occurrence of a particle after a nominal that forms a compound with the following nominal

L - Non-occurrence of a particle in light verb constructions

In addition, nominals can be combined with copula *ita* or appear at the end of a phrase or a sentence without the copula in Korean. These predicate nominals have been annotated separately from other nominals. When a nominal is repeated by mistake with or without a particle, these erroneous nominals are separately marked and excluded from counts of particle realization and ellipsis. Separate features are given to handle these cases.

P- Predicate nominals combining with copula *ita*. It also marks a nominal standing alone without *ita*, as answering utterance.

ER - Errors including a repeated nominal by mistake or an incomplete utterance

as long as there is one particle realized in either the content noun or the classifier, we do not count it as case ellipsis.

[8] E: Everyday Conversations; M: Monologues, D: Debates; L: Lectures; PE: Personal Essays; N:Novels; P:Newspapers, A:Academic Texts

3.4 Principles of Annotating Particle Omission and Inter-Annotator Agreement

Our annotation principles of missing particles are presented as follows:

- With respect to missing particles, we annotate only obligatory case particles and conjunctive particles while excluding discourse/modal particles. This captures the minimum needed for a particle prediction system.
- In the process of recovering elided forms, there are cases in which more than one particle could be correct. Instead of selecting a single best particle, we present a set of multiple candidates without preference ranking.
- Particle stacking is allowed in Korean. We annotate stacked particles as single units without separating them into smaller particles. However, their segmentation is specified under the annotation feature of realized particle type. Missing particles, however, exclude stacked particles. Most particle stacking includes a discourse/modal particle that adds its specific meaning to the attached nominals.

Based on our annotation scheme and guidelines, two experienced annotators manually annotated realized particles, missing particles, and their types on the spoken and written corpora separately and cross-examined each other's annotation. Difficult cases were picked out and discussed with each other to reach an agreement. In order not to overly inflate the values with words that do not take particles, we removed words that do not belong to the nominal categories (nouns, pronouns, bound nouns, and numbers). The realized particles were provided to the annotators with the morphological analysis. Thus, we decided to compute the inter-annotator agreement on only 466 nominals with no particles within 5000 *Ecels* (before cross-examination). The kappa statistic on the case ellipsis by the two annotators is 91.23% for the specific particles. The agreement rate is much higher than we expected, but can be attributed to the annotation guidelines, which were clear and limited recovery of particles to case particles not including auxiliary and discourse particles. The two annotators were highly trained, having over two years of experience with particle annotation tasks.

4 Corpus Analysis

Table 2 summarizes the results of particle annotation of all the nominals, and Table 3 focuses on particle realization and ellipsis. Table 2 shows all nominal realizations with particles and without. Zero particles include both bare particle ellipsis and bare nominals including nominals that do not require particles as a component of compound nominals (N) and nominals that appear without particles in the corpora although they may optionally (E). In addition, the spoken corpora include bare nominals used as vocative phrases without particles. These cases have been counted separately. Erroneous usage of nominals only appears in the spoken corpora. Light verb combinations here only include cases that may allow realization of subject or object case particles, whose numbers are significantly high both in the spoken corpora and the written corpora.

As we see in Table 3, the overall case ellipsis rates are not that high across the two registers, but the difference between the spoken and the written corpora is significant (χ^2=851.78, p <.001).

Spoken	E	M	D	L	Total
Realized	71%	88%	93%	95%	88%
Ellipsis	29%	12%	7%	5%	12%
Written	PE	N	P	A	Total
Realized	98%	98%	97%	99.7%	98%
Ellipsis	2%	2%	3%	0.3%	2%

Table 3. Particle Realization vs. Ellipsis

Furthermore, genre plays an even more significant role within the spoken corpora. Particle ellipsis in everyday conversations is significantly more frequent than in monologues, debates, or lectures using a Bonferroni adjusted alpha level of .008 per comparison (.05/6). (χ^2(1)=266.64, p<.001; χ^2(1)=571.19, p<.001; χ^2(1)=746.93, p<.001). Particle ellipsis in monologues is significantly more frequent with debates or lectures (χ^2(1)=61.66, p<.001; χ^2(1)=126.59, p<.001). In contrast, particle ellipsis between debates and lectures shows a lower chi-square value than the other cases, although the value is still significant. (χ^2(1)==11.72, p<.001).

Table 4 presents the annotation results of case particle realization and ellipsis including subject and object particles.

Particles	Spoken					Written				
	E	M	D	L	Total	PE	N	P	A	Total
SUBJ +	63% (539)	88% (776)	93% (927)	95% (848)	85% (3090)	97% (743)	97% (840)	92% (635)	99.7% (588)	98% (2806)
SUBJ −	37% (318)	11% (97)	7% (67)	5% (48)	15% (530)	3% (25)	3% (24)	3% (18)	0.3% (2)	2% (69)
OBJ +	51% (398)	73% (535)	85% (698)	89% (771)	75% (2402)	94% (967)	95% (1066)	99% (1050)	99% (1026)	97% (4109)
OBJ −	49% (389)	27% (198)	15% (121)	11% (92)	25% (800)	5% (56)	5% (53)	1% (13)	1% (9)	3% (131)
CONJ +	92% (57)	68% (54)	90% (89)	98% (137)	88% (337)	100% (133)	100% (113)	97% (226)	99.7% (276)	99% (748)
CONJ −	8% (5)	32% (26)	10% (10)	2% (3)	12% (44)	0% 0	0% (0)	3% (7)	0.3% (1)	1% (8)
OTHERS +	81% (549)	90% (634)	95% (859)	97% (1174)	92% (3213)	99% (1778)	99.5% (1739)	93% (1680)	100% (2173)	98% (7370)
OTHERS −	19% (131)	10% (74)	4% (39)	3% (42)	8% (286)	1% (17)	0.5% (9)	7% (127)	0% (0)	2% (153)

Table 4. Realization and Ellipsis of Case Particles

Overall dropping rates of subject particles and object particles show a difference between the spoken and the written corpora. Object particle dropping is significantly more frequent in the spoken corpora than in the written corpora (χ^2 =797.03, p<.001). Within the spoken corpora, there is also some variation according to genre. Both subject and object dropping rates increase as the genres become less formal. In everyday conversations, the dropping rate of object particles reaches 49% and the dropping rate of subject particles is 37%. While the dropping rates of both particles decrease in the formal registers of the spoken corpora, the dropping rate of the object particles is consistently higher than the dropping rate of the subject particles at each register. In parallel, conjunctive particles and other case particles are more frequently dropped in the spoken corpora than in the written corpora.[9]

Our findings can be summarized as follows:

- In Korean, particle ellipsis is not very frequent. The particle dropping rate for subjects is 12% in the spoken corpora and 2% in the written corpora.
- The effect of register variation on particle ellipsis (everyday conversations vs. debates & lectures) demonstrates that particle dropping is less preferred in formal contexts. However, formality per se is not the deciding factor, but a partially related factor.[10]
- Across the spoken corpora, object particles drop more frequently than subject particles. (χ^2 =115.17, p <.001)
- Other case and connective particles are also more frequently elided in the spoken corpora.

5 Linguistic Properties in Particle Ellipsis

The frequent case particle ellipsis in the spoken corpora suggests that discourse need to be further investigated. This implies that discourse factors contribute to particle ellipsis, as suggested in Lee and Thompson (1989). Using the corpus annotation, we can explore linguistic properties involving in particle ellipsis.

5.1 Definiteness and Specificity

A case particle is likely to be dropped when the preceding noun is definite or specific (Kim, 1991). The definite NP *ku haksayng* 'that student' can drop subject case. This contrasts with the fact that the indefinite expression *etten haksayng* 'some student' cannot appear without the subject particle.

[9] Unexpectedly, conjunctive particles drop more frequently in monologues than in everyday conversations.

[10] This can be supported by the fact that register variation does not affect particle dropping in the written corpus.

(5) a. ku haksayng-i/-Ø na-lul chacawa-ss-e.
that s tudent-SBJ/Ø I-OBJ visit-PAST-END
'That student visited me.'
b. etten haksayng-i/*Ø na-lul chacawa-ss-e.
some student-SBJ /Ø I-OBJ visit-PAST-END
'Some student visited me.'

In our annotated corpus, the particles that are attached to personal pronouns and *wh*-pronouns are frequently dropped. This implies that definiteness is a crucial factor for licensing particle dropping.[11]

5.2 Familiarity and Salience in Discourse

Particle ellipsis is also based on discourse properties of familiarity (background).[12] In the following example, it is more natural to drop the object particle from *tampay* 'cigarette' when speaking in a convenience store. This is because selling cigarettes is already familiar knowledge shared among the discourse participants.

(6) tampay-[?]**lul/-Ø** cwu-seyyo.
cigarette-OBJ-Ø give-IMPERATIVE
'Please give me cigarette.'

However, when the object particle is used in (6), the object cigarette is exclusively designated or highlighted. This contrasts with the fact that the speaker commonly uses a nominal referring to discourse participants such as *you* and *I*, proper names, or titles without a particle in order to catch the attention of the listener(s). Also, when a subject or object nominal is scrambled out of its original position and appears at the sentence initial or final position, the particle disappears to emphasize the salience of the nominal element, as in (7).

(7) a. philyohan-n kel hanato mos tule, na-Ø.
necessary- REL thing anything not take I-Ø
'I cannot take anything that is necessary.'

b. saylo o-n sensayng-**Ø (ul)**, ne alla?
newly come-REL teacher-Ø (OBJ) you know
'Do you know the new teacher?'

Examination of our annotated corpora strongly suggests that particle ellipsis is associated with two contrastive discourse properties, familiarity and salience, and also that it interacts with other grammatical mechanisms such as word order, lexical category, and possibly prosody.[13]

6 Final Remarks

In this study, we presented our annotation work on particle realization and ellipsis using spoken and written corpora in Korean. A new annotation scheme and principles were presented, along with challenging issues and solutions, such as the recovery of missing particles and the distinction between ellipsis and non-occurrence of particles. In order to evaluate the effect of register variation on particle ellipsis, we incorporated four different genres. Our major finding is that the rate of particle ellipsis in Korean is not as high as generally assumed and register variation is a significant factor only in spoken corpora. The more informal dialogs are, the more often particles are elided. Our corpus annotation suggests that particle ellipsis is related to activated semantic/pragmatic constraints among discourse participants, which include definiteness, specificity, familiarity and salience.

The implication of these findings is significant not only for linguistic theory, but also for language processing, Korean language teaching, and translation. Particle ellipsis will be a more serious issue for computational modeling that incorporates informal spoken dialogs than for computational processing on written texts. In language teaching, particles need to be emphasized more for formal writing and formal speaking based on their frequency in the given register (Lee et al., this volume). Next, we plan to run error detection software on our corpus to verify the consistency of our annotation (Dickinson and Meurers, 2003), to prepare for releasing the data with guidelines, to further analyze the results of the annotation, and to address more elaborate linguistic implications in the annotated data.

[11] Lee (2006, 2010) argues that case ellipsis of subjects and objects interacts with the definiteness of nominals. The rate of case ellipsis for strongly definite subject NPs is significantly higher than the rate for weakly definite NPs. However, object case ellipsis works in the opposite direction. It is difficult to identify definiteness of a nominal in Korean, where definite and indefinite articles do not exist. We have not annotated definiteness features in our corpora, but intend to as part of future work.

[12] Similarly, Lee and Thompson (1989) propose that "sharedness between communicators" is the pragmatic factor determining object particle ellipsis in discourse.

[13] Case ellipsis and realization have been also examined within information structure-based analyses such as Lee (2006, 2010) and Kwon and Zribi-Hertz (2008)

References

Markus Dickinson and Detmar Meurers. 2003. Detecting Errors in Part-of-Speech Annotation. Proceedings of the 10th Conference of European Chapter of the Association for Computational Linguistics (EACL-03). Budapest, Hungary.

John Fry. 2001. Ellipsis and 'wa'-marking in Japanese conversation. Doctoral Dissertation. Stanford University.

Noriko Fujii and Tsuyoshi Ono. 2000. The Occurrence and Non-Occurrence of the Japanese Direct Object Marker *O* in Conversation. Studies in Language, 24(1): 1-39.

Jeanette K. Gundel, Nancy Hedberg and Ron Zacharski. 1993. Cognitive Status and the Form of Referring Expressions in Discourse. Language, 69: 274-307.

Young-joo Hong. 2009. Syntactic Relation between Two Nominals in NP and Non-occurrence of の/uy (*Myengsakwu Nay-uy Cenhang Myengsa-wa Hwuhang Myengsa-uy Thongsacek Kwankey-wa の /uy-uy Pisilhyen*, In Korean). Japanese Study (*Ilbon Yengoo*), 40: 639-653. The Institute of Japanese Studies. Seoul.

Paul Hopper and Sandra A. Thompson. 1984. The Discourse Basis for Lexical Categories in Universal Grammar. Language, 60: 703-752.

Ji-Eun Kim. 1991. A Study on the Condition in Realizing Subject without Case Marker in Korean, Hangul, 212.

Kun-hee Kim and Jae-il Kwon. 2004. Korean Particles in Spoken Discourse-A Statistical Analysis for the Unification of Grammar. Hanmal Yenku, 15: 1-22.

Eon-Suk Ko. 2000. A Discourse Analysis of the Realization of Objects in Korean. Japaenese/Korean Linguistics, 9: 195-208. Stanford: CSLI Publication.

Jae-il Kwon. 1989. Characteristic of Case and the Methodology of the Case Ellipsis, Language Research, 25(1): 129-139.

Song-Nim Kwon and Anne Zribi-Hertz. 2008. Differential function marking, case, and information Structure: Evidence from Korean. Language, 84(2): 258-99.

Hyo Sang Lee and Sandra A. Thompson. 1989. A discourse account of the Korean accusative marker. Studies in Language, 13: 105-128.

Hanjung Lee. 2006. Parallel Optimization in Case Systems: Evidence from Case Ellipsis in Korean. Journal of East Asian Linguistics, 15: 69-96.

Song-Nim Kwon and Anne Zribi-Hertz. 2008. Differential Function Marking, Case, and Information Structure: Evidence from Korean. Language, 84:2:258-299

Hanjung Lee. 2010. Explaining Variation in Korean Case Ellipsis: Economy versus Iconicity. Journal of East Asian Linguistics, 19: 292-318.

Seon-woong Lee. 2005. A Study on Realization of Nominal Arguments (*Myengsa-uy Nonhang Silhyen Yangsang*, In Korean).

Sun-Hee Lee. 2006. Particles (*Cosa*). Why Do We Need to Reinvestigate Part of Speeches? (in Korean): 302-346.

Sun-Hee Lee, Markus Dickinson, and Ross Israel. 2012. Developing Learner Corpus Annotation for Korean Particle Errors. In Proceedings of the Sixth Linguistic Annotation Workshop (this volume). Jeju, Korea

Minpyo Hong, Kyongjae Park, Inkie Chung, and Ji-young Kim. 1998. Elided Postpositions in Spoken Korean and their Implications on Center Management, Korean Journal of Cognitive Science, 9(3): 35-45.

Yoon-jin Nam. 2000. A Statistical Analysis of Mondern Korean Particles (*Hyentay Hankwuke-ey tayhan Kyelyang Enehakcek Yenkwu*). Thayhaksa.

Ho-Min Sohn. 1999. The Korean Language. Cambridge University Press. Cambridge, UK.

Yongkyoon No. 1991. A Centering Approach to the *[CASE][TOPIC] Restriction in Korean. Linguistics, 29: 653-668.

Yu-hyun Park. 2006. A Study on the Particle '-ka''s Non-Realization in Modern Korean Spoken Language. Emwunlonchong, 45: 211-260.

EnricVallduví and Maria Vilkuna, M. 1998. On Rheme and Kontrast. The Limits of Syntax, eds. Peter Culicover and Louise McNally, 79-109. New York: Academic Press.

Shuichi Yatabe. 1999. Particle Ellipsis and Focus Projection in Japanese. Language, Information, Text, 6: 79-104.

Annotation of Adversarial and Collegial Social Actions in Discourse

David B. Bracewell, Marc T. Tomlinson, Mary Brunson, Jesse Plymale, Jiajun Bracewell, and Daniel Boerger
Language Computer Corporation
Richardson, TX 75080
{david,marc,mary,jesse,jiajun,dan}@languagecomputer.com

Abstract

We posit that determining the social goals and intentions of dialogue participants is crucial for understanding discourse taking place on social media. In particular, we examine the social goals of being collegial and being adversarial. Through our early experimentation, we found that speech and dialogue acts are not able to capture the complexities and nuances of the social intentions of discourse participants. Therefore, we introduce a set of 9 social acts specifically designed to capture intentions related to being collegial and being adversarial. Social acts are pragmatic speech acts that signal a dialogue participant's social intentions. We annotate social acts in discourses communicated in English and Chinese taken from Wikipedia talk pages, public forums, and chat transcripts. Our results show that social acts can be reliably understood by annotators with a good level of inter-rater agreement.

1 Introduction

Discourse over social media presents a unique challenge for discourse processing, which has traditionally been focused on task- (Grosz, 1978; Traum and Hinkelman, 1992) and formal meeting- (Shriberg et al., 2004) based discourse. In contrast, the discourse taking place over social media is focused more on the social engagements between participants. These social engagements are often driven by the social goals of the participants and not by a common goal or task.

Social goals focus on the efforts of individuals to fulfill roles and maintain or alter relationships with others in a group. There are a great number of social goals a discourse participant may undertake, such as: maintaining the role of an authority or power (Bramsen et al., 2011; Mayfield and Rose, 2011); or trying to gain a new rule, such as by pursuing power (Tomlinson et al., 2012);

In this paper, we focus on the social goal of an individual (actor) maintaining a relationship (intention) with a second single individual (target). In particular, we wish to address the intentions of individuals whose goal is related to a ***collegial*** (+ valence) or ***adversarial*** (- valence) relationship.

Collegiality is defined as cooperating with others in order to reach a common goal or ideal. Collegiality has importance at a personal, interpersonal, and group level. At the personal level, collegiality can be an indicator of the degree of social support a person has. Social support can be physical or emotional and can have effects on job satisfaction (McCann et al., 1997) and, in some cases, quality of life (Shapiro et al., 2001). Collegiality is key for a productive discourse and collaboration. Studies show that people who are put together in groups are more likely to be collegial (Tajfel and Turner, 1979). Collegial groups are more likely to have increased performance (Little, 1982) and are more likely to reach their goals (Campion et al., 1996).

In contrast to collegiality, adversarial behavior is meant to explicitly point out opposition or dislike for other participants. Adversarial individuals often are not following the cooperative principle of dialogue as formulated in Grice's maxims (Grice, 1975). Moreover, due the anonymity that social media provides adversarial participants often also do not follow the social norm of taking face into account, such as Boella et al. (2000) suggest. The dialogue only progresses due to the social intentions of the other discourse participants in reaction to the adversarial individual, e.g. defending one's honor.

We adopt the Grosz and Sidner (Grosz and Sidner, 1986) theory of discourse, which breaks discourse into three constituents: (1) linguistic structure; (2) intentional structure; and (3) attentional state. We address linguistic structure by segmenting the discourse based on topical shifts (Cassell et al., 2001), which can be accomplished using methods such as (Blei et al., 2003) or (Ambwani and Davis, 2010). For attentional structure, we borrow from research on local coherence by Barzilay and Lapata (2005). The most crucial of the three constituents for the understanding of social goals is the intentional structure.

As a first attempt at capturing the intentional structure indicative of collegial and adversarial behavior, we looked at using the prevailing methods in discourse processing. Namely, we examined mapping dialogue acts (Allen and Core, 1997; Stolcke et al., 1998), which pertain to the intentions of the discourse, into these higher level social goals. However, we found that dialogue acts are not capable of capturing the nuances of the social intentions of the discourse participants.

Instead of focusing solely on the discourse, the intentional structure of social discourse must also focus on the discourse participants and how their social goals constrain their dialogue. We argue that to capture these social goals it is necessary to understand the social intentions of the discourse participants and how they perceive the social intentions of others. We define a social intention as the intention of an individual to affect their social status or relationships within a group. In doing so, we consider the social cognition of the discourse participants, it is from cognition that the participants' social intentions are transformed into linguistic utterances.

We identify a set of 9 social acts, listed in section 3, that capture common social actions performed by individuals whose social goal is the maintenance or altering of a collegial or adversarial interpersonal relationship. These social acts come from literature in the fields of psychology and organizational behavior and are motivated by work in discourse understanding. We present the results of annotating these 9 social acts for discourses communicated in Chinese and English. In total, the corpus is made up of 215 English and 292 Chinese discourses.

2 Related Work

The two areas of research most related to this paper are in social relationship extraction and discourse processing. Work in the area of social relationship extraction can be divided into several areas. The field of socio-linguistics boasts well-established studies of interpersonal relationships. For example, Eggins and Slade present a thorough linguistic analysis on causal conversations that covers topics such as humor, attitude, friendliness, and gossip (Eggins and Slade, 1997). This is accomplished through a comprehensive analysis of the dialogue at multiple levels. In contrast, however, research using Natural Language Processing to automatically identify social relationships in text is still in its infancy.

Strzalkowski et al. (2010), examine identification of social goals by breaking them down into mid-level social language uses. They focus on the use of discourse features (e.g. topic control) to identify language uses (Strzalkowski et al., 2010) that might be indicative of some social constructs.

Another area of research that is along the lines of determining adversarial and collegial actions is the detection of agreement and disagreement. Wang et al. (2011) identify agreement and disagreement in English using conditional random fields. Similarly, Hillard et al. (2003) detect agreement and disagreement in speech transcripts using prosodic features.

The closest work to a general view of social acts is by Bender et al. (2011). The researchers created an annotated corpus of social acts relating to *authority claims* and *alignment moves*. We propose that social acts are instead a broad class of speech acts that cover a wide variety of social interactions. However, this paper focuses on social acts which correlate to a positive and negative valence for interpersonal relationships.

Research understanding the intentionality of dialogue and discourse has a long history. Some of the earliest work in discourse processing is on speech acts. Speech acts are actions performed by individuals when making an utterance. Austin (1962) formalized the concept of speech acts by separating them into three classes: (1) *locutionary*, (2) *illocutionary*, and (3) *perlocutionary*. Locutionary acts the prosody, phonetics, and semantics of the utterance. Illocutionary acts are the intended functions of the utterances of the speaker. Perlocutionary acts are illocutionary acts that produce a certain effect in its addressee, e.g. scaring and insulting. Much of the work in speech acts has been focused on illocutionary acts due to the work of Searle (1969).

Dialogue acts are illocutionary speech acts extended to include the internal structure, such as grounding and adjacency pairs, of a dialogue. There are a number of schemes for coding dialogue acts, such as DAMSL (Allen and Core, 1997) and VERBMOBIL (Jekat et al., 1995). The DAMSL coding scheme defines dialogue acts that are forward looking, which are extensions of speech acts, and which are backward looking, which relate the utterance to previous utterances. Likewise, we define social acts to reflect the social intention of an utterance. Social acts serve a function to inform individuals about social relationships. For example, in the statement "get me a cup of coffee", speech acts would focus on identifying the set of actions that would result from the utterance - presumably the target of the utterance physically going to get a cup of coffer for the speaker. In contrast, social acts focus on the social implicature of the statement, that the speaker is indicating their power over the target.

Other work has focused on the coherence of discourse(Barzilay and Lapata, 2005; Byron and Stent, 1998; Hobbs, 1979; Mann and Thompson, 1988). Mann and Thompson (1988) introduce Rhetorical Structure Theory (RST), which was originally developed during the study of automatic text generation. They posit that the coherence of a text is attributed to the rhetorical relations between non-overlapping texts called the nucleus and satellite. The definition of the relations are not morphological or syntactic, but instead are focused on function and semantics.

Barzilay and Lapata (2005) cast the local coherence problem as a ranking problem. They take a set of alternative renderings for a discourse and rank them based on local coherence. Inspired by Centering Theory they use an entity-based representation where the role that the entities fill is taken into consideration.

3 Social Acts Expressing Adversarial and Collegial Intentions

Social interaction is the foundation of discourse. Even task oriented discourse has many social implications. One of the most common social implications of language is the expression of a desire to establish or maintain a bond between the individuals, i.e. a collegial relationship. Here we also consider its opposite, to sabotage others, i.e. playing the adversary.

Collegiality is defined as cooperating with others in order to reach a common goal or ideal. Interpersonal collegiality is often born out of group collegiality, as the group defines the common bonds, shared focus and common purpose that serve to unite the individuals (see Gomez et al, 2011). An individual maintains their collegial relationship with the other members through collegial expressions, such as supportive behavior and solidarity.

In contrast, adversarial behavior is meant to explicitly point out opposition or dislike for other participants. An individual establishes his/her opposition to a group or an individual through such means as disrespect and undermining the other's efforts.

We label the discourse segment purpose, or the social intentions of an utterance, as social acts. Social acts are pragmatic speech acts that signal a dialogue participant's social intentions. Social intentions can range from establishing mutual bonds to asserting dominance over another individual. These social acts can be signaled with a variety of cue phrases as well as through a discourse participants observation or violation of social norms, or expectations of socially appropriate responses.

For informing a participant's intentions to be adversarial or collegial toward others, we define a set of 9 social acts, listed in figure 1. The set of acts presented below have been derived from work in psychology on conflict and cooperation (Brewer and Gardner, 1996; Deutsch, 2011; Jehn and Mannix, 2001; Owens and Sutton, 2001).

3.1 Agreement & Disagreement

Agreement can act as an affordance to an individual or as a means to establish solidarity between individuals. Likewise disagreement can act as a way of undermining or challenging credibility. However,

Agreement	Statements that a group member makes to indicate that he/she shares the same view about something another member has said or done.
Challenge Credibility	Attempts to discredit or raise doubt about another group members qualifications or abilities.
Disagreement	Statements a group member makes to indicate that he/she does not share the same view about something another member has said or done.
Disrespect	Inappropriate statements that a group member makes to insult another member of the group.
Offer Gratitude	A sincere expression of thanks that one group member makes to another.
Relationship Conflict	Personal, heated disagreement between individuals.
Solidarity	Statements that a group member makes to strengthen the groups sense of community and unity.
Supportive Behavior	Statements of personal support that one group member makes toward another.
Undermining	Hostile expressions that a group member makes to damage the reputation of another group member.

Figure 1: The set of 9 social acts that capture social moves by individuals exhibiting adversarial behavior.

because of the special status of agreement and disagreement we consider them as two separate social acts.

Agreement can be manifested through simple phrases, such as "I agree", through negations of disagreement, such as "I am not disagreeing with you", and through more complex phrases, such as "What Adam says is in principle correct." Similarly, disagreement is manifested through simple "I disagree" phrases as well as negations of agreement, such as "I definitely do not agree with what you said."

An example of agreement in Chinese is 同意 A所言，所以還是先繼續保護著吧。 ("I agree with what A said, so just keep the protection."). An example of disagreement in Chinese is 恕本人不認同。 ("sorry, I can not agree.").

3.2 Challenge Credibility

Challenging credibility can be used by an individual to lower the status of other group members (Owens and Sutton, 2001). These challenges can be in demands to prove credibility, such as "prove your lies" and aggressive accusing questions, such as "what does that have to do with what we are talking about?". Challenging credibility can also occur through gossip, such as "X doesn't know what he is talking about". This tactic can be used by group members to moderate the power of a leader who has overstepped their boundaries (Keltner et al., 2008).

An example of Challenge Credibility in Chinese is 不知可有其他依據？("I do not know if you have other evidence?").

3.3 Disrespect

Disrespected individuals often feel they have been unjustly treated due to the disrespectful action, causing a social imbalance between them and the perpetrator (Miller, 2001). This social imbalance causes a power differential between the two individuals, thus giving the perpetrator power over the individual. Examples of disrespect include "You are a gigantic hypocrite you know that?" and "Do you speak English well?"

An example of Disrespect in Chinese is 你有种的话，请表明你的教派身份。 ("if you have the guts, show your religious status.").

3.4 Offer Gratitude

There is psychological validation for the consideration of attitudes expressed by one individual towards another. Even in the absence of any major differences within a group, the expression of an in-group bias and out-group bias (Brewer, 1979) between individuals still takes place. Individuals within a group are more likely to possess positive feelings for another individual within the group and to rate him or her more highly than an individual outside of the group.

An example of Offer Gratitude in Chinese is 回應：谢谢你的意见。("response: thanks for your opinion").

3.5 Relationship Conflict

Relationship conflict is a personal, heated disagreement between individuals (Jehn and Mannix, 2001). Individuals exhibiting relationship conflict are being adversarial. Examples of relationship conflict include "your arrogant blathering" and "I consider it offensive for you to assert that I insist on turning every interaction into a personality conflict."

An example of Relationship Conflict in Chinese is 久違認為也有可能是閣下眼睛有問題，沒看見來源。("I think it is possible that you did not see the sources because your eyes have a problem.").

3.6 Solidarity

Further, language indicative of a desire for group solidarity encapsulates the establishment and maintenance of shared group membership. Group membership can be expressed at either the relational level (e.g. Father, co-worker, etc.) or the collective level (e.g. single mothers) (Brewer and Gardner, 1996). Language indicative of a desire for group solidarity demonstrates that an individual identifies with the group, an important characteristic of leaders (Keltner et al., 2008) and cooperators (Deutsch, 2011). This solidarity can be expressed explicitly (e.g. "We're all in this together"), covertly (e.g. as through the use of inclusive first-person pronouns), or through unconscious actions and linguistic cues, such as the use of in-group jargon, certain syntactic constructions, and mimicry.

An example of Solidarity in Chinese is 生日快乐！("Happy birthday!").

3.7 Supportive Behavior

By definition, supportive behavior, or cooperation towards a common goal, is an example of collegiality. This type of behavior lies at the center of group dynamics. Cooperation is correlated with both overall group performance and managerial ratings of group effectiveness (Campion et al., 1996).Evidence for cooperation manifests itself in many different ways. Classically, there is the notion of cooperation on a physical task (e.g. one person helping another lift a heavy weight), or cooperation through social support (e.g. Mary says, "John's decision is excellent").

There are also more subtle, unconscious examples of cooperation between individuals, which can demonstrate a certain degree of collegiality between the individuals. One example is cooperation for the effective use of language and the building of dialogue (Garrod and Pickering, 2004). Dialogue is a complicated interaction that requires commitment from both parties. In order to maintain a stable conversation, participants must be willing to expend cognitive effort to listen, understand, and form a relevant response that advances the dialogue. The degree to which participants are able to maintain a cohesive dialogue should be reflected in the collegiality of the participants. If one participant is not cooperating, the dialogue will not progress.

An example of Supportive Behavior in Chinese is 加油啊。("do your best.").

3.8 Undermining

By definition undermining is meant to damage or weaken. Undermining a goal is meant to erode the support or weaken the stance of the goal. Individuals who are undermining another are demonstrating a form of hostility, which is in direct opposition to being supportive. Examples of undermining include "And people you quoted aren't historians," "This is making a mountain out of a molehill," and "So you will delete anything that YOU don't like?"

An example of Undermining in Chinese is 就像某人说这条目是他建的就不让其他任何人修改一样荒谬。("it is ridiculous that certain people said that he built the item and he will not let other people edit it.").

4 Data Collection & Annotation

Annotations were performed on social discourses extracted from Wikipedia talk pages, public forums, and chat transcripts. A collection of 215 discourses communicated in English and 292 discourses communicated in Chinese were annotated. Each discourse was annotated by 2 native-language annotators.

Annotation was performed at the sentence level with each sentence acting as an utterance. The sentences were presented in the order that they appeared in the social discourse and included speaker information. Annotators were given the option to label each sentence with zero or more social acts. An example of a discourse communicated in English annotated with social acts is shown in Figure 2 and an example in Chinese is shown in Figure 3.

Annotators were given the list of social acts with their associated definitions, as shown in figure 1. Annotation began on a small set of data with each annotator labeling sentences based on their own intuition. After this small set of data was annotated (10

Turn 1] Propose that this page be moved to East Timor Defence Force as this is the closest translation of Foras de Defesa de Timor Leste. I have worked in Timor Leste as a government advisor, including with FDTL, and have never heard anybody ever refer to the FDTL as Military of East Timor. P1

Turn 2] As I understand it, 'East Timor Defence Force' is considered outdated. **While it was commonly used when the force was established, almost all english-language publications now use 'F-FDTL'. 'Military of East Timor' is a generic name, and I agree that it's rarely used and not a great title.**[Agreement] I'd prefer 'Timor Leste Defence Force' as this seems to be the direct translation, but this would be inconsistent with the other Wikipedia articles on the country. **Should we be bold and move this article to 'Timor Leste Defence Force'**?[Solidarity] P2

Turn 3] **I so totally agree with you. [Agreement] 'Timor Leste Defence Force' is it.** [Agreement] **The only reason I did not propose that was the failure to change the country page from East Timor to Timor Leste, a decision that I feel was extremely discourteous of Wikipedia considering the government's specific request that it be referred to as Timor Leste.**[Solidarity] If you have worked there you will know that everybody uses 'Timor Leste', even the ADF but the Australian DFAT uses East Timor although the more enlightened Kiwi embassy call it TL. I suggest we leave it for 48 hours to see if anyone has any strong feelings and then change it to ' Timor Leste Defence Force' with diverts from F-FDTL and FDTL P1

Turn 4] **I agree with that approach.** [Agreement] In the interests of consensus editing, I've posted a note at Talk:East Timor (in lieu of a Wikiproject on the country) to seek other editors' views. P2

...

Turn 8] **As no-one has raised any objections, I've just made the move.**[Supportive Behavior] P2

Turn 9] **Good move, well done**[Supportive Behavior] P1

Figure 2: An example discourse communicated in English with social acts labeled.

S) 1. 使用的博客经过了实认证，特别是名人博客. [*Establish Credibility*]

"1. The blogs we used, especially famous people's blogs implemented real-name authentication. [*Establish Credibility*]**"**

2. 百科内的某些观点正是缘于博客，却禁止对该博客的引用. 不加入 Blog 地址的话会使得来源更难于验证. [*Establish Credibility*]

"2. Some comments in wiki came from blogs, but it was forbidden to cite the blogs. It is more difficult to confirm the sources without adding the blog address.[*Establish Credibility*]**"**

3. 这些内容根本不需要大众媒体验证即可确信是代表某个知名人士的言论，反之也不会有媒体整天围着博客转来报道这些博文. [*Establish Credibility*]

"3. It can be known that these contents represent certain famous person's comment without the authentication of mass media. On the contrary there is no media monitoring these blogs all day long and reporting these posts.[*Establish Credibility*]**"**

T) 基本上认为博客不是第二手来源。[*Disagreement*] 如果真要加入博客中的论点，最好找别的媒体报道这篇博客中的看法的文章作为来源。[Managerial Influence]

"Normally it is considered that blogs are not second hand sources.[*Disagreement*] **If you really want to use the comments in the blog, it is the best to use the articles written by other media that reported the comments in these blogs.**[*Managerial Influence*]"

Figure 3: An example discourse communicated in Chinese with social acts labeled.

discourses) each group of annotators, i.e. one group of 2 Chinese annotators and one group of 2 English annotators, worked together to formulate guidelines for what constitutes an instance of each social act in their respective language. After the creation of the guidelines the annotators went back to working independently.

The English portion of the corpus consisted of 21,067 sentences of which 4,486 (21.3%) were annotated with one or more of the nine social acts. The Chinese portion of the corpus ended up with 24,339 sentences for which 4,260 (17.5%) had one ore more of the nine social acts annotated.

The set of nine social acts can be naturally split into those that are adversarial and those that are collegial. Thus, we first examined how well the annotators were able to distinguish between sentences containing adversarial and collegial social acts. We defined the set of adversarial social acts as: Challenge Credibility, Disagreement, Disrespect, Relationship Conflict, and Undermining. The set of collegial social acts were defined as: Agreement, Offer Gratitude, Solidarity, and Supportive Behavior. Table 2 shows the mutual F-Measure for adversarial an collegial social acts. In addition, we examined the annotators ability to agree when a sentence had no adversarial or collegial social act present.

Tables 2 and 3 show the mutual F-Measure for agreement on adversarial, collegial, and neither (no social act present) for English and Chinese respectively. The English annotators had high agreement (close to 90%) for determining if a sentence had a collegial social act (89.7%) or neither collegial or adversarial social act (89.4%). Their agreement for

	English			Chinese		
	♯ Annotated	Kappa	F-Measure	♯ Annotated	Kappa	F-Measure
Agreement (+)	295	0.38	76.5%	315	0.50	54.5%
Challenge Credibility (-)	1,113	0.36	33.8%	409	0.38	45.4%
Disagreement (-)	434	0.46	71.0%	555	0.07	13.1%
Disrespect (-)	367	0.24	53.5%	214	0.36	41.5%
Offer Gratitude (+)	108	0.44	79.9%	300	0.88	89.9%
Relationship Conflict (-)	399	0.13	21.3%	93	0.42	56.8%
Solidarity (+)	100	0.52	41.2%	574	0.41	44.0%
Supportive Behavior (+)	269	0.36	68.1%	1,034	0.84	88.2%
Undermining (-)	1,401	0.35	49.3%	766	0.49	58.0%

Table 1: The number of annotations, kappa, and F-Measure per social act. The valence of the social act is denoted in parentheses next to the social act name, e.g. (+) for positive valence and (-) for negative valence.

	F-Measure	No. of Sentences
Adversarial	79.9%	3,714
Collegial	89.7%	772
Neither	89.4%	16,581
Average	87.8%	–

Table 2: The mutual F-Measure for adversarial and collegial social acts in discourse communicated in English.

	F-Measure	No. of Sentences
Adversarial	73.0%	2,037
Collegial	85.5	2,222
Neither	79.9%	20,079
Average	80.3%	–

Table 3: The mutual F-Measure for adversarial and collegial social acts in discourses communicated in Chinese.

adversarial social acts was almost 80%, which is still quite high. The Chinese annotators had their highest agreement for collegial social acts (85.5%) followed by sentences with neither collegial or adversarial social acts (79.9%). The agreement for adversarial social acts was 73.0%, which is still acceptable. In general, we hypothesize that natural discourse is predominately collegial and because of this annotators have an easier time identifying and agreeing upon collegial social acts.

After determining that annotators can agree on whether a sentence contained an adversarial or collegial social act, we examined their ability to identify individual social acts. Table 1 shows the number of sentences annotated for each social act as well as the kappa (Cohen, 1960) and mutual F-Measure. The kappa values range from 0.13 to 0.53 for English and 0.07 to 0.90 for Chinese. Relationship conflict was the most difficult to reach consensus on for English and Disagreement was the most difficult for Chinese. While the kappa values seem low, they are comparable with other work in social acts and work done in dialogue acts.

Kappa values for dialogue acts have been reported as high as 0.76 for ANSWER and as low as 0.15 for COMMITTING-SPEAKER-FUTURE-ACTION (Allen and Core, 1997). Other work in social acts have seen kappa values in a similar range, such as Bender et al. (2011) who report kappa values from 0.13 to 0.63. Given the complexities presented by annotating the social intentions of dialogue participants, we believe that the kappa values reported here are acceptable.

5 Conclusion

In this work we have addressed the creation of a multilingual corpus of utterances annotated with social actions relating to being adversarial and being collegial. In doing so, we introduced a set of 9 social acts designed to capture the social intentions of discourse participants. Our results show that annotators can reliably agree and distinguish adversarial and collegial social actions. Moreover, we also believe that the agreement rates obtained for most of the individual social acts are adequate given the complexity of the task.

Acknowledgement

This research was funded by the Office of the Director of National Intelligence (ODNI), Intelligence Advanced Research Projects Activity (IARPA), and through the U.S. Army Research Lab. All statements of fact, opinion or conclusions contained herein are those of the authors and should not be construed as representing the official views or policies of IARPA, the ODNI or the U.S. Government.

References

J Allen and M Core. 1997. Draft of DAMSL: Dialog Act Markup in Several Layers.

Geetu Ambwani and Anthony R. Davis. 2010. Contextually-mediated semantic similarity graphs for topic segmentation. In *Proceedings of the 2010 Workshop on Graph-based Methods for Natural Language Processing*, TextGraphs-5, pages 60–68, Stroudsburg, PA, USA. Association for Computational Linguistics.

J L Austin. 1962. *How to do things with words*, volume 7 of *The William James lectures*. Harvard University Press.

Regina Barzilay and Mirella Lapata. 2005. Modeling local coherence: an entity-based approach. In *Proceedings of the 43rd Annual Meeting on Association for Computational Linguistics*, ACL '05, pages 141–148, Stroudsburg, PA, USA. Association for Computational Linguistics.

Emily M. Bender, Jonathan T. Morgan, Meghan Oxley, Mark Zachry, Brian Hutchinson, Alex Marin, Bin Zhang, and Mari Ostendorf. 2011. Annotating social acts: authority claims and alignment moves in wikipedia talk pages. In *Proceedings of the Workshop on Languages in Social Media*, LSM '11, pages 48–57, Stroudsburg, PA, USA. Association for Computational Linguistics.

David M. Blei, Andrew Ng, and Michael Jordan. 2003. Latent dirichlet allocation. *JMLR*, 3:993–1022.

Guido Boella, Rossana Damiano, and Leonardo Lesmo. 2000. Social goals in conversational cooperation. In *Proceedings of the 1st SIGdial workshop on Discourse and dialogue - Volume 10*, SIGDIAL '00, pages 84–93, Stroudsburg, PA, USA. Association for Computational Linguistics.

Philip Bramsen, Martha Escobar-Molano, Ami Patel, and Rafael Alonso. 2011. Extracting social power relationships from natural language. In *Proceedings of the 49th Annual Meeting of the Association for Computational Linguistics: Human Language Technologies - Volume 1*, HLT '11, pages 773–782, Stroudsburg, PA, USA. Association for Computational Linguistics.

Marilynn B. Brewer and Wendi Gardner. 1996. Who is this "We"? Levels of collective identity and self representations. *Journal of Personality and Social Psychology*, 71(1):83–93.

Marilynn B. Brewer. 1979. In-group bias in the minimal intergroup situation: A cognitive-motivational analysis. *Psychological Bulletin*, 86(2):307–324.

D. Byron and A. Stent. 1998. A preliminary model of centering in dialog. In *Proceedings of the 36th Annual Meeting of the Association for Computational Linguistics and 17th International Conference on Computational Linguistics - Volume 2*, ACL '98, pages 1475–1477, Stroudsburg, PA, USA. Association for Computational Linguistics.

M.A. Campion, E.M. Papper, and G.J. Medsker. 1996. Relations between work team characteristics and effectiveness: A replication and extension. *Personnel psychology*, 49(2):429–452.

Justine Cassell, Yukiko I. Nakano, Timothy W. Bickmore, Candace L. Sidner, and Charles Rich. 2001. Non-verbal cues for discourse structure. In *Proceedings of the 39th Annual Meeting on Association for Computational Linguistics*, ACL '01, pages 114–123, Stroudsburg, PA, USA. Association for Computational Linguistics.

Jacob Cohen. 1960. A Coefficient of Agreement for Nominal Scales. *Educational and Psychological Measurement*, 20(1):37–46, April.

M. Deutsch. 2011. Cooperation and competition. *Conflict, Interdependence, and Justice*, pages 23–40.

Suzanne Eggins and Diana Slade. 1997. *Analysing casual conversation*. Cassell.

Simon Garrod and Martin J. Pickering. 2004. Why is conversation so easy? *Trends in Cognitive Sciences*, 8(1):8–11, January.

Angel Gómez, Matthew L Brooks, Michael D Buhrmester, Alexandra Vázquez, Jolanda Jetten, and William B Swann. 2011. On the nature of identity fusion: Insights into the construct and a new measure. *Journal of Personality and Social Psychology*, 100(5):918–933.

H. P. Grice. 1975. Logic and conversation. In Peter Cole and Jerry L. Morgan, editors, *Syntax and semantics*, volume 3. New York: Academic Press.

Barbara J Grosz and Candice L Sidner. 1986. Attention, Intention, and the Structure of Discourse. *Computational Linguistics*, 12(3):175–204.

Barbara J. Grosz, 1978. *Understanding Spoken Language*, chapter Discourse Analysis. Elsevier Science.

Dustin Hillard, Mari Ostendorf, and Elizabeth Shriberg. 2003. Detection of agreement vs. disagreement in meetings: training with unlabeled data. In *Proceedings of the 2003 Conference of the North American*

Chapter of the Association for Computational Linguistics on Human Language Technology: companion volume of the Proceedings of HLT-NAACL 2003–short papers - Volume 2, NAACL-Short '03, pages 34–36, Stroudsburg, PA, USA. Association for Computational Linguistics.

Jerry R. Hobbs. 1979. Coherence and coreference *. *Cognitive Science*, 3(1):90–67.

Karen A Jehn and Elizabeth A Mannix. 2001. The Dynamic Nature of Conflict: A Longitudinal Study of Intragroup Conflict and Group Performance. *Academy of Management Journal*, 44(2):238.

Susanne Jekat, Ra Klein, Elisabeth Maier, Ilona Maleck, Marion Mast, Tu Berlin, J. Joachim Quantz, and J. Joachim Quantz. 1995. Dialogue acts in verbmobil. Technical report.

D. Keltner, G.A. A Van Kleef, Serena Chen, and M.W. W Kraus. 2008. A reciprocal influence model of social power: Emerging principles and lines of inquiry. *Advances in experimental social psychology*, 40:151–192.

Judith W Little. 1982. Norms of Collegiality and Experimentation: Workplace Conditions of School Success. *American Educational Research Journal*, 19(3):325–340, January.

William C Mann and Sandra A Thompson. 1988. Rhetorical Structure Theory: Toward a Functional Theory of Text Organization. *Text*, 8(3):243–281.

Elijah Mayfield and Carolyn Penstein Rose. 2011. Recognizing Authority in Dialogue with an Integer Linear Programming Constrained Model. In *Computational Linguistics*, pages 1018–1026. Association for Computational Linguistics.

B S McCann, J Russo, and G A Benjamin. 1997. Hostility, social support, and perceptions of work. *Journal of occupational health psychology*, 2(2):175–85, April.

D.A. Owens and R.I. Sutton. 2001. Status contests in meetings: Negotiating the informal order. *Groups at work: Theory and research*, 14:299–316.

John R. Searle. 1969. *Speech Acts: An Essay in the Philosophy of Language*. Cambridge University Press.

S L Shapiro, A M Lopez, G E Schwartz, R Bootzin, A J Figueredo, C J Braden, and S F Kurker. 2001. Quality of life and breast cancer: relationship to psychosocial variables. *Journal of Clinical Psychology*, 57(4):501–519.

Elizabeth Shriberg, Raj Dhillon, Sonali Bhagat, Jeremy Ang, and Hannah Carvey. 2004. The ICSI Meeting Recorder Dialog Act (MRDA) Corpus. In Michael Strube and Candy Sidner, editors, *Proceedings of the 5th SIGdial Workshop on Discourse and Dialogue*, pages 97–100, Cambridge, Massachusetts, USA, April. Association for Computational Linguistics.

Andreas Stolcke, Elizabeth Shriberg, Rebecca Bates, Noah Coccaro, Daniel Jurafsky, Rachel Martin, Marie Meteer, Klaus Ries, Paul Taylor, and Carol Van Ess-Dykema. 1998. Dialog Act Modeling for Conversational Speech. In *Applying Machine Learning to Discourse Processing*, pages 98–105. AAAI Press.

Tomek Strzalkowski, George Aaron Broadwell, Jennifer Stromer-galley, Samira Shaikh, Sarah Taylor, and Nick Webb. 2010. Modeling Socio-Cultural Phenomena in Discourse. In *Internation Conference on Computational Linguistics (Coling)*, number August, pages 1038–1046.

Henri Tajfel and J. C. Turner, 1979. *An integrative theory of intergroup conflict*, pages 33–47. Brooks/Cole.

Marc Tomlinson, David B. Bracewell, Mary Draper, Zewar Almissour, Ying Shi, and Jeremy Bensley. 2012. Pursing power in arabic on-line discussion forums. In *Proceedings of the Eighth Conference on International Language Resources and Evaluation*.

David R Traum and Elizabeth A Hinkelman. 1992. Conversation acts in task-oriented spoken dialogue. *Computational Intelligence*, 8(3):575–599.

Wen Wang, Sibel Yaman, Kristin Precoda, Colleen Richey, and Geoffrey Raymond. 2011. Detection of agreement and disagreement in broadcast conversations. In *Proceedings of the 49th Annual Meeting of the Association for Computational Linguistics: Human Language Technologies: short papers - Volume 2*, HLT '11, pages 374–378, Stroudsburg, PA, USA. Association for Computational Linguistics.

Author Index